PREFACE

Home Geography. — In the Introductory volume of the Tarr and McMurry series of geographies, as issued ten years ago, more extensive acquaintance was urged with the fundamental ideas of geography before the child enters upon a study of the earth as a whole. Such preparation was advocated in the preface in the following words:

"**Necessity of Home Geography.** — The final basis for all study of geography is actual experience. Yet text-books on that subject rarely treat Home Geography at all, and those that do, devote but few pages to it. This subject should, we think, receive far more careful attention.

"**Necessity of Other Basal Notions.** — Home experience alone, however, cannot offer a complete basis for the later study of geography, because no one locality presents all the features required. From this it happens that the best books have contained some definitions and illustrations, as of mountain, river, valley, harbor, and factory, and have planned to build the later text upon the ideas these gave as a foundation. Such conceptions are certainly necessary in the early part of geography; but mere definitions fail to produce vivid, accurate pictures. The average pupil who has pursued geography for a year, has little notion of the great importance of soil, of what a mountain or a river really is, of the value of good trade routes, and why a vessel cannot find a harbor wherever it will cast anchor along the coast. Yet such ideas are the proper basis for the study of geography in the higher grades. The fact that they are so often wanting is proof that our geography still lacks foundation.

"**How these Needs are Met.** — The first 110 pages of this volume attempt to supply this foundation by treating first, such common things as soil, hills, valleys, industries, climate, and government, which are part of every child's environment; and secondly, other features, as mountains, rivers, lakes, and the ocean, which, though absent from many localities, are still necessary as a preparation for later study. Definitions, however, are not relied upon for giving the child this extra knowledge, but detailed descriptions and discussions instead. This by no means involves neglect of the child's own environment from the time the unfamiliar matter is introduced, for throughout the geographies home experiences are frequently used. We believe that our plan gives a fuller guarantee of fitness for advanced study than has heretofore been furnished."

While this plan was a radical innovation in text-book production at the time, the authors have seen no reason for receding from any portion of it. On the contrary, they have greatly enlarged this portion of the book, devoting to it eighty-five pages of the present volume. The chief additions have been two new chapters, one at the beginning on Food, Clothing, and Shelter — in which man's dependence upon the earth is somewhat extensively treated; and one on Country and City — in which life in the two places is contrasted.

Relationship to Man. — In the former preface the authors defined geography as the science " which treats of the relation between man and the earth," and the text was written upon this basis. It was difficult ten years ago to apply this idea extensively, because so little had been previously accomplished in this direction. The authors feel that one of the most important improvements in the present volume has been effected at that point. Every topic has been *approached*, and receives its entire consideration, from the point of view of man's interest in it. Descriptions of continents and countries offered without reference to human relationships are likely to be colorless and tiresome to the young mind.

Our point of view may be illustrated by the treatment of Asia, for instance. That continent is declared, at the beginning of its presentation, to be the largest and most populous of all the continents, and also to have the oldest civilization. In addition it lies next to Europe. Yet, possibly next to Africa, it is the least known of all the continents. Why it should be so little known becomes then a question of real interest; and the answer, as presented in pages 216–218, involves consideration of its surface features, climate, and inhabitants. Likewise in the case of China, as an example of an individual country, the former

progress of its inhabitants first receives attention. This is contrasted with their present backwardness. Then, since the future progress of the Chinese is one of the live · questions of the day, the area and population of the country, the variety of its climate, its surface features, and resources, are all considered with reference to this one problem. Then the recent advances of China are discussed and its principal cities located. Thus, as far as possible, each continent and country has been approached from the point of view of the learner, and the questions raised at the beginning control the presentation that follows.

Organization of Subject-matter. — The close relation of this method of presentation to organization is evident. Good literature is organized around ideas of live interest to man; and any text whatever, intended for children, should be organized on the same basis. Most geography text, however, has attempted to follow the scientific organization, which is that of the mature mind supposed already to be interested in the subject. But even though the attempt has been made, it has not heretofore been followed in full, for, owing to the immaturity of children and to want of space, many of the connecting facts — that reveal the relationship of facts and tend to arouse interest — have had to be omitted, until a mere heterogeneous lot of statements has been all that has occupied many a page.

Believing that good organization is necessary to successful study, the authors have endeavored earnestly to secure it. With this object they have done two things.

First, for each page, more or less, they

have fixed upon some central thought that should tie together the details underlying it, and secure their unity. What this central idea is in each case is clearly shown in the marginal heading; and by grasping it early, the child is enabled to master a lesson much more quickly and easily than otherwise. It is surprising how many pages of geography and history for children lack such a central idea. A portion of text may read easily and appear simple; but it shows serious want of organization when you cannot find the one thought with which it deals. Many a lesson is found difficult by children because, while each sentence may be clear, each page, more or less, treats of several things instead of one, and there is nothing to hold these parts together.

It is hardly advisable that all texts for children be provided with marginal headings, for children should have practice in finding these themselves. But it is highly important that enough texts contain such headings to accustom pupils to dividing their lessons up into well-rounded units, or to studying by "points."

In the second place, the authors have selected for the unifying thoughts, not merely scientific facts, but ideas likely to prove of peculiar interest to young students. Africa, beginning on page 231, well illustrates this, as well as Asia and China, to which reference has already been made. In consequence of these two characteristics, the authors believe that the subject-matter in this volume is more completely organized, and organized on a better basis, than is customary in common school geography texts.

Amount of Detail. — Part Two, as well as Part One, of this book has been greatly enlarged. The main reason for this is that more detail seemed necessary in order to make the subject interesting and clear. The most difficult text to study, or to teach, is one that contains too little detail to clothe its skeleton. A child can memorize or understand ten pages of good literature as easily as he can one or two of the ordinary geography, and will enjoy himself far more in the process. One important reason for this is that the literature offers enough detail to establish a close relation among the ideas and thus secure the story form. Any good text must follow the model set by literature in this respect. Books are thereby made thicker, to be sure; and longer lessons may, therefore, have to be assigned. But the "length" of a lesson is determined by other things, as well as by the number of pages; and two pages of an interesting, properly organized text may easily make a shorter lesson than one page of a different kind of text.

Method of Study by Children. — While there is no reason why a text-book in geography, more than any other text, should offer suggestions about methods of study, every one knows that children's ways of studying are often extremely crude, involving great waste. On this account it seemed advisable to include here some suggestions on this subject, applicable both to this and to other books. These are found on pages 10, 30, 53, 66, and 80. These occupy little space; but they will have accomplished much, if they are influential in leading children to do the things suggested, and if, in addition, they direct the attention of both children and teachers to a fuller consideration of proper methods of study.

Size of Page. — It is with much regret that the small size page has had to be abandoned in this revision; but the length of the line involved seemed mandatory. If the old form of book had been retained, the additional subject-matter would have compelled a much wider page, or else a book so thick that the difficulties of binding would have become serious. Meanwhile, agitation in favor of a line not over three inches in length has become so active, and has seemed so fully justified, that both authors and publisher have felt convinced of the advisability of adopting a larger style of book.

Maps and Illustrations. — The maps in this book have been made by The Williams Engraving Company. Half-tones from photographs are used whenever possible, and these have been selected with great care, from collections of many thousands, and are in all cases introduced not as mere pictures, but as illustrations of topics treated in the text. It is expected that they will be studied as well as the text. It is believed that the book is as thoroughly illustrated as is desirable for the needs of the student, and the authors have used care not to overillustrate by throwing together a heterogeneous mass of pictures unrelated to the text. It is our idea that a geography should not be a picture album.

From the preceding statements it is evident that the " Introductory Book in Geography," published ten years ago, has suffered radical revision in this edition. There is hardly a page that has not been greatly altered, and most of the volume has been completely rewritten.

TABLE OF CONTENTS

LIST OF COLORED MAPS

PART I. HOME GEOGRAPHY

SECTION I. FOOD, CLOTHING, AND SHELTER

I. AMONG THE PEOPLE OF OUR OWN COUNTRY

1. Food

IN the spring, men begin to work the soil. Those who have small gardens **What the farmers do** break up the ground with such tools as spades and forks. Those who live on farms turn the soil over with plows drawn by horses. In these ways the soil is loosened and made soft, so that seeds and plants can grow in it. After the planting is done, the weeds must be killed and the soil must be loosened. In places where little rain falls, other ways of watering the plants must be found.

Later, in the summer, the crops are ready to gather. This is the harvest season, and it is a very busy time for the farmers. They often begin work at four or five o'clock in the morning, and sometimes do not stop before eight o'clock at night.

They raise much more than they need for themselves, and what they do not want they sell. Those of us who live in the city eat at every meal some of the **How their work is of value** things that have been grown on farms.

FIG. 1.— A herd of dairy cows in pasture.

This shows how important the work of farmers is to every one of us.

One of their most valuable crops is grass. It is not a food for people, yet it helps to give us food. Can you tell how? If you cannot answer this question, perhaps Figure 1 will help you. Make a list of the different kinds of food that you eat in one day, and find how many of them come from farms.

1

A very great number of men are kept busy raising food for other people to eat. They are called farmers. How would you like the work of a farmer? What are some of the pleasant things about it?

Many other people are at work changing the farm crops into food. For ex-
Preparing our food   ample, milk is made into butter and cheese, oats into oatmeal, and sugar-cane into sugar. Can you tell the story of a loaf of bread?

2. Clothing

Every one must have *clothing* as well as food. The Indians dressed very

FIG. 2. — Picking cotton in a cottonfield in the South. The white patches are fluffy cotton out of which cotton goods are made.

lightly in summer; but in winter they had to wear much heavier clothing made out of the skins of animals.

We wear much more clothing than the Indians did, both in summer and
Materials for our clothing, and where they come from   winter, and it is of many more kinds. Most of the materials for it come from the soil, as our food does.
For example, girls' dresses are often made of cotton. In some places

cotton is one of the farmers' greatest crops. Fields of cotton (Fig. 2) are as common in the South as cornfields are in the North.

Linen handkerchiefs, collars, and cuffs are made out of flax. This plant is also raised in large fields, much as wheat and oats are grown.

Some of the materials for our clothing come from animals that feed on plants. For example, a boy's coat, if not made of cotton, is usually made of the wool that grows on sheep. Find such a coat.

The leather for your shoes came from the hide of some animal, probably a cow. Name several things that you wear, and tell, if you can, from what material each has been made.

Cotton, wool, and hides are called *raw materials*. Much work is necessary to change
Work necessary to change raw materials into clothing   such raw materials into clothing. For example, cotton and wool must be spun into yarn and woven into cloth. Perhaps you can tell what else must be done before a dress or coat is finished. What are some of the things that must be done with hides before they become shoes or gloves?

The work of preparing our clothing keeps many, many thousands of men and women busy both winter and summer. Do you know any persons who do such work?

3. Shelter

Shelter, as well as food and clothing, is very important.

Why shelter is necessary

We must have houses to protect us against rain; also, against the heat of summer and the cold of winter. We must have fuel, too, such as coal, or wood, or gas, to keep our houses warm.

The Indians often lived in tents called wigwams (Fig. 3). These are pleasant enough in summer, but are very cold in winter.

Materials used for shelter in our country

FIG. 3. — An Indian wigwam, the home of the Indian girl who stands in the front of the picture.

Sometimes the Indians built much better houses, using wood in some places and stone or clay in others.

What are some of the materials that we use in building our houses? Make as full a list of them as you can. Where does the wood for the floors and for other parts of a house come from? The stone? Where is the material for brick found? For nails? Can you tell where the other materials in your list come from? Where is coal found?

Most of the men in our country are engaged in some one of these three kinds of work, that is, in preparing *food*, or *clothing*, or *shelter*. People living in other countries have the same kinds of work to do. But in many other countries the food, clothing, and shelter are very different from ours, for reasons that you will now learn.

II. AMONG THE NEGROES OF CENTRAL AFRICA

Central Africa, the home of the Negroes, is a part of the earth where the people live in a very strange way. Have you ever thought what a difference it would make with us, if we had summer all the time? Central Africa is just such a land. Every day in the year is hot.

The heat and rain in Central Africa

In some parts of Central Africa the air is damp or muggy, as it is here on our most unpleasant summer days; and heavy thunder-storms are common. Central Africa is one of the rainiest places on the earth.

Where there is so much heat and rain, plants grow very rapidly. You have, perhaps, noticed how grass and plants thrive on warm, damp days. Because there is just such weather all the time in **The vegetation that grows there** this part of Africa, plants grow there in vast numbers. Giant trees are found in the forests, and vines, trees, and other plants grow so close together that one cannot make his way through them without cutting a path.

Many fruits and vegetables grow wild there; and since there is no winter in

sheep, and goats, or from wild game, such as the buffalo and antelope.

It is also easy to provide clothing in this region. One reason is that not much of it is wanted. Figure 4 shows how little clothing is needed in the hot country of Central Africa. Sometimes skins of animals are used; but the common material is cloth made from the bark and fiber of trees and plants that grow in that land.

FIG. 4. — Negroes of Africa sitting in front of their grass-covered huts.

Since there is no winter, one might think that houses **Their shelter** would not be needed; but the heat and rain make shelter of some sort very necessary. Sometimes the people live in trees, or in caves, as the Swiss Family Robinson lived for a time. Sometimes they stick branches of trees into the ground in the form of a circle, fasten the upper ends together, and then cover the sides and top with such materials as brush, mud, grass,

that land, there is no season when all the vegetation stops growing and loses its leaves.

It is very easy for people to obtain food, clothing, and shelter in such a land. **What the people eat and wear** Food is plentiful. Bananas or other fruits can be plucked from the trees and bushes at any time of year. Or if beans, peas, and corn are wanted, one has only to scrape a hole in the soft earth and plant the seeds. There is plenty of meat to be had, too, from cattle,

and straw (Fig. 4). Their huts are always very simple; they usually have no windows, and are only one story high. A savage Negro, when he first saw one of our houses, cried out, "This is not a hut; it is a mountain with many caves in it!"

You can see that the Negroes who live in the hot, damp part of Central Africa do not have to work hard for food, clothing, and shelter. Are they fortunate to have such an easy time? Would you like to live in such a country and in such a way?

III. AMONG THE ESKIMOS

Far to the north of us is the home of the Eskimos. They have both summer and winter. But the sum-mer is so cold that the ground does not thaw except at the very surface. The winters are bitterly cold. Heavy snows then fall, the ground freezes to a great depth, and thick ice forms on the sea (Fig. 5).

The cold and snow in the Far North

In such a country no trees can grow. The Eskimo children have never seen trees of any kind. Only small plants are found there, such as mosses, grasses, and very low bushes; and the plants that

Plants and animals found there

in fishing and in hunting the seal and walrus; and now and then they catch sea-birds and the polar bear. They have very little food except the flesh of these animals. Even that is difficult to get, especially in winter when the sea is frozen over with thick ice.

These sea animals supply oil for heat and for light in the long, dark winter. The seals have a layer of fat under the skin which helps to keep them warm in winter. This seal fat, or blubber, is burned in small lamps for both heat and light. But the Eskimos do not do much cook-ing. They are fond of raw meat and like to eat it even when it is frozen!

Other uses of animals

FIG. 5. — Eskimos on sledges drawn by dogs on the frozen Arctic Ocean.

grow wild furnish no food except a few small berries.

With so little vegetation there can be few wild animals on the land, for they would have nothing to eat. There are a few reindeer, foxes, and wolves, but scarcely any other land animals.

What, then, can the Eskimos them-selves find to eat? Not very many things, to be sure. They have to look to the sea, not to the land, for their food. From one year's end to another, they are engaged

What the Eskimos eat

In summer the Eskimos go hunting in small canoes, or *kayaks*, that are easily upset in storms. In winter they often go on long and dangerous journeys over the ice on sleds, or sledges, drawn by five or ten dogs (Fig. 5). Can you give reasons why horses are not used in the land of the Eskimo?

The sleds and canoes are not made of wood, like ours. The reason is that no forests grow in that country. The only wood the Eskimos have is that which drifts ashore from distant, forest-covered lands, or from the wrecks of vessels. There is so little of this that pieces of wood are highly prized. An Eskimo will gladly exchange valuable furs for a small amount of wood.

Parts of the bodies of animals take the place of wood in many ways. Their bones are used to build the framework of the sledges and kayaks, and their

ent that is from the clothing worn by the Negroes of Central Africa!

The Eskimo houses seem even stranger than their clothing. Although there is plenty of stone for building, **Why the Eski-** it hardly pays to build stone **mos build snow** houses because the Eskimos **huts** have to move from place to place in order to find food. Very often whole

FIG. 6.— An Eskimo igloo made of blocks of snow. In the upper right-hand corner is a little figure showing the inside of the igloo.

skins are stretched over these frames in place of boards. Bones are also used to make spears, fishhooks, pipes, and even needles; and skins are made into harness for the dogs.

The Eskimos need the warmest kind of clothing. Their boots are made of **What the** the skins of animals, with **Eskimos wear** the fur on. Their clothes are also made of fur; and in that cold land they need to wear these furs both in summer and in winter. How differ-

villages must be moved many miles on this account.

In summer, therefore, the Eskimos live in tents made of skins, which are easily taken down and moved about. In winter they live in huts made of snow. There is always plenty of snow at hand, no matter where the people happen to be; and in an hour or two they can build an *igloo*, as the Eskimo snow hut is called.

Figure 6 is a picture of one of these igloos. It is about forty feet around the outside, and is made of blocks of snow piled one on another, till it is high **How these huts are built** enough on the inside for a man to stand up. The entrance is through a snow tunnel about ten feet long, and so low that the Eskimos have to crawl through it on their hands and knees. The purpose of this tunnel is to keep the cold winds out of the hut; and when all the persons are inside, the tunnel is tightly closed, so that no draught can enter.

A stand, made of snow, is used for the lamp, that gives both light and heat. Low benches of snow, covered with furs, are used for beds. A whole family, and sometimes two families, live in a single hut that is no more than ten or fifteen feet across.

You might think that a snow hut is not very comfortable; but the snow **The warmth in such huts** keeps out the cold, and even when it is stinging cold outside, the Eskimos in the igloo are warm enough. The heat of their bodies, and of the small blubber lamp, warms the air in the igloo, so that it is often too warm for comfort. Of course, with so many people in a single small room, the air becomes very close.

If a family decides to remain in one place a second winter, a new hut has to be built, because the old one melts down during the summer. No wonder that the huts are small!

The Negroes of Central Africa have little work to do to find food, clothing, and shelter at any season. But the Eskimos must work hard for these things even in summer; and in winter all the people of a village may starve to death. Are people in our own country better off or worse off than the Eskimos?

IV. Among the People of the Desert

While parts of Central Africa are hot and wet, northern Africa is somewhat cooler, and very dry. In fact, so little rain falls there **The desert of northern Africa** that very few plants can grow. On that account it is a desert land, called the *Desert of Sahara*.

One might travel hundreds of miles in that desert without seeing a tree, or a house, or even a patch of **The vegetation found there** green grass. He might find nothing except sand and rock and a few half-starved plants (Fig. 7).

A little rain falls now and then even in the driest part of the desert, and grass and flowers quickly spring up whenever that happens. To be sure, these soon wither for want of more rain. But a few kinds of plants, like the acacia, are able to live a long time even in such a place. These store up water in their roots, or leaves, or stems, whenever it rains, and this keeps them alive till the next rain comes.

Here and there one finds trees and green grass. For in some places streams flow from the mountains out into the desert, and in other places springs occur. These springs and streams wet the desert soil near by, so that grass can grow; and if the supply of water lasts throughout the year, trees like the date palm can thrive. Such green places in the desert are called *oases*, and on them are found gardens and villages. The oases are like beautiful islands, many miles apart, in a great ocean of sand and barren rock.

People live on the oases year after year. Indeed, good-sized towns have been built upon some of them. The fruit that these families most commonly The food of eat is the date, from the people on the date palm tree; they also oases raise figs and wheat, and keep cattle, camels, sheep, and goats.

Some people who live in the desert, however, have no fixed homes. They The nomads of spend their time in tending the desert herds of cattle, sheep, and goats. As soon as these animals eat the grass in one place, they must be

The nomads can get other food from the people who live on the oases. Can you name something that they could obtain from them? What food might the nomads give in exchange?

Food can also be brought from other countries. For, although there are no railroads across that desert, How food is and no rivers large enough brought from for boats, there is a way of other countries carrying goods from place to place. That is by means of the camel (Fig. 8).

Fig. 7. — A barren desert, and some nomads with the tents in which they live.

driven to another section. Thus these herders, like the Eskimos, must move about and take their families with them. They spend their lives wandering about with their herds. For this reason they are called *nomads*, or wanderers (Fig. 7).

For food, these nomads of the desert have plenty of meat and milk from The food of their camels, cattle, and the nomads goats. They make butter, too; but it is so warm in the desert that the butter is sent, melted, to market in goatskins. In some places the people drink the melted butter.

This animal, often called "the ship of the desert," can carry a heavy load on its back, and can travel a long distance without drinking. Indeed, the camel has in his body a sack which is filled when he drinks, and which holds enough water to last for several days. The camels are driven across the desert in droves, called *caravans*.

The dress of the people of the desert, as we might expect, is very different from that of the Negroes. The clothing of The days are very warm, the people for the sky is almost always clear, and

Fig. 8. — A nomad of the desert.

the sun shines brightly. Figure 9 shows the kind of clothing that is worn. The strange covering for the head is called a turban. It protects the head against the sun and the fine sand that is driven about by the winds.

Although the weather is hot during the day, it becomes rapidly cooler as soon while to build such houses, when they might be used only a few days. Like the Eskimos in summer, therefore, the nomads live in tents (Fig. 7) that can easily be taken down, carried about, and set up again. The skins of animals, or blankets that the nomads weave, are used as covering for the tents.

FIG. 9. — A street in a town on an oasis in northern Africa. Notice the house made of sun-dried clay.

as the sun sets, and the nights are quite chilly. On account of the cool nights these people need much more clothing than the Negroes, and they must sleep under heavy blankets. Their herds supply plenty of wool for cloth; and other materials for clothing are brought by the caravans.

The people living on the oases remain in one place, building houses of sun-dried **Why the nomads** mud or clay (Fig. 9). But **live in tents** mud huts are not suited to the nomads. It would not be worth

We have now learned some facts about the Negroes in Central Africa, about the Eskimos, the people of the desert, and ourselves. From **What food,** what has been said it is plain **clothing, and** that people do not have their **shelter depend** own way fully in choosing what they **upon** shall eat and wear, and the kind of houses they shall have. These depend very much upon the amount of heat and rain. In which of these sections is there too little rain? In which too much cold? In which too much heat?

In studying this book it is a good plan first to read a number of pages without stopping, just as you would read any story. For instance, the first three pages — up to the part telling about the Negroes — might first be read without pause, for the purpose of finding out what it is all about. Then you might read the same part through a second and a third time, watching each heading that is printed near the margin to see if you are getting its answer. When the part about our country has been studied in this way, the part telling about the Negroes of Central Africa should be studied in a similar way; and so on through the book.

About how to study

1. Name some of the things that farmers and gardeners do. 2. How is their work of importance? 3. Give examples of other kinds of work that are necessary in preparing our food. 4. Out of what materials is our clothing made? Where do such materials come from? 5. Tell about the work necessary to change these raw materials into clothing. 6. Why is shelter necessary? 7. What materials are used for shelter in our country? 8. Where do these materials come from? 9. What can you tell about the heat and rain in Central Africa? 10. What sort of vegetation grows there? 11. What do the people who live there, eat and wear? 12. What kind of shelter have they? 13. What about the cold and snow in the Far North? 14. What plants and animals are

Review Questions

found there? 15. What is the food of the Eskimos? 16. What other uses do they make of animals? 17. What do the Eskimos wear? 18. Why do they build huts of snow? 19. How are such huts built? 20. Why is it not cold in the igloos? 21. What about heat and rain in the Desert of Sahara? 22. Describe the vegetation there. 23. What is the food of the people? 24. What are the oases? Who live on them? What kind of houses have they? 25. What is meant by the nomads of the desert? 26. What food do they eat? 27. How is food brought to them from other countries? 28. What kind of clothing is worn by the people of the desert? 29. Why do the nomads live in tents? 30. Why is there so little plant and animal life in the Far North, and in the Sahara Desert, while there is so much of each in Central Africa? 31. Why do the Eskimos have so few kinds of food, clothing, and shelter, while we have so many?

1. If you have visited some garden, or farm, in the spring, tell how the ground is prepared for planting. 2. What kinds of work are done later in the season? 3. Make a list of products that some gardener or farmer near you is raising. 4. What things that your grocer sells have come from some garden or farm? 5. Make a list of the many kinds of work that you have seen men doing, and find how many on the list have to do with food, clothing, and shelter.

Suggestions for study at home and out of doors

SECTION II.　LAND, WATER, AND AIR

I. The Land

1. Soil

HEAT and rain are very important, as we have seen. But they are not of much value alone. There is a third thing that must go with them in order that people may have food, clothing, and shelter; and that is the *soil*, or dirt, in which plants grow.

As soon as the warm spring weather comes, thousands and thousands of men in our own country begin to work the soil, in gardens and on farms (Fig. 10). Indeed, more than one third of all the people in the United States live on farms. They spend their lives in raising plants, and animals that feed on plants, such as cows, sheep, hogs, and chickens. What they do not need for themselves they sell to other people. Our flour, potatoes, and sugar, the cotton for our clothing, and hundreds of other things come from the soil.

The value of the soil in our country

FIG. 10. — Men plowing a field in which wheat is to be sown.

The dense forests of Central Africa, and the fruits and vegetables of that
Its value in other places land, all spring from its soil, warmed by the hot sun and kept moist by the rains. It is the warm soil again, watered by streams and springs, that makes life on the oases of the desert possible.

On the other hand, it is the cold in the land of the Eskimos that freezes the soil and prevents the growth of trees and crops. It is the frozen soil that drives the Eskimos to the sea for food.

The dirt under your feet may seem hardly worth thinking about; but it is
Why soil is of so great importance really one of the most important things in the world. If there were no soil, there could be no grass, no flowers, no trees, around your home. Without grass and grain there could be no cattle, horses, or sheep; in fact, few animals, such as are found upon the land, could live; for what would they eat? What, then, would you find to eat? There would be no fruits or vegetables, no bread, no butter and milk, and no meat. We could not live if there were no soil.

Since the soil is so important, it is worth while to study about it. How it has been formed, how plants make use of it, and what men do to increase its value to plants, — these are all very interesting questions that every one should be able to answer.

If you have ever made mud pies, or played in the dirt in other ways, you have, perhaps, sometimes won-
What the soil is made of dered what the soil is made of. It has not always been dirt or mud. You know that the wood in your desk has not always been a part of the desk; it used to be a part of a tree, and has a long story to tell about itself before it was brought to your school. So, also, the soil has a long story to tell about itself. Let us see what that story is.

When mud dries upon your hands, and you rub them together, you can notice an unpleasant, gritty feeling. This is caused by hard bits of something in the soil that scrape together. If you rub some of this dirt upon a smooth piece of glass, you can perhaps hear it scratch the glass. This shows that these little bits must be very hard; for if they were not, they could not scratch anything so hard as glass. They must be even harder than a pin, for you cannot scratch glass with a pin.

It will help you to find out what these bits are, if you examine some sand. The grains of sand are tiny bits of rock, large enough to be clearly seen. When they are rubbed against glass, they scratch it, because they are very hard and sharp.

Sand is made of rock that has been broken up into fine pieces. Soil is also made of rock; but the pieces are still finer than sand. The soil that you have seen, such as that in the school yard, or by

FIG. 11. — A stump of a tree decaying, or rotting.

the side of the walk, or in a flower-pot, was once a part of hard rock.

Soil has been made in several ways, which you may learn about How soil is　　later; but most of it made from rock has been formed by the decay of rock. You know that the stumps of trees and the boards in sidewalks, after a long time, become so soft that they fall to pieces. Perhaps you have called it "rotting," but that means the same as decaying. The picture (Fig. 11) shows such a stump.

Other things, even harder than wood, decay in much the same way, although

perhaps more slowly. Bright and shiny nails decay until they become a soft, yellow rust. Tin cans and iron pipes rust until holes appear in them and they leak.

You may not have thought that stones also decay, but they do. The headstones in old graveyards are often so crumbled that the letters can scarcely be read;

FIG. 12. — A rock cliff showing the cracks that extend through the rock; also, at the base of the cliff, a large pile of rock fragments that have been loosened by frost, and have fallen down the steep slope.

and sometimes the stones have fallen to pieces. The decay of rock may also be seen in old stone buildings, bowlders, and rock cliffs. Have you ever noticed this?

There are several causes for this decay. All rocks have cracks in them (Fig. 12).

Usually some of these cracks are so large that they can be plainly seen; but **What causes the decay of rock** there are many others so small that they cannot be seen without a magnifying glass. When it rains, the water steals into the cracks, and by eating into and

FIG. 13. — A cut into the earth. In this figure notice the *soil* on top, partly decayed rock lower down, and *solid rock* below that.

rotting the rock, this water very slowly changes it into a powder.

The water may also freeze in the cracks and pry the stone apart. Perhaps you have seen iron pipes or water pitchers that have been burst by water freezing in them. This shows how much the freezing water expands; it will even break rocks apart. Some of the pieces of rock broken off in this way are very small, others are quite large (Fig. 12).

Plants help the water to break up the rock. Their hairlike roots push into the cracks, and remain there until they grow so large that they pry off pieces of rock.

The earthworms that one often sees on a lawn after a heavy rain also help in crumbling the rock. In order to get food, they take soil into their bodies and grind the coarse bits together until these become very fine.

Rock changes to soil most rapidly near the surface. This is because the

rain, roots of plants, and earthworms can reach it there most easily. For this reason the deeper you dig **Why solid rock is found beneath the soil** into soil that is formed by the decay of rocks, the less you will find the rock changed (Fig. 13); and no matter where you live, if you dig deep enough, you will come to solid rock.

Figure 14 shows the soil a little less than two feet deep. Sometimes there is much more than this, and **Why the soil is of different depths** men may even dig deep wells without finding rock. But in many places there are only a few inches of soil, and in others there is not enough even to hide the rock.

One reason why the soil is deeper in one place than in another is that some kinds of rock decay much more easily than other kinds. Another reason is that in some places the rain washes the bits away as fast as the rocks crumble. This may leave the rock quite bare in one place, and make very deep soil in the places where the water leaves the broken bits.

FIG. 14. — A cut in the earth, showing the soil resting on the solid rock.

Having learned how the soil is made, let us see how plants make use of it.

An acorn that has been planted in the soil sprouts and sends up a tiny stem.

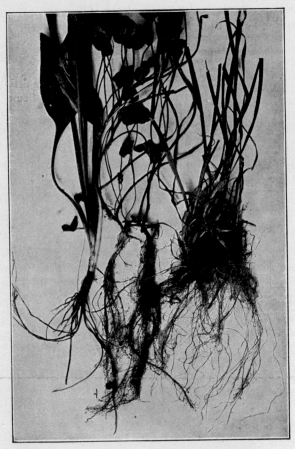

FIG. 15. — A photograph of four weeds, showing the great number of long, hairlike roots.

The use that plants make of the soil

This grows taller and taller, and sends out one branch after another until the little tree becomes a mighty oak. What a lot of material has been used to make such a tree ! Where has it all come from ?

Some of it has been taken out of the air by the leaves, but much of it has been taken from the soil by the roots. While the stem, branches, and leaves have been growing above ground, the roots have been growing underground, where we cannot see them. These roots have spread out in all directions (Fig. 15) and have extended deep into the soil, in search of things needed by the tree. Dig up a weed, in order to see how its roots have pushed their way in and out through the soil.

The value of the hairlike roots

Roots have no eyes, to be sure ; but they burrow about, and in their own way find what they need. It is not the large or old roots, however, that do this. That is the work of the young roots, many of which are not much larger than hairs (Fig. 15).

If you dig up a weed, or any other plant, very carefully, you will see that it has a great many such hairlike roots. It is these that take the materials from the soil, while the older, larger roots merely pass these materials on to the part of the plant above ground. Every tree, every blade of grass, every weed and vegetable, depends upon such tiny roots for its life.

What plants take from the soil

One of the things that the roots of plants seek in the soil is water. Plants need water as much as you do ; and a plant in a flower-pot will soon wither and die if it is given no water. Try it, to see for yourself. That is the reason we water our lawns during dry weather in summer.

Roots take other substances from the soil, called *plant food*. This plant food is a part of the soil itself, and is as necessary to plants as food is to you. It is carried, in the sap, to all parts of the plant and used to make stems, leaves, flowers, fruit, and seeds, as the blood in your body is used to make bones and flesh. Every blade of grass and every limb of a tree contains some of this plant food that was once a part of the rocks. When a piece of wood is burned, some of this rock material is left behind in the ashes.

Every person, even, has some plant food in his body; your bones and teeth are partly made of it. But you did not take it directly from the soil; the plants took it for you, and you received it from them in the flour and other foods that you have eaten.

Plants do not all need the same kind of food, any more than all animals do.

Why different kinds of soil are needed

Horses eat hay and grain; dogs eat meat. So, also, some plants need one kind of food, others another. These different kinds of plant food are found in the different kinds of soil.

There are many different kinds of soil. Sometimes the rock has crumbled into very small bits, making a fine-grained

What causes different kinds of soil

soil; again the pieces are so large that the soil is coarse. In fact, in some soils the pieces of rock are so large that some of them are pebbles. Then, too, there are many kinds of rock, such as granite, marble, and sandstone; and when they crumble they make different kinds of soil.

In some places the soil has plenty of plant food in it. To raise good crops

Fertile soil

in such soil, men have to do nothing beyond plowing, planting, and hoeing. Central Africa has a great deal of that kind of soil, and so has the United States. Soil of this kind, with plenty of plant food in it, is said to be rich, or *fertile*.

There is also much soil that has little plant food in it, and that is said to be

Sterile soil

poor, or *sterile*. One reason for sterile soil is that the rock from which the soil has come may contain little plant food. On that account one farm may be much more sterile than another next to it.

Soil that was once fertile may become sterile, because plants are always taking some of the plant food out

How fertile soil may become sterile

of it. They must do this in order to grow. When weeds and trees fall and decay on the spot where they grew, they pay back what they took away. But if plants are carried away from the spot where they grew, there is danger that fertile soil may be made quite sterile.

Now this often happens. Farmers send away their wheat to make flour, and take their corn, hay, and oats to market. Indeed, they have to do this in order to make a living. Some farmers have sent their crops away year after year, without putting anything back in the ground to take the place of what was carried away. The result is that the soil has become really worn out, or sterile, and the farmers are no longer able to support their families on such land.

The wise farmer takes care to put some plant food back upon the soil, to replace what his crops have

How this danger can be avoided

taken from it. Then he can continue to raise good crops. That which he puts back upon the soil is called a *fertilizer*, because it keeps the soil fertile. People in the city often spread a fertilizer on their lawns, to feed the grass and thus make it grow.

Millions of dollars are spent in the United States every year for fertilizers. If this were not done, the crops would not be nearly so valuable. Then the farmers would suffer; and since we all depend upon the products which they raise, we should all suffer. Farming is the most important industry not only in our country, but in the whole world. Therefore, what is important to the farmer, is important to every one.

Review Questions 1. Why is the soil in our country so valuable? 2. What about its value in other places? 3. Why is the soil one of the most important things in the world? 4. What is the soil made of? 5. How has it been made? 6. What causes rock to crumble? 7. How does it happen that solid rock is everywhere found beneath the soil? 8. Why is the soil of different depths? 9. What use do plants make of the soil? 10. What is the work done by the hair-

2. Plains

If the soil that rests on the rock had a smooth and level surface like a floor, it would be unfit for farming. For the water, after a heavy rain, would then stand in a thin sheet upon the ground. This would drown the crops and prove unhealthful for both people and animals.

Why gently sloping land is the best for farming

Land with steep slopes is also unfit for farming. The rains wash away much of the soil on these slopes, until

FIG. 16. — Farmers cutting wheat on the broad plains of the West.

like roots of plants? 11. Name two things that plants take from the soil. 12. Why is it important that there should be different kinds of soil? 13. What causes the different kinds? 14. What is meant by *fertile* soil? 15. By *sterile* soil? 16. How may fertile soil be made sterile? 17. How can such danger be avoided?

Suggestions for study at home and out of doors 1. Find a place where men are digging a ditch, or a cellar, and see how the dirt looks below the surface. 2. Find a bowlder, cliff, or old stone wall, that is crumbling away. 3. Collect several different kinds of soil. 4. Find out what trees and vegetables grow best near your home. 5. Visit a greenhouse to find out what kind of soil is used there, and what is done to keep it fertile. 6. Make a drawing of the roots of some weed that has been carefully dug up.

only a rough, thin soil is left; sometimes even the rock is uncovered. The crops, too, are often washed away from such steep slopes by the heavy rain. It is very difficult, also, to do the work of planting, plowing, and harvesting on a steep hillside.

Land that has gentle slopes is better for farming. The water runs off more slowly, without washing the soil away or injuring the crops; more of the water soaks into the soil, leaving it moist; and the farmer can work, or *cultivate*, the soil more easily.

Land of this kind, with slopes so gentle that it is nearly level, or slightly rolling, is called a *plain*. A very large part of our country consists of such plains, and this is one reason why the The extent of plains in the United States United States is one of the finest farming countries in the world (Fig. 16).

If you were to cross our country on the railroad you might travel for two or three days over nearly level plains, with no mountains, and not even any high hills, in sight. On either side of the track you would see one farmhouse after another, each surrounded in summer by fields of waving grain, and by green

There are thousands of swamps in our country, and it is quite common for a farm to have one or more of them upon it. Swamp land cannot be cultivated until it is *drained;* that is, until the water is made to run off. Drainage of the land, therefore, becomes a very important matter.

Swamp soil is usually very fertile. For this reason, when there is no natural slope to carry off the What is done with swamps water, men often set to work to make one. For this purpose they

Fig. 17. — An open ditch dug through a swamp in order to drain off the water.

pastures in which horses, cattle, and sheep were feeding. Now and then the train would pass through a village or a city; but everywhere else, for hundreds of miles, you would find only fertile farms.

In many places, even from a train, one can easily see that there are slopes The importance of slopes on this great plain, down which the water runs freely. But in parts of the plain the slopes are so gentle that the surface seems to the eye to be perfectly flat. Yet the fact that the water runs off, proves that even here the land has a slope.

Here and there, however, the surface is so level that the water does not all run off, but makes wet places, called *swamps.*

dig ditches with sloping bottoms that allow the water to run away to some lower place.

Sometimes the ditches are left open, as shown in Figure 17. More often tiles are laid along the bottom, forming a kind of pipe, and then the ditch is filled up with earth. The water finds its way into these pipes and thus flows away. Such drainage is expensive, but it usually pays well, for it makes good fertile farm land out of land that before was useless.

A *plain* is a nearly level, or gently rolling, part of the land. Definitions

A *swamp* is wet land from which the water does not run off freely.

c

Review
Questions
1. Why is gently sloping land the best kind for farming? 2. What about the extent of such land in the United States? 3. Why are slopes of great importance? 4. Why are swamps drained? 5. How is this done?

Suggestions
1. Find some ground near your home that seems nearly level. In what direction does it really slope? 2. Where is the longest slope in your neighborhood? Would you call it a part of a plain? Why? 3. Find out whether or not there are any swamps near you. If so, tell how you might plan to drain one of them. 4. Why should a farmer use tile and fill up a ditch, rather than leave it open?

No matter in what direction you look, in a hilly country, the scenery changes. The view from the top, or *summit*, of a hill that requires only a few minutes to climb, is very different from the view at its base (Fig. 18). Can you explain why?

The higher hills, which may require several hours to climb, furnish even finer views. From the summit of such a hill one can see hilltop after hilltop, with valleys between, stretching out for miles in the distance. The valleys wind in and out among the hills, with perhaps rugged cliffs too steep to climb on one

FIG. 18. — A view in a hilly country, with a lake in the valley. Here some of the slopes are too steep for farms, and are, therefore, still covered by forests.

3. Hills and Valleys

The beauty of a hilly country

Plains are usually so level that one can see for miles across them in every direction. The surface is so flat that, no matter where one looks, he sees the same kind of scenery.

It is very different in a region where the slopes are steeper. The higher parts are called *hills*, and the lower parts, between the hills, are called *valleys*.

side, and long wooded slopes on the other. In the bottoms of the valleys one can possibly see brooks or rivers winding about. If you live among hills, describe some of the walks and views that you have enjoyed.

Uses made of hills

The soil on hills may be deep and fertile; and then, even though it is difficult to cultivate the ground, the hilly land, like the plains, is used for farms.

Many people build their houses upon

hills in order to enjoy the beautiful views. Another reason for doing this is that the air is cooler and fresher there in summer.

A third and even more important reason is that it is more healthful to live on high ground. Where the land is low, the slope is often so gentle that the water cannot flow off readily. Houses in such places often have cellars that are damp, and the people living in such houses are in danger of fever, and of other kinds of sickness caused by this dampness. But the water generally runs away quickly from a hill, so that the ground there soon becomes dry even after a heavy rain.

In large cities, where land is very expensive, people build almost anywhere. Here the low places are carefully drained, like swamps on farms; drain pipes, or sewers, being used to carry off the water.

The bottoms of valleys, unlike hills, usually have a gentle slope. This fact has had a great influence upon the roads of every country (Fig. 20). For in order to get from one place to another, it is easier to travel in a valley than to go up and down across the hills. On that account, when white men first came to

The use of valleys for roads and railways

FIG. 19. — The ruins of castles, built on the crests of steep hills in the Rhine Valley in Germany.

In times past, when war was more common than now, men built great castles, with thick walls, on the summits, or crests, of hills (Fig. 19). From these they could look out over the country for a long distance, and spy approaching enemies in time to prepare for them. Besides this, the steep sides of the hills were difficult for the enemy to climb.

Some of the Indians used to build their towns upon the tops of steep hills, in order to be safe from other Indians. For the same reason the early settlers in New England placed their churches and villages upon the hilltops. At present, hills are little needed for protection against enemies.

this country, and settled among the hills, they built their roads in the valleys. The same thing is still done.

Railroads have also been built in the valleys. Trains cannot be drawn up steep slopes, and therefore the railroads must either cut through the hills or else follow the valleys. The latter is much the cheaper plan, so that in a hilly country railroads wind in and out, often making sharp curves in order to follow the valleys (Fig. 20).

FIG. 20. — A road and a railway winding their way up a mountain valley.

large enough for boats are also found in many of the larger valleys. Can you give reasons why people choose to live along such highways of travel?

It is because valleys are such important highways that many of our towns and cities have grown up in them. Some of the largest cities are found where two or more valleys come together. In such places roads and railways, coming from different directions, meet and thus make a good center where people may trade, and from which they may ship goods (Fig. 21).

When we think of a valley, we usually have in mind a small one, across which

Where the country is nearly level, as upon a plain, it is easier to travel in a straight line. Even in such a place, however, both the wagon roads and the railways are often built round a small hill rather than over or through it.

While many people build their houses upon hills, many **The use of valleys for homes** more live in the valleys. Farmers often live in the valleys because the best soil is usually found there. The soil is washed into the valleys by the rains and is therefore deeper than on the hill slopes. There is also more moisture in the valleys, so that the crops grow better there.

Another important reason why people live in valleys is the fact just mentioned, that the roads and railways are so often built there. Rivers

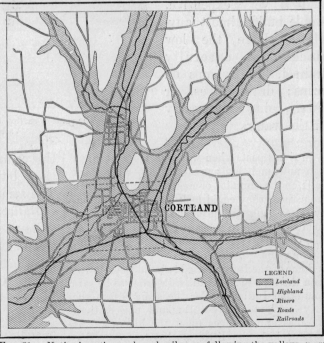

CORTLAND

LEGEND
Lowland
Highland
Rivers
Roads
Railroads

FIG. 21. — Notice how the roads and railways, following the valleys, meet at this point. Because this is a center, a city has grown up here.

a person can easily see, for the valleys

The size of valleys that one commonly sees are both narrow and short.

But valleys are of all sizes. Many are so narrow that a person can easily toss a stone across them. Probably there

FIG. 22. — Trace the *divide* on the roof of this house.

are some of this kind near your home, and if you search you may find one.

Other valleys are several miles across, and some are far larger. Indeed, there are some so great that one could not travel their whole length or width, even if he were to spend all day and all night upon a fast train. There is one such in our country, called the Mississippi Valley, which is over three thousand miles long, and nearly as wide.

Valleys as large as this must, of course, have very gentle slopes. On that ac-

The Mississippi Valley count many people living in the Mississippi Valley scarcely know that they are in a valley. The Mississippi River flows through the lowest part, but the homes of many people are so far from that river that they may never have seen it. The land all about them is so level that it does

not seem to form a part of any slope. It is, in fact, a vast plain. Yet, when the rain falls there, it flows on and on in brooks and rivers, till it reaches the great river, thus proving that the plain is a part of the Mississippi Valley.

Not all the slopes of this valley are smooth and even. There are smaller valleys of many different sizes within this great valley, and some of them are hundreds of miles long.

The more important valleys have names, just as people have; **How one valley** for instance, there is the **is separated** Mississippi Valley, the Hud- **from another** son Valley, and the Connecticut Valley. Can you name others? It is important that there be some way of fixing the boundaries of such a valley, so that one can know where it begins and ends, and how much land is included within it. Usually this is easily done.

When the rain falls upon the roof of a house (Fig. 22), the water is divided along the highest part, some flowing down one side, some down the other.

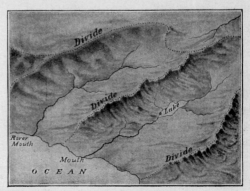

FIG. 23. — A map to show the divides between valleys. Trace the divides.

Water falling upon the highest land between two valleys is divided in a similar manner. Because the water parts, or divides, at the highest place between two valleys, this place is called a *divide*, or *water parting*, or sometimes a *watershed*. The dotted lines in the picture (Fig. 23) show some divides. Notice how irregular the lines are.

A divide sometimes stands out as sharply as on the roof of a house. In other places it is difficult to find, because the land is so nearly level. Can you point out such a place in Figure 23?

Since the divides are the boundaries of the valleys, it is easy to determine how far it is across any valley. How would you do it?

When it rains slightly, the water soaks into the soil and disappears; but when there is a heavy rain, not all of the water can sink into the ground. Some begins to flow away. One little stream, perhaps less than an inch wide, begins at one point; another joins it; soon several of them unite; and after a little while a good-sized brook or creek is formed.

Have you not noticed this flowing water in the school yard, in the roads, or on the sides of hills? If you have, you have surely noticed that the water

Fig. 24. — Little valleys cut in the soil by the rains.

The divides on the two sides of the Mississippi Valley are many hundreds of miles apart. But there are, no doubt, some valleys near your home whose divides are not one hundred feet apart. See whether you can find one; and if you do, try to trace its divides.

People sometimes speak of the " everlasting hills," but they are not everlasting. **How hills and valleys have been made** The hills and valleys that you have seen were not always here, and will not remain forever. They have all been slowly made. Let us see how this has been done.

did not flow off without taking something with it. It was muddy. This means that soil had become mixed with the water and was being borne away by it. Every heavy rain bears along much soil, cutting little channels, washing out roads, and perhaps even destroying the beds of railways, so that trains must stop running for a time.

During such a rain little channels, or *valleys*, are carved in the soil, leaving tiny *hills* and *ridges* between (Fig. 24). No doubt you have seen these formed many times. If not, you can easily make them by pouring water from a sprinkler upon a pile of loose dirt.

There are many heavy rains every year, and in a lifetime their number is very large. During many hundreds of years, then, the water could wash away an enormous amount of soil and rock. This soil the large streams and rivers would carry away to the sea. It is by such very simple means that even deep valleys have been formed, with the hills between them. It has all been done in much the same way as the rain water cuts the tiny channels in the soil of the school yard.

What a change water must have made in the surface of the earth during the thousands of years that have passed! No doubt there were hills and valleys in the very beginning; but every year these have been slowly changing, so that they are now very different from what they once were. After many more years they will be very different from what they are now, for they are even now slowly changing.

This is the way in which most hills and valleys have been formed. Some of the very largest valleys, however, like the Mississippi, have not been made entirely by running water. They have been partly caused by the sinking or the rising of the land. We shall learn more about this when we study about mountains.

Definitions   A *valley* is the low land between higher lands, as between hills or mountains.

A *divide* (also called *water-parting* or *water-shed*) is the place between two valleys where the rain water parts, or divides, that on one side flowing into one valley, that on the other flowing into the neighboring valley.

Review Questions   1. Why does a hilly country look more attractive than a plain? 2. Of what use are hills? 3. Show how valleys are of use for roads and railways. 4. Why are they of use for homes? 5. What about the size of valleys? 6. Tell about the Mississippi Valley. 7. How is one valley separated from another? 8. How have hills and valleys been made?

Suggestions   1. Where is the highest hill near your home? 2. What views do you most enjoy in your neighborhood? Describe them. 3. Find pictures of castles, showing their location on hills. 4. Find the divide, or watershed, of some valley near you. Trace it as far as you can. 5. Watch the water carrying off soil after a rain. 6. Find a washout after a heavy rain. 7. Show that streets and roads are so made that they have a watershed. Why is that done? 8. Do you know any roads or railways that follow valleys and wind about among the hills? If so, tell about them. 9. Make a drawing showing the appearance of a hilly country.

4. Mountains

Hills are seldom more than a few hundred feet high; but in some parts of the world the slopes rise thousands of feet. Such high places are called *mountains*.

You may never have seen mountains, but you have certainly seen something that looks quite like them. **Appearance of mountains** Often, on a summer evening, the sun sets behind great banks of clouds that reach far up into the sky. Some of them have rough, steep sides and great rugged peaks; others have more gentle slopes and rounder tops. Often there are many of them together, and they appear so real that it seems as if one might climb their sides, if he could only reach them.

This is very much as snow-covered mountains appear in the distance. In fact, in a mountainous country one must often look carefully to tell whether he sees real mountains or only some clouds.

FIG. 25. — A view in a region of low mountains, with forests covering the lower slopes. —

The mountains in Figure 25 are much like hills, except that they are larger.

The size of mountains They are two or three thousand feet in height. Some mountains are so low, and their slopes so gentle, that one is easily able to climb to their tops. Such mountains are often called hills; but many mountains are even two or three miles in height. The tops, or *peaks*, of these may rise far above the clouds, and are often wholly hidden by them.

Usually where there is one mountain peak, there are others in sight (Fig. 26). They often extend in lines, forming what is called a *mountain chain*, or a *mountain range*, which may be hundreds of miles in length. Besides peaks, there are many deep valleys and steep slopes in such a mountain chain.

Perhaps you know that it is colder on the summit of a high hill than at **The temperature on mountains** its base. When going to the top of the Washington Monument, which is five hundred and fifty feet high, if one

FIG. 26. — Snow-covered mountain peaks in the Alps, many thousands of feet high.

takes a thermometer with him, he finds that it is about two degrees cooler at

FIG. 27.—A mountain on whose summit snow has just fallen, while no snow fell at its base.

the top than at the base. One might not notice any difference in temperature when climbing low hills, but it is easily noticed on high ones. If your home is near such a hill, you can prove this.

People who live among high hills observe that it often snows upon their summits (Fig. 27), while it rains in the valleys below. How can you explain this?

Many mountains rise so high that it is *much* colder at the summit than at the base. In fact, it is so cold on very high mountains that the snow never quite melts away. No rain ever falls there; but it snows instead, both summer and winter, and it is far too cold for trees to grow. Such mountains, therefore, are always white with a thick blanket of snow.

Even in hot Central Africa some of the mountains rise so high that they are always covered with snow. On these peaks it is as cold as in the land of the Eskimos, although the Negroes living at the base of the mountains need hardly any clothing.

Because of the cool climate and beautiful scenery, many people spend part

of the summer among the mountains. Even the lower mountains, which are covered with woods all the way to the top, and have no snow in summer, are so much cooler than the lowland that they often attract thousands of visitors during hot weather.

The use of mountains as summer resorts

Railroads now lead to many of the mountains, and sometimes even go completely across them. Following a valley, such a road rises higher and higher until it comes to what is called a *mountain pass* (Fig. 28).

FIG. 28.—A railroad train crossing a pass in the lofty, snow-covered Alps.

This is nothing more than a valley between two mountain peaks. Then, after going over the pass, the railroad leads down the valley on the other side. Or, quite often, if the way to the pass is too steep, a railroad winds about, in many curves, until it can climb no higher; then it tunnels directly through the hard mountain rock. Some of the tunnels in mountains are several miles long, and have several thousand feet of rock directly overhead.

There are often good roads in the mountains, and some of the visitors amuse themselves by driving. There are also paths in many directions, leading to points of interest; and many people spend a part of their time in mountain climbing.

Why mountain climbing is difficult, and even dangerous

This sport, however, is often difficult and sometimes dangerous. It may not seem difficult to climb to the top of a mountain, but it usually is.

In the first place, a long distance must be traveled. It might require a whole day of steady climbing to reach the summit of a mountain only one mile high. We cannot go straight up into the air. That is impossible. Instead, we must walk up the slope of the mountain and go several miles before we reach the summit.

Most mountains are so steep that one would grow very tired climbing directly up their slopes; therefore a much longer, zigzag path is usually followed. In addition to this, there may be some steep cliffs, or *precipices* (Fig. 29), that could not be climbed even if one wished to do so; and it is necessary to travel round these, to find a place where the slope is less steep.

For these reasons it may be necessary to walk ten miles, or even more, climbing uphill all the time, in order to reach the top of a mountain only a mile high. One would need to stop often for breath and rest.

There may be danger, at some points, especially in climbing very high mountains. One may lose his way, or, since the path is often wet and rocky, with perhaps a steep precipice close to it,

FIG. 29. — Steep rock precipices, up whose face one cannot climb.

one's foot may slip, causing him to fall upon the rocks far beneath. Or great masses of stone and snow may suddenly come crashing down the mountain side, destroying everything in their path. The dangers to be met in climbing high mountains are shown in the following description.

The climbing of Mont Blanc, in Switzerland

Many people cross the ocean to visit the Alps Mountains in Switzerland. Mont Blanc, one of the best-known peaks in the Alps, is nearly three miles in height.

It is so difficult and dangerous to climb this mountain that persons wishing to do so must employ guides, to show them the way and help them over the worst places.

The round trip usually takes two nights and three days; and as there is no place to obtain food, it is necessary to carry it. Overcoats and blankets are also needed; for even though the journey be made in the hottest summer weather, it is bitterly cold upon the mountain top.

Suppose that we are making such a journey. We start early in the morning, so as to have a long day. Each of us carries a few light articles, but the guides and porters take most, for they are strong and used to climbing. At first we walk along a pleasant path in a beautiful wood; a house is now and then passed, and perhaps a green field, but soon there are no more houses and fields, and we meet no people. The trees become smaller and smaller, until the line is reached above which it is so cold that no trees can grow. This is called the *tree line*, or *timber line*.

From this point on, no plants larger than bushes are seen, and after a while even these disappear. Meantime the soil and grass have become more scarce, while here and there banks of snow are found in the shady hollows. Soon we have climbed to the *snow line*. This is the line above which snow is found all the year round. Now, no matter in what direction we look, rocks and snow are everywhere to be seen, and the snow is often *hundreds* of feet deep.

What a wonderful view is before us! It repays us for all the hard work. We look down upon the woods through which we have just passed, and over them to the deep valleys, with the green fields, pretty houses, and villages far below us. Beyond are seen other steep mountains upon the opposite side of the valley.

A guide takes his place in front of us, and often tells us to stop while he goes ahead to examine the way. It may be that the snow has bridged over and hidden a deep and narrow chasm, and if we were to step upon this snow bridge, we might break through and fall a hundred feet or more.

Sometimes the guides lift us over a dangerous place; and when it is steep or slippery, they fasten all the members of the party together with ropes, so that if one falls, the others may hold him (Fig. 30).

As we advance higher and higher, it is often necessary to take a narrow path on the steep side of the mountain. On the right we can look hundreds of feet almost straight downward; on the left are huge stones and masses of snow almost directly overhead.

Fig. 30. — Mountain climbers, fastened together by ropes, on the way to the top of Mont Blanc.

The snow sometimes slips, forming *snow slides*, or *avalanches*, which are very dangerous. They come tearing down the sides of the mountains with a terrible roar, at times burying whole villages beneath them. You have seen the same thing, on a much smaller scale, when snow has slid from the roofs of houses on warm winter days.

After one night spent in a little house about halfway up the mountain side (Fig. 31), and after much hard work on the next day, we reach the summit. Here, in spite of our heavy wraps, we are all shivering, for upon high mountain tops there are fierce winds which seem to go through even the thickest clothing.

FIG. 31. — Rest house on the slopes of Mont Blanc, above the snow line.

Perhaps you already know that the rocks inside the mountains sometimes contain gold and silver. Iron, lead, and other *metals* are also obtained there. The metal in the rings, watches, and silver coins that you have seen, and even the iron parts of your school desk, may have come from the rocks of some mountain.

Other uses of mountains

Rock that contains metal is called *ore;* and it may look so much like common rock that you might not note the difference. You might have a

On this barren mountain top there are no birds, no trees, no grass, — nothing but snow and rock (Fig. 32). But if it is a clear day and there are no clouds clinging to the mountain sides below us, we may be able to look down into the beautiful green valleys only a few miles away. There the birds are singing, flowers are blossoming, and men working in the fields are complaining of the heat.

very valuable gold ore in your hand and not know that it contained any gold. In order to get the metal out of the ore, much work is necessary. Many men in mountainous countries are employed in mining ore and in getting the metal out of it (Fig. 33).

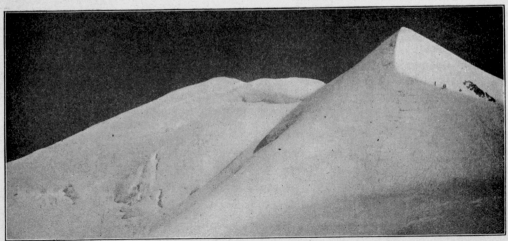

FIG. 32. — The summit of Mont Blanc, always covered with a deep coat of snow.

The trees in the mountain forests are also valuable. The most common kinds are evergreens, such as the pine, hemlock, and spruce. These are green even through the winter, and can live on the

there is much ice and snow upon some of them; and that upon the higher mountains there is so much that it never melts away, no matter how hot the summer may be.

During hot weather, many streams in the plains dry up; but at such times the ice and snow of the mountains melt the faster. Then the streams which flow forth from these mountains are even more swollen than usual. This water may run along for many miles, until it finally reaches towns and cities where people need it to drink. Do you know of any city that gets its drinking water from such a river?

You have learned that most hills have been slowly made by running water, which cuts out val-

FIG. 33. — In these buildings metal is obtained from the ore that is mined in the mountain rocks far below the surface.

cold mountain sides as far up as the timber line (Fig. 34). The land upon a mountain side is usually too steep and rocky for farms, but even where there can be no farms, trees may grow, covering the mountains for miles and miles with dense forests. These trees may be cut down and sawed into lumber, from which all sorts of wooden articles are made. Possibly the very seat in which you are sitting was once part of a tree that grew on the side of a mountain.

Mountains are of further use because of the water they supply. We have already seen that

FIG. 34. — The forest-covered slopes of lofty mountains, which shut in a mountain valley. Point out the timber line.

leys and leaves high places between. Most mountain ranges have *not* been made in this way. They are really parts of the land that have been slowly raised, until some portions are much higher than the

How mountains have been made

surrounding country. When mountains are thus raised, the rocks are bent, broken, and folded in a very irregular way (Fig. 35). You can imitate this folding of the mountain rocks by bending, or crumpling, a number of sheets of paper. When the rocks of mountains are folded, the crumpling extends for a great distance, sometimes even for thousands of miles. Such a region of folded rocks, a hundred miles or more wide, and perhaps a thousand miles or more long, is called a *mountain system.*

FIG. 35. — Beds of rock, in the mountains, that have been bent up in an arch when the mountains were raised.

Of course running water cuts valleys in a mountain region as well as in a hilly country. In fact, most of the valleys and many of the peaks and ridges in mountains, have been carved out by running water. The land is slowly raised by folding, and then valleys are cut into it by the water that flows down the slopes.

About how to study　While it is well, first, to read even several pages of the text without pause, as before stated, it is necessary in further study to stop here and there to think over what has been read.

For this purpose some stopping places are better than others. Probably the best stopping place, for every page or two, is found at the end of the answer to each question that is suggested in the headings at the side of the page. At this point, each time, the thought turns to another topic, and it is therefore a good place to make a stop. One can then look back over what he has just read, or think it through without looking at the book.

In preparing for recitation it is not necessary to try to remember the *exact words* of the book. In fact, it is much better to tell what has been learned in one's own words, just as a person does in writing a letter.

Definitions　A *mountain* is high land, where masses of rock have been pushed up above the level of the surrounding country.

A *mountain peak* is a high part of a mountain. It is a sort of large hill in the mountains.

A *mountain range* is a long, rather narrow belt of mountain country.

A *mountain chain* is a group of mountain ranges, one beside the other, and often nearly in a line.

A *mountain system* is an even larger group of mountains, often including two or more mountain chains.

A *precipice* is a steep rock cliff, often found in a mountainous country.

An *avalanche* is a great mass of snow, ice, or rock falling down a mountain side.

The *timber line* (or tree line) is the line above which no trees grow.

The *snow line* is a line above which snow remains all the year round.

A *mountain pass* is a gap, usually a valley, across the crest of a mountain range.

Review Questions　1. Describe the appearance of mountains. 2. What about the temperature on mountains? 3. Why are mountains of use as summer resorts? 4. Why is mountain climbing difficult and sometimes dangerous? 5. Tell about the climbing of Mont Blanc. 6. State other uses of mountains. 7. How have mountains been made?

8. What is meant by a plain? Swamp?

Valley ? Divide ? Mountain ? Mountain peak ? Mountain range ? Mountain chain ? Mountain system ? Precipice ? Avalanche ? Timber line ? Snow line ? Mountain pass ?

Suggestions 1. If you have made a visit to the mountains, describe what you saw, to the class. 2. Watch for clouds that resemble mountains. 3 Make a collection of pictures of mountains. Note the timber line, the snow line, and other points of interest. 4 Represent a mountain by the use of sand, stones, twigs, and chalk dust. Show the woods and the timber line ; the snow line ; precipices. 5. Ask some one who has climbed a mountain to tell you about it 6 Write a story relating the adventures you might expect in climbing a mountain. 7. Describe some of the views you would expect to enjoy.

II. Water

1. Rivers

We have seen how very important valleys are; and we have also learned that they have been formed by the work of running water. We shall next study the running water that has carved out the valleys, and that makes the rivers.

How rivers begin Every heavy rain causes the water to collect here and there, and to flow down the slopes. At first only tiny rills are formed, but these unite to make little streams and brooks. The brooks and small streams, in turn, unite to form rivers. Thus rain alone may cause a river; but as soon as all the rain water runs off, such a river would become quite dry if there were not water from some other source.

Rivers usually have a more regular supply of water. Some of them, as we have seen, start in the high mountains, where the snows never entirely melt away. Others have their beginnings, or *sources*, in lakes and swamps.

It should be remembered, too, that there is a great deal of water in the ground, for some of it sinks into the earth during every rain. It is this water that men find when they dig wells. The underground water trickles

Fig. 36. — Icicles formed in winter where water from underground slowly oozes out from cracks in the rock.

slowly through the soil, and through crevices in the rocks (Fig. 36), often bubbling forth as a *spring*, weeks after it has fallen as rain somewhere else. Many rivers have their sources in such springs, and most large rivers receive water along their courses from hundreds and even thousands of them.

How a river changes and grows as it advances Let us take a journey from the source of a river to its lower end, or *mouth*, and see how it changes. Our river has its source in a small spring in the mountains, where the clear, cold water bubbles out of the **1. Its upper part** ground at the base of a rock cliff.

For a short distance it flows through a grassy meadow (Fig. 37), and is so narrow that you can easily step across it. The water is so clear that you can see the speckled trout swimming about in a deep hole near one side, or *bank*. A smaller branch, or

FIG. 37. — A meadow brook — that later forms a river — near its source.

tributary, enters the brook from another small valley, and makes it somewhat larger and deeper.

Soon the brook leaves the meadow and begins to tumble down a steeper slope. Here it changes greatly. In some places it is narrow and deep; in others, broad and shallow; here it flows swiftly, there slowly.

We put a toy boat upon the water. It floats along quietly for a time, and then, coming to a swift part of the current, called a *rapid*, it is whirled along roughly and upset. We rescue it and set it right again, but soon it comes to a place where the water falls several feet from the top of a ledge (Fig. 38). In tumbling over this *waterfall* the boat is again upset, and dashed against the rocks.

As the water rushes along, beating itself into foam, it is here and there joined by other tributaries, some very small, others nearly as large as the brook itself. Thus the stream gradually grows broader and deeper.

Often the water must rush around or leap over large bowlders that lie directly in its path; and often it

FIG. 38. — Here the water, shut in by steep walls, leaps from ledge to ledge, each time forming a waterfall.

FIG. 39. — The stream, shut in by towering cliffs. The large bowlders in its bed have fallen from these cliffs.

stream until they are worn into smooth, round pebbles. These pebbles are borne on downstream, and are slowly ground up into grains of sand and bits of clay.

The bed of the stream and the rock cliffs by its side are ground away at the same time. It is this grinding that has made the gorge so deep and caused its sides to rise so steep and high. The scenery here is wild and grand, with towering cliffs on either side (Fig. 39). Now it is too difficult to follow the stream, and we leave it, to join it again many miles below.

Here the river has left the mountains and flows in a broad valley through a hilly country. Some of the slopes are steep and covered 2. Its middle part with forests; others, more gentle, are cleared of trees and dotted with farms, farmhouses, and barns.

The current is not so swift now, although there are still some rapids and falls; and instead of rocky cliffs the banks are low (Fig. 40). In fact, in

falls directly downward for many feet, with a roar. The stream is now in a deep gorge, with the rocky cliffs extending high on each side, and shutting it in like walls (Fig. 38). It seems quite helpless, with the great, hard rocks all about it. Yet it is really getting the better of this rock, for pieces of stone are often loosened and fall from the steep cliffs into the water. Then the torrent hurls them against one another, and grinds them against the bottom, or *bed*, of the

D

FIG. 40. — The river is now large, and its banks are low and bordered by farm land.

some places these are not much higher than the water. Here and there a tributary, itself almost a river, pours its flood into our stream.

It has now been many days since this water left the mountains. The river has become so deep that we cannot touch its bed with a long pole, and so

has greatly changed. In the mountains the water rushed rapidly and noisily onward, dragging along bowlders and pebbles; in its middle part it flowed fast enough to carry only sand and mud; but now the current is so gentle that it can carry only the finest bits of rock mud. These bits are so tiny that, if you were

FIG. 41. — Here the river is so broad that a very long bridge is needed to cross it.

wide that bridges are needed to cross it (Fig. 41). We can now drift along easily in a boat, watching the men at work in the fields, and the towns and villages that we pass.

At one point, however, the current grows swifter, and finally the water tumbles in a great fall. We must leave the river at this point and pass around the fall. Here is a large city with many mills and factories. From this point on, the stream is so broad and deep that large steamboats can travel upon it; it has now become a great river.

It is still several hundred miles to the river mouth, and since other rivers, both

3. Its lower course large and small, continue to join it, our river steadily grows deeper and broader. The banks become lower, and they are occupied by many towns and cities, with farms between.

In this part of its course there are no rapids and falls. Indeed, the current

to place some of the muddy water in a glass, it would take hours for all of them to settle and leave the water clear.

At last we are approaching the river mouth, toward which the water has been steadily flowing for weeks. The river is now a full mile in width, and moving very slowly. It never dries up, because there is always a supply of water from its thousands of springs, and it drains so great a country that rain is nearly always falling into some of its hundreds of tributaries.

Not only river-boats, but ships from the ocean are now passing up and down the river. Now the water divides into several streams, each flowing into the ocean along a separate course (Fig. 43). Each of these pours its fresh water into the salt water of the sea, and beyond their mouths no land is to be seen, — nothing but water everywhere (Fig. 42).

How other rivers differ from this one

Other rivers may differ from this one in many ways. Instead of having their sources in springs among the mountains, they may start from swamps or lakes. They may have low, soft *system* (Fig. 43). For instance, we speak of the Mississippi River System, meaning the Mississippi River and all its tributaries.

FIG. 42. — Mouth of a large river where it pours its water into the ocean.

banks near their sources, instead of high rocky ones, and they may have no rapids or falls. Instead of emptying directly into the ocean, they may enter other rivers as tributaries, or they may pour their waters into lakes. But, in spite of such differences, other rivers are much like this one in most respects. If there is a river near you, how does it resemble the one described? How does it differ from it?

The meaning of *river system* and *river basin*

We have seen that from its source to its mouth a river may receive water from hundreds of tributaries. Thus the rain that falls in places even hundreds of miles apart may at last be brought together in a single main stream. Such a main stream, with all of its tributaries, is called a *river*

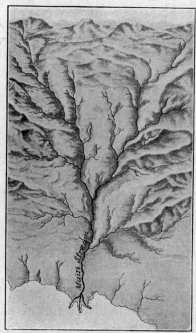

FIG. 43. — Map of a river system. Point out the source; the mouth; the main stream; several tributaries.

All the country that is drained by a single main stream is called a *river basin*. Thus all the land drained by the Mississippi River and its tributaries forms the Mississippi Basin. In what river basin is your home located?

What rivers do with their sediment

Very great quantities of soil are carried away by rivers, and much rock is ground up and carried off by them. This load of rock bits that rivers carry, is called *sediment*. Some of it comes from the pebbles that are rolled about in the stream bed, and some comes from the stream bed itself. What becomes of it all?

If you have seen a sidewalk, or a field,

flooded with water, you perhaps remember that a thin layer of sand or fine mud was left when the flood **1. Flood plains** disappeared. The sand and mud were borne along by the current, land (Fig. 45) between the stream and the hills that rise at some distance on either side. But in large valleys, like the Mississippi, the flood plains are many miles in width.

FIG. 44. — A river which has overflowed its banks in time of flood. The tree is completely surrounded by the flood.

Flood plains make the best kind of farm land. The soil is very fertile; the surface is so level that it can be easily cultivated; and, being so near the water, it has plenty of moisture for the roots of plants.

Not all the sediment that a river carries is used to build flood plains along **2. Deltas** its banks. Much of it is drifted on to the river mouth, where it enters a lake or the ocean. Here the water is usually quiet, so that even the finest mud sinks to the bottom. At first only enough sediment is collected to form

until they reached a place where the water did not move swiftly enough to carry them any farther. Then they slowly settled.

After heavy rains, or when the snow melts rapidly, rivers often rise so high that they overflow their banks (Fig. 44). At such times the water spreads out in a thin, slowly moving sheet, on both sides of the main current. Then, as just described, this slowly moving water allows a thin layer of mud to settle. Each flood adds another layer, making the land a little higher, until, after many years, it is built above the usual level of the river. Such land is generally a level plain; and, since it is made by river floods, it is called a *flood plain*.

This is one of the ways in which plains are made. Near small streams such plains are generally narrow strips of

FIG. 45. — A narrow flood plain bordering a small stream, which in time of flood overflows the plain.

low, swampy land. But, like the flood plains, this is slowly built higher and higher, by a layer of mud from each flood, until it becomes high enough to make dry land.

Such plains at the mouths of rivers form what are called *deltas* (Fig. 46). Many rivers have deltas so wide that one cannot see across them, and the great quantity of sediment from which they are made has come from the fields, hills, and mountains, perhaps hundreds of miles away. Such delta lands, like flood plains, are very fertile and make excellent farms.

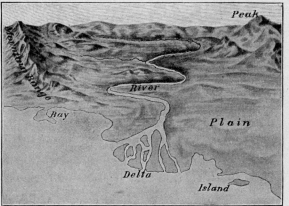

FIG. 46. — The delta of a river.

Rivers are of importance in other ways besides carving out valleys and building flood plains and deltas. Each river is really a great open ditch for draining the surrounding land.

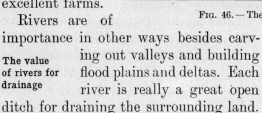

The value of rivers for drainage

rapidly. If it were not for rivers, this water could not run off so quickly. People in towns and cities along a river bank also owe a special debt to the river, because it quickly carries away all sewage.

While rivers drain the land, and thus keep it healthful, they also bring the much-needed water to plants, animals, and man. We have already learned in our study of the Sahara Desert how necessary water is to plants. In desert countries men lead water from the streams many miles, through ditches or pipes, and let it spread out over the

Their value for the water they supply

FIG. 47. — A large ditch, in western United States, in which water is led from a river to be used in watering crops in the desert.

Its work in drainage is always of value to the farmers who live in the valley through which it flows; but its importance is most plainly seen when heavy rains fall, or when the snow melts thirsty soil, so that plants can thrive (Fig. 47). That is called *irrigation*, and in many places, including some parts of our own country, no crops can be raised without it.

Again, many animals and people depend upon rivers for the water that they drink. Even whole cities often

FIG. 48. — An old-fashioned water wheel used to give the power for grinding grain into flour in a grist mill.

obtain their drinking water from rivers. Find out where your own drinking water comes from, if you do not already know.

The water of rivers is also used for turning water wheels (Fig. 48).

Their use for manufacturing You have, perhaps, noticed how windmills work. The *wind* blows the large wheel round and round, and it may be so connected with other wheels that it can pump water, or turn a saw for sawing wood, or grind corn. *Steam* is also used for power; for example, to turn the wheels of a railway engine, so that it can drag the heavy cars along.

River water is made to do work in much the same manner. Where there is a swift current, or where there are waterfalls, such as the Niagara Falls, it is often easy to run some of the water off to one side through a ditch or pipe. The water, racing rapidly along, or falling with great force, strikes a wheel (Fig. 48) and makes it whirl round. This wheel, being connected with others, causes them to turn also, much as one wheel in a clock causes others to move.

Thus machinery is set in motion by which logs are sawed into lumber, grain is ground into flour, cotton is made into cloth, and many other kinds of work are done.

Water that furnishes the power to turn the wheels is called *water power;* and the buildings in which such manufacturing is carried on are called *factories*, or *mills* (Fig. 49).

The water in most rivers does not flow fast enough to strike a wheel with much force. Water power is found

FIG. 49. — A large mill beside a waterfall that supplies the water power for running the machinery in the mill.

mainly in rivers with swift currents, and especially near rapids and falls. There mills have been built (Fig. 49), and then cities have often sprung up. We found one such city on our journey down the river, described on page 34.

There is one other way in which rivers are very valuable. It has always **Their use for** been difficult to find an easy **navigation** means for carrying goods from one place to another. In some places there are no roads, and even where there are roads, they are often hilly, rough, and muddy.

much as scores of wagons or cars (Fig. 50), and many boats can go up and down at the same time, so that a large river is equal to several railroads. Besides, such a river may lead a long distance into a country. For example, one can travel by boat for thousands of miles up the Mississippi River and its tributaries.

For these reasons, carrying goods by boat upon rivers, or *river navigation*, is a very important business. Indeed, it is so important, that broad ditches, called *canals*, have been dug in many places (Fig. 51) in order to improve it.

Fig. 50. — A large steamboat on the Mississippi River.

Yet most of the things that we use, such as sugar, flour, oil, meat, coal, lumber, and clothing, must be carried long distances, sometimes thousands of miles. Even if the roads were excellent, it would take a great deal of time, and cost much money, to haul these materials in wagons. To ship them by railway takes less time, but is expensive.

A broad, deep river is really one of the finest highways in the world. To be sure, no wagons or cars can be drawn over it, but boats are easily moved upon it. A large river boat can carry as

Sometimes these canals have been extended around rapids or waterfalls for the use of river boats. In other places they have been built many miles across the land, so as to connect one river with another.

Before the time of railways, — which is no longer ago than when your great-grandfathers were boys, — boats were used for carrying all sorts of articles. Even to-day, when there are so many good wagon roads and railways, it is cheaper to carry many things on boats than in cars.

It is easy to see, then, why many people have chosen to build their homes near rivers. A farmer prefers to live near a good wagon road, or near the

A *river basin* is the land drained by a river and all its tributaries. The divide surrounding it forms its boundary.

A *tributary* to a river is another stream that flows into it.

Fig. 51. — A canal boat in a canal dug around some rapids in a river.

railway station, so that he may easily send his crops to market; and for the same reason, people have always liked to live near a river, which is a good highway, or *waterway*. It is partly on this account that many of the large cities of the world stand on the banks of large rivers. Do you know of any such cities?

Definitions　　A *river source* is the place where a river starts.

A *spring* is water flowing forth from the ground.

A *river bank* is the land that borders a river. Each river has two banks.

A *river channel* is the part of a valley that a river occupies.

A *river bed* is the bottom over which the water flows.

A *rapid* is a part of a river where the water flows so swiftly that it is tossed about.

A *waterfall* is a part of a river where the slope of the bed is so steep that the water falls nearly straight down.

A *river system* is a main stream with all its tributaries.

The *mouth* of a river is its lower end. It is usually the part where its waters empty into a larger body of water, such as another river, a lake, or the ocean.

A *flood plain* is the plain along the banks of a river that has been built up by the sediment that settles during floods.

A *delta* is the plain formed at the mouth of a river by sediment that the current can carry no farther.

1. How do rivers begin? 2. Describe the upper part of a river. 3. Describe its middle part. 4. What is the condition in its lower course? 5. How **Review Questions** may other rivers differ from the one described? 6. What is meant by a river system? By a river basin? 7. Where are flood plains found, and how are they formed? 8. Where and how are the deltas of rivers formed? 9. How are rivers of importance for drainage? 10. How are they of value for supplying water? 11. For manufacturing? 12. For navigation?

13. What is a river source? A spring? River bank? River channel? River bed? Rapid? Waterfall? River system? River basin? Tributary? River mouth? Flood plain? Delta?

1. Why are the rocks in river beds usually so smooth and round? 2. What is meant by "up a river"? By "down a river"? By "right bank"? By "left bank"? 3. Find a spring. Why is its water cool? 4. Find a flood plain. 5. What are the causes of river floods? 6. Do you know of some city that gets its water from a river or a lake? If so, how is the water brought to the city and distributed to the houses? 7. Make a water wheel, and arrange for a stream of water to turn it. 8. Make a collection of pictures of rivers, and notice as many facts as you can about them. 9. Make a drawing of a river, showing its source, mouth, tributaries, and flood plains.

2. Ponds and Lakes

How ponds and lakes are formed

If you build a dam of sticks and mud across a small brook, the water soon fills the little basin that you make, and then flows out over the dam. In this way you can make a very small pond (Fig. 52).

wood, or stone, across much larger streams (Fig. 53). They do this because the rivers that supply towns and cities with drinking water, or with power for manufacturing, often become too low to

FIG. 52. — A boy making a small pond by building a dam in a roadside gutter.

furnish the amount of water needed. By means of the dam a large basin is formed;

FIG. 53. — A dam built across a stream in order to make a lake for storing water.

In order to make ponds or small lakes, men often build dams of earth, and when the river is high, enough water may be collected in it to last through the dry season. If you have seen such a pond or lake, describe it to the class.

Most ponds and lakes have been caused in much this way. That is, the water has collected behind dams that have been formed across streams. This is true even of the large lakes, some of which are two or three hundred miles long and fifty miles or more wide. Usually, however, these dams have not been built by men.

Some of the dams have been made by beavers (Fig. 54). There used to be a great many beavers in our country, and some are still left.

been widened by the forming of a dam. The stream flows into this body of water at one end. This end is really a little higher than the other end, and is called the *head* of the lake. The water flows out at the lower end, which is called the *foot* of the lake. The stream that flows into a lake is called the *inlet*, and that which flows out is called the *outlet*.

Names for parts of a lake

Some lakes have no outlet, because there is so little water that the basin cannot fill and overflow. The water in such lakes becomes

Fig. 54. — A dam of sticks placed by beavers in a swift stream, in order to make the pond in which they live.

Since they prefer quiet, shallow ponds in which to live, they gnaw down small trees and make dams with the sticks. Then they build their houses in the ponds thus formed.

In other places, as among mountains, where the sides of the river valleys are steep, great avalanches of rock and earth have fallen, and blocked, or dammed up, a stream. These are some of the simplest ways in which dams have been made across valleys, to form ponds and lakes. In your later study of geography you will learn about other ways in which ponds and lakes have been made.

From what has been said, it is clear that a pond or lake is usually nothing more than part of a stream that has

salty. Perhaps you have heard of the Great Salt Lake, in Utah. Its water is so salt that no one could drink it, even if he were dying of thirst.

Why some lakes become salt

The reason why such lakes become salt is as follows. There is some salt in all water, even in that which we drink, although so little that we do not notice it. When water flows into a lake, the salt is carried with it. If there is no outlet, the water cannot flow out, but it escapes, because every day some of it dries away; that is, it is changed into vapor and carried away in the air. The salt cannot pass off in this manner. It remains, therefore, and slowly collects, until the water of the lake becomes salt.

You have heard of the Sea of Galilee, and of the Dead Sea; both of them are in Palestine.

The Sea of Galilee is a fresh-water lake, with the Jordan River for its outlet. This fresh-water river finally empties into the Dead Sea, a lake that has no outlet. The air in that desert country is so dry that fully as much water passes off from this lake in vapor as enters from the river. On that account the Dead Sea cannot overflow, and it has become one of the saltest lakes on the earth. It is so salt that fishes cannot live in it, and that is the reason it is called the Dead Sea.

tant waterways. Upon the Great Lakes, in the northern part of the United States, hundreds of vessels are engaged in carrying passengers, grain, coal, lumber, and countless other products. On this account many people have settled on the shores of large lakes, and as a result many towns and cities have been built there. Do you know of any?

FIG. 55. — The result of a morning's fishing from a canoe in a lake in Canada.

Like rivers, ponds and lakes are of use to men in many ways. They help to keep the ground moist near their shores; they furnish water to cities, to factories, and to farmers for irrigation. Besides this, many valuable food fish are caught in lakes; and in cold countries much ice, for use in summer, is cut from their surface.

The uses of ponds and lakes

Again, lakes, like rivers, are impor-

Another reason why lakes are important is because their shores are often very beautiful; and the air there is usually cool in summer. Because of this many persons go to lakes, as they do to mountains, to spend part of their summer vacation. There they can enjoy the hunting, fishing (Fig. 55), canoeing, and bathing, as well as the walks along the sand and pebble beaches and in the woods along their shores.

1. How are ponds and lakes formed? 2. Give names for the parts of a lake. 3. Why do some lakes become salt? 4. What are some of the uses of ponds and lakes?

1. Find a pond or small lake and examine the dam that caused it. 2. What dangers do you see from lakes, when the dams made by men have not been well built? 3. Find out more about beavers. 4. What is meant by "up a lake"? By "down a lake"?

travel, if you went far enough, you would come to it.

If you wished to go to the home of the nomads of the desert, or of the Negroes of Central Africa, you would have to travel across the ocean; and even if you went on a fast steamer, it would be many days before you arrived there. All the time you would be out of sight of land, with nothing but the level ocean

FIG. 56. — The vast ocean, with no land in sight. The sailboats are fishing vessels.

3. The Ocean

The great rivers, starting as tiny brooks, grow into larger and still larger streams, until, after days and perhaps weeks, they mingle their waters in the sea or ocean. No doubt much of the rain that falls near your home finally reaches the sea in this way, and if you could float along upon it in a boat, you, too, would in time reach the ocean.

We can see across most lakes, and can sail across even the largest in a day or two; but the ocean is far larger. One could sail upon it, in the same direction, for many days without coming to land (Fig. 56). Indeed, the ocean is so large that it surrounds all the land on which people live, and no matter in what direction you might

about you. Every day would be somewhat warmer than the day before, until finally you reached the hot country of Africa.

To reach the land of the Eskimos you would also go by ship on the ocean, and travel for days upon it. On this journey every day would be a little cooler than the day before, and finally you would come to a region where it is so cold that there is ice on the sea even in summer.

If your home is not near the ocean, you might have to make a journey of one or two, or even three or four, days to reach it. It might be necessary to go up hills and across valleys, to pass around lakes, and possibly even to cross great ranges of mountains. You would be surprised to find how much land there is, and how many farms, villages, towns, and cities there are. Find out how long it would take to reach the ocean from your home.

Although there is so much land, there is far more water. In fact, there is

ocean. Since plants, animals, and men must all have water, the ocean is of value to all living things on the land. It is in supplying water for rain that the ocean is of greatest importance.

Fig. 57. — A mackerel. Mackerel are usually from one to one and a half feet long

nearly three times as much water as land. The ocean is so immense that the great rivers in all parts of the earth pour their water into it. Their mouths may be thousands of miles apart, yet the sea stretches far enough to reach them all.

The water of the ocean is too salt to drink, but river water is fresh. Since there are many thousands of rivers entering the sea, you might expect that their water would make the ocean less salt. It does do so near the mouths of great rivers, but soon the fresh water becomes mixed with and swallowed up in the salt water; for the ocean is so large that all the river water that enters it is not enough to make it fresh.

Plants, animals, and men all owe much to the ocean, for without it very

Value of the ocean in furnishing water for rains

little rain would fall. Moisture is always rising into the air from the ocean, and being carried about by the winds. When it falls from the clouds, we have rain. Even rain that falls thousands of miles inland comes largely from the

There are other ways in which the ocean is of value. One of these is in supplying food. You know

Value of the ocean as a source of food

(p. 5) that almost all the food that the Eskimos eat, such as seal, walrus, and fish, comes from the sea. Fish from the ocean, or salt-water fish, as they are called, are a very important food for other people also, and many men make their living by going out in boats and catching them. Great numbers of fish are sometimes found close to the land; but often they are caught far out in the sea, so that the fishermen must remain out of sight of the land for days at a time (Fig. 56).

Instead of hooks and lines, long nets are often used, and so many fish are sometimes caught in these nets that the boats are soon filled with them. No doubt some of the mackerel (Fig. 57) or herring that you have eaten have been caught in this way. Halibut also come from the sea, and so do codfish (Fig. 58), which may be seen in almost any grocery store. Picture 56 shows a fishing vessel that is used in catching salt-water fish. | makes the seashore a pleasant place to spend the summer.

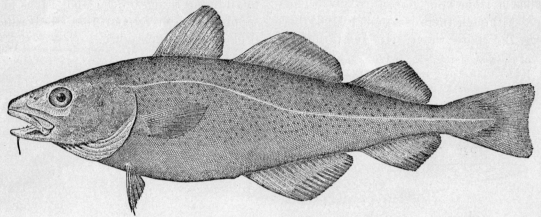

Fig. 58. — A codfish. Codfish are often three or four feet long.

Value of the ocean as a pleasure resort The ocean water is cooler than the land in summer, and for that reason the breezes that blow from the ocean are cool. This | The views at the seashore also attract people. The silvery sheet of water, stretching out as far as the eye can reach, is often dotted with white sails. Sometimes its color is green, again it is blue; when the clouds hang over it,

Fig. 59. — The ocean waves dashing into foam on the rocky coast of New England.

it is dark and gloomy. There are beautiful sunrises and sunsets to watch, and one can see the storms come and go, with the waves dashing into the whitest of foam against the rocks (Fig. 59), or rolling high upon a sandy beach.

In fact, the water, the sky, and the coast are always changing in appearance. This is true of the lake shores, too; but the ocean is so much larger than the greatest lake, that the scenery on the seashore is far grander than that on the lake shore.

For these reasons many people go to the seashore in summer, just as others go to the mountains or to the lakes. There they spend their

known. Coney Island and Asbury Park are two such resorts near New York City, and Atlantic City is another near Philadelphia. Can you tell anything about any one of them ?

Where the winters are warm, as in the South, the seacoast is a *winter* resort. Many persons spend a part of the winter on the warm southern coasts or on small islands in the sea. Some of these, like Bermuda, lie far out in the ocean. At these winter resorts there is no frost or snow. Flowers blossom all winter, and people dress in light clothing, enjoying themselves out of doors, while at their own homes the ground is covered with snow and the weather is bitterly cold.

Fig. 60. — Hundreds of people bathing on the sandy beach at Atlantic City, New Jersey.

time climbing over the rocks, walking upon the clean, sandy beach, bathing in the cool salt water (Fig. 60), and looking at the scenery.

Many houses, and even cities, have been built at the most attractive places along the seashore. There are large hotels for the visitors which are often crowded in summer, but few people are found at these summer resorts during the winter.

Resorts of this kind are very common near large cities, and some of them have become well

Different parts of the ocean have different names. For instance, the *Atlantic* Ocean is the part lying between the United States and the land, called *Europe,* where the English, Irish, Germans, and other peoples live. We buy many articles from these peoples, such as linen and woolen cloth, sugar, silk, oranges, and olives; and they likewise purchase articles from us, such as cotton, wheat, meat, iron and steel goods, and

Value of the ocean for navigation

leather. Hundreds of millions of dollars' worth of these articles are sent across the ocean every year. Thousands of passengers also cross the ocean every year, some coming to this country to live, others men are engaged in it. A single large steamship may employ five or six hundred men, and carry as many as three thousand passengers. Many of the ships are great steamers, each costing mil-

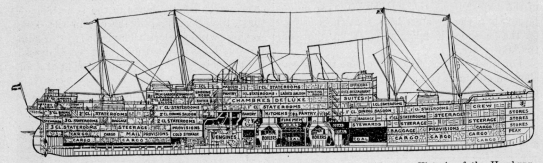

FIG. 61. — A section through one of the largest ocean steamers — the *Kaiserin Auguste Victoria* of the Hamburg-American Line. Note the position of the engines, where the coal is stored, the places for the cargo, passengers, etc.

going to Europe to travel, or to visit friends. The fastest steamers need only five or six days for the voyage.

Every part of the ocean is a great highway, and thousands of ships are always traveling upon it in all directions, carrying people, fruit, iron, different kinds of machines, mail, and many other things (Fig. 61). Although there are so

FIG. 62. — A picture to show how deep a large steamer sinks into the water.

many ships, the ocean is so large that a person may sail for days upon it without even seeing another ship.

Ocean navigation is, therefore, a very important business, and thousands of

lions of dollars. Some of these travel at the rate of twenty miles or more an hour; others are sailing vessels pushed along by the wind, going fast when the wind blows hard, and hardly moving at all when it is calm. Many of the ships used on the ocean are far larger than vessels upon lakes, and they sink deeper into the water. The largest, when loaded, reach down thirty feet or more below the surface.

One of the difficulties that ships meet is in loading and unloading the goods that they carry. Wagons can be driven alongside a railway car and be quickly filled or emptied. But a large ship sinks down into the water so many feet (Fig. 62) that it is difficult to find a place where it can come close to shore. If it should strike the bottom, it might be wrecked. Besides this, a boat cannot load and unload where there are large waves.

Difficulties and dangers for vessels

Again, upon both lakes and the ocean,

FIG. 63. — The great storm waves on the open ocean.

vessels meet with dangers of many kinds. Storms are often severe, and the waves are so high that sometimes they sweep over, and for a moment almost cover up even the very large vessels (Fig. 63). When far out from land, large, well-built ships are not in serious danger in such weather, but smaller vessels, especially those that are old or poorly built, may be destroyed.

When approaching land, however, sailors of all vessels must be careful. The shores of large lakes and of the ocean are often quite irregular, and the depth of the water may change very quickly. In some places there are dangerous shallows, in others hidden rocks, or *reefs*, that lie near the surface (Fig. 64).

There are also currents that may float a vessel out of its course; and fogs are often so dense that a person can see only a short distance ahead. It is then very easy to lose one's way at sea. In addition to all this, strong winds and high waves may drive a ship in the wrong direction, in spite of all that can be done to prevent it.

Not all these difficulties and dangers can be overcome, but much is done to make shipping both easy and safe. The irregular shape of the coast itself helps

How such difficulties and dangers are met

FIG. 64. — The wreck of an ocean steamer that ran aground in shallow water during a storm.

toward this end. Very often the land partly surrounds a body of water, as in

1. **Harbors**

Fig. 68, forming what is called a *bay*. Some of these bays are very large, being even hundreds of miles long, but many more are quite small. Many of the small bays have an

FIG. 65. — Rio Janeiro harbor.

opening large enough for vessels to enter easily, but small enough to shut out most of the fierce waves. If the water is deep, as is often the case, such a small bay makes a fine *harbor* (Fig. 65); that is, a place where vessels may enter and be protected from storms and waves.

For the purpose of loading and unloading ships, piers of wood or stone, called *wharves*, are built from the shores of the harbor out into the deep water. Even large vessels can be firmly fastened, or moored, to these wharves, and wagons can be drawn out on them close to the side of the vessels.

Thus a convenient and safe way is found for handling goods that are carried on vessels.

Harbors are so important that they are sometimes made on coasts where there are no good natural harbors. This is very expensive work, but it pays. Walls of rock are built in such a way as nearly to inclose a body of water, much as the water of a bay is inclosed by land. Such a wall is called a *breakwater* (Fig. 66), because it breaks the force of the waves and prevents them from entering the space behind.

It often happens that harbors are not as deep as they need to be. The vessels now used are much larger and sink deeper into the water than those formerly used. On that account many harbors that were once deep enough are now too shallow. All the time, too, the waves and tides are bringing

FIG. 66. — Breakwaters built at Chicago to form a harbor where ships may be safe from the waves.

sediment that settles in the harbors, slowly filling them up.

Vast sums of money have to be spent, therefore, in deepening harbors. The loose sand and mud are scraped out by dredges; but when the bottom is solid rock, it has to be blasted out. This work is of so great importance to so many people, that the United States govern-

Fig. 67. — A lighthouse built on a small island at the tip of a cape.

ment spends millions of dollars every year in doing it.

So long as a ship lies in a good harbor, it is safe from most dangers. But when **2. Lighthouses** it is outside, on its way **and light-ships** from one harbor to another, dangers are ever present. Did you ever stop to think how a vessel finds its way on the great ocean?

While a ship is out of sight of land, its officers must guide it by the position of the sun or of certain stars, using the compass and other instruments. But during storms and foggy weather, the winds and currents may cause even a large steamship to drift far out of its course. Then as a ship approaches land, the chief help is from the *lighthouses* (Fig. 67), which are built in many places along the coast.

Often the land extends out into the water, forming what is called a *point* or a *cape*, or if large and almost surrounded by water, a *peninsula* (Fig. 68). Lighthouses are placed far out on such points or capes or peninsulas, or on islands near the mainland, so that their lights may be seen a long distance over the water. They are also built elsewhere, wherever the danger requires.

In some places there are dangerous shallows, or *shoals*, where it is impossible to build a lighthouse. In such cases, ships with lights on their masts, called *light-ships* (Fig. 69), are securely anchored near by to give warning to sailors.

When the captain sees the light of a lighthouse or light-ship, he knows that he is nearing land and must be very careful. How can he tell which light he sees when there are so many light-

Fig. 68. — Find here and describe a harbor; a bay; a point; a cape; a peninsula; an island: an isthmus; a strait.

houses? That is not difficult, for the lights are not all alike. Some are white, others red; some give a steady light, others turn around and, as they turn, send out flash after flash. There are many different kinds, and the maps, or *charts*, that all ships carry, tell the captain where each is placed. He also knows the special kind of lighthouse to be found at the entrance to the harbor for which he is bound.

In case of heavy fog, when the lights cannot be seen, powerful horns and whistles are

might be wrecked. It is necessary, therefore, that the channel be clearly marked. This is done by placing hollow iron buoys here and there. These float on the surface, but are anchored firmly in their places. They are guideposts to the sailor, pointing out the way.

Dangerous rocks and shoals are also marked by buoys; and many of these are so made that they send out a shrill whistle, or ring a bell every time they are moved by the waves. On this account they are called *whistling buoys* or *bell buoys*. Have you ever seen any of these on the water?

Fig. 69. — A light-ship on which men live, keeping the light on the mast burning at night, and the fog whistle blowing in foggy weather.

blown for a warning. The lighthouses and light-ships are well provided with these, and they are blown every few seconds, or minutes, according to the need. When sailors approach the coast during foggy weather, they always listen for the sound of the fog horn.

By such helps as these a vessel finds its way to the entrance of its own port. What a lonesome life those people who live in the lighthouses and light-ships must lead, attending to the lamps and giving warning in the fogs! But how important their work is in saving ships from destruction on the wave-beaten coasts!

3. Buoys The entrance, or *channel*, to a harbor is often narrow, and sometimes on each side there are reefs and shoals on which a vessel

4. Pilots It is so important that no mistake be made in entering a harbor that men, called *pilots*, make a business of guiding, or piloting, ships into harbors. They go out in small boats, often out of sight of land, to watch for an approaching vessel. And when they see one, they sail toward it as fast as they can. In stormy weather it is exciting to see a pilot come up in his little boat, tossed about by the huge waves, and clamber up the side of the ship. It seems a wonder that he is not washed into the sea, and that his small boat is not dashed to pieces against the sides of the big vessel.

In spite of all the care that is taken to guide ships safely into harbors, one is now and then wrecked on the coast, especially in foggy and stormy weather (Fig. 64). Then, of course, the lives of sailors and passengers are in danger. Hence it is important that some means be provided for saving shipwrecked people. This is done through life-saving stations. Here and there along the coast such stations are found, where several men spend their time in keeping a sharp lookout for shipwrecks, and in going to the rescue. At such times they boldly launch their lifeboats through the surf and perform many acts of bravery.

5. Life-saving stations

FIG. 70. — Ships at the wharves in New York harbor.

A harbor is also called a *port*, and a city on a harbor is called a *seaport*. Seaports often grow to be great cities. New York City is an example; it is the largest in North America, and the second in size in the world. Philadelphia is another example; Boston and San Francisco are also seaports. Can you name any others?

Why seaports often become large cities

The fact that each of these great cities is located on a good harbor is one important reason for its size. The ocean connects a good harbor with all parts of the world, and if the country back of the seaport is fertile and thickly settled with people, the port becomes a gateway for travel and for the shipping of goods. To such a port vessels may come by hundreds (Fig. 70), bringing goods that are wanted, taking others away, and carrying passengers back and forth. Hundreds of vessels may be seen in New York harbor at all times, and every year many thousands of them enter that port alone.

When studying the lesson, it is important to know that not all the sentences in the text are to be remembered alike, for they are not all of the same value. Neither are the paragraphs all of the same value, nor the pages. On the contrary, in any text there are always some sentences, paragraphs, and pages that are far more important than others, and one of the principal things to do in studying a lesson is to discover what the most important parts are.

About how to study

For instance, on pages 44 and 45, telling about the size of the ocean, there are more than a score of sentences, and seven different paragraphs. What are the most valuable parts? They are not the first paragraph, nor the last, for both of these could be omitted and the main thought would remain fairly clear. But look at the second and the sixth paragraphs. These two contain the principal fact. Read them to see what it is. The other paragraphs are less important, aiming merely to help make this main thought plain. They can be remembered most easily, too, by thinking of the most important fact.

In all study of the text, it is best to find the most important statement as quickly as possible, and then think of the others along with it, in order to hold it the more firmly. To test this, pick out the one or two main sentences in the paragraph about the value of the ocean in furnishing water for rains. Do the same with other parts of the text.

Definitions   An *island* is a body of land entirely surrounded by water.

A *peninsula* is a body of land almost surrounded by water; the word means "almost an island."

A *cape* is a small body of land extending out into the water.

A *bay* is a large body of water partly inclosed by land.

A *harbor* is a small body of water so shut in by land, or by breakwaters, that vessels entering it are protected from winds and waves.

Review Questions   1. Give proofs that the ocean is very large. 2. How is the ocean of value in furnishing water for rains? 3. Of what value is it in furnishing food? 4. What is its value as a pleasure resort? 5. How is it valuable for navigation? 6. What difficulties and dangers do vessels meet on the ocean? 7. State the main facts about harbors. 8. About lighthouses and lightships. 9. About buoys. 10. Pilots. 11. Life-saving stations. 12. Why do seaports often become large cities? 13. What is an island? A peninsula? A cape? A bay? A harbor?

Suggestions   1. What might be the effect, if there were much less ocean and much more land? 2. Examine pictures of bluefish, herring, and halibut in the dictionary, and make a drawing of each. Find the real fish at some fish market or elsewhere. 3. In what direction would you go to reach the ocean at the nearest point? Find out how far it is.

4. Have some one tell you about a voyage across the ocean. 5. Have some one tell you about a visit to a summer resort on the seashore. 6. Read the description of the storms on the ocean, found in the story of Robinson Crusoe. 7. Do you know of any views that are made more beautiful by the presence of water? If so, where are they? Describe them. 8. Which is probably the most important use of the ocean? Why? 9. Which is probably its least important use? Why? 10. Make a drawing illustrating island, peninsula, cape, bay, and harbor.

III. The Air

Resting upon the solid earth is the air, or, as it is often called, the *atmosphere*. It surrounds the earth completely, much as a cover surrounds a ball, and it extends upwards many miles above our heads.   *Extent of the atmosphere*

This air cannot be seen, though we can see birds, and sometimes balloons, floating about in it, much as fish float in water. We know that air is all about us, because we can feel it striking against our faces and hands whenever the wind blows; and when it blows very hard, the air may move with force enough to overturn trees and even houses.

The air is of the greatest importance to all plants, animals, and people. It is even more important than the heat and the soil, about which we have already learned. Plants and animals cannot live without it; and we ourselves cannot live more than a few minutes, if we do not have it to breathe. Drowning means nothing more than sinking under the water, where there is no air to breathe.   *The importance of air to life*

The air is of great use to us in still another way. Without it there could be no fire; for wood, coal, and gas cannot burn without air. So without the air we could have no light from kerosene or gas, no fire for cooking or heating, and no steam for running factories and engines.

The movements of the air, which we call winds, are of great importance, for

FIG. 71. — A sailing vessel driven through the water by the wind blowing against the sails.

the winds do work of many kinds. For **The work of the winds** example, they drive sailing vessels through the water (Fig. 71), and they turn windmills, which are often used to pump water from wells. They also remove smoke, dust, and foul air from crowded cities.

Far more important than this is the work the winds do in carrying water from place to place over the earth. The air takes up water from the ocean in the form of vapor, which we cannot see, and the winds bear it about, sometimes a few miles, sometimes hundreds and even thousands of miles. The winds carry the vapor in all directions, and often hold it for many days before letting it fall.

It requires an enormous amount of water to keep the soil damp, the lakes full, and the rivers flowing; far, far more is needed than all the wagons, boats, and trains in the whole world could

haul. But the winds do that vast very easily, and much of the time quietly. Thus it is by the help of the winds that the rocks are made wet and changed to soil, that plants are able to grow, and that animals and people are furnished with water to drink.

What causes the air to move, and do such a mighty work? Heat has much to do with it. If **The cause of winds** you watch smoke in a room where there is a lighted lamp, you will see that it moves toward the lamp, and then, being heated, rises above it (Fig. 72).

In the same manner the air in a room moves toward a hot stove, and then, being heated, rises above it. This is why in winter, when there is a hot fire, the air near the ceiling of a room is much warmer than that near the floor and at some distance from the stove.

FIG. 72. — Smoke of a burning match rising above a lighted lamp.

The reason for this upward movement of the air is first, that air is made lighter when it is warmed; and second, that the colder air all around, being heavier, crowds in and pushes the warm, lighter air upward. The warm air is forced upward just as a light cork that is sunk in water is forced to the surface by the heavier water all about it.

The movements of the atmosphere that surrounds the earth are quite like those of the air of the heated room. If the atmosphere is warmed in one place, cool, heavier air rushes in and pushes it up. That causes wind, first toward the warmer place, and then upward.

For example, people on the seashore often enjoy a cool sea breeze on hot summer days. This is because the hot sun warms the land more than the water; then the cooler air from over the sea blows in toward this warmer place. It is these cool sea breezes that greatly help to make the seashore a pleasant summer resort.

Such differences in the warmth of the air are the main cause of winds everywhere. Winds that blow even hundreds of miles in one direction are caused in much the same way as the very gentle draughts about a lamp or a stove. What wonderful results follow from the fact that there are always some places warmer than others!

Water is always rising from the ocean surface, as well as from rivers and lakes. **How the air is able to take up water** In fact, enough water to fill thousands and thousands of barrels is leaving the ocean every second and floating away in the atmosphere; and at all times there is enough water in the air to fill many large lakes. What causes so much water to rise into the air? And why can we not see it there?

You have no doubt watched a kettle of water boil, and have seen that "steam" rises from it. Perhaps you know, too, that if it boils long enough, all the water will boil away, leaving the kettle quite dry. All the water in the kettle has then passed into the air, where it cannot be seen.

The reason for this is that heat has changed the water, which is a *liquid*, into a ███████████, has no color and ca███████████s gas is called *water* ███████████ light that it floats ███████████That explains how th███████████ke up" water and carr███████████without our being able to see it.

It is not necessary, however, to boil water in order to change it to vapor. All over the earth, wherever there is water, vapor is rising into the air every minute. You can prove this for yourself by noticing that muddy streets and wet clothes soon become dry, even in winter. Or you can place a shallow pan of water on a table and observe, after some days, how much of it has gone.

People say that the water has *evaporated*, which means simply that it has changed to vapor. It is in **What causes the air to give back this water** this way that so vast an amount of water is always rising from the ocean into the atmosphere. Perhaps after many days, and after traveling hundreds of miles from the ocean, the air gives back some of its water vapor in the form of rain. What causes it to do this?

Have you ever noticed a glass, or a pitcher of ice water, "sweat" (Fig. 73) on a hot summer day? The water that collects on the outside of a glass of cold water has not leaked through, for there are no holes in the glass. What has really happened is that the air around the cold glass has been cooled by it, and this has caused the vapor in the air to collect in drops on the cold surface of the glass. Drops would gather, or *condense*, just the same on any cold glass, even if no water were in it.

The window panes of a kitchen are often covered with drops of water from vapor, which rises from the kettles and is condensed into a liquid again on coming close to the cold glass. The vapor in your breath will be condensed in the same way when you breathe against a cold window pane.

From these facts you see that when air loaded with vapor is cooled, some of the vapor is changed back to water.

Fig. 73. — Drops of water that have gathered on the outside of a cold glass on a hot summer day.

that blow against mountains are often chilled so that the vapor is condensed, forming clouds (Fig. 74) and rain. This proves clearly that mountains are an important help in causing rain. Indeed, the mountains are usually the rainiest parts of a country.

Vapor may also be condensed into clouds and rain when a cold wind blows against a warm, damp one. Again, on hot summer days, the warm air near the earth often becomes so light that it rises high above the earth to a place where the air is cold; and then the vapor is cond___ ___ into raindrops. The summer thunder-showers, which often come on hot afternoons, are caused in this way. Such days are usually "muggy," and muggy air is really air with much water vapor in it.

There are several different forms that the vapor in the air takes when it changes to water. For example, when

Fig. 74. — Clouds that have formed on the mountain sides as the damp winds are chilled by the cold mountains.

Heat will cause water to change into vapor, and cold will change it back again.

There are several ways in which winds may be cooled. You know that mountains are colder than the lower lands (p. 25). Therefore, winds

you breathe into the air on a cold, frosty morning, your breath forms a little cloud, or *fog*. The cold air has made the vapor in your breath change to tiny drops of water, so small that you cannot see a

The forms into which vapor is condensed

single one, though hundreds of them together make a thin mist. You have, no doubt, seen fogs in valleys, on lakes, or over the ocean. These are always made of tiny drops of water condensed from vapor in the air.

We have learned that water may be either a liquid or a gas. We know, too, that it may also be a solid, for ice is the solid form of water. When vapor condenses at a temperature below 32°, or the *freezing point*, it takes the solid form. Then either *snow* or *hail* is formed instead of rain. Have you ever ex-

FIG. 75. — A view from a mountain top, looking down on the clouds.

Most *clouds* are also made of tiny fog and mist particles. These particles, too, are caused by the cooling of the air, as when winds blow against mountain slopes. When climbing a mountain one may pass through such a cloud, and it then seems to be no more than a fog or a mist. Viewed from below, however, it is seen to be a cloud; and if you go high enough, you may even climb above it. Then, looking down on its upper surface, you can see clearly that it is a cloud (Fig. 75).

The *raindrop*, which falls from the clouds, is another form of condensed vapor. Raindrops commence as tiny mist or fog particles, but as they grow in size, they become so heavy that they can no longer float. They must then fall to the earth.

amined the beautiful snow *crystals*, or *snowflakes* as we call them ? (Fig. 76).

Drops of water often collect at night on the cold ground, on grass, and on leaves. This we call *dew*. The dew gathers because the ground

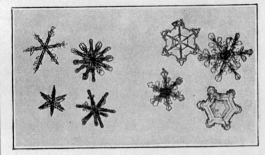

FIG. 76. — Photograph of snow crystals, showing their beautiful starlike forms.

and plants cool quickly after the sun sets. These in turn chill the air next to them, until some of the vapor in it changes to water. If the temperature is below the freezing point, *frost* is formed instead of dew.

Our weather depends very much upon our

winds. Winds from certain directions, as from the ocean, are likely to bring rain, while others bring none. You would find it interesting to observe this for yourself. If you should keep a record every day of the direction of the wind and the kind of weather it brings, you would soon learn which of your winds cause rain, and which cause fair weather. You might also notice the clouds, and look at the thermometer each day, to see what the temperature is. By this means you can learn something about the weather near your home. A record of this kind, which is called a *weather record*, might be kept somewhat as follows: [1] —

Meaning of weather records, and how to keep one

Date	Time of Day	Direction of Wind	Kind of Weather	Temperature
March 10	8 A.M.	Southeast	Cloudy	55°
March 10	6 P.M.	Calm	Gentle rain	60°
March 11	8 A.M.	Strong west wind	Clear	30°

[1] Some teachers may consider it profitable to introduce at this point an elementary study of the daily weather maps, at least to the extent of reading the predictions, and noticing how nearly correct they are.

Review Questions

1. What is the extent of the atmosphere? How do we know that there is air all about us? 2. Of what importance is air to life? 3. What work do the winds do? 4. State the cause of winds. 5. How is the air able to take up water? 6. What causes the air to give this water back? 7. Into what forms is the vapor in the air condensed? 8. What do you understand by a *weather record*? How would you keep one? 9. Tell what happens to a raindrop from the time it leaves the ocean to the time it returns to it.

Suggestions

1. Name other ways besides those mentioned in the text in which air is important. 2. Why does smoke go *up* chimneys? 3. Make a drawing, showing how a hot stove causes a movement, or circulation, of air in a room. 4. How many examples of evaporation can you observe about you? 5. What examples of the condensing of vapor can you find? 6. Why do clouds often surround mountain tops? 7. What winds usually bring your rain? 8. Where have they probably obtained their vapor? How far is that from you? 9. Prove that air is a real substance by thrusting an open bottle upside down into a pail of water.

SECTION III. INDUSTRY, COMMERCE, AND GOVERNMENT

I. INDUSTRY AND COMMERCE

IN your study about the Eskimos you found that they live in a very simple way. If an Eskimo needs a house, he builds it. If he wants food, he catches a fish or kills a seal. If he needs clothing, he takes a sealskin and makes it. If he wishes to have a sledge, or a boat, he makes that. Thus, he depends entirely upon himself for his food, clothing, and shelter.

How the Eskimo supplies his wants

The Eskimo does not think of going to a store to buy anything, for such a thing as a store is unknown to him. He has no money, because he has no use for it; there is nothing he can buy with it. He has never seen a horse and wagon, nor a railroad train, nor a city; nor does he know anything about post offices or the telephone or the telegraph.

Not many hundred years ago there were no stores in this country where we live. Then, like the Eskimo, every man had to depend largely or wholly upon himself for his food, clothing, and shelter.

How our early settlers supplied their wants

Our first white settlers came from Eu-

rope, and they made their homes along the eastern coast, because that was the
1. Location of homes first land they came to after crossing the Atlantic Ocean. Soon people, called *pioneers*, began to push into the wild country farther west. Often several families settled together, many miles away from other people; but sometimes a family went off alone and made a home ten or fifteen

Fig. 77. — The log house of a pioneer.

miles from the nearest neighbor. Most of the United States was first settled by such families as these.

Usually the first thing they had to do was to cut down trees in order to make
2. House and furniture room for a house and garden. The house was built of logs, and mud was used to stop up the cracks (Fig. 77). The house often had no floor except the earth, and only a single room. The beds were made of posts driven into the ground and joined together with cross-pieces. The chairs were three-legged stools, and the table was part of a log supported upon four legs.

Wheat was raised for bread; and corn, which often took the place of wheat, was made into corn bread. **3. Food** Tea was often made from roots found in the forest, and most of the meat was obtained by shooting wild game.

Many families kept sheep, and the wool was made into yarn, blankets, and cloth. If a boy needed a new suit **4. Clothing** of clothes, his mother might weave the cloth, cut it out, and sew the parts together. Such a suit was called *home-spun*. Or if there were no sheep, the clothing might be made out of the skins of animals. Many boys wore trousers made from deerskin, and used moccasins for shoes, when they did not go barefoot.

There were no schools, and whatever the children learned from **5. Schools and study** books was generally taught by the mother. There was little time for reading during the day, and the only light at night was that which came from the burning wood in the great fireplace. Ink was made from some colored root, such as brier root, and pens were cut from the quills of fowls. There were few books, however, and there was little time for reading or writing.

As a rule, each man raised more of some things, such as wool, wheat, or hogs, than his own family needed. **6. Necessary journeys** There were other articles that he had to buy, such as powder, sugar, salt, pepper, and coffee.

Sometimes a pioneer stayed at home and bought nothing, or he waited till some trader came along and then exchanged skins for the things that he wanted. More likely, however, he made a journey, once or twice a year, to the nearest town, which was perhaps a hundred miles distant. He then took with him the products of the farm and exchanged them for such articles as he needed.

These trips had to be few, not only on account of the distance, but because the roads were rough and muddy. It might take two weeks to haul a load of grain to town and bring back the things he wanted. The journey was dangerous also, for in those days savage Indians often lurked in the forest.

7. Independence of such life The life that such pioneers lived was, in many ways, as independent as that of the Swiss Family Robinson, or of Robinson Crusoe. Of course, when a man started out into the wilderness, he took some articles with him, such as a gun, with powder and bullets, some clothing, and some blankets. But when he reached his new home, he found himself alone, with no one to look to for help. Then, like Crusoe, he was forced to rely upon himself. In spite of the trips to the cities, most of the things that a family used had to be obtained by the family itself, and each member had many kinds of work to do. In some parts of the world, where there are few settlers, people still live in this manner.

8. Dependence on others, later Our country was settled so rapidly that each family soon had neighbors. A number of people would build their houses near together, so as to form a little village,

and one of them would start a general store. Then the families living some distance away would come to this center to trade, bringing their farm products and the skins of animals, and taking back other articles.

As the number of people in such a place grew larger, each man did fewer kinds of work. Perhaps one of them built a sawmill, and sawed lumber for the others when they needed it. Another spent part of his time at carpentry work for his neighbors. A third built a gristmill, and ground grain into flour.

From Inman's "The Old Santa Fe Trail," by courtesy of the publishers, Crane & Company.

FIG. 78.—A trapper and his horse.

A fourth made shoes a part of the time, or served as a doctor, or taught school, along with other work.

A few of the men might spend all their time at one kind of work. For example, the blacksmith might be kept busy shoeing horses, and repairing wagons, while the storekeeper did nothing but buy and sell goods. Now and then the storekeeper would make trips to the nearest city, to buy such supplies as he thought his neighbors would require, like matches, boots, shovels, axes, calico, and drugs. These he would keep in his store for sale. Sometimes he received money for them, but more often he took eggs, meat, wool, and grain for his pay. These he would send to the nearest large town for sale.

In this way it was no longer necessary for each farmer himself to go to a distant town or city, for he could usually get what he wanted from the store. He could also sell his products to the storekeeper, and with the money received pay the blacksmith, or doctor, or teacher. Thus each man came to do fewer things for himself, and to depend more and more upon others for many things.

Each year more people came to this country, and the villages grew to be towns How our wants and cities, with many mills are supplied and factories. Then people in our country began to live as we now do. That is, not a few men only, but *every* man began to do only one, or at most, very few kinds of work.

At present some men do nothing but farm ; others, nothing but dig coal or iron ore from the mines. Some spend all their time at fishing ; others spend it in making cloth, or needles, or shoes. The work that one man does may be of a very simple kind. For example, he may only drive a team, or make screws, or saw shingles, or tie up sacks of flour, or put in the heads of barrels.

With the money received for such work he buys the many things he wants, and these articles have been made by hundreds, perhaps thousands, of other people. Think how many men have had a share in the work of preparing the food that you have on your table each day, or the shoes that you wear, or the house in which you live ! How different our ways are from those of the pioneers !

As a rule, each town or city is especially interested in one, or, at most, a few kinds of business. For example, a town near the forest is likely to have an important lumber industry. Another, in the midst of mountains, may have mining for its special work. A third, near great wheat fields, may have immense flour mills.

The articles that these cities produce are sent away in all directions; and other things, that the people need, are brought to them from the hundreds of places in which they are produced. In what kinds of work is your town chiefly interested ? What are some of the articles that are brought to it?

When each man does only one kind of work, and depends upon others for most of the things that he needs, good roadways, or *highways*, become of very great importance. This is especially true when goods have to be carried long distances, as in a large country like ours. If we live in the East, and the best wheat is raised more than a thousand miles away, in Dakota, it is of little use to us unless it can be brought to us. If the best shoes are made in New England, they are of little value to the people of the South, unless they can be easily

FIG. 79. — A pack train carrying supplies up a mountain trail in western United States.

filled in. Streams had to be crossed by wading across, or *fording* (Fig. 80) them in places where the water was shallow. This was often difficult, and even dangerous, especially when the streams were swollen after heavy rains; therefore bridges were built as soon as the people were able to do so.

Many of our country roads are still very poor. They are rough or steep in places, **4. Our roads** and at some seasons of the year the mud is so deep that it is difficult for a team of

shipped there. It is of the highest importance, therefore, that we have good highways leading in all directions.

When a country has not advanced very far, the highways are usually poor. For example, the **2. Trails** routes of travel in some of the regions of Africa are merely paths that have been made by goats and barefooted people, and are less than a foot wide.

The Indians in this country, likewise, had only narrow paths, or *trails*, for roads. They often used the trails made by the bison. Wagons could not be drawn over these, and goods could be carried only on the backs of men, or of horses. A number of horses carrying packs formed a *pack train* and these trains may still be seen in some places (Fig. 79).

The pioneers at first had only trails, and one of their hardest tasks was to **3. Roads of pioneers** cut roads through the dense forests. Trees had to be cut down, stumps and stones removed, steep places leveled, and swampy places

FIG. 80. — Horses and wagon fording a swift mountain stream.

horses to draw even an empty wagon. Our roads are being rapidly improved, however, and some of the states are spending large sums of money each year in making them smooth, hard, and level. Perhaps you have seen some of this work and can tell how it is done.

In cities there is so much hauling of heavy loads that the streets must be paved. For this purpose bricks are often used, or paving stones, which are larger than bricks; and sometimes asphalt, or blocks of wood are used. But the most common pavement, especially in the country, is called *macadam*, after the Scotchman who invented it. It consists of broken stones, scattered to a depth of from six to ten inches, and pressed together as closely as possible. What kinds of pavement, if any, are to be found in your neighborhood?

You have already learned that lakes and rivers are important for travel and **5. Rivers, lakes, and canals** for transportation of goods. When the pioneers were settling the Mississippi Valley, it was the custom to carry many

FIG. 81. — Freight yard of a railway, showing a large number of freight cars loaded with coal and other freight.

of their goods down the Ohio and Mississippi rivers, a thousand miles or more, to New Orleans for sale. In many parts of our country the rivers were at that time the best routes of travel. These *waterways* are still generally the cheapest, and every year the government spends great sums of money in keeping them clear of logs, stones, and mud, so that they may be in good condition for boats.

Where there are waterfalls or rapids in rivers, canals have sometimes been built so that boats may go up and down the river. Canals have also been made to connect lakes and rivers with one another. Much money has thus been spent in improving the natural waterways of the United States.

In our country, railroad trains have largely taken the place of wagons, and also of river boats, as carriers for long distances. This is **6. Railroads** because trains are so much faster than wagons or boats. Even on the finest of roads, wagons can seldom be drawn more than forty miles a day. Boats can travel somewhat faster; but trains can go from five hundred to one thousand miles per day. Moreover, they carry both passengers and freight far more cheaply than these could be taken in wagons.

As we ourselves travel on passenger trains, we are apt to think that the chief business of railways is to carry people; but that is not usually the case. Their main business is to carry freight, such as grain, cattle, groceries, coal, oil, and machinery (Fig. 81). For this reason on most railways there are many more freight trains than passenger trains; and there are many more cars in each freight train.

The fast trains also carry express packages, newspapers, and letters. Before railways were built, the mail was carried in stage coaches, or on horseback. Now many passenger trains have one or two cars that are used for this purpose alone; and most of our mail is carried in this way.

The ocean is the greatest highway of all, connecting us with the most distant countries, as well as joining

7. The ocean different parts of our own land (Fig. 82). Before the invention of the steam engine, the ocean was so difficult to cross that it kept the people of different countries apart. Sailing vessels were then the only ships in use, and they were very slow. The invention of the steam engine made steamships, as well as locomotives, possible. Now thousands of steamships carry passengers, freight, and mail rapidly by water, just as trains do by land.

Thus people have improved upon the trail, the stagecoach, and the sailing vessel, until all parts of the world are brought into close touch with one another.

The people of the United States are busy

The great producing
occupations many things, and sending them from place to place. Although each man does only one kind, or, at most, very few kinds of work, there are scores of different kinds all together. Most of these, however, are included under seven great occupations. These are (1) *agriculture*, including farming, gardening, and the grazing of cattle, sheep, and horses; (2) *fishing*; (3) *lumbering*; (4) *mining*; (5) *manufacturing*; (6) *trade*, or buying and selling; and (7) *transportation*, or the carrying of goods.

1. The first five The greatest of these in-
of these dustries is *agriculture*, about which you have already studied in the first and second sections of this book. One man out of every three in the United States is engaged in agriculture of some kind.

Fishing is far less important. Still, along the shores of the lakes and the ocean, there are thousands of men who spend all their time at this work.

Lumbering is not carried on in as many places as it used to be, because many of the forests have been cut down. Yet, every house you see is built partly

FIG. 82. — Vessels coming and going in New York Harbor.

of wood on the inside, and many are made of wood on the outside as well. Besides this, wood is used for many other purposes, as for making furniture and paper. From this you can understand that great numbers of men must be engaged in cutting down trees and sawing them into lumber.

Mining is a great industry employing hundreds of thousands of men. There are many kinds of mines, the most important of which are coal, iron, copper, gold, silver, and lead mines. *Quarrying*, or taking out stone from the earth, may be considered a part of mining.

F

Manufacturing is a still more important industry than mining. Note how many things about you have been carefully made somewhere. This book that you are reading is one example. The desk, at which you sit in school, much of your food, and your clothes, are other examples.

These *five* occupations serve mainly to supply proper *food, clothing,* and *shelter.* They are often called the *five great industries,* and you will find them mentioned again and again in your later study of geography. These *five,* however, merely *produce* articles. The first four produce the raw materials, or *raw products ;* the fifth changes, or *manufactures,* these raw products into articles ready for use.

2. The other two great occupations — There are thousands of people engaged in shipping the raw products and manufactured articles, as we have just seen in our study of highways. If there were not, these articles would be of little use. Nor would they be of much use if there were not other thousands of people buying and selling them in stores, so that we can get them when we wish.

There are, therefore, the two other occupations of (1) *trade,* or buying and selling ; and (2) *transportation.* These two together are called *commerce.*

The commerce within our country is called *home,* or *domestic commerce.* The commerce between the United States and other countries is called *foreign commerce.* In your study of geography, you will find that domestic and foreign commerce are very important.

No doubt you can think of some occupations, such as teaching, that do not belong either under commerce, or under any one of the five great industries. However, the seven great occupations cover *most* kinds of work that men do ; and they are the chief kinds that need to be studied in geography.

About how to study — It takes much practice to discover the most important thought of a page quickly. Yet, one can get his lessons more easily by learning to do that.

Here is an example. The first page of this chapter tells how the Eskimo supplies his wants. The main thought here is found at the end of the first paragraph, in the words, *"He depends entirely upon himself for his food, clothing, and shelter."* The rest of the two paragraphs merely makes this central thought clear by giving examples, as follows : he builds his own house, finds his own food, makes his own clothing; there are no stores where he can buy anything; he has no money to buy things with, for he has no use for money; he has never seen a city ; nor even a horse and wagon, nor a train; and he knows nothing about telephoning, or telegraphing, or writing for what he wants.

Here are many facts, and it is difficult to remember them until one finds the leading thought that binds all the others together. Then it becomes easy to remember most of them. Since lessons are more easily mastered by getting the leading fact quickly, stop often, after reading a paragraph, to see whether you can state its principal thought. Do this in a few words ; if possible, in a single sentence. Then add as many other statements as you remember which explain the chief thought. Practice getting your lessons in this way.

Review Questions — 1. How does the Eskimo supply his wants ? 2. Tell about the location of the homes of the early settlers. 3. About their houses and furniture. 4. Their food. 5. Their clothing. 6. Their schools and study. 7. Why were journeys necessary ? 8. How was their life an independent one ? 9. State how people later became more dependent. 10. How are our own wants supplied ? 11. What about special kinds of work for each town or city ? 12. Explain the importance of highways. 13. Tell about trails. 14. The roads of the pioneers. 15. Our roads. 16. Show the importance of rivers, lakes, and canals as highways. 17. Of railroads. 18. Of the ocean. 19. Name the great occupations.

20. Describe the first *five*.   21. Describe the other two.

1. What articles would you expect to find in a general store in a village ?   2. How are department stores in large cities **Suggestions** like such general stores ?   3. The last syllable in the names of many towns and cities is *ford*, as Hartford, Stamford, Rockford. What does that fact suggest to you ?   4. Find out more about the ways in which money is spent on rivers to make them more useful for navigation ?   5. Write a story describing an early pioneer's journey to the nearest large town.   6. What men do you know who are engaged in some one of the seven great occupations ?   7. Make a list of articles that you use which were brought from a distance, on the railroad or by water.   Which of these belong to domestic commerce ?   Which to foreign commerce ?   8. Is there any one of the seven great occupations that we could somewhat easily do without ?   If so, name it, and give your reasons.   9. How can good roads and waterways help to prevent famines ?

II. Country and City

The kinds of work that people are doing lead some to live in the country, **Kinds of work in country and in city** others in the city.   The farmer, for instance, lives in the country because he must have a great deal of land in order to raise his crops.   The lumberman must live in the country where there are forests.

Persons engaged in the five other leading occupations usually live in towns and cities.   Miners, for example, must have their homes near the entrance to the mines where they work ; and the workers in a single mine, together with their families, often make a large town. Men who work at manufacturing must live near the factory.   A single factory may employ several thousand men ; and since there are often many large factories near one another, many thousands of people may thus be brought together. These people, together with others engaged in commerce and other kinds of work, form great cities, sometimes with hundreds of thousands of persons.   These cities are usually located at some point where the shipping of goods is easy, as on a river, a large lake, an ocean harbor, or a railway center.

Life in the great cities is so different from that in the country, that it will be interesting to see what some of the differences are.   Since **The country** life in the country is very simple, and since more than half of all the people in the United States live there, we will study country life first.

A farmer needs land enough for a house, a barn, and other buildings ; for a garden and an orchard ; and for fields in which various kinds of crops can be **1. The space needed by a farmer** raised.   This means that he must have a large tract of land.

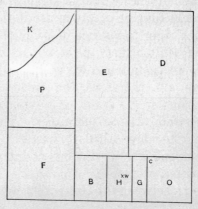

Fig. 83. — Plan of a farm in Ohio.

Figure 83 shows a plan of a farm in the state of Ohio.   It includes 160 acres, which is the amount of land in many farms in that section.   One side of this farm is half a mile long ; and

FIG. 84. — A farmer's house and barn.

from this you can easily tell the entire distance around it. The house and yard, shown by the letter *H,* are close to the road that runs along one side of the farm. The barnyard and barn, lettered *B,* are on the left. *G* is the garden, and *O* is the orchard. The rest of the land is divided into fields, *D* containing corn, *E* oats, *F* grass, and *P* pasture. At *K* there is a small wood lot, from which firewood is obtained. Can you tell about how long and wide some of these fields are ?

The house is of two stories and a half, and is built of wood (Fig. 84). Close to it is a wood shed in which piles of wood are kept for burning. On many farms, where wood is scarce, coal is used instead.

The barn is only a short distance from the house, and is larger than the house. In it are kept the horses, cows, and other farm animals, and the wagons, plows, and other farm implements. Much hay and grain is stored there, to be sold later, or to be fed to the animals in winter when they cannot graze in the pasture.

In one corner of the orchard (at *C*) is a henhouse in which from one hundred to two hundred hens are usually kept; and near the henhouse is a pen for a few pigs. Besides these animals, there are some turkeys, ducks, and geese.

Vegetables and strawberries are

FIG. 85. — A farmer's children playing in the hayfield.

raised in the garden, and there are also small patches of raspberry, blackberry, currant, and gooseberry bushes. Besides apple trees in the orchard, there are pear, plum, and peach trees. Altogether a great many kinds of fruit are raised on the farm.

The yard about the house is large, and the grass is kept closely cut. There are several elm and maple trees in the yard, as well as some flowering bushes and flower beds, which the farmer's wife cares for with much pride.

Most of the other farms near this one are of about the same size, though some are larger and others smaller. What can you say, therefore, as to how far apart houses in the country must be?

2. The farmer's water, light, and heat Near the house is a well (*W*), from which the farmer obtains his water. On this farm the water is pumped by a windmill into a tank, from which some is piped to the house, and some to the barnyard for the animals; but on many farms the water is pumped by hand.

At night, light is supplied by lamps that burn oil. This house is heated by stoves placed in several of the rooms, though some farmhouses are heated by furnaces.

3. Schools in the country Although there are not many children on each farm, it is important that they go to school. All the children who live near enough together to attend one school may not number more than twenty-five or thirty, and even then some may have to walk several miles. On fine days such a walk is pleasant enough, but since there are no sidewalks, it is not so pleasant in rainy weather, and the walk is very

difficult when there is much snow. On account of the distance, every child usually takes his lunch along, and remains at school all day.

Since there are so few pupils, the building is generally small, with only one room (Fig. 86). There is but one teacher, and children of all ages, from six to nineteen or twenty years, study

FIG. 86. — A group of school children in front of a country schoolhouse.

and recite in the same room, and to the same teacher.

You might think that such a school could not be very good, yet some of our best-known men and women have attended such a country school. Perhaps you can name one of our Presidents, or some other great man, who once went to a country school.

The city

1. The space used by a family in a large city In a great city, as many as twenty thousand persons are sometimes found living within a space no larger than the single farm just described. The buildings, therefore, must cover almost all the ground, leaving little or no room for yards and lawns.

In some of the larger cities the buildings have from four to fifteen or twenty stories, and sometimes even more than that. In such a building a single family occupies only a small part of one floor, called a *flat* or *apartment*, which has from two or three to eight or ten rooms. Other families live in other flats on the same floor, and in the stories above and below. Thus several hundred persons may have their homes in a single large building.

The factories, stores, office buildings, and other places where the city people work, are also very large. Hundreds, and even thousands, of persons work in them every day. Some of the office buildings in New York City are over thirty stories high (Fig. 87).

a large farm, not many families can afford to have such houses. With land so costly, a small barn for a horse or cow, or a garden and a chicken house, are not to be thought of. It is difficult even to take care of a pet dog, or a cat, in a crowded city. Usually there can be no yard, and the street is the only place where the children may play (Fig. 88).

2. Water, light, and heat in the city

It would be impossible to have wells enough to furnish water for all the people in a city. Besides that, the water might not be fit to drink. Instead of coming from a great number of wells, therefore, the water is brought to the city, in large pipes, from some distant source such as a lake or a river. It is then led in smaller pipes through each street and into each house. When one wants water, all that he needs to do is to

Copyright, 1906, by Moses King, New York.

FIG. 87. — The Singer Building in New York, one of the highest buildings in the world. It is 612 feet high, has 41 stories, and there are offices even in the lofty tower.

There are, it is true, houses of two and three stories in the large cities, just as in the country. However, since the land on which such a house stands is often worth several times as much as

turn a faucet, and the water flows freely; and there is enough to supply all, although thousands may want it at the same time.

Lamps for light cause much trouble even in the country. In the city, where there are so many people in one building, and where the buildings are so close to one another, lamps may be dangerous. Why? Gas and electricity usually take their place.

For heat, furnaces are commonly used. They burn coal, and heat the houses by means of steam, or hot water, or hot air. In the larger buildings, furnaces big enough to heat a great number of rooms at once are placed in the basement, and, by means of pipes, steam is carried to each room.

3. Food in the city The farmer himself raises much of the food that his family needs, such as vegetables, fruit, meat, and often the grain for flour. Other things that he uses he buys at the village store. In a great city, on the other hand, little or no food is produced, so that the problem of feeding the hundreds of thousands of people who live there is a very serious one.

Trains, ships, and wagons, loaded with all sorts of food, are all the time moving toward a large city. For example, milk is brought every day in special milk trains that start perhaps a hundred miles or more away. At each station they take on cans filled with milk from surrounding farms, and in this way car after car is filled by the time the city is reached.

Most of the city people buy food at the stores in very small quantities, because they have no room in which to keep large amounts. For instance, they may buy three or four pounds of sugar at a time, or a small bag of flour, or two quarts of potatoes. The farmer, on the other hand, has whole barrels of potatoes, apples, and turnips stored in his cellar, and often buys sugar and flour by the barrel.

From all this you can see how the city depends upon the country for food.

FIG. 88. — A crowded street in the East Side of New York City.

If anything should prevent food from reaching a city for a few weeks, the people would starve. Even when a heavy snowstorm blocks the freight trains for a day or two, there is suffering in the larger cities.

4. Schools in the city The people are so crowded in a great city that there are often enough children in one block to fill a large school. Sometimes a thousand, and even two or three thousand children, go to school in one building. The schoolhouse may have from twenty-five to seventy-five large rooms in it, with a teacher for every room. Scores of such schools may be found in a single city (Fig. 89).

The children usually need to walk only a few minutes to reach their school,

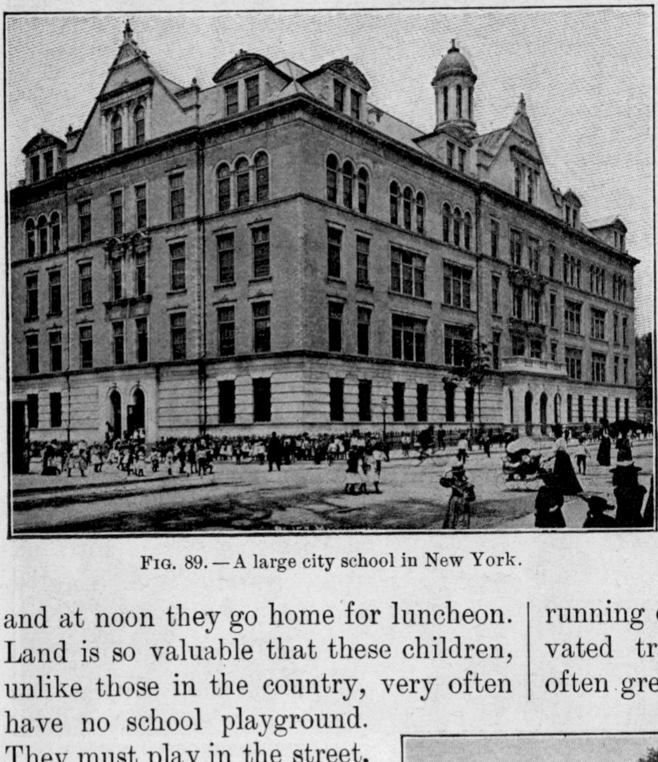

FIG. 89. — A large city school in New York.

and at noon they go home for luncheon. Land is so valuable that these children, unlike those in the country, very often have no school playground. They must play in the street, dodging horses, wagons, and street cars as best they can.

People in the country walk short distances to visit one **Transportation** another, or to **in country and** work. They have **in city** horses, which they can use for hauling goods or for driving. The roads are never crowded (Fig. 90), and where they are well made, it is a pleasure to drive over them.

Transportation in a large city is a very different matter. In spite of the fact that each building holds so many people, many persons live too far from their places of work to walk there. Street cars, therefore, carry many of them.

In the largest cities the distances are often too great even for riding on street cars. They go slowly and cannot carry half of the people, even though they run only a minute apart. This is especially true in the mornings, when tens of thousands of persons start for their places of work, at about the same time, and in the evenings, when they return home.

In great cities, therefore, like New York, Chicago, and Boston, railroads are built over the streets. These are called *elevated railroads* (Fig. 91). They carry great numbers of passengers, the trains running every few minutes; yet the elevated trains, like the street cars, are often greatly overcrowded.

FIG. 90. — Driving on a country road.

To meet the needs of transportation further, in New York, Boston, and some other cities, electric railroads, called *subways*, have been built in tunnels dug underground (Fig. 92). They even run under rivers, and carry thousands of passengers every day.

Thus it happens that in some parts of New York there may be an electric car in the street, a train directly overhead, and another train directly underground, all filled with people, and rushing along as fast as they can in the same direction.

In the near future, many more tunnels for carrying passengers and freight will have to be built in the great cities. This will be necessary, because even now some of the streets are so crowded with street cars, wagons, carriages, and automobiles, that these can scarcely move at all (Fig. 93); and foot passengers find it difficult and dangerous to cross the streets.

Copyright, 1905, by Detroit Photographic Co.

FIG. 91. — An elevated railway in New York City.

Copyright, 1904, by Detroit Photographic Co.

FIG. 92. — An underground railway, or subway, in New York.

Attractions of country and of city

1. The country A person who likes the trees and the green grass, who loves to watch the birds, and who finds pleasure in wild flowers, and fruits, and nuts, should live in the country. So should any one who likes to skate and coast, to hunt and fish, to keep cats, dogs, and other pets, and to take long walks in the quiet woods and fields. There is plenty of room there for all such pleasures. In the great cities, on the other hand, there are children who have never seen a bird, except, perhaps, the English sparrow, nor a cow, nor a pasture, nor a field of grain.

It is true that life in the country seems lonesome to many. But it is much less lonesome now than it used to be, since the postman now carries mail to the farmer's door every day, and the farmer is able to have the telephone in his house, just as people have in the city. Then, too, the country roads are being improved every year, so that it is now easier and more pleasant to drive over them, and to visit neighbors. In many parts of the country, also, there are electric car lines, running through the farming region on their way from one town to another.

Although families in the country live far apart, they are usually much better acquainted than those who live close together in the city. It is common, in a large city, for families that have lived for years in the same building, with only a brick wall a foot thick between them, not to know one another by name, nor to speak when they meet. A farmer might be much better acquainted with a neighbor living ten miles away. Many people in the city, as well as some in the country, lead lonesome lives.

kinds; and art museums, filled with statues and pictures. There are concerts, fine churches, and large stores. A single store sometimes employs a thousand clerks, and contains almost everything that a person can want.

On the whole, there are many more kinds of pleasure in the city than in the country; but the country offers most attraction to those who like to live out of doors, and who want quiet.

FIG. 93. — A street in New York City, crowded with carts and wagons.

These facts explain why many city people flock to the country in summer. It is a treat for them to get away from the noise, the bad air, and the crowding of the city. It is also clear why country people like to visit the city; for there are always many new and interesting sights for them there. Which place do you prefer for a home, and why?

Many people live in towns and villages (Fig. 94). Here the houses are Life in towns usually from and villages one- to three-story buildings, placed far enough apart to

Large cities also have many attractions. Beautiful parks are set aside here and there, where children are 2. The city allowed to play, and where people can enjoy the birds, flowers, and trees, and watch the squirrels frisking about. There are gardens, where wild animals from all parts of the world are kept, and thousands of children visit these gardens each week, often taking their lunches so as to remain all day. There are great natural history museums, containing stuffed animals of many

allow good light all around. A man can have a lawn and a garden if he wishes them, and also a barn where he can keep a horse or a cow.

If the town is large enough to require street cars, these are seldom crowded, and the streets are wide enough to meet all needs. Such foods as milk, eggs, and potatoes are easily obtained from the surrounding farms, and the open country can be reached, from any point in the town, by a few minutes' walk (Fig. 94).

FIG. 94. — A village nestled in a valley among the hills of New England.

Unless a town is quite small, it supplies itself with water and light in the same way as these are supplied in cities; but in most respects towns and villages resemble the country, more than they do the large city.

Review Questions 1. Which great occupations must be carried on in the country? 2. Which ones in towns and cities? 3. Explain why farmers need a large amount of land. 4. How do they get their water, light, and heat? 5. Tell about schools in the country. 6. What about the space used by a family in a large city? 7. How are the water, light, and heat obtained in such a city? 8. What about food in the city? 9. What do you know about the schools there? 10. How is transportation provided in country and in city? 11. What are some of the attractions of the country? 12. Of the city? 13. Tell about life in towns and villages.

Suggestions 1. Boys and girls living in the country usually have much work to do helping their fathers and mothers. Make a list of things that they have to do. 2. Is it an advantage or a disadvantage for city children that they have little work of this kind to do? 3. Make a drawing of some farm that you know, showing the buildings upon it, and how it is divided up. 4. Make a collection of pictures of buildings and streets in the city. 5. Write a composition telling whether you prefer to live in the city or country, and give your reasons. 6. If your home is in a city or large town, find out about the lighting system; the transportation; the parks; the museums; the protection against fires.

III. GOVERNMENT

Meaning of voting and of elections Every boy and girl has heard men talk about *voting*, and has noticed how interested they often become as *election* day draws near. Do you know what is meant by voting and by election?

Suppose that all the members of your class, or of your school, wished to form a club, and to choose one of your number president. How would you go about it?

Probably the names of two or three children, who seemed best fitted for the place, would first be suggested. Then each of you would write the name of the one you preferred upon a slip of paper, and drop it into a box. After that, all the slips, or *votes*, would be counted, and the boy or girl who received the greatest number of votes would be elected.

In such a case you would be voting, and having an election at school. When you dropped the name of the one you preferred into the box, you cast a *vote;* and the *election* was nothing more than the choosing of some one for the position. Quite possibly some of you would become just as much interested in such an election as men do in their elections.

Men hold their elections in much the same way. Ask your father, or some man old enough to vote, to tell you exactly what he does when he votes.

People hold elections and vote on all sorts of questions, but usually when one **Matters that** speaks of voting and of elec-**elections de-** tions he means the choosing **cide** of officers for our government. We do not hold elections to decide how a farmer shall manage his farm, for it is best that he should do that about as he pleases. He builds fences, puts in certain crops, sells his grain, or feeds it to his stock, as seems to him best. So, also, the miller builds a large or a small mill, uses old or new machinery, grinds much or little corn, and makes repairs as he chooses. In each of these cases one man owns and uses the property.

There are many things, however, that no one person owns, and in which a large number of people are about equally interested. That is true, for instance, of roads. Many people drive or walk over them, but no one person owns them. The people together have to decide, or vote, where and how they shall be built and repaired, and who shall do the work. That is, they hold elections to make laws about the roads, and choose officers to carry out such laws.

The schools, likewise, are not owned by any one person, and are of great interest to everybody. So questions about the schools are also voted upon at elections.

What shall be done with thieves and disorderly persons? This is another question of great interest to everybody. Laws must be made to control such people, and officers must be selected to carry out such laws. There are many other questions that interest large numbers of people. Can you not name some of them? Ask your father, or some friend, to tell you what will be some of the questions to be voted on at the next election.

Elections, therefore, deal with matters of general interest. They provide for laws on such matters, and for the selection of officers to enforce them.

Some of the matters that are voted on at elections concern only those persons who live in a small sec- **Questions to be** tion, as in a small town or **voted upon by** village. For instance, the **small groups** kind of streets that you shall **of people** have, and the men who shall take care of them, are questions of no special interest to people in other towns or cities, but they interest all the voters in your section.

It is also very important that you have a good school building, with a large yard, and good teachers. People living at a distance have little interest in *your* school, but those who live near you are very much interested in it. The people to vote on such a question, therefore, would be those who have a special interest in it.

Thus there are many matters that are mainly of interest to the persons living in one neighborhood. They are called *local questions*, and are voted upon only by the few voters in that section. Ask some one to tell you of other local questions.

There are some matters that are of interest to the people in a much larger section.

Matters that concern the people of a whole state For example, a railway company might charge too much for passengers and freight. In such cases, laws may need to be passed, forcing them to charge lower rates. Since a railway may be hundreds of miles long, the people of a single town or city could do very little with such a company. In that case it would be necessary for men, living perhaps hundreds of miles apart, to unite in some way to make laws.

Again, it is important that there be buildings in which blind people may be cared for; others in which the deaf and dumb may be educated; and still others in which insane people may be kept. There must also be strong prisons where criminals may be sent. There are not many such persons in any one small section, and it would prove very expensive and difficult to take proper care of only a few of each kind. Therefore, all the people in a large section, called a *state*, unite to make proper laws, and provide buildings and officers for the care of such people. What is the name of your state?

The voters of a state cannot, of course, all come together at one place to discuss such matters. Even if all could make the journey at a time agreed upon, there would be so many thousands **How laws are made and officers chosen for a state** that it would not be possible for all to hear those who spoke, and little business could be done. Besides, new laws are needed every year, and the voters would have to spend too much time on such work.

For these reasons it is the custom for one man to be elected to *represent* many others in the making of laws. Where there are great numbers of people, he may represent many thousands, and vote in place of them all. Suppose, for instance, that there are a million persons living in one state, and that one man is elected to represent every ten thousand. There would then be one hundred such men chosen, and it would be their duty to come together and make laws for the whole million.

Such men, being elected to represent others, are called *representatives;* and because they legislate (which means "make laws"), the whole body is called the *legislature*. Find out who is the representative to the state legislature from your district; also who is your state senator.

The city where the legislature meets is called the *capital* (which means "head city") of the state. The capital is often located near the center of the state, and it usually has a fine, large building, called the *state capitol*. It is here that the representatives hold their meetings.

FIG. 95. — The beautiful capitol building at Washington.

The chief officer of the state, who is elected to see that the state laws are carried out, or enforced, is called the *governor.* Who is your governor? He is elected by voters in *all* parts of the state, while each representative is elected by a small section of the state. There are also other state officers, such as a state treasurer, a state superintendent of schools, and judges. Some of these officers are elected by the people; others are appointed by the governor.

How laws are made and officers selected for cities In large cities, laws are made through representatives, just as in states, and for the same reasons. The representatives chosen to make the laws in cities are usually called *aldermen* or *councilors;* and the highest officer, elected to carry out, or *execute,* the laws, is called the *mayor.* All these officers are chosen by the voters at elections. If your home is in a city, learn the name of your mayor and that of your alderman or councilor. Find out what some of their duties are.

The building in which these representatives meet, and in which the mayor has his office, is called the *city hall.* While the city is governed in some matters by its own laws and officers, the same as any small town, it also forms part of the state and elects representatives to the state legislature.

Questions that concern the people of the United States In our country there are forty-eight states, and there are some questions that no one state can decide alone, because the others are equally interested in them. For instance, it would be a great hindrance to trade and travel if each state made its own money, for each state might then have different coins. In that case, every time a traveler passed from one state to another, he might be obliged to take the time and trouble to exchange his money for a new kind.

Again, in case of war, the country would be weak if each state acted alone.

Perhaps you can give some of the reasons why. Mail is another matter that

FIG. 96. — President Wilson.

concerns all the states, and there are others besides. Can you mention some?

So it is clear that we need a *United States Government* as well as state, city, and town governments. The reason for calling it the United States Government is also plain, for the *states* have really *united*, in order to have one central government for many important matters.

If the people in a single

How laws are made and officers chosen for the United States

state cannot meet in a body to make laws, certainly the people of the entire United

States cannot do so. Therefore, representatives are elected, and sent to one place, from all the states of the Union. Here they consider questions of interest to the whole nation.

The place where they meet is WASHINGTON, and this city is, on that account, the *capital of the United States*, or the *national capital*. At Washington there is a magnificent capitol building (Fig. 95) in which the meetings are held; and there are many other fine government buildings there.

The representatives from the forty-eight states of the Union form what is known as *Congress*. This corresponds to the legislatures of the state, for the congressmen make laws for the nation, as the legislators do for the state. The members of Congress are called *senators* and *representatives*.

The chief *executive officer* of the United States, corresponding to the mayor of a city, and the governor of a state, is called the *President* (Fig. 96). He lives in Washington, and his residence is called the Executive Mansion, or White House, since it is white in color (Fig. 97). Who

FIG. 97. — The White House, where the President lives.

is now President of the United States? Who was the first President? What do you know about each?

Besides these officers, who are elected by the people, there are a great many others who are appointed by the President to carry on the government work. Many live in Washington, but some, such as postmasters, live in other places.

We have seen that our representatives, and other officers, are elected by votes that are cast for them. Be-

Why our government is called a *democracy* and a *republic*
cause the people thus have the power to make their own laws, our government is called a *democracy*. The first part of this word means "people," and the last part "government," so that

FIG. 98. — General George Washington, first President of the United States.

the whole word means "government by the people." Because the people do not really make the laws themselves, but elect representatives to do that for them, ours is often called a representative government, or a *republic*.

It is often said that our form of government makes us "free and equal." People are by no
Other forms of government
means so free and equal in all countries. Under some governments, in Europe and Asia, the people have very little to say about the laws that shall govern them. Nor do the laws protect them all equally; for some of the high officers say freely what they think, while others dare not do this. Many must obey their rulers blindly, just as little children are expected to obey their parents.

Such a government cannot be called a democracy, or a republic; it is really a *despotism*, or an absolute *monarchy*. This means that the ruler is a *despot*, or a monarch, having complete power to do what he chooses. For instance, he may put men to death without any trial, a right that the laws of our country do not allow.

In many countries that have kings, however, the people have much power. For example, there is a king in England, but the English people are quite as free as we are.

In studying a lesson it is not best to spend all of your time with your book in hand. After carefully read-
About how to study
ing the text through two or three times, you might select some topic that you think would prove interesting to your mother, or to some of your friends, or that they could tell you more about. Then, during the meal hour, or at some other time when others present

FIG. 99. — The Washington Monument, erected in Washington in memory of our first President.

have nothing special to talk about, bring up this topic. Tell what you have read, and ask the others some questions about it.

Talking over a part of a lesson in such a way is one of the very best ways of studying it, and it is also one of the best ways of pleasing your parents.

Review Questions 1. What do you understand by *voting*, and by *elections?* 2. What kind of questions do elections decide? 3. Give examples of local questions, or questions that are voted upon by small groups of people. 4. Give examples of questions that concern the people of a whole state. 5. How are laws made for a whole state, and who are some of the officers elected for the state? 6. How are laws made for large cities, and who are some of the officers elected for cities? 7. Give examples of questions that concern the people of the United States. 8. How are laws made, and who are some of the officers chosen for the United States? 9. Why is our government called a democracy? Why a republic? 10. Tell about other forms of government.

Suggestions 1. Name some officers that you know about, and find out whether they represent the local, state, or national government. 2. What officers look after your school, and how are they chosen? 3. What is the capital of your state, and where is it? 4. In what respect are the town hall, city hall, state capitol building, and United States capitol alike in their use? 5. Why should the capital of a state be near the center of the state, if possible? 6. What does U. S. stand for?

SECTION IV.   MAPS

IT is often important to represent a country upon a map, so as to tell at a glance what its shape is, and where its mountains, rivers, and cities are. Such a drawing can be made of any place, no matter how large or small it may be.

How a map of a schoolroom can be drawn Suppose, for instance, we desire to make a map, or drawing, of a schoolroom (Fig. 100). The room we have chosen is thirty-two feet long and thirty-two feet wide. It would not be easy to find a piece of paper so large as that; but it is not necessary to have so large a piece in order to make the drawing. A small piece will do just as well, if we let one inch on the paper stand for several feet in the room.

In this case let one inch stand for sixteen feet. Since the room is thirty-two feet on each side, the drawing will be just two inches long and two inches wide. To place the desks and aisles properly, we shall need to use a ruler with the inches divided into sixteenths; for one foot in the room represents one sixteenth of an inch on the ruler.

The ends of the room are on the north and south, and the sides on the east and west.

FIG. 100. — Photograph of a schoolroom.

The teacher's desk is three and one half feet in front of the north wall. There is a row of desks about four feet from the west wall. The desks are just two feet long, with eight in a row one and one fourth feet apart. There are seven rows, and the aisles between them are each one and one fourth feet wide. The piano is on the west side of the teacher's desk.

G

Here is a map of the schoolroom (Fig. 101). Measure each part to see whether it has been drawn correctly, using a foot rule that shows the sixteenths of inches. How large is the teacher's desk? The piano?

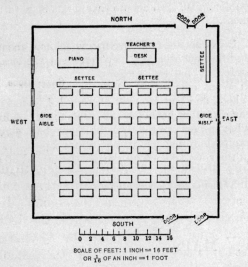

FIG. 101. — Map of a schoolroom.

When a person draws in this way, letting a certain distance on the paper

Meaning of drawing "according to a scale"
stand for a greater distance, he is said to use a *scale*, or to make a map *according to a scale*. In the schoolroom just described (Fig. 101) the scale is one inch to sixteen feet.

FIG. 102. — Picture of the schoolhouse and yard represented in the map (Fig. 103).

In the next drawing, that of the school yard (Fig. 102), the number of feet which an inch

represents must be still greater, because the yard is much larger than the room. Here one inch represents one hundred and forty feet. According to that scale, find out how large the yard and the school building are

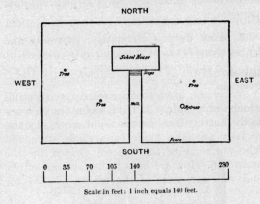

FIG. 103. — Map of a school yard.

(Fig. 103). Find how far the trees are from each other; from the nearest fence; from the building.

All maps are drawn according to a scale, just as these two are. It makes no difference whether they represent a school yard, a state, the United States, or even the entire earth; all are drawn to a scale. In Part II of this book there is a map of North America (Fig. 133); to what scale is it drawn? Look at some other maps to find out their scales.

Can you not make a map of your own schoolroom? What scale will you use? You might put in your own desk, **Maps that you might draw** but omit the others. You might also draw a map of your school yard. If you prefer to do so, find its size by stepping, or *pacing*, off the distance, making each of your steps about two feet long. Measure the building in the same way. After having finished these two maps, you might draw a third one, including in it not only the school yard, but also a few of the streets and houses near by. The scale for this third map might perhaps be one inch for every five hundred steps.

Maps are used a great deal to show the location of places and the direction **Ways of finding directions out of doors** of one place from another. To use them properly, a person must first understand what is meant by north, south, east, and west. Probably you already know that. One of the easiest ways to find the direction is by a compass (Fig. 104).

A compass is a piece of steel, called a needle, which easily swings around, and always points to the north. This needle is a magnet, like the

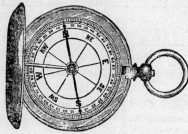

FIG. 104. — A small compass.

horseshoe magnets that you have seen. It points northward because some force within the earth draws it in that direction. No one knows certainly just what this force is, but it is called *magnetism*.

Another way to tell direction is by the stars. When the stars are shining, one can tell which direction is north by the help of the Great Dipper. The two stars on the edge of the Dipper point toward the North Star. This star can be easily found, and it always lies to the north of us.

One can also find direction by the help of the sun. At noon it stands exactly south of us; and twice each year, about the 21st of March and the 21st of September, it rises exactly in the east, and sets exactly in the west. Where does it rise in winter? In summer? When you face the east, which direction is on your right? Which on your left? Answer the same questions when facing the west; the south.

Northeast (N.E.) means halfway between north and east; southeast (S.E.) halfway between south and east. What, then, do northwest and southwest mean?

Point north, east, west, south, southwest, northeast, northwest. Walk a few feet in each

of these directions. What is the direction from your desk to the teacher's desk? To the desk of one of your schoolmates? To the door? What direction is your home from the schoolhouse? From certain other houses? In what directions do some of the streets extend?

Now let us tell directions on the map. Lay your drawing of the schoolroom upon your desk so that the **Directions on a map** line representing the north side of the room is on the north side. Also place yourself so that you face directly north as you look at the map. Now north on the map is also north in the room, and the other directions correspond with those in the room. In which direction, on the map, is the door from your desk? From the teacher's desk? Place your map of the school yard in the same position, and give the directions.

You see that the north side of this map is the side farthest from you. The east side is on your right, the south side is nearest to you, and the west side is on your left. When a map is lying before us, the directions on it are usually the same as these.

Of course it is not always convenient to have a map lying flat. This is especially true in the schoolroom, where the large maps must be hung up, so that the whole class may see them.

Let us hang up one of these maps, taking particular pains to place it upon the *north wall*. Which direction on the map is north now? You see, of course, that the north side must be the upper side, east is on the *right*, south is the lower side, and west is on the *left*.

You should drill yourself to understand directions on maps. Give directions from one place to another while

When you read such a letter, you think of the place and have some idea of how it looks. So, when you look at a map, you should think about the country, how it looks, and how far apart the places are.

There is more than one kind of map. Figure 133 (in Part II), **Two kinds of maps** for example, is a map of North America. This shows the shape of the continent, the position of the mountains, the large rivers, and the principal cities. It does not show the height of the mountains, nor of the hills and valleys, but represents the whole continent as entirely flat. Such a map may be called a *flat map*.

Figure 111, however, is a different kind of map. It shows how the continent might appear if

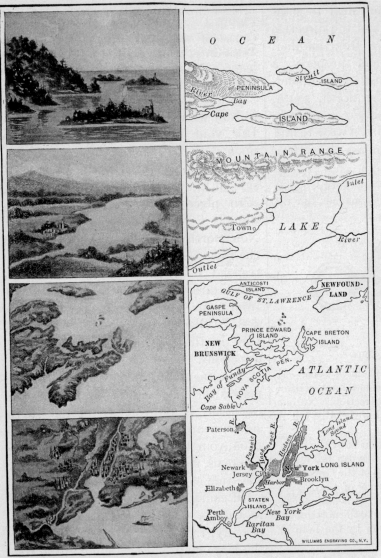

Fig. 105. — To illustrate the meaning of a map. The left-hand figures show the country as if you were looking down upon it; the right-hand figures represent the same country by maps. Tell what you see in each of these.

the map is hanging up. Put up the map of the school yard, and any others that you may have, and tell the directions from place to place.[1]

It is clear now what a map is. It is a drawing telling something about a country, just as a letter may be some writing telling what a place is like.

[1] After the children are quite at home in using the map when it is hung on the north wall, hang it on the other sides of the room and have them give the directions. This is very easy work if properly graded; but careless work at this point, in regard to directions on the map, often so confuses children that they never fully recover from their confusion. At the proper time, but much later than this, show that toward the top of the map is not always north. See Figure 272.

you looked down upon it from some point far above. On this map the plains appear level, as they should, while the mountains stand out in relief. You can easily see where the mountains, plains, and valleys are. Such a map as this is called a *relief map*, because it gives you some idea of the height of different portions of the land, or of the *relief*.[1] In

[1] Some teachers will find it useful to introduce the study of contour maps of the home region at this point. Such a study is not difficult, and will serve many useful purposes. A limited amount of modeling in sand may also be introduced; but the most important thing to do at this stage is to have the children understand the *meaning* of maps, so that these may be properly used in the class work. The best results from geography study cannot be gained without a knowledge and constant use of maps; and much use of the globe should be made, the moment children begin the study of continents and countries.

Figure 105 you can easily see the difference between these two kinds of maps. There are other kinds of maps, which you will learn about later.

Review Questions

1. How can a map of a schoolroom be drawn? 2. What is meant by drawing "according to a scale"? 3. Tell how you have drawn some map of your own. 4. What are some of the ways of finding directions out of doors? 5. What are the directions on a map? 6. What two kinds of maps do you know?

Suggestions

1. Examine a compass. 2. Find the Great Dipper and the North Star. 3. Show how you can tell the north direction by your shadow at 12 o'clock, noon. The east direction. The west. 4. Using sand, make a relief map of some piece of land that has some slopes.

PART II. WORLD GEOGRAPHY

I. GENERAL FACTS ABOUT THE EARTH

1. Form and Size of the Earth

Hundreds of years ago, before America was discovered, men thought that the earth was flat. It certainly *seemed* flat to them, just as it does to us. A few learned men, however, believed the earth to be a round ball, and that, if a person should travel straight on in one direction, he would, in time, return to the place from which he started. You can see how this would be if you push your finger straight around on the outside of an orange, until it comes back to the starting point.

The form of the earth

At that time men were in the habit of going to a land called India, for spices, silks, and jewels. To reach India from Spain they traveled thousands of miles *eastward*. Christopher Columbus (Fig. 108) was one of the men who believed that the earth was round. So he thought he could reach India just as well by going *westward* across the ocean. He also thought that the distance would be much less. He therefore went to the king of Spain and asked him for ships and men to make the journey.

The king refused the request because the plan seemed foolish, but Queen Isabella came to Columbus's aid. At last, on Aug. 3, 1492, he sailed westward from Spain out into the open Atlantic Ocean (Fig. 109). Almost every one thought that he was going on a voyage from which he would never

FIG. 108. — Christopher Columbus.

return; but after a journey of several weeks, and many adventures, he discovered land on October 12 (Fig. 110).

Thinking he had reached India, Columbus called the natives Indians; but, instead of India, he had discovered some

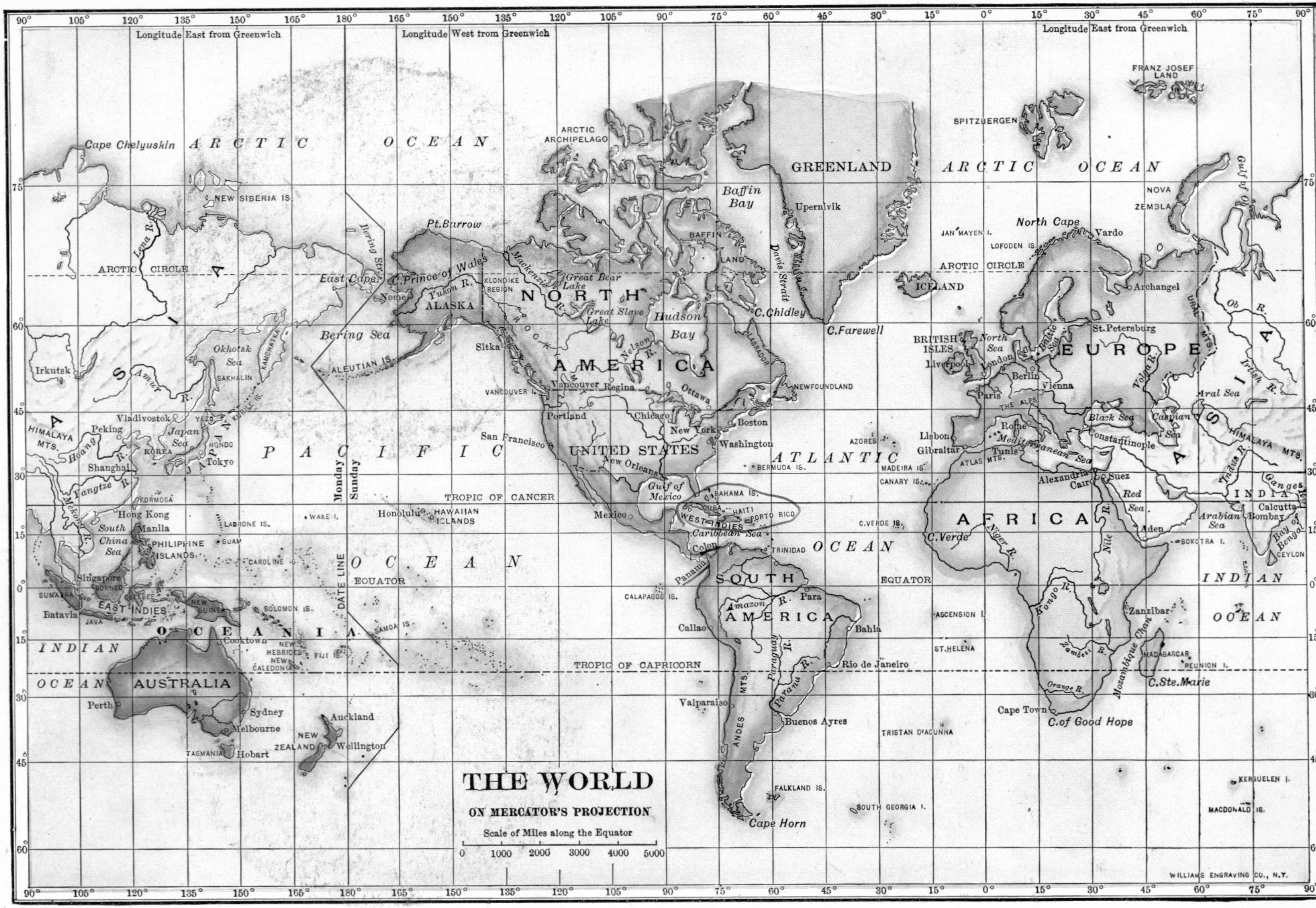
THE WORLD
ON MERCATOR'S PROJECTION
Scale of Miles along the Equator
0 1000 2000 3000 4000 5000
Longitude East from Greenwich
Longitude West from Greenwich
ARCTIC OCEAN
PACIFIC OCEAN
ATLANTIC OCEAN
INDIAN OCEAN
GREENLAND
NORTH AMERICA
SOUTH AMERICA
EUROPE
ASIA
AFRICA
AUSTRALIA
OCEANIA
UNITED STATES
ALASKA
ARCTIC CIRCLE
TROPIC OF CANCER
TROPIC OF CAPRICORN
EQUATOR
DATE LINE
Monday
Sunday
Hudson Bay
Baffin Bay
Davis Strait
Bering Sea
Gulf of Mexico
Caribbean Sea
WEST INDIES
EAST INDIES
PHILIPPINE ISLANDS
JAPAN
ICELAND
BRITISH ISLES
SPITZBERGEN
FRANZ JOSEF LAND
NOVA ZEMBLA
NEW SIBERIA IS.
NEW ZEALAND
Cape Chelyuskin
C.Farewell
C.Chidley
Cape Horn
C.of Good Hope
C.Verde
C.Ste.Marie
WILLIAMS ENGRAVING CO., N.Y.

FIG. 106.

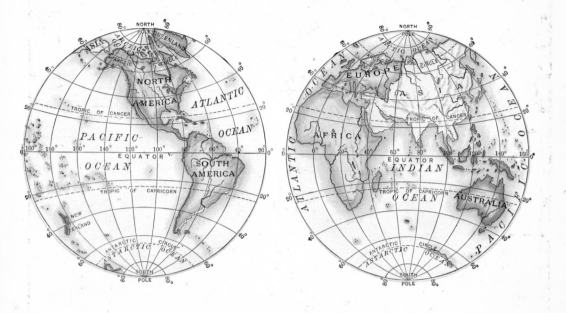

FIG. 107.

The Eastern and Western Hemispheres.

islands in the West Indies, on the coast of our own continent of North America.

Fig. 109. — A copy of the *Santa Maria*, on of the ships that Columbus had on his first voyage to America.

He did not know that a continent and a large ocean still lay between him and India.

After Columbus had returned in safety, other men dared to explore the *New World*, as it was called, to distinguish it from the *Old World*, where all white men then lived. One of these explorers, named Magellan, started to sail entirely around the earth. He was killed when he reached the Philippine Islands, but his men went on with the ships and

completed the voyage. This was in the year 1520, and it was the first time that any one ever sailed entirely around the earth. Since then many people have made the journey, in various directions, and the earth has been studied so carefully that every one now knows that it is round.

The great round earth is a huge ball, or *sphere*, called the *globe*. The reason why it does not appear round **Why the earth** to you is that you see so little **does not seem** of it at a time. If you see **round** very little of an orange, for example, it will not look round. To prove this, place a piece of paper with a small hole in it, upon an orange, so that none of the surface of the orange is seen, excepting that which shows through the hole. You will then observe that this part of the orange appears to be flat, not round.

If we could get far enough away from the earth to see a large part of it at once, we could easily observe that it is

Fig. 110. — Columbus taking possession of the newly discovered land in America.

round (Fig. 111). We know that the moon is round, because we look at it from a great distance; and the earth has the same shape as the moon.

NORTH POLE

SOUTH POLE

FIG. 111. — A map of half the earth as it might appear if seen from a great distance above it.

Our globe is very large; in fact, it is much larger than the moon. A lofty mountain seems to us very high, but even the highest mountains are only a very small part of

The size of the earth

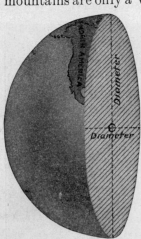

FIG. 112. — Figure of the earth cut in two, to show the *diameter* — a line passing through the center of the earth.

the great earth; when compared to the whole earth, they are no larger than a speck of dust compared to an apple. The loftiest mountains are rarely more than three or four miles high, but the *diameter* of the earth (Fig. 112), or the distance from one side to the other, through the center, is nearly *eight thousand miles*.

The distance around the earth, on the outside, called the *circumference*, is about twenty-five thousand miles. This distance, as you see, is a little more than three times the diameter. The circumference of any sphere is always a little more than three times its diameter. How can you prove this with an orange?

2. Daily Motion of the Earth

It does not seem to us that the earth is moving, but the ground on which you stand is really moving faster than any passenger train that you ever saw. The whole earth is whirling around like a top, at a tremendous rate. This motion is called its *rotation*. Since the earth turns completely around, or makes one complete rotation, every twenty-four hours, this motion is called its *daily rotation*.

The daily motion of the earth

FIG. 113. — The light from the candle lights only half of the apple that the boy is holding, just as the sun lights only half of the earth.

It is this daily rotation that causes day and night. A lamp can light only one half of a ball at a time, as you know (Fig. 113). The sun is a kind of lamp for the earth ball, for all the light of our

How rotation causes day and night

day comes from the sun. The sun, then, can light only one half of the great earth at a time.

This being the case, if our globe stood perfectly still, it would always be day on the side facing the sun, and night on the other side.

Since the earth rotates, the part that is getting the light is always changing. Thus, while the sun is always setting for some people, it is always rising for others. When it is noon where you live, it is midnight at the point opposite you, on the other side of the earth.

This is why there is a period of daylight, and a period of darkness, at the place where you live. These two periods together must last twenty-four hours, because the earth makes one complete rotation in that time.

The daily rotation also causes sunrise and sunset. Our earth *seems* to be stand-

How this motion causes sunrise and sunset

ing still, while each day the sun *seems* to rise in the east, to pass over us, and to set in the west. Yet we have just seen that the earth is not standing still by any means. Neither does the sun really "rise" and "set." The reason that the sun *seems* to rise in the east is that the earth is always rotating *toward* the east. We first get the light of the sun from that direction because the earth is turning in that direction. The sun seems to set in the west because, as the earth continues to rotate, we see the sun last in the west.

Although men speak of the sun "rising" in the east and "setting" in the west, they really know better. They express their thoughts in that way, simply because it is the easiest way. It would be difficult to think of any better way. Can you? Hundreds of years ago, however, all people thought that the sun really rose, and

that after moving across the heavens, it really set in the west. Our use of the words *sunrise* and *sunset* has come down to us from that time.

Since the earth is rotating with so great speed, why can we not notice it? The answer is simple. Everything on the earth is moving with it, including ourselves. On that account there are no objects near by for us to rush past; yet the only way of seeing that we are moving, would be to observe that we were passing the objects about us.

Why are we not all hurled away from the earth? When the string breaks by which a stone is being **Why rotation** whirled around, the stone **does not hurl** flies off. Why, then, do not **us away** we, and other objects, such as the water in the ocean, fly away into space?

The reason is that *the earth draws everything toward it,* and holds it there. If you push a book from your desk, it falls to the floor; and when you spring upward into the air you quickly return to the ground. All objects are drawn downward because the earth is pulling upon them. It attracts them much as a horseshoe magnet attracts a piece of iron. This force, which draws all objects to the earth, is called *gravity,* and you see how very important it is.

You have perhaps watched a wheel spin about on a rod or pin, the rod or pin holding it in place and **Meaning of** carrying its weight. The **axis and poles** earth spins around in much **of the earth** the same way; but no rod is necessary to hold it in place. What a mighty rod it would have to be, if there were one! A spinning top does not turn around a rod, either. It turns around a line running through its center, which is called its *axis* (Fig. 114). The earth also *rotates around,* or as we say, *on its axis.*

The axis of the earth is really nothing that you can see. It can be represented, however, by a straight line that runs through the center of the earth, and extends to the surface in both directions. Such a line is called the *axis of the earth*

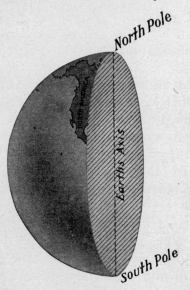

Fig. 114. — A drawing of the earth, cut in two, to show the position of the axis extending from pole to pole through the center of the earth.

(Fig. 114), and the two ends of the line are called the *poles of the earth*. One end of the axis is the *north pole*, and the other, the *south pole*.

You can understand this better by running a long, slender stick, or needle, through the center of an apple. The stick represents the axis, and the places where its two ends appear at the surface, represent the two poles of the earth. You can then spin the apple very much as the earth spins around on the line called its axis (Fig. 114).

If you were to go directly north from the place where you live, you would pass through the land of the Eskimos; and if you could go on, you would, in time, come to the north pole. Or, if you should travel due south, and went far enough, you would come to the south pole.

Many men have tried to cross the icy seas that surround the north pole; but, until 1909,

no one had been able to get quite so far as the pole. In that year Commander Peary, after many trials, at last reached the north pole; and Captain Amundsen discovered the south pole in 1911. Of course, Commander Peary did not find anything at the pole to mark the place. He was able to tell that he was there by the position of the sun. Had he been there during the night he would have found the *north star*, towards which the earth's axis points, almost directly over his head.

Midway between the poles we think of another line, drawn around the earth on the outside (Fig. 115). This is called the *equator*, because all parts of it are equally distant from each of the poles. The distance

Meaning of equator

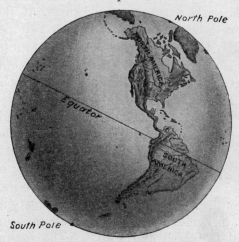

Fig. 115. — A drawing of that half of the sphere that includes the New World, — to show the position of the poles and the equator.

around the earth was given on page 88. What, then, is the length of the equator?

As the earth spins on its axis, all points on the surface must go with it, just as every part of the skin of an apple turns with the apple. Since the earth makes one complete turn each day, a man at the equator travels twenty-five thousand miles in twenty-four hours. What a whirling motion that is! It is at the rate of over one thousand miles an hour, while the fastest trains travel little more than sixty miles an hour!

3. The Zones

The hottest part of the earth is near the equator. The reason for this is

The zones and their boundaries

1. The torrid zone

that the sun, at midday, is directly over the heads of the people who live in that region.

You know that the sun's rays feel warmer at noon than in the early evening, because the sun is more

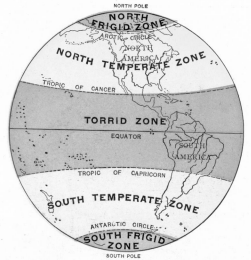

Fig. 116. — A map of the zones. The colors suggest *sharp* differences between the zones on the two sides of the boundaries; but you should remember that the changes are really *very* gradual.

nearly overhead at noon. For much the same reason the sun seems warmer in summer than in winter, because in summer it rises higher in the heavens. At the equator, however, and for many miles to the north and south of it, the sun is high in the heavens both in summer and winter. Thus there is a wide belt, extending all the way around the earth, that never has any winter; it is hot there every day in the year, as it is in summer where we live.

The northern boundary of this hot belt is called the *Tropic of Cancer* (Fig. 116);

it is about fifteen hundred miles north of the equator. The southern boundary, which is likewise fifteen hundred miles from the equator, is called the *Tropic of Capricorn*. In all the vast space between these two lines, or *tropics*, the sun is straight overhead during a part of the year; and it is never, on any day, very far from that.

Point out these two tropics on Figure 116. How wide is this belt? Over all this vast region the heat is intense, or *torrid*, and for that reason this is called the *torrid zone*. It is also called the *tropical* zone, or the *tropical belt*, because it is bounded by the two tropics.

People who live within the torrid zone wear only the very lightest clothing. We have seen that this is true of the Negroes of Central Africa, whose homes lie within this belt. Point out Central Africa on Fig. 107. Does any part of North America lie within the torrid zone? Walk toward that zone.

North of the torrid zone, the sun, even at noon, *never* stands directly overhead; and the greater the

2. The two temperate zones

distance from the equator, the greater is the slant at which the sun's rays shine upon the earth. Exactly the same is true as one goes south of the torrid zone.

There is a belt, then, on each side of the broad torrid zone, where it is neither very hot nor very cold. The climate there is called *temperate*, and in these belts the summers are warm and the winters cold. The belt north of the torrid zone is called the *north temperate zone*. It extends all the way from the Tropic of Cancer to the Arctic Circle (Fig. 116). How much of the United States lies within this zone?

Here, at noon, even in summer, you find your shadow pointing north, for the sun is south of you. Notice the direction and length of your shadow at midday, and the position of the sun at that time. Do you know whether your shadow is longer in summer than in winter, or shorter? Which must it be, since the sun stands higher in the heavens in summer than in winter?

The belt south of the torrid zone is called the *south temperate zone*, as you might expect. It extends from the Tropic of Capricorn to the Antarctic Circle. People living there find their shadows at noon always pointing south, since the sun is north of them. Their seasons, also, are just the opposite of ours; when we have summer, they have winter; and when we have winter, they have summer.

3. The two frigid zones Near the poles the rays of the sun reach the earth at a still greater slant, much as they do with us early in the morning, or late in the afternoon. Even in the middle of the day the sun lies low in the sky, near the horizon, and the shadows are very long. Therefore, the climate there is very cold, or *frigid;* the ground never thaws out; and the ice never entirely disappears from the sea (Fig. 117). Indeed, there is never any warm summer near the poles, just as there is never any winter near the equator.

The two regions around the poles are called the *frigid zones*. That about the north pole is called the *north frigid zone*, and the other the *south frigid zone*. Since they surround the poles, they are also sometimes called the *polar zones*. The north frigid zone is the home of the Eskimos, but there are no people living in the south frigid zone.

The hemispheres Since the equator is midway between the poles, it divides the earth, or sphere, into two equal parts, called *hemispheres* (*hemi*=half). The half of the earth north of the equator is called the *northern hemisphere*, and that south of it the *southern hemisphere*. In which of these hemispheres is the United States?

Fig. 117. — A ship in the ice that covers the sea in the cold, or frigid zone.

The earth may also be divided into halves by a circle running north and south through both poles. The western half, in which the New World lies, is called the *western hemisphere*. The eastern half, containing the Old World, is called the *eastern hemisphere*. You will find these two hemispheres represented in Figure 107. In which of them is your home?

4. Latitude and Longitude

How places are located on the earth If we learn that a certain place is in the torrid zone, or in one of the other zones, we know something about its location; yet we do not know very much about it, because each zone is so wide and long.

To help locate places more exactly, other circles than those already men-

1. Finding their latitude tioned are used upon maps and globes. Some of these circles extend east and west, on each side of the equator, as you can see in Figure 107. The distance between them is measured, not by miles, but by degrees, each of which is equal to almost seventy miles. How many degrees are there from one of these circles to the next, in Figure 107? About how many miles is that? We can thus quickly learn how far any place that is on or near one of these circles is from the equator. For example, how many degrees north of the equator is New York City? Chicago? How many miles would that be?

Instead, however, of saying that a place is a certain number of degrees north or south of the equator, we say that it is in so many degrees *north or south latitude.* Latitude means simply the distance north or south of the equator. Places north of the equator are in *north latitude,* and those south of it, in *south latitude.* The circles running east and west, which are drawn to show the latitude of places, are called *circles of latitude.* By their help, find the latitude of New Orleans; of Boston.

Other circles, extending north and south, from pole to pole, help to locate places in an east and west direction. A line that extends through England is agreed upon as the starting point in measuring. Places

2. Finding their longitude east of this line are said to be so many degrees in *east longitude;* places west of it, so many degrees in *west longitude.*

Longitude, as you see, simply means the distance east or west of this principal line; and these circles are called *circles of longitude.* In what longitude is New York City? Give both the latitude and longitude of Chicago. Locate other places, for example your own home, in the same way.

FIG. 118. — A map to show the land in the northern hemisphere that nearly surrounds the north pole.

5. The Continents

On page 45 you learned that there is about three times as

The five continents much water as land upon the surface of the earth. By examining the globe you can see that most of the land lies in the northern hemisphere. It almost surrounds the north pole, as you can see from the globe, or by looking at Figure 118.

There are two great masses of land here, one called Eurasia and the other North America. Besides these, there are three other great divisions of land — South America, Africa, and Australia. Point these out on the globe. Thus there are five great divisions of land upon the earth, and each of them is called a *continent*.

The continent of *North America* is the one on which you live. Notice its form,

North and South America

1. Their shape and climate

which is clearly shown in Figure 119. It is quite broad near the north pole, and tapers down almost to a point just north of the equator. This gives it the shape of a triangle. Make a drawing of it.

What part of this continent is in the frigid zone? In the torrid zone? In the temperate zone?

FIG. 119.—The continents of North and South America.

South America also has the form of a triangle. Draw its outline by using only three straight lines. Which of the American continents seems to have the more irregular coast line? Which, therefore, has the greater number of bays, capes, and peninsulas?

In what zones does South America lie? Point to parts of both North and South America where there is never any snow. Point to a part of North America where there is always snow.

Where must the Eskimo girl, Agoonack, one of the Seven Little Sisters, have lived (Fig. 120)? How would the climate change if you were to travel from the northern part of North America to the southern tip of South America? What differences would you expect to find in the plants? In the clothing of the people? Write a story about such a journey.

These two continents together are called the *two Americas*. They form what is known as the *New World*, which Columbus discovered.

FIG. 120.—An Eskimo child, dressed in furs, although the picture was taken in August.

You can see by the map that the two Americas are connected by a long, narrow neck of land, called an *isthmus*. This is the *Isthmus of Panama*. Any vessel that happens to be on one side of these continents, and which must reach the other side,

2. The Isthmus of Panama, connecting the two

has to pass all the way around South America. If this isthmus were not in the way, a ship might sail directly between the two continents. To save so long a journey, the United States government, by the help of many thousands of men, is now digging a channel, or *canal*, across this isthmus. When finished, it will be broad and deep enough to let ocean vessels pass through. Then ships going from the eastern to the western coast of our country will save a journey of thousands of miles.

The *Old World*, which includes Eurasia and Africa, contains much more land

FIG. 121.— A map of Eurasia and Africa.

The western part of Eurasia is called *Europe*. Long ago, before Columbus made his voyage to the New World, the most civilized people lived in Europe. The homes of Jeannette and Louise, two of the Seven Little Sisters, were in that country. If you have read the story, can you tell something about each of them?

2. Europe

Europe is usually considered one continent, and Asia another; but, as you can see from Figure 107, they are far less separated from each other than the other continents are. For this reason Europe and Asia are often classed together as one continent, and this is called Eurasia. The name is made of "Eur" from Europe, and "Asia."

3. Reason for the name Eurasia

than the New World (Fig. 121). The largest mass, which is almost entirely surrounded by water, is called *Eurasia*. You will notice that it is connected with Africa by a narrow isthmus. This isthmus, called the *Isthmus of Suez*, already has a ship canal across it. Thus vessels may go from one ocean to the other without having to travel all the way around Africa, as they used to do.

Eurasia

This is the largest continent in the world. You see that it is very irregular, even more so than North America. Point toward this continent. Walk toward it. Which is probably its warmest part?

The northern part of Eurasia lies in the north frigid zone, on the opposite side of the north pole from North America (Fig. 118). The continent extends a great distance east and west, as you see. Find for yourself how far south it reaches, and through what zones it extends. The eastern and larger part of the continent is called *Asia*. Read in the "Seven Little Sisters" about Pen-se, the Chinese girl, whose home was in Asia (Fig. 122).

1. Asia

FIG. 122. — Chinese children.

South of Europe is the continent of *Africa*. Draw its outline and compare

Africa
it with that of South America. Is its coast line regular or irregular? In what zones does it lie?

The Desert of Sahara, where the nomads live, is in the northern part of Africa (Fig. 123).

FIG. 123.—Children of the desert.

It is in this continent that the Negroes have their home; and here lived Gemila, the child of the desert, and Manenko, the little dark girl (Fig. 124), two of the Seven Little Sisters. The Negroes of our country are descendants of people who were brought from Africa many years ago.

Look on a globe to see in what direction you would have to travel if you were going to Africa. Could you reach it by going in more than one direction?

The many large islands south and southeast of Asia are called the *East

The East Indies and Australia
Indies;* and the central one of the peninsulas on the south side of Asia is called *India*. In Figure 106 find this peninsula, and these islands.

It was this part of the world that Columbus hoped to reach, when he sailed westward from Europe on his wonderful voyage. Can you show on a globe that, if the New World had not

been in his way, he might have reached India and the East Indies?

None of the East Indies is large enough to be called a continent. Just south of them, however, is an island, called *Australia*, so large that it is generally classed as a continent. It is the smallest of the continents, and

FIG. 124.—Negro school children and teacher in Africa.

is the only one that lies wholly in the southern hemisphere.

Find Australia on the globe; also in Figure 107. Is the northern or the southern part the hotter? Why should you expect any difference in temperature from north to south?

6. The Oceans

The ocean water forms only one body of water; but for long distances some parts are largely separated from others by the continents. These separate parts are given different names.

The parts of the ocean that are of most importance to us are those that lie to the east and west of

The Atlantic Ocean
the United States. That on the east, between North America and Europe, is called the *Atlantic Ocean*

(Fig. 125). This is the water that must be crossed in going to Europe; and it brought to us across the Atlantic from the Old World, and we send many of our products across this ocean to Europe.

FIG. 125. — Map of the Atlantic Ocean.

On Figure 125 observe that the Atlantic Ocean extends far to the south, between South America and Africa, as well as far to the north. In what part must the water be warmest? In what parts is it cold, and perhaps covered with ice? On the globe find which continents border this ocean.

The part of the ocean lying west of North America is called the *Pacific Ocean* (Fig. 126). What continents border it (Fig. 106)? It is the largest of the oceans, and covers more than one third of the earth's surface. Walk toward it. In what zones does it lie?

The Pacific Ocean

Not so many products are brought across the Pacific Ocean for our use as across the Atlantic. Yet Japan, China, and the Philippine Islands are on its farther side, as you can see on the map. We ship some articles to these countries, and they send some to us. Many Chinese and Japanese have come across this ocean to the United States. Where might they land?

On Figure 107 you will find a third great body of water, called the *Indian Ocean* (Figs. 121 and 127). What continents border it? Notice that it lies directly south of India, the peninsula in Asia which Columbus was seeking (p. 86). In what zones does this ocean lie?

The Indian Ocean

There are two other oceans, making five in all. One of these is the *Arctic Ocean*, which extends around the north pole,

The Arctic Ocean

FIG. 126. — Map of a part of the great Pacific Ocean.

was this ocean that Columbus crossed. Many things to eat and wear are

H

FIG. 127. — The Indian Ocean and the western part of the Pacific Ocean.

and is almost shut in by Eurasia and North America (Fig. 118). Notice that it is connected with the Pacific Ocean by only a very narrow body of water, or *strait*, called Bering Strait (Fig. 106). North America and Asia come close together at that point.

The Arctic Ocean has a freer connection with the Atlantic on the east. Huge masses of ice, called *icebergs* (Fig. 128), often float

down from the Arctic into the Atlantic Ocean. Sometimes there are so many that they are dangerous to vessels sailing between North America and Europe.

Figure 129 shows the *Antarctic Ocean*, which surrounds the south pole. As you see, there is a great mass of land around that pole. It is large enough to be called a continent; but, since no

The Antarctic Ocean

FIG. 129. — Map of the Antarctic Ocean, which surrounds the Antarctic continent.

FIG. 128. — Large numbers of icebergs floating in the water of the Arctic Ocean.

one lives upon it, and since it is covered with snow and ice all the year through, very little is known about it.

This ice-covered land is surrounded by the Antarctic Ocean, on which there is always much floating ice. Observe that this ocean is not separated from the three great oceans by land, as the Arctic is. Are the Arctic and Antarctic oceans of more, or less, importance to us than the other oceans? Why?

The water in the ocean occupies great hollows on the surface of the earth. **The depth of the ocean** The depth of this water varies greatly, though it is a little over two miles deep on the average. In many places, however, the ocean is more than four miles deep; and in one place, in the Pacific Ocean, the depth is nearly six miles. If the highest mountain in the world could be placed in the water at this point, its peak would not rise above the level of the sea.

Beneath the oceans there is solid rock, just as there is beneath the soil of the land. This **The bottom of the ocean** rock is covered with a coat of mud made of the shells of tiny animals, most of them smaller than the head of a pin. They have lived near the surface of the sea, and upon dying, their shells have slowly dropped to the bottom. Some of the chalk used in schools was once just such mud, before it was raised to form layers of chalk on the dry land.

The bed of the ocean lies so deep below the surface of the water that it is as dark there as our darkest night. Yet fish are living in these

FIG. 130. — A fish caught on the bottom of the deep ocean, where no sunlight ever reaches.

dark ocean depths (Fig. 130). Since there is no sunlight, they have little use for eyes, and some of them have no eyes. Others see by means of the light that they themselves make, called *phosphorescent* light. This is like the light that the firefly gives out at night.

The bottom of the ocean is, for the most part, a level plain. In many **The islands in the ocean** places, however, there are islands rising from the sea floor, as a glance at the map will show.

Many of these islands are *portions of mountain chains*. They are like the mountains on the continents, with only the highest peaks rising above the water. Other islands are the peaks of *volcanoes*. These have been made of melted rock, or *lava*, that has been forced up from inside the earth. Still others are what are known as *coral islands*. These have been formed in the following interesting way: —

Some of the tiny creatures that live in the ocean are called *coral polyps*. They build hard,

FIG. 131. — Coral growing in the sea.

limy coral (Fig. 131), such as you have no doubt seen; it is as hard as rock. Where the ocean water is warm, as in the torrid zone, these animals live in immense numbers, millions of them around a single island.

Each polyp helps to build the coral, which is a sort of house in which it lives. When it chooses to do so, the polyp can draw itself into the little cave that forms its home. It can thus escape enemies that might devour it.

At other times the polyp stretches out beyond the surface of the hard coral, spreading out like a fully blossomed flower. The polyps differ greatly in color, being white, pink, purple, red, yellow, brown, and other colors. It is a truly beautiful sight to see them spread out in the water, giving the appearance of a flower garden in the sea.

When these coral animals die, the hard, stony

homes that they have built, remain. Then other polyps build upon these remains, and this continues until the polyps build the coral up to the surface of the water. It is in this way that coral islands are formed (Fig. 132), and there

FIG. 132. — A ring-shaped coral island in the open ocean.

are thousands of them in the warm oceans, especially in the Pacific and Indian oceans.

FORM AND SIZE. 1. What did people formerly think about the form of the earth? 2. What is its form? 3. Relate the story of Columbus. 4. Why did he call the savages Indians? 5. Why was the land he discovered called the New World? 6. What makes Magellan's voyage important? 7. Explain why the earth does not appear to us to be a sphere. 8. What is meant by the diameter of the earth? By the circumference? What is the length of each?

Review Questions

DAILY MOTION. 9. Describe the daily motion of the earth. What is this motion called? 10. How does this motion cause day and night? 11. How does it cause sunrise and sunset? 12. Why can we not observe that the earth is rotating? 13. Why is not every loose object hurled from the earth by this rapid motion? 14. What is meant by the axis of the earth? By the poles of the earth? 15. Walk toward each of the poles. 16. What is meant by the equator? How long is it?

THE ZONES. 17. Give the cause of the great heat in the torrid zone. 18. How wide is that zone, and what are its boundaries? 19. Where are the two temperate zones? 20. Why is the heat less there than in the torrid zone? 21. Where are the frigid zones? 22. What is meant by the northern hemisphere; by the southern hemisphere? 23. What is meant by the eastern and the western hemispheres?

LATITUDE AND LONGITUDE. 24. How are places located on the earth? 25. What is latitude? Longitude?

THE CONTINENTS. 26. Name the five continents, counting Eurasia as one. 27. Write their names. 28. Walk toward each. 29. What is the shape of North and of South America? Show the shape of each by a drawing. 30. Tell about the climate of each. 31. Of what importance is the Isthmus of Panama? 32. What can you tell about Eurasia? Why this name? 33. Tell what you can about Africa. 34. Locate and give the principal facts about Australia. 35. What part of the world, near Australia, was Columbus hoping to reach?

THE OCEANS. 36. What two oceans are of most importance to us? 37. What do you know about each of them? 38. Where is the Indian Ocean? 39. Where are the Arctic and Antarctic oceans? 40. Why are they of little importance to us? 41. What can you tell about the depth of the ocean? 42. About the ocean bottom? 43. What are the three causes for islands in the ocean? 44. What is the result of the work of the coral polyps? 45. What oceans touch North America? 46. Name the five oceans. Write their names.

1. Trace Columbus's voyage on a globe. Find India and see how one can go by water from Europe to India by sailing eastward; by sailing westward. **Suggestions** 2. Make a sphere in clay. Measure its diameter with a needle, and its circumference with a string. 3. Locate the poles on such a sphere; and also represent the equator. 4. Use a horseshoe magnet to see how it attracts iron. 5. With a globe or an apple, and a lamp, show how it is day on one side of the earth while it is night on the other side. Show also why the sun appears to rise in the east. 6. Who were Atlas and Aurora? 7. Where did people, long ago, suppose that the sun went at night? 8. Write a story telling the kinds of clothing you would need in going from the north to the south pole. 9. In passing southward on such a journey, in what different directions would you look at noon to see the sun? 10. Would you expect a sudden change in temperature in crossing the Tropic of Cancer or of Capricorn? Why? 11. If there were no watches or clocks, how could you learn the time

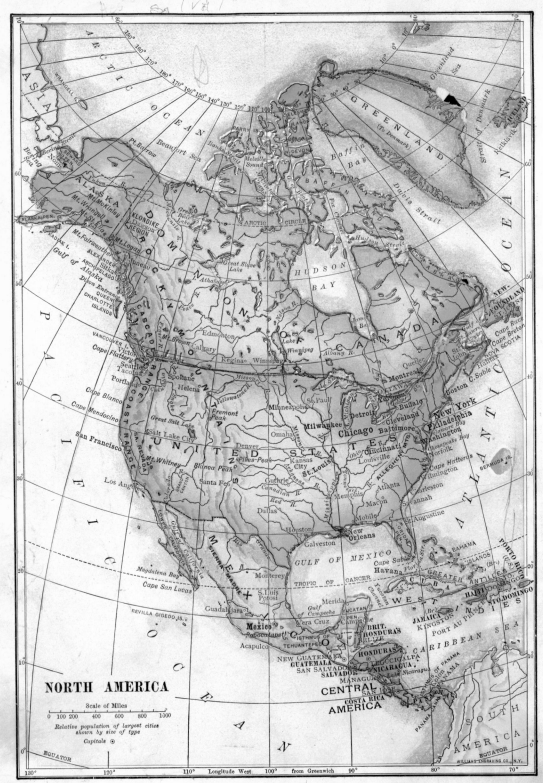

NORTH AMERICA

Scale of Miles

0 100 200   400   600   800   1000

Relative population of largest cities shown by size of type
Capitals ⊙

FIG. 133.

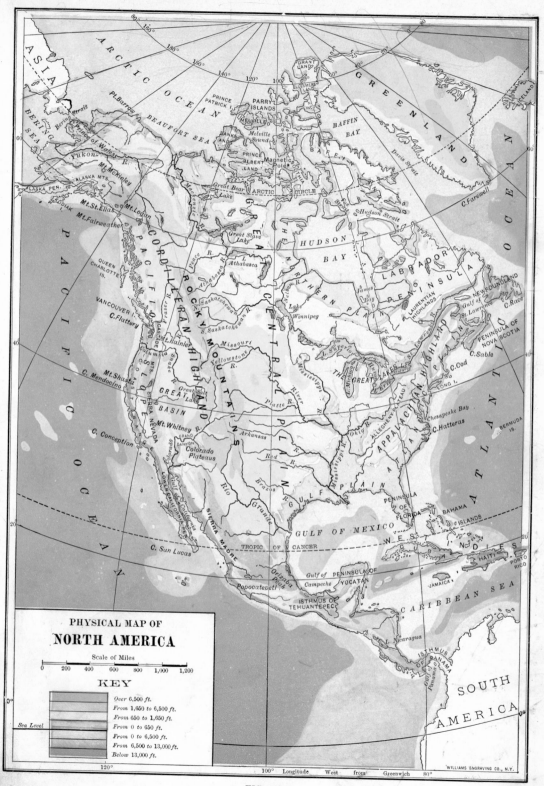

PHYSICAL MAP OF
NORTH AMERICA

Scale of Miles

0   200   400   600   800   1,000   1,200

KEY

Over 6,500 ft.
From 1,650 to 6,500 ft.
From 650 to 1,650 ft.
From 0 to 650 ft.
From 0 to 6,500 ft.
6,500 to 13,000 ft.
Below 13,000 ft.

Sea Level

120°   100°   Longitude   West   from   Greenwich   80°

WILLIAMS ENGRAVING CO., N.Y.

FIG. 134.

of day from your shadow? 12. Find out about some of the men who have tried to reach the north pole. 13. In which zone would you prefer to live? Why? 14. Examine a piece of coral. If possible, secure a piece for the school collection.

II. NORTH AMERICA

The principal divisions of North America If you look on the map of North America (Fig. 133), you will see that the continent is divided into several countries. In the center, extending from ocean to ocean, is the *United States*. North of our country is *Canada*, and northwest of that is *Alaska*. South of us lies *Mexico*, and southeast of that is *Central America*. Make a simple drawing of North America, and upon it mark off each of these sections.

Some reasons for these divisions **1. Mexico and Central America** You remember that Spain was the nation that helped Columbus to make his discovery of America. After his voyage, many Spaniards came over and settled in the southern part of the continent. They occupied the parts now marked Mexico and Central America. All this section, and some of the land to the north of it, now a part of the United States, was for many years owned by Spain. Indeed, at one time it all bore the name of *New Spain;* but the government by Spain was so very bad that the people rebelled against it, and, by war, secured their independence.

Although the Spanish language is still spoken in all this section, it is now divided into several independent countries. The larger part of it, called *Mexico*, is under one government; the part of it marked *Central America* is divided into several little nations. The only reason for calling this part of the continent Central America is its central position between two continents. There is really no country of that name.

The small country of *Panama* occupies the narrow Isthmus of Panama, which joins Central America with South America. It is here that the Panama Canal is being dug to connect the Atlantic and Pacific oceans (p. 163).

2. The United States Other nations besides Spain sent explorers to America, and made settlements. Chief among these were the English and the French. The English settlers at first made their homes along the eastern coast, as in Massachusetts and Virginia. The French chose the valleys of the St. Lawrence and Mississippi rivers. Find these rivers on the map. As the result of war, the English obtained control of the French territory, and English became the principal language of all the continent north of Mexico.

Even now, however, one is reminded of the old French rule. French is still heard in New Orleans, near the mouth of the Mississippi River, and it is the common language in the city of Quebec, on the St. Lawrence River. Point out these cities.

The names of many places in the Mississippi and St. Lawrence valleys, such as New Orleans, St. Louis, and Montreal, are French. They were given when these places belonged to France.

For many years the colonies in America were governed by England; but finally many of the colonists became dissatisfied with English rule. As a result, a war for independence broke out, which lasted several years, under the leadership of General George Washington (Fig. 98). The colonists declared themselves independent on July 4, 1776, a date whose anniversary you celebrate every year. Independence was not gained, however, until later, after several years of hard fighting and much suffering.

Our ancestors, who fought in this war, formed a government of their own which they called the United States. At first there were only thirteen small states in the Union, all near the Atlantic coast. Gradually other states and territories were added, until our country now extends across the continent, as you see.

England was able to keep a large part of the continent, which is called **3. Canada and Newfoundland** the *Dominion of Canada.* This country, which is still a British colony, is a union of states, or *provinces*, like our United States.

You observe, on the map, the large island of *Newfoundland*, in the extreme eastern part of the continent. This also was kept by England and is still a British colony; but it has never joined the Dominion of Canada and has, therefore, a separate government.

The extreme northwestern part of North America, called *Alaska*, was first explored by the Russians, **4. Alaska** and they owned it for a long time. Russia finally sold it to the United States, and it still belongs to us.

Of course, where two countries lie side by side, as do Canada and the **The boundaries of these countries** United States, there must be some place where one country ends and the other begins. Such a place is called a *boundary.* The boundary lines between the different nations are marked on the map (Fig. 133) by heavy lines. Point them out.

In some parts you will see that a *natural boundary*, such as a river or a chain of lakes,

has been chosen to separate two neighboring countries. In other places the boundary does not follow any natural line. In some cases it is even a straight line, cutting across rivers, lakes, and mountains. Examine the boundary of the United States to see how much of it is natural.

Where the boundary is only a straight line, it is marked by a row of posts or stone pillars, a few rods apart. These you could easily see if you were to cross from one country to another, where there is such a boundary. On your drawing of North America, mark those boundaries of the United States which are natural.

Figure 133 is a map of North America showing the boundaries of **Study of maps** the different countries, and **1. Political** the location of the largest **Maps** rivers and cities. Such a map is called a *political map.*

Find Greenland on this map. Would you expect it to be an important island? Why? Trace the Mississippi River. Three other great rivers of North America are the St. Lawrence, the Mackenzie, and the Yukon. Find each. What would you say about the importance of the Mackenzie and Yukon rivers, in comparison with that of the St. Lawrence and the Mississippi? Why?

Figure 134, a *physical* map, is a very different kind of map from **2. Physical** Figure 133. Its purpose is **Maps** to show the height of the land, or the high and low parts of the continent.

What great mountain system, or highland, do you find in the western part of North America? What great highland in the east? In what direction does each of these highlands extend? Which is the broader? Which the higher? Trace, as nearly as you can, the boundaries of each.

Where is the lowest land between these two highlands? Show the length and width of the Mississippi Valley. Notice the slope east of the Appalachian

UNITED STATES
WESTERN PART
Scale of Miles

0   50 100   200   300   400   500

WILLIAMS ENGRAVING CO., N.Y.

115°   Longitude   West   110° from   Greenwich   105°   100°   95°

FIG. 136.

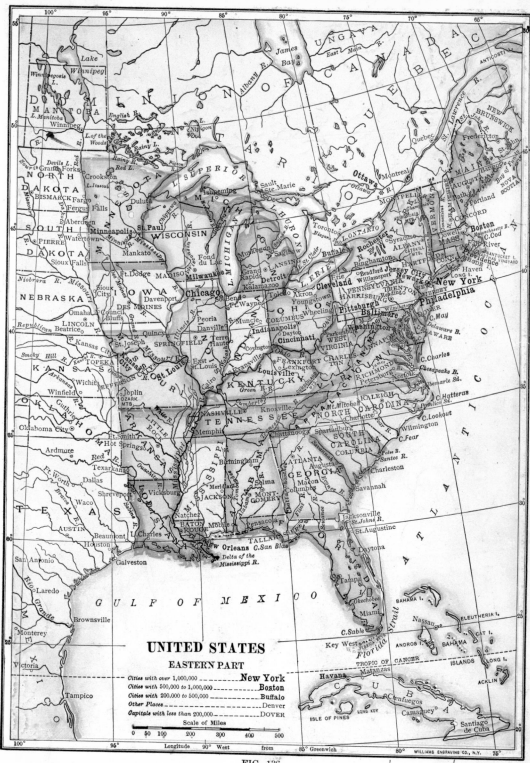

UNITED STATES

EASTERN PART

Cities with over 1,000,000	**New York**
Cities with 500,000 to 1,000,000	Boston
Cities with 200,000 to 500,000	Buffalo
Other Places	Denver
Capitals with less than 200,000	DOVER

Scale of Miles

0   50   100   200   300   400   500

100°   95°   Longitude   90° West   from   85° Greenwich   80°   WILLIAMS ENGRAVING CO., N.Y.   75°

FIG. 136.

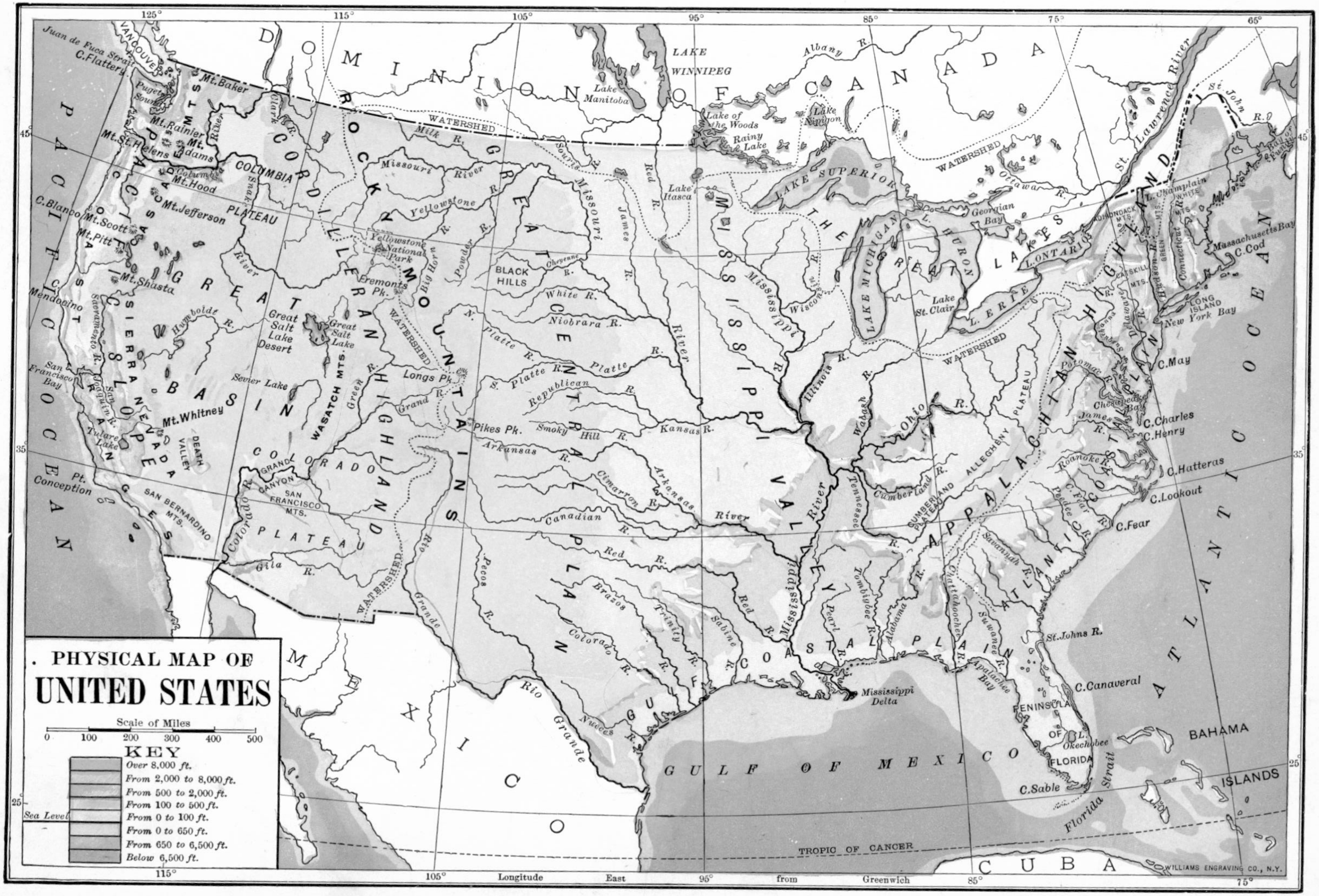
PHYSICAL MAP OF
UNITED STATES
Scale of Miles
0 100 200 300 400 500
KEY
Over 8,000 ft.
From 2,000 to 8,000 ft.
From 500 to 2,000 ft.
From 100 to 500 ft.
From 0 to 100 ft.
From 0 to 650 ft.
From 650 to 6,500 ft.
Below 6,500 ft.
Sea Level
DOMINION OF CANADA
ROCKY MOUNTAINS
CORDILLERAN HIGHLAND
GREAT CENTRAL PLAIN
MISSISSIPPI VALLEY
THE GREAT LAKES
APPALACHIAN HIGHLAND
ATLANTIC COASTAL PLAIN
GULF COASTAL PLAIN
GREAT BASIN
COLORADO PLATEAU
COLUMBIA PLATEAU
PACIFIC SLOPE
CASCADE MTS
SIERRA NEVADA
COAST RANGES
PACIFIC OCEAN
ATLANTIC OCEAN
GULF OF MEXICO
MEXICO
CUBA
BAHAMA ISLANDS
TROPIC OF CANCER
Longitude East from Greenwich
WILLIAMS ENGRAVING CO., N.Y.

FIG. 137.

FIG. 135. — A section across the United States from the Atlantic to the Pacific ocean, showing the highlands and lowlands.

Mountains (Fig. 135). Is it longer or shorter than that west of the western Highlands? What are the main slopes in North America? Upon which of these slopes do you live? Point as nearly as you can to the place where your home is.

On Figure 133 find New York and San Francisco. If you were to travel westward from the former to the latter place, you would have to pass over many hills, valleys, and mountains. Some of the slopes would be short and gentle; others would be very long, sometimes gentle, sometimes steep. Make a drawing showing the chief slopes you would cross in making that journey.

Review Questions
1. Name the principal divisions of North America. Write these names. 2. State some of the reasons for such a division of the continent: (*a*) for Mexico and Central America; (*b*) for United States; (*c*) for Canada and Newfoundland. 3. What do you know about Alaska? 4. What natural boundaries has the United States? 5. What do you understand by a political map? By a physical map? 6. What are the principal slopes in North America? 7. Name the principal mountain ranges. 8. The principal rivers. 9. The largest lakes. 10. The largest islands, peninsulas, and gulfs and bays. 11. Make a drawing of the continent, putting in the names of all these.

III. THE UNITED STATES

Map study
1. What bodies of water border the United States? 2. What countries? 3. Find the Appalachian Mountains. 4. What are the names of the mountain chains in western United States? 5. Make a drawing of the Mississippi River and its larger tributaries. 6. Make a drawing of the United States, putting on it the largest rivers and lakes, with their names; also the largest cities. (You will find a list of them in the Appendix, p. 256.)

If you look on Figure 136 you will see that its scale is about 325 miles to the inch. Knowing this fact, find how many miles it is across our country from north to south, measuring from our northern boundary to the mouth of the Rio Grande. Find the width of our country in an east-west direction, from New York to San Francisco. The United States is not quite so large as Canada. How does it compare with Mexico in size? **The extent of the United States**

As we have seen, the states that formed our Union after the War of Independence were thirteen in number. These were New Hampshire, Massachusetts, Connecticut, Rhode Island, New York, New Jersey, Pennsylvania, Delaware, Maryland, Virginia, North Carolina, South Carolina, and Georgia. Find each of these states on the map, Fig. 136. How many of them do not border on the ocean? What a small part of the United States they now form! **Steps in the growth of the United States** **1. The thirteen original states**

Our flag still has its thirteen red and white stripes, to remind us of these thirteen original states. At first there were only thirteen stars in the blue field of the flag. But a star has been added for each new state, until now there are many more. Count the stars in the flag to see how many states there are now.

To form all these new states, several great sections of land have been added, at different times, to the original thirteen states (Fig. 138). **2. States of the Mississippi Valley**

At the close of the War of Independence, all the land east of the Mississippi River belonged to the Union, except Florida and a narrow strip along the coast west of Florida. For many years, however, the part between the Appalachian Mountains and the Mississippi River was not made into states. Indeed, it was a wilderness about which very little was known, because the Appalachian Mountains were like a great wall, shutting people out of the Mississippi Valley.

Trappers and traders first forced their way into this valley. Among these were David Crockett and Daniel Boone, who had many thrilling adventures with the Indians, some of which you may have read about. Then, when it was learned what an attractive region this was, settlers rapidly followed, and states were soon formed. Name some of these states.

Pioneers soon pushed across the Mississippi River, over the *Great Plains*, as far as the Rocky Mountains. Nearly all the vast region between the Mississippi River and the Rocky Mountains, except Texas, was bought from France in the year 1803. Name some of the states that have been formed from it.

Florida, together with a narrow strip of land along the Gulf of Mexico, was **3. Florida and Texas** bought from Spain in 1819. Texas, which had once been a part of Mexico, obtained its independence from that country; and later it entered the Union.

The highlands of western United States are much broader and more difficult to cross than the Appalachian Mountains, and **4. States west of the Rocky Mountains** for a long time few men were daring enough to try to reach the Pacific coast. When rich gold deposits were discovered near the west coast, however, many thousands started in haste for that region. Partly by purchase, and partly by war with Mexico,

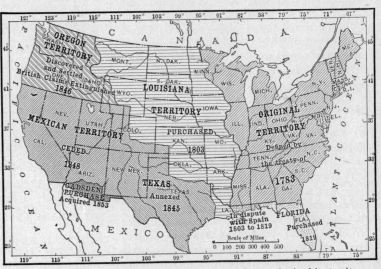

FIG. 138. — Map to show when and how the United States obtained its territory.

our country had already obtained possession of this western land; and, as it became rapidly settled, states were formed from it. Name some of them.

At the close of the War of Independence, in 1783, there were only about three million white persons **Our growth in population** living in the United States. Now we have about ninety-two million, or more than are found in all the other countries of North and South America together. We have more people than France, or Germany, or any European nation except Russia. It should be remembered, too, that those countries are very old, and had been settled for centuries when America was discovered. Dating the birth of our nation from 1776, how old is it?

One reason for this rapid growth in population is the fact that our country

Reasons for this growth
1. Our temperature

is situated in the *temperate zone*. The great heat in the torrid zone makes it difficult to work and unhealthful to live there. On the other hand, the extreme cold of the frigid zone makes it difficult to get a living, no matter how hard one works. In the temperate zone, we find neither of these drawbacks. There is not too much heat for comfort or health, and yet there is plenty for the growth of plants.

Our country is so large that there is much difference in temperature between one part and another. In southern Florida, there is never any frost or snow, and such crops as bananas and pineapples can be grown, as in the torrid zone. Cotton, sugar cane, rice, and oranges, which require a warm climate, are also grown in our Southern States. Farther north we can produce the more hardy crops, such as wheat and oats, that thrive in a cooler climate. There are few countries in the world that have such variety of temperature as ours.

Over a large part of our country there is plenty of rain for farming and

2. Our rainfall

gardening. In several of the Western States, however, there is so little rain that no crops can be grown without irrigation. In fact, some parts of the West are true deserts, with farming only on the oases, as in the Sahara. In spite of their dryness, a large portion of these sections is useful for grazing; and the western part of the United States is one of the most important regions in the world for sheep and cattle. Thus the differences in rain-

fall, as well as temperature, help to give us a variety of products.

Fertile soil, as well as heat and rain, is necessary in order that people may have food, clothing, and shelter. Few countries in

3. Our soil

the world have as much deep, rich soil as our own. There are many kinds, too, so that many different crops can be raised.

On the whole, the climate and soil of our country are so favorable, and so varied, that the United States produces almost all the crops necessary for food, clothing, and shelter.

The mineral products, from the rocks beneath the soil, are also of great value. In our western mountains are gold, silver, lead, and

4. Our minerals

copper mines of untold richness. Enormous amounts of copper and iron ore are mined in the states that border Lake Superior. Coal, too, is abundant in many of our states, so that there is plenty of fuel for manufacturing these various metals into useful articles. In addition, we have valuable building stone of many kinds, and clays, salt, and other useful mineral products. All together the rich supply of minerals found in the United States is one of the most important reasons for our remarkable growth as a nation.

It is of great importance that we have so many different kinds of land in our country. There are the

5. Our plains and mountains

coastal plains, that lie between the Appalachian Mountains and the sea. Here the land is so level and fertile that farming is easy. Far larger than these are the *central plains*, through which the Mississippi River and its tributaries flow. This level country makes one of the finest farming sections in the world. There are also many smaller plains, and much gently rolling and hilly land suited to agriculture.

The higher hills, mountains, and plateaus are valuable in a different way. They cause the moisture in the air to be condensed into rain and snow, which keep the rivers filled with water. In addition, they are the source of valuable minerals, and they are often covered with forests, which supply us with the lumber that we need for so many purposes.

6. Our conveniences for transportation The minerals and other raw products have to be transported from the mines to the factories, and then the manufactured articles must be distributed far and wide over the country. It is important, therefore, that there be abundant means for shipping goods.

The railroads now do much to supply this need, but our natural highways, or waterways, have met it well from the beginning. First of all, note (Fig. 136) how the Mississippi River and its tributaries make it possible for boats to reach the ocean even from the heart of our country. Trace some of the larger of these rivers, and write their names.

The Great Lakes, on the north, are other important waterways on which vessels may travel for many hundreds of miles. How many such lakes are there? There are also many smaller rivers and lakes of importance for transportation. Can you name some of them, and point them out on the map?

It is important to send some goods to foreign lands, and to bring others from foreign countries to our shores. Here again the United States is fortunate.

One of our coasts faces Europe, and is well supplied with excellent harbors. Trace this coast line, to see how irregular it is, thus making fine harbors possible.

Our Southern coast, too, has some excellent harbors, from which ships can easily reach Europe, the West Indies, Mexico, and the countries of South America. Vessels may also go from port to port along our coast, carrying goods from one place to another.

Our Western coast faces Asia, where there are enormous numbers of Chinese, Japanese, and other people. This coast likewise has some excellent harbors, from which steamship lines now run to many ports on the Pacific and Indian oceans.

No other country has so favorable a situation for trade with all parts of the world as ours. In fact, no other large country has a seacoast, with an abundance of good harbors, on both the Atlantic and Pacific oceans.

7. Our free land There have been still other powerful attractions to our country. One of these has been the free land. Any one who has cared to come here and live for a few years could obtain a good-sized farm to live upon. That has been a help indeed to many a man. So many people have been attracted to our country, that almost all the free farm land has now been taken up.

Even where there was no land to be given away, it has often been possible to buy it at a very low price, — only a few dollars an acre, — which even a poor man, with energy, could hope to pay. Millions of people have been attracted to the United States by the free and the cheap farm lands.

In some countries of Europe many of the people are still in ignorance. In the United States, on the other hand, an effort is made to give every one an education. One of the first things our forefathers did was to establish schools, and now there are schools, colleges, and universities all over the land. Most of this education is free, and any one can obtain it. Our excellent system of education is one of the chief causes of our rapid advance, for educated people can do things which ignorant people cannot do.

8. Our free education

Another great attraction to many persons has been our free government. In some countries the rulers do not let the people share in the making of laws. They seize private property; they arrest men and throw them into prison, or drive them from the country, or put them to death, without trial.

9. Our free government

After the War of Independence, our forefathers established a government called a *democracy*. In this, the people elect some men to make laws, and others to execute them. That is the kind of government we now have. All the officers are thus really *servants* of the people, and not masters; and they are paid for their work by the people. The object of this government is to help every one, as far as possible, and not to worry or oppress any one.

Millions of men have died fighting against a despotic form of government; and it is no wonder that other millions have braved great hardships to reach a land where they were free from despotic rulers. There is, perhaps, no country on the earth where an honest man, with ability and energy, can prosper so easily as in the United States.

These are some of the more important reasons why our population has increased so rapidly. Aside from the people who have been born in this country, millions have come from Europe and Asia; and they still come in almost every ship that carries passengers. Such people are called *immigrants,* and most of them land at New York.

Immigrants to the United States

From that city they scatter in all directions, and settle in every part of our country. These immigrants have greatly helped to develop our land, and to make the United States one of the great powers of the world. They have been eager to come here, and most of them have been eager to stay, for they have learned to love this land. You probably know some immigrants yourself, for they are all about you. Ask some of them why they came here, and whether this country is as good to live in as the one they left.

1. What is the size of the United States? How does it compare in size with other countries? 2. Name the first thirteen states of our Union, and locate them. 3. What great sections of land have been added to these, to make the number of states that we now have? 4. Tell about our growth in population. 5. Show that our temperature is one reason for so great a population. 6. How is our rainfall a second reason, and our soil a third? 7. How are our minerals a fourth reason? 8. Show that our plains and mountains are a fifth reason. 9. How have our conveniences for transportation helped our growth? 10. How has our free land helped? 11. Our free education? 12. Our free government? 13. Tell about the immigrants to the United States.

Review Questions

1. Read the life of Daniel Boone or David Crockett. 2. Find out what steps a man has had to take, in order to get possession of free land in this country. 3. Learn what is done with the immigrants when they land at Ellis Island in New York Harbor. 4. Do you see any dangers to this country in allowing all people to come here from other countries who desire to come?

Suggestions

IV. THE NORTHEASTERN STATES

1. Name these states. Write the names. 2. Which has no seacoast? 3. Which state extends farthest east and north? **Map study** Which farthest south? Which farthest west? 4. What natural boundaries do you find between them? 5. What mountain system crosses these states (Fig. 137)? 6. Which states are most mountainous? 7. Name and locate the chief rivers. 8. Find New York City. Using the scale, about how far is it from New York City to Boston? To Philadelphia? 9. Walk toward New York City. 10. In what direction would one have to sail from New England, in order to reach England?

In order that our country may be more easily studied, we divide the states into groups. The first group of states to be studied are those in the Northeast. They include the *New England States* and some of those along the middle part of our Atlantic coast, usually called the *Middle Atlantic States*. These nine states together are here called the *Northeastern States*.

Of these nine states the six farthest northeast are called *New* **The area of these states** *England*. What are their names? What are the names of the other three? On the map of the United States (Fig. 136) you can see what a small part of our country these states make. All of them together are much smaller than Texas, yet they form nearly one fifth of our whole number of states.

Which is the smallest of these states? It is the smallest state in the Union. One of the New England States is about as large as the other five together. Which one is it? Even this, however, is much smaller than New York, the largest of the Northeastern States.

In spite of their small area, these states contain about twenty-six million inhabitants, or about one **Their population** fourth of the people in the United States. One of them, New York, has more inhabitants than any other state in the Union. It also contains

Fig. 139. — A view in the White Mountains of New Hampshire, showing a railroad winding along a valley at the base of a steep, rocky mountain side.

the largest city in the New World. Pennsylvania is next to New York in population, as well as in size.

It is interesting to learn why so many people have crowded to- **Why so great a population** gether in this small section. What special kinds of work can have attracted them here?

The principal occupations are the same as those found elsewhere; namely,

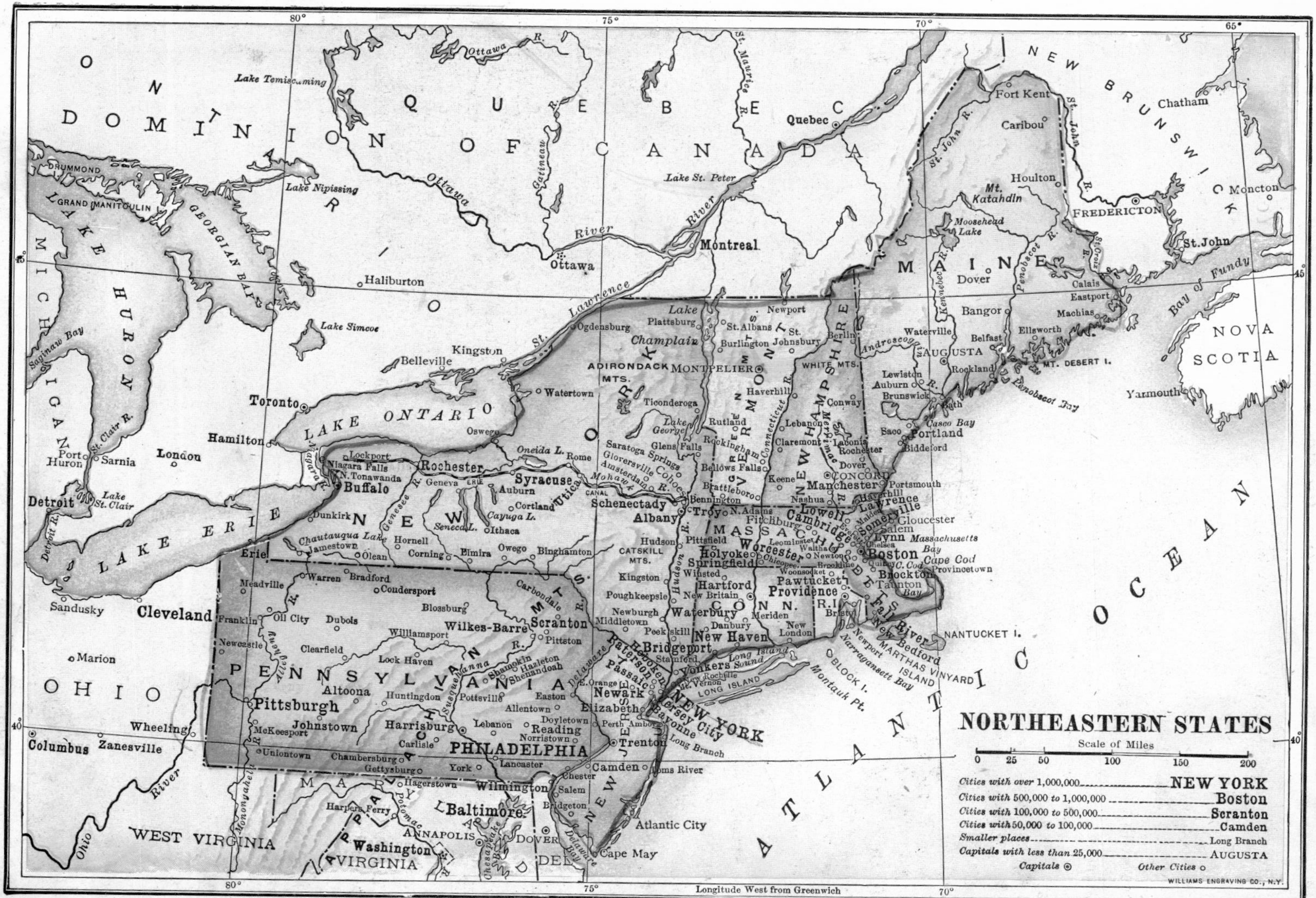

NORTHEASTERN STATES

Scale of Miles

Cities with over 1,000,000 ———— **NEW YORK**
Cities with 500,000 to 1,000,000 ———— **Boston**
Cities with 100,000 to 500,000 ———— **Scranton**
Cities with 50,000 to 100,000 ———— Camden
Smaller places ———— Long Branch
Capitals with less than 25,000 ———— AUGUSTA
Capitals ⊙ ———— Other Cities ○

WILLIAMS ENGRAVING CO., N.Y.

FIG. 140.

Longitude West from Greenwich

arming, lumbering, fishing, mining, manufacturing, and commerce. Among these occupations, however, some have here become far more important than others, and we shall now find out which they are.

Strange to say, farming, the most important occupation in the world, is not so prominent in these states

FIG. 141. — A view in the hilly region of New England, dotted with patches of woodland and of land cleared for farming.

land (Fig. 139). On Figure 140 trace the main mountain ranges. In what directions do they extend? Name the states that contain mountains.

Even in sections where there are no mountains, the country is often so hilly and rocky that much of the land cannot be farmed. The slopes are too steep (Fig. 139), or the soil is too thin and stony. There are so many people living in these states, however, that even much land with thin, stony soil and steep slopes is cultivated.

In so hilly a country farming on a large scale is seldom possible. The land is cut up into small fields with patches of woodland here and there (Fig. 141).

Among the most common products are those fruits and vegetables that find a ready market in the large cities near by. This kind of work is known as *truck farming;* for the many things that are raised, such as tomatoes, onions, beans, peas, corn, berries, apples, and radishes are called *truck*.

2. Farms mainly small, and often used for truck farming

Many farm animals, such as pigs, ducks, chickens, turkeys, and geese are also raised for food. Eggs are, therefore, an important product. One of the chief farming industries is *dairying*. The many inhabitants in this section require great quantities of milk, butter, and cheese. Where other crops will not flourish, the land produces grass; hence wherever one travels through these states, he is likely to see beautiful pastures and fine cattle.

3. Dairying and raising of domestic animals

Besides dairy products, the cattle furnish meat for food, and hides for leather. Many horses and sheep are also raised, the sheep furnishing meat, wool, and skins.

There are many sections in which the farm land is of the very best quality. This is true, for instance, of the Connecticut Valley, in which much grain and tobacco are raised. Trace the Connecticut River. It is true, again, of the southern half of New Jersey and eastern Pennsylvania. Here the climate is milder than in New England, so that such crops

4. Some of the most fertile sections

as grapes and peaches are raised. Apples, grapes, and other fruits also thrive on the fine farm land of western New York, especially near Lakes Erie and Ontario. There is much excellent farm land in New York.

While a great deal of food is raised in the Northeastern States, there is not
5. Need of food from other places nearly enough to feed the people. Therefore much is brought from the more fertile farming states of the Mississippi Valley. Wheat for bread is shipped to these states in great quantities; so are meat, sugar, and other common foods.

Most of the land in the Northeastern States was once wooded; but most of the
**Lumbering
1. Where forests are found** trees have been removed from those parts that could be made into farms. Forests are now mainly found, therefore, upon the mountain slopes and upon the hilly, rocky land (Figs. 139 and 141).

Lumbering does not employ a great number of men; on this account not
2. Importance of lumbering many people live where it is carried on. Yet the industry is very important, because there are so many people in these states who need articles made of wood. Among these are tables, chairs, and paper. Add to this list as many more objects as you can.

Lumbering is extensively carried on in Maine (Fig. 142); in the Adirondack
3. Centers for this industry and Catskill mountains in New York; in the Appalachian Mountains; and in the plateau region of western Pennsylvania. Find each of these regions on the map.

In and near these forest-covered sections are many lumber mills, and many paper mills, in which wood is ground into pulp for making paper. Much of the paper used for books, newspapers, letters, and wrappings is made from wood. Probably a large part of the paper that you use has been manufactured from the trees of the forest.

Fishing is another occupation of much importance, though it employs few men. Along the eastern coast are **Fishing** found cod, halibut, mack- **1. Kinds of fish** erel, herring, bluefish, clams, and other food fish. At the time of the early settlements, these food fish were abundant close by the rocky New England shore; but so many have been caught along the coast, that they are now far less common.

To-day, in order to catch large quantities of cod, halibut, and mackerel, it is necessary to go far from **2. How caught** land. Men go out to sea in two-masted sailing vessels, or *schooners* (Fig. 143); and when they leave port they often expect to be gone for weeks, and to travel many hundreds of miles. They carry either salt or ice with which to keep the fish, and when they return, the vessel may be full of fish either salted or on ice.

3. Fishing centers The principal fishing port in the United States is GLOUCESTER, in Massachusetts, from which hundreds of schooners sail every year. Fishing vessels also sail from BOSTON, PORTLAND, and other seacoast towns. Find the places named. The fish brought into these and neighboring ports

FIG. 143. — Fishing schooners on the stormy ocean far from land.

are sent to all parts of the United States, and even to foreign countries.

Quarrying and mining Quarrying and mining in these states employ a great number of men. Note, from the following description, how many kinds of mineral products are found here.

1. Stone and clay Each of these states produces *granite:* Maine, Massachusetts, and Vermont supply the greatest quantity. More than half the granite used in the entire country comes from the Northeastern States.

Marble is found in some parts of these states, especially near RUTLAND, Vermont. Here are quarries of fine *white marble* that is much used for monuments.

Slate, used for roofs of houses, for writing slates, and for other purposes, is found in several of the Northeastern States, especially in Pennsylvania and Vermont. There is much *sandstone* that is good for building; there is *clay,* for making bricks, drainpipes, flowerpots, and tiles; and there is limestone for the manufacture of lime and *Portland cement.*

2. Salt *Salt* is another very important mineral product of this region. Since this is the one mineral that *everybody* must have, it was fortunate for the early settlers that salt springs were found in central New York. To these springs the wild animals and the Indians had long been in the habit of going for the salt they needed. The white men found the salt springs so valuable that the production of salt soon became an important industry at that point, and it caused the beginning of the city of SYRACUSE.

The salt water of these springs flowed from a great bed of salt that lies underground, beneath a large part of central New York. By boring down through the soil, and some layers of rock, the salt bed itself can be reached. Many such borings have been made, and much salt is now obtained through them.

3. Oil and gas *Mineral oil* and *natural gas* are two other important mineral products of these states. These two substances lie imprisoned deep down in the rocks, and when a hole is bored down to them (Fig. 144), they escape to the surface, sometimes in great gushing fountains.

Fig. 144. — A view in the oil fields of western Pennsylvania. Each of these small towers, or derricks, stands over an oil well. The derricks were used in boring the wells.

The natural gas is then piped, even hundreds of miles, to be used for lighting cities and as fuel in factories and houses. The oil, or *petroleum,* is also allowed to run in pipes, like water, to *refineries,* where it is changed to kerosene oil, gasolene, naphtha, vaseline, and other valuable products.

The pioneers knew nothing about either of these substances. When they came to this country, they used either candles or lamps, in which some animal oil, such as whale oil, was burned. Very likely, even your great grandfather, when he was a boy, did not know of kerosene oil.

There is much *iron* produced in the Northeastern States. It is obtained from

4. Iron and coal
    iron ore, which looks very little like iron; it often looks like reddish earth, and must be melted before the iron can be obtained from it.

When the pioneers pushed across the Appalachian Mountains, they discovered rich beds of iron ore. In the same region they found large quantities of coal. As coal is a good fuel, it thus became possible to get the iron from the ore easily, and to make articles of iron. So there grew up a great iron industry in this part of the country.

Most of the iron ore mined in these states comes from Pennsylvania and New York. Soft or *bituminous coal* is mined in western Pennsylvania, near Pittsburgh and Allegheny, now united with Pittsburgh (Fig. 145); and hard coal, or *anthracite,* is found in the eastern part of the state, among the mountains near Scranton and Wilkes-Barre.

Much coal is needed, also, for stoves and furnaces in houses, for use on railways, and for producing steam in factories. There is, therefore, a great demand for it, and every year it is shipped by thousands of car loads to New York, Philadelphia, and elsewhere. Indeed, the prosperity of every city in all this region depends largely on the coal and iron.

Manufacturing is even a greater industry in these states than mining. It is, in fact, more important
    Manufacturing
here than in any other section of the United States, and is one of the chief reasons why there are so many people in the Northeastern States.

The raw materials mentioned in the last few pages, especially coal and iron,

FIG. 145. — Miners working far underground in a bituminous coal mine near Pittsburgh. The machine, in front, is drilling a hole in the thick coal seam that forms the wall on the right.

FIG. 146. — Niagara Falls, whose power is made to produce electricity for use not only near the Falls, but in many cities and towns in central and western New York.

are one important cause of so much manufacturing. The iron is shipped to many cities and made into stoves, engines, guns, ships, knives, and a thousand other things. See how long a list you can make of iron and steel articles.

1. In Pennsylvania, New Jersey, and New York

PITTSBURGH, in western Pennsylvania, is especially noted for iron and steel manufactures; also READING, HARRISBURG, the capital of Pennsylvania, and PHILADELPHIA on the coast.

In New York State, water power, as well as steam, is much used for running the machinery of factories. For instance, Niagara (Fig. 146), which is the greatest waterfall on the continent, furnishes water power for extensive manufacturing near the Falls. BUFFALO, the second city in size in the state of New York, is also supplied with Niagara power, although it is twenty miles from the Falls. Indeed, this power is carried by wire, in the form of electricity, even into central New York.

ROCHESTER, at the falls of the Genesee River (Fig. 147), has many flour mills and other factories run by water power. The cities on the Mohawk River are also engaged in manufacturing. What are their names?

All the cities in this section, both large and small, are engaged in manufacturing. Some of them make a specialty of one or two articles. For instance, near ALBANY, the capital of New York, is TROY, where the making of shirts, collars, and cuffs is the leading industry. In other cities many kinds of articles are manufactured.

In New England it is more difficult to obtain coal for steam, because very little coal is found there. 2. In New England It has to be shipped there from Pennsylvania and elsewhere.

On the other hand, water power is abundant. Many of the rivers of New England are short and swift, and their courses are interrupted by rapids and falls. In one (1) *How power is obtained*

FIG. 147. — Falls in the Genesee River at Rochester, used for power in the flour mills and other factories at Rochester.

respect this is not an advantage, for vessels cannot go far upstream; but it is a great advantage for manufacturing.

On account of this water power, manufacturing developed very early here. The principal rivers used are the Connecticut, the Merrimac, and the three largest rivers in Maine. Trace the course of each of these five from source to mouth. Make a drawing of New England, putting in these rivers and locating upon them the large cities.

Cotton has long been shipped here from the Southern States, to be made into many kinds of cloth. *(2) Kinds of manufacturing, and centers for them* MANCHESTER, LOWELL, NEW BEDFORD, and FALL RIVER have large cotton factories. Many cities are engaged in the manufac-

FIG. 148. — A room in a large watch factory at Waltham, Mass., in which great numbers of men and women work at making watches.

ture of woolen goods. Two of them are LAWRENCE and PROVIDENCE, which are also important cotton manufacturing centers. LYNN, BROCKTON, and other cities manufacture the hides of cattle, and of other animals, into boots, shoes, gloves, and leather goods of all kinds.

A great amount of metal, such as iron, copper, gold, and silver, is shipped to New England for manufacture. The metal is made into needles, watches, jewelry, fire-arms, fishhooks, nails, wire, and countless other things. WORCESTER, BRIDGEPORT, SPRINGFIELD, HARTFORD, and NEW HAVEN are engaged in such manufacture. Locate each of these cities.

The forests have led to manufacturing industries in which wood is used. BANGOR, in Maine, is one of the most

noted of the lumber manufacturing cities; and in several of the cities along the coast wooden ships are still built.

The way in which manufacturing is now carried on is very different from the old way. In the olden days, all the wool for cloth, *3. Great changes in methods of manufacture* for instance, was obtained from sheep that were raised near by. It was *(1) The old way of manufacturing* brought to the house, and was first made into yarn by means of a spinning wheel (Fig. 149) run by one's foot, as a sewing machine is now run. Then it was woven into cloth, and this cloth was made into garments by the mother and daughters of the household, during the long winter evenings. It was then the custom for everybody to wear "homespun," or cloth made at home. Likewise, when the men were not too

FIG. 149. — An old-fashioned spinning wheel.

busy with farm work, they made shoes for their families. Or some one traveled from house to house, making boots and shoes. Pieces of leather for the uppers were cut from hides of animals, raised near by, and sewed together by hand; then the thick soles were tacked on, again by hand. Most kinds of work, indeed, were done by hand.

Now, most of the wool that is used is raised far away, perhaps on the sheep (2) *The present way* ranches of the Western States, and is brought to these states in boats, or in freight trains. At the factory it is put into machines and quickly spun into long threads of yarn that are wound upon spools by machinery. This yarn is then woven into cloth, also by machinery.

To-day, also, most of the hides for use in making shoes are brought a long distance, often from the cattle ranches of the West. The hides are first tanned, and then the leather is cut into proper shapes by machines. After that the pieces are sewed, or nailed, together by machinery.

Everywhere machinery has taken the place of hand work. As now done, the work is carried on not in the home, but in factories in which hundreds, or even several thousands, of persons may be employed. All these men and women, and boys and girls, are kept busy from morning till night running the machines. It is an interesting sight to watch the throngs of workers pour out of one of these factories at the close of the day.

In former days it took a long time to make a piece of cloth, or a pair of shoes, which can now be made in a few minutes. (3) *The variety of work* One of the most striking changes, though, is in the *kind* of work that each person does; for now one person usually has only a very small part of the work to do. He may spend all of his time, day after day, tending a machine that only cuts out soles for shoes, or that sews certain pieces of leather together.

How different it was when a man plowed ground one day, acted as a carpenter in building a shed on a second day, and made shoes a third! Were former days really worse than the present, or better?

The transportation of goods is another occupation that has helped to attract so great a population to the Northeastern States. To *Transportation of goods* take the raw products to the factories, and then to distribute the manufactured goods in all directions, calls for an enormous number of workmen.

Good harbors along the coast are one of the first aids to such commerce. Many things must be received from foreign countries, and many others must be shipped abroad. Also, in these states, many articles can best be sent from city to city by boat along the coast. *1. Harbors*

For such shipping, harbors are necessary. If you examine the map, you will see that this coast is very irregular, with many bays, both large and small. These form excellent harbors all the way from Maine to Pennsylvania. Draw this coast line, showing the chief bays and capes. Write in their names.

The chief rivers in New England have already been mentioned (p. 114). Recall their names. On the map find the Hudson, the principal river in New York; the Susquehanna, the principal one in Pennsylvania; and the Delaware River. *2. Rivers and canals*

Most of these rivers are too shallow for large boats to go far upstream; and in some cases, travel by boat is prevented by rapids and falls. The Hudson River is the one notable exception; for large steamboats can go up

Fig. 150. — The broad and deep Hudson River as seen from West Point.

About the time the Erie Canal was finished, the locomotive was invented, and rail- **3. Railroads** roads began to be built. After that, there was no pressing need for more canals, since railroads could take their place.

Railroads extend from north to south through these states; but most of the great railroads run from the coast westward, toward the interior of the country. The Appalachian Mountains have been a great hindrance in building them. Why? Yet several fine roads now cross these mountains (Fig. 151). One of the first was the New York Central, running from New York City to Buffalo. It follows the Hudson River to Albany, then takes the same course westward that the Erie Canal does. All the important cities of these states are now connected by rail.

The half-dozen occupa- **Why trade is** tions thus far named could **especially im-** not be carried on, of course, **portant** without a large amount of buying and

the Hudson as far as the mouth of the Mohawk River (Fig. 150).

The wide mouths of these rivers make excellent harbors, as is proved by the large cities there. Name and locate some of these cities.

The need of more waterways into the interior led very early to the digging of canals. Several have been built, the longest and most important of which is the *Erie Canal* (Fig. 140) extending from the Hudson River, near Troy and Albany, to Buffalo on Lake Erie. Measure its length. This canal is especially important, because it connects the Great Lakes with the ocean by way of the Hudson River. On that account it has been a great highway of commerce. Name several cities along its course.

Fig. 151. — A broad horseshoe curve where the Pennsylvania Railroad ascends the steep grades in crossing the Appalachians.

selling, or *trade*. This is the final great occupation that has brought so many people together in these states.

The 26,000,000 inhabitants living here produce so many things, and need so many others, that there is a very large amount of trade. In addition, there are many more millions living to the west of these states. Across the oceans are Europe, Africa, Asia, Australia, and South America, where hundreds of millions of other people live. The people in all parts of the

the coast. The products of the country west of them, and the ease with which goods can be carried back and forth, have had much to do with the size of such cities.

Great centers of manufacture and commerce

GREATER NEW YORK is the largest of all these cities; in fact, London is the only city in the world that is larger. New York, which includes BROOKLYN as a part

1. Greater New York and vicinity

Copyright, 1907, by Detroit Publishing Co.

FIG. 152. — A view of lower New York, showing the lofty buildings, or "sky scrapers."

United States have goods to sell to the inhabitants of these continents across the oceans; and these foreign countries have things to sell us.

The harbors of the Northeastern States are used for a large part of this trade between the United States and foreign lands. This *foreign commerce* keeps scores of thousands of men and women busy all the time, mainly in the large cities, such as New York, Philadelphia, and Boston.

The largest cities have naturally grown up around the excellent harbors along

of it, contains nearly five million persons, Across the Hudson from it, in New Jersey, but using the same harbor, are JERSEY CITY, NEWARK, PATERSON, and several other cities.

The largest vessels from all parts of the world can enter New York harbor. Also, goods can be shipped by water, along the Hudson River, the Erie Canal, and the Great Lakes, all the way to Duluth at the western end of Lake Superior (Fig. 136). About how far is this? In addition, railroads run in all directions, so that transportation is well provided for.

Because of these unusual advantages for shipping, thousands of factories have been located in or near New York, and in them are made almost all kinds of manufactured articles that people want. Probably the greatest manufacturing industry is the making of clothing. The refining of petroleum is one of the important industries in Jersey City and in Brooklyn. Paterson is noted for the manufacture of silk. Large quantities of iron and steel goods are also made in this neighborhood.

the third city in size in the country. As is the case near New York, there are other large cities near by. Among these are CAMDEN and TRENTON in New Jersey, the latter being noted for its manufacture of fine pottery.

The products of Pennsylvania and New Jersey, such as fruit, lumber, iron, coal, and oil, together with the manufacture of iron and other goods, have helped make Philadelphia a great city. This port, like New York, has much foreign commerce, with steamship lines to all parts of the world, and railroads connecting it with the interior.

FIG. 153. — A part of Boston, with its fine harbor beyond.

Merchants from all parts of the United States come to New York to purchase goods for their stores. Many great buildings in the city are given up entirely to this kind of trade, called the *wholesale trade.* A number of the buildings in New York are as many as thirty stories in height, some are forty or more, and one, including its tower, is fifty stories high. It is no wonder that New York City is called the *metropolis,* or great city, of the United States.

2. Philadelphia and vicinity Only ninety miles southwest of New York is PHILADELPHIA, situated as far up the Delaw~~~ River as large vessel~

3. Boston and other New England ports The largest city northeast of New York is BOSTON, which is the fifth in size in the United States. It has an excellent harbor (Fig. 153), and although there is no water route toward the west, numerous railroads lead from it to the north, west, and southwest. Boston has a large amount of manufacturing, and ranks next to New York in foreign commerce. Near by are several important manufacturing cities, such as CAMBRIDGE, ~~~thers whose names cannot be ~~~ small a map.

NEW HAVEN in Connecticut, PROVIDENCE in Rhode Island, and PORTLAND in Maine are the other principal coast cities in New England. Locate each.

Review Questions

1. Name the six New England States. Name the three Middle Atlantic States included in this group. 2. What can you say about the total area of these states? About the area of Rhode Island? Of Maine? Of New York? 3. What do you know about the population of these states? 4. Name the principal occupations. 5. Why is farming not especially prominent? 6. What are the chief kinds of farming? Why? 7. Name some of the most fertile sections. What are their products? 8. Tell about the lumbering. 9. The fishing. 10. Name the chief mineral products of these states. 11. State the principal facts about the quarrying. 12. About salt. 13. Oil and gas. 14. Iron ore. 15. Coal. 16. What about the manufacturing in Pennsylvania, New Jersey, and New York? 17. In New England? 18. What changes have there been in methods of manufacture? 19. What can you say about the number and excellence of the harbors? 20. About the rivers and canals? 21. The railroads? 22. Why is trade especially prominent in these states? 23. State the principal facts about Greater New York and vicinity. 24. Philadelphia and vicinity. 25. Boston. 26. Name and locate other New England ports. 27. Which of the seven great occupations are especially prominent in the Northeastern States? Give reasons. 28. What reasons can you now give for the dense population of these states? 29. Name the principal seaports, and locate each. 30. Locate several other important cities in these states.

Suggestions

1. Make a drawing of New York State, showing the Hudson River and the Erie Canal. 2. How does it happen that New York City and Buffalo, at opposite ends of the state, are such large cities? 3. What cities do you find on the Erie Canal? Why so many? Put their names on your map. 4. How can a canal be built where land is not level? 5. Make drawings of some of the more common fish. Fill in the colors. 6. Visit a fish store to see the kinds of fish mentioned in the text. 7. Make a collection, for . . . of some marble, granite, slate . . .

coal, and iron ore. 8. What names beginning with *New* do you find on the map? How can you explain such frequent use of this word? 9. Write the abbreviation for each of the states in this group. 10. Draw an outline map of the Northeastern States, putting in the rivers and cities mentioned. 11. Name and locate the capital of each state in this group.

V. THE SOUTHERN STATES [1]

Map study

1. In which states of this group are there mountains? 2. What are the names of the mountains? 3. Where are the plains (Fig. 137)? 4. Which is the largest river? 5. Locate Chesapeake Bay. What rivers enter it? 6. What large cities are on it? 7. How is Texas separated from Mexico? 8. Which is the largest state? Which the smallest? 9. Which state is largely a peninsula? 10. How far distant are the southern points of Florida and Texas from the Tropic of Cancer? What does this suggest about the climate of the Southern States? 11. What waters lie east and south of these states?

These states are not always grouped together as Southern States. Sometimes Kentucky is considered one of the Central States, which is the next group to be studied; and Delaware, Maryland, Virginia, and West Virginia are often classed with New York, New Jersey, and Pennsylvania, as the Middle Atlantic States. Name the sixteen states of this Southern group.

States included here

These sixteen states have more than five times the area of the Northeastern States; and Texas alone, the largest state in the Union, is larger than the entire group of Northeastern States.

Area and population

[1] Any division of the country into groups of states is unnatural, because state boundaries rarely follow natural lines. This present grouping is adopted in this first book because it makes it possible to study related industries more effectively. It is, as . . . ter of fact, more natural to include these states . . . to follow the usual grouping of . . . etc.

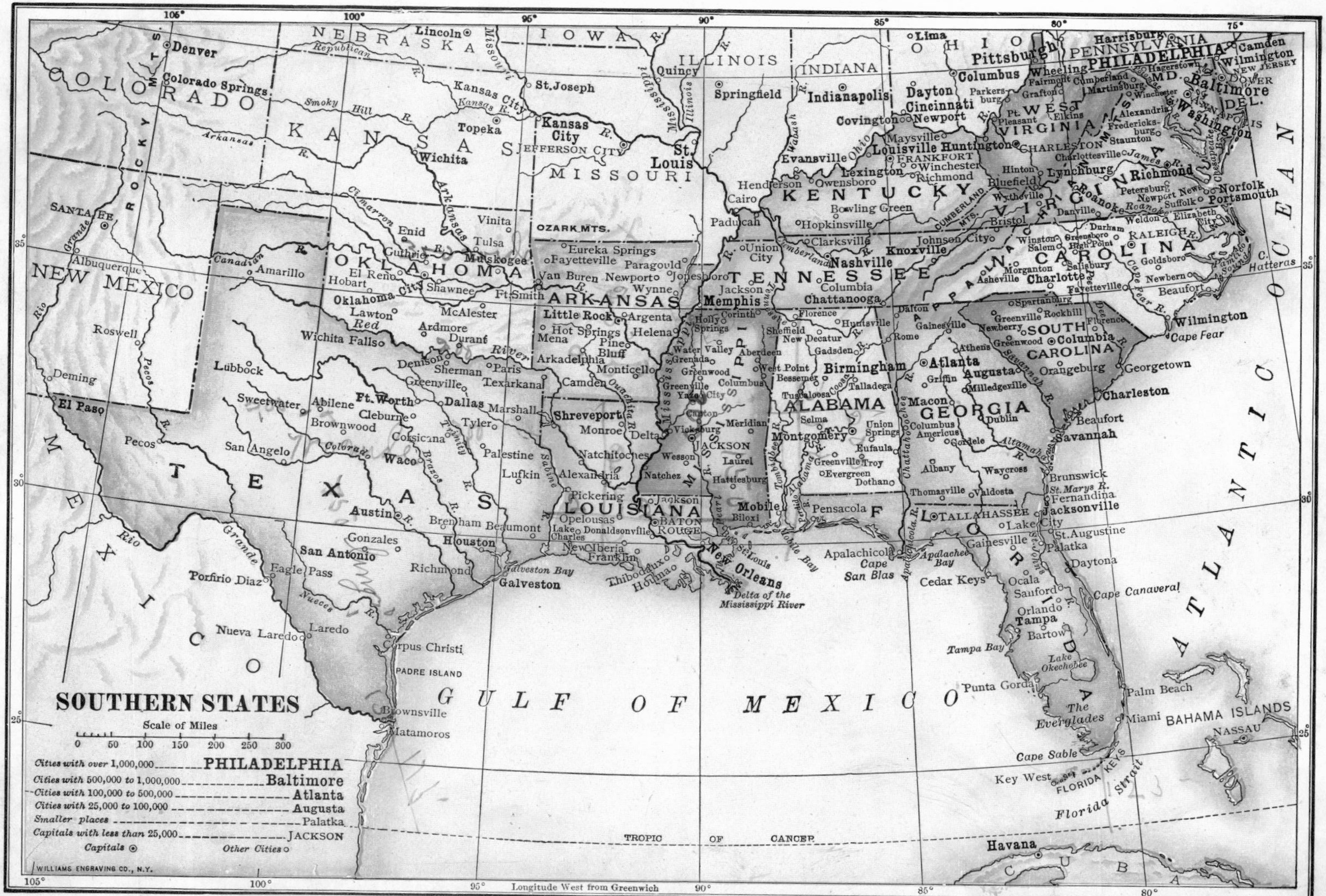
SOUTHERN STATES
Scale of Miles
0 50 100 150 200 250 300
Cities with over 1,000,000 PHILADELPHIA
Cities with 500,000 to 1,000,000 Baltimore
Cities with 100,000 to 500,000 Atlanta
Cities with 25,000 to 100,000 Augusta
Smaller places Palatka
Capitals with less than 25,000 JACKSON
Capitals
Other Cities
WILLIAMS ENGRAVING CO., N.Y.
Longitude West from Greenwich
GULF OF MEXICO
ATLANTIC OCEAN
TROPIC OF CANCER
MEXICO
TEXAS
LOUISIANA
ARKANSAS
OKLAHOMA
NEW MEXICO
COLORADO
KANSAS
NEBRASKA
IOWA
MISSOURI
ILLINOIS
INDIANA
OHIO
KENTUCKY
TENNESSEE
MISSISSIPPI
ALABAMA
GEORGIA
FLORIDA
SOUTH CAROLINA
N. CAROLINA
VIRGINIA
WEST VIRGINIA
PENNSYLVANIA
MD.
DEL.
NEW JERSEY
BAHAMA ISLANDS
CUBA
ROCKY MTS.
OZARK MTS.
CUMBERLAND MTS.
PADRE ISLAND
Delta of the Mississippi River
Denver
Colorado Springs
Santa Fe
Albuquerque
Roswell
Deming
El Paso
Pecos
Lincoln
St. Joseph
Kansas City
Topeka
Wichita
Jefferson City
St. Louis
Springfield
Quincy
Indianapolis
Dayton
Cincinnati
Columbus
Pittsburgh
Harrisburg
PHILADELPHIA
Camden
Wilmington
Baltimore
Washington
Richmond
Norfolk
Portsmouth
Louisville
Lexington
Frankfort
Nashville
Knoxville
Chattanooga
Memphis
Little Rock
Shreveport
New Orleans
Baton Rouge
Jackson
Vicksburg
Mobile
Montgomery
Birmingham
Atlanta
Augusta
Macon
Savannah
Charleston
Columbia
Wilmington
Charlotte
Raleigh
Tallahassee
Jacksonville
Pensacola
Tampa
Key West
Havana
Nassau
Houston
Galveston
Dallas
Ft. Worth
Austin
San Antonio
Waco
Corpus Christi
Brownsville
Matamoros
Laredo
Nueva Laredo
Eagle Pass
Porfirio Diaz
Oklahoma City
Tulsa
Muskogee
C. Hatteras
Cape Fear
Cape Canaveral
Cape Sable
Florida Strait
Florida Keys
Lake Okechobee
The Everglades
Tampa Bay
Galveston Bay
Mobile Bay

FIG. 154.

The population of all the Southern States together is only three million more than that of the Northeastern States. This fact suggests that the chief occupations may be different from those in the states already studied. Let us see to what extent this is true.

The rest of this great section, however, consists mainly of plains. From western Texas to the Appalachian Mountains there is little else than fairly level land (Fig. 155). Along almost the entire coast there is a broad strip of low, level land known as the *coastal plains*. Between

FIG. 155. — Much of the South is level land like that in the picture, which shows an immense peach orchard on the plains of Florida.

We have seen that much of the land in the Northeastern States is so mountainous or hilly that it is not well suited to farming. The Appalachian Mountains extend also across some of the Southern States, as you can see from the map. Name the states that these mountains cross. There are also low mountains in western Arkansas and in eastern Oklahoma; and a portion of the Rocky Mountains extends across western Texas. These mountainous parts, of course, are little suited to farming, except in the valleys.

Agriculture
1. Amount of level land

this and the Appalachian Mountains there is a very fertile, rolling country called the *Piedmont* (meaning "foot of the mountain") region.

Higher plains are found in Texas and in some parts of the Mississippi Valley. Along the rivers, especially the Mississippi, there are broad flood plains protected from the river floods by banks, called *levees*. Notice especially the Mississippi delta. Can you explain why the land at this point extends so far into the Gulf of Mexico?

In some parts of these plains the soil is too sandy for farming, being fit only

for the growth of timber; but in most

2. Soil and climate sections the soil is very fertile.

The climate is much more favorable to farming than that of New England. There is more rain in nearly all parts except in western Texas, where the chief industry is grazing.

The temperature is especially favorable, for the winters are not severe, and the summers are longer than in the Northeastern States. Therefore, many kinds of plants can be grown here that cannot live in the North; and it is easier to keep cattle and other live stock. They can be left out of doors in winter, and can find grass to eat when the ground in the North is frozen and covered with snow.

On account of the climate, three crops can be raised here that are not produced in the North. The most important of

3. The three special crops of the South

(1) *Cotton*

these is *cotton*. Every person has use for cotton; for calico dresses, underclothing, thread, and, indeed, hundreds of things are made of it. More than one half of all the cotton raised in the world is grown in our Southern States. The large farms on which it is cultivated are called *plantations* (Fig. 156), and often contain hundreds of acres. It is the principal crop all the way from North Carolina to central Texas.

The cotton plant grows to a height of from two to four feet. It has a blossom that is at first white, and then turns pink. Later it develops into a small pod which enlarges until it ripens and bursts into a white ball, called a *cotton boll*. This looks somewhat like a milk-

weed pod, after it has burst open, and presents a beautiful sight when seen in thousands on the plantations.

The fiber, or cotton, in the bolls is picked in the autumn by men, women, and children. After picking, it is placed in a machine, called the *cotton gin*, to remove the seeds. The cotton is then pressed into large bales, like hay. About one sixth of it is manufactured in the South, and the remainder is shipped to New England, to England, and to other European countries to be manufactured.

Cotton is the most valuable farm product in the South. The amount

FIG. 156. — Picking cotton on a plantation in Arkansas.

raised in one year is usually worth more than all the gold and silver mined in the whole world in a year. It is also worth as much, or more, than all the wheat produced in the United States in a year. Even if there were no other crop, cotton alone would make the Southern States of great importance.

A second crop that is produced nowhere else in the United States but in the South is *sugar cane*. It grows in tall stalks (Fig. **(2) *Sugar cane*** 157), that resemble corn and that are valuable on account of the sweet juice they contain. This juice is pressed out and made into sugar and molasses.

Sugar cane can be grown only in a warm climate and in fertile soil. The district most noted for its production is the delta of the Mississippi River in southern Louisiana; but it is also raised in Texas, Alabama, and other Southern States.

now raises even more than Virginia, and these two states together produce more than one half of the entire amount grown in our country. Yet tobacco raising is an important industry in nearly every one of the Southern States,

FIG. 157. — Workmen cutting the sugar cane on a sugar plantation in Louisiana.

Rice is the third of our crops raised only in the Southern States. Like sugar cane, this **(3) Rice** plant requires a warm climate and fertile soil. In addition, it needs a great amount of moisture, and the fields must be flooded a part of the time.

Until quite recently rice has been grown only on the low, wet coastal plains. Now, however, it is produced in higher lands in Louisiana, Texas, and other states. A few years ago these lands were altogether too dry for rice, but now they are flooded by means of irrigation. The amount of rice raised in the Southern States has thus been greatly increased. Most of it is produced in Louisiana and South Carolina.

When white men first came to America, they found the Indians smok- **4. Tobacco** ing a weed called *tobacco*. The white men soon learned the habit from the Indians, and introduced it into Europe, so that a great demand for tobacco soon arose. From that time on, one of the principal crops of Virginia has been tobacco. Kentucky

and some is raised in the Northern States, even as far north as the Connecticut Valley (p. 109).

Besides the crops that have been named, almost all the farm products common to other parts of **5. Other important farm products** the country are raised in the South. For instance, great amounts of corn, wheat, and oats are grown, as well as fruits and vegetables.

Truck farming and gardening are also profitable industries. In the warm South, fruits and vegetables ripen earlier than in the North, and these early products can be sent North for sale long before the season for them there. There is so great a demand for these early fruits and vegetables, that gardening has rapidly developed in recent years. Whole train loads of tomatoes, strawberries, peaches, green peas, potatoes, and other fruits and vegetables are sent to Northern cities during early spring and summer.

In the most southerly part of this group, especially in Florida, fruits that require an almost tropical climate are grown. Among these are the orange (Fig. 158), lemon, and grapefruit; and in southern Florida, the pineapple, cocoanut, and banana.

FIG. 158. — An orange tree, loaded with fruit, in a Florida orange grove.

The South is a wonderful farming country, and many products besides those mentioned

Live stock, such as cattle, sheep, horses, mules, and hogs are raised on the plantations in all the states, while the dry plains 6. Ranching of western Texas are given up almost wholly to grazing. The grass there furnishes excellent feed for cattle, horses, and sheep, and the work of raising these animals is one of the leading industries of the state. The land over which a man's cattle or sheep roam is called a *ranch* (Fig. 159), rather than a farm or a plantation, and the business of raising them is known as *ranching*.

If you look on the map, you will see few names of towns or cities in western Texas. The reason for this is that it takes only a small number of people to carry on ranching, since a few men can look after several thousand cattle, horses, or sheep. Great numbers of cattle are sent eastward by rail, from FORT WORTH, to be used as food.

Figure 160 shows how extensive the forests are in the Southern States. Not

FIG. 159. — Cattle grazing on the broad plains of western Texas.

are raised there. For instance, tea plantations have been started, quantities of peanuts are grown, and groves of pecan nuts are planted and cared for like orchards.

all the land marked as forest on this map is covered with woods, to be Lumbering sure, for, as we have just seen, farming is a very great industry. The map is intended merely to show that *much timber* grows in all these states. As a matter of fact, about twice as much land is covered with forest as is taken up by farms.

fenced in by stakes, and are owned and cared for as carefully as ordinary farms are. One of the best oyster sections in the country is Chesapeake Bay, with its many shallow branches; but oysters are raised as far north as Cape Cod, in Mass., and as far south as the Rio Grande.

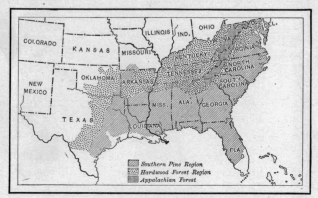

FIG. 160.— The forest regions of the Southern States.

There is a great amount of hard pine on the coastal plains, and on the higher lands such hardwoods as oak and hickory thrive. In which states are these higher lands found? Name some of the uses to which these different kinds of wood are put. Nearly one half of all the timber now cut in the United States comes from the South. From this you can see that lumbering is one of the prominent industries here.

There is much fishing here, as in New England, but the kinds of fish are

Fishing
different. Cod and halibut are not found, because they live only in the colder waters. There are, however, oysters, shad, bluefish, and a number of other kinds of food fish.

Oysters thrive so well in these warm Southern waters, and they are so highly prized for food, that the culture of oysters is given careful attention. There are many "oyster farms"; that is, patches of shallow water in which young oysters are placed, to be gathered when they have grown to full size. These "farms" are

From what has been said, you can see that *farming* and *lumbering* are among the Growth of leading industries of the South the South. Yet neither of these industries requires a dense population, or causes the growth of large cities. From this it is clear why people are more scattered in the Southern than in the Northeastern States.

Of late years, however, other industries have been rapidly developing in the South; the population has been increasing very fast, and seems likely to increase much more in the near future.

Mining is one of the industries that have been rapidly developing, and many valuable minerals are found. Among these minerals, the Mining most important is soft, or 1. Coal bituminous coal, which is mined in large quantities. The states where this coal is found are shown on the map (Fig. 161). What are their names? Note also what states have lignite, or brown coal. This is not so good as the bituminous coal, but is of considerable value.

Iron ore is mined in several of the Southern States, especially Tennessee and Alabama; but Alabama 2. Iron ore supplies nearly as much as all the others together. Only two other states in the country, Minnesota and Michigan, produce more iron ore than Alabama.

Both petroleum and natural gas have been found in several of these states. Indeed, the oil fields of Texas, Oklahoma, and West Virginia are among the most remarkable in the country, and millions of barrels of oil are now produced by that section every year.

3. Oil and natural gas

More petroleum comes from Oklahoma than from any other state in the Union, except California. West Virginia produces less than one fourth as much. But its oil is of finer quality, and hence brings a higher price than that from Oklahoma.

There are deposits of building stones, including granite, sandstone, limestone, and marble; important deposits of clay for bricks and pottery; and of limestone for Portland cement. Besides these, some gold and silver, as well as other metals, are produced. The South, therefore, has a great deal of mineral wealth.

4. Other mineral products

There are so many valuable raw products in the South, that there are great

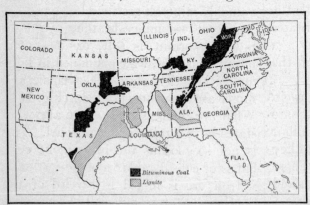

FIG. 161. — The coal fields of the Southern States.

opportunities for manufacturing. Among these products are cotton, sugar cane, corn, wheat, cattle, sheep, lumber, and iron ore, from each of which useful articles can be made.

Manufacturing

More important still, there is an abundance of coal for power. Besides that, there are many rivers and mountain streams that can furnish water power, as in New

1. Conditions favorable to manufacturing

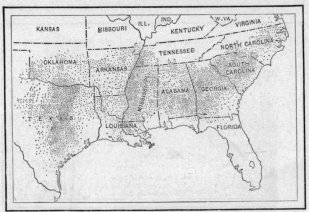

FIG. 162. — The cotton belt. Each dot represents 1,000,000 pounds of cotton.

England. In many places, this water power is used to run factories. Much of it is made to produce electricity, as at Niagara Falls in New York. The electricity is then conducted by wires to factories in all directions.

For a long time most of the manufacturing in the United States was done in New England. Great quantities of cotton, and other raw products, were sent there from the South and West; then some of the finished articles were shipped back.

2. Cotton manufacturing

Until very recently many persons believed that the South could not compete with New England in the manufacture of cotton goods. To be sure, it seemed strange that the place where the cotton was grown should not be the place where it was made into cloth. Yet it was supposed that the Southern climate was unfavorable to that kind of work, and that the cotton must be manufactured somewhere else.

This notion is now given up (Fig. 163). It is true that the South still ships much cotton to New England and Europe; but much is kept for manufacture at home. Indeed, in the year

steel. In a few years Birmingham has become a thriving city, and it is often called the *Pittsburgh of the South*.

Farther north in these states there are several other noted centers of iron manufacture. BALTIMORE, in Maryland, is one; WILMINGTON, in Delaware, is another. To each of these cities both

FIG. 163. — A Southern cotton mill at nighttime. Power is obtained from the river.

1906 the Southern mills used more cotton than the mills of the North. Even some of the large mill owners in New England are now building cotton mills in the South, so as to be able to compete with the Southern manufacturers.

The principal states engaged in cotton manufacture are North and South Carolina and Georgia; but all through the cotton belt the industry is rapidly growing.

A great amount of iron ore is found near BIRMINGHAM, in Alabama, and coal

3. Iron and steel and limestone for making **manufacturing** it into iron and steel are also abundant near by. Because these three products lie so close together here, there is hardly a better place in the world for the manufacture of iron and

coal and iron can be easily shipped. Baltimore makes many kinds of iron goods; Wilmington is noted especially for the manufacture of cars, heavy machinery, and ships. Other centers of iron manufacture are RICHMOND, in Virginia; WHEELING, in West Virginia; ATLANTA, in Georgia; LOUISVILLE, in Kentucky; and KNOXVILLE, CHATTANOOGA, and other cities in Tennessee.

There are many other kinds of manufacturing in the South, and most of them are rapidly increasing in importance. For example, the abundance of timber has led to the manufacture **4. Other manufactures** of furniture; and the wood and iron ore together have led to the making of many farm implements. Cotton seeds are made into cottonseed oil; hides into leather and leather goods; sugar cane into sugar and molasses; the sap of the pine tree into turpentine, tar, and resin;

wheat into flour; and tobacco into cigars and other forms for use. There is now almost every kind of manufacturing in the South.

The irregular coast line of parts of the Southern States shows that there are

Transportation
1. Harbors

many harbors there. Good harbors are especially numerous in the northern part. Observe how far the waters of Chesapeake and Delaware bays extend into the land. The cities of BALTIMORE and WILMINGTON, on these bays, have much the same advantages for shipping goods that Philadelphia has. NORFOLK and RICHMOND, in Virginia, are also good shipping points.

Farther south, although the water in some of the bays is shallow, and sand bars are common, there are many good harbors; and the United States government is spending much money in deepening and improving others, so that the largest ships may enter them.

The commerce of the states bordering the Gulf of Mexico is greatly aided by the Mississippi River. This

2. Rivers

mighty river, together with its tributaries, drains a vast area, inhabited by millions of people. Name the principal tributaries, and trace them to their sources. On Figure 213 note how far up these rivers boats can go. Since transportation of goods is cheapest by water, a large amount of freight is sent up and down these waterways (Fig. 164). No wonder, therefore, that the United States government is spending large sums of money improving them.

In addition to the waterways, there are railways connecting all important points in these states, and reaching out to all parts of

3. Railroads

our country. These carry great quantities of freight, as well as many passengers.

The principal cities in the South, as in the North, are those that

Principal centers of manufacture and commerce

have grown up at the best shipping points, or at points especially favorable to manufacturing.

BALTIMORE, the largest of all, is the seventh city in size in the United States, having over half a million inhabitants. It has

1. Baltimore

an excellent harbor, far inland, in the fertile state of Maryland, near the head of Chesapeake Bay. Coal and iron can easily reach it from the Appalachian Mountain region; and, like New York and Philadelphia, it has a large amount of manufacturing and commerce. It is further noted as a center of oyster fishing and shipping.

FIG. 164. — Even the small streams and canals are used for shipping freight Here, for example, are six thousand bales of cotton on a barge in the Houston Canal, in Texas, bound for the seacoast, to be placed on vessels for shipment to England.

RICHMOND, the capital and largest city of Virginia, is located on the James River. It is a

2. Richmond, Norfolk, and Wilmington

hriving center, noted especially as a obacco market. NORFOLK, at the mouth of Chesapeake Bay, is a shipping point of growing importance.

WILMINGTON, on the Delaware River, s the largest city in Delaware. Like

FIG. 165. — Loading Mississippi River boats from the levee.

Camden, it should be associated with Philadelphia as an important manufacturing center.

Among Southern cities, the one next to Baltimore in size is NEW ORLEANS, on the Mississippi River about one hundred miles above its mouth. Large ocean vessels can reach this port, and river boats (Fig. 165) can travel from it as far up as Pittsburgh on the Ohio River, and a great distance, also, up the Mississippi and Missouri rivers. On Figure 154 measure the distance from New Orleans to Pittsburgh.

3. New Orleans and other cities on the Mississippi River and tributaries

Quantities of cotton, cotton-seed oil, sugar, molasses, and rice are shipped from here. Manufactured goods, such as cloth and shoes; and foods, such as meat, wheat, and corn, are collected here and then distributed in all directions. Since New Orleans is so good a shipping point, it has, of course, much manufacturing.

Far up on the Ohio River is LOUISVILLE, the fourth city in size in the Southern States, and the largest in Kentucky. It is a leading center for tobacco manufacture and trade, as well as for the manufacture of iron goods and other articles.

On the Mississippi River, midway between New Orleans and Louisville, is

FIG. 166. — A view on the water front at Savannah, where much lumber is shipped.

MEMPHIS, in Tennessee, another of the large cities in these states. It is in the midst of the cotton and hardwood sections,

K

and is noted for its cotton and lumber trade.

NASHVILLE, on the Cumberland River, is the capital of Tennessee. It is a manufacturing and trade center, and is distinguished for its fine schools and colleges.

Find BATON ROUGE, in Louisiana; VICKSBURG and JACKSON, in Mississippi; LITTLE ROCK, in Arkansas; and GUTHRIE, in Oklahoma. These are all centers of trade in the states where they are situated. Which of them are state capitals?

Several well-known cities besides those already mentioned are found along the coast east of the Mississippi River. The most important are SAVANNAH, Georgia (Fig. 166), and MOBILE, Alabama, both of which handle much cotton. Find WILMINGTON, North Carolina; also CHARLESTON and JACKSONVILLE farther south. The last is one of the chief shipping ports for Florida fruit. TAMPA and PENSACOLA, on the west side of Florida, ship much lumber. Tampa also has important trade with the West Indies.

4. Other cities, east of the Mississippi River

Another leading city of the South, ranking next to Louisville in size, is ATLANTA, near the southern end of the Appalachian Mountains. It is a great railway center and is in the midst of a country of rich resources. Cotton is abundant, there is plenty of lumber, and both coal and iron ore are not far distant. Atlanta has, therefore, become a manufacturing center.

BIRMINGHAM as a manufacturing center has already been mentioned, as have CHATTANOOGA and KNOXVILLE. There are other important inland manufacturing cities in the South that you will learn about later.

Florida deserves special mention, because it has so many small towns and cities that are noted as winter resorts. The mild winter climate attracts thousands of Northern visitors, for it is never very cold, and flowers blossom all winter. MIAMI, JACKSONVILLE, and ST. AUGUSTINE are among the best known of these resorts. KEY WEST and TAMPA, also winter resorts, are extensively engaged in tobacco manufacturing.

GALVESTON ranks second in importance among the seaports of the United States. Baltimore and New Orleans are also important shipping ports. Galveston is the outlet for a great amount of cotton and other goods, produced to the north and west of it. HOUSTON, DALLAS, FORT WORTH, SAN ANTONIO, and AUSTIN are other leading cities of Texas.

5. Other Cities, west of the Mississippi River

Oklahoma, one of the newest of our states, includes what was formerly called Indian Territory, a region reserved as the home of several Indian tribes. It is a state of splendid resources, and as soon as the government opened the land to settlement by white men, large numbers of settlers went there. Within a few years so many people have made their homes in Oklahoma that it has been changed from a territory to a state. It already has four thriving cities, — Oklahoma City, the capital, Muskogee, Shawnee, and Guthrie, — and there are other rapidly growing cities.

WASHINGTON, on the Potomac River, not far from Baltimore, is the third largest city in the South; but it is unlike any of the others that have been mentioned. While manufacturing and commerce are, as a rule, the occupations that make great cities, Washington is noted for neither of these.

6. Washington in the District of Columbia

The importance of Washington is due to the fact that it is the capital of the United States. It is a great business merely to carry on the government of our country, and this is done in Washington. The main buildings there are government buildings, not factories or stores. A large number of the people are engaged in some kind of government work, such as making the laws, or acting as clerks in the many departments of our government.

Since it is the capital of our country, much care has been taken to make the city attractive. The streets are broad (Fig. 167) and bordered with trees, and good taste has been shown in planning

Fig. 167. — Pennsylvania Avenue, in Washington, showing the Capitol at the farther end.

most of the government buildings. It is the most beautiful city in the United States, as it should be (Figs. 95 and 97).

The *District of Columbia,* in which Washington is situated, is a tract of land about eight miles square. It is not a part of any state, but is controlled directly by the government of the United States. The Capitol was located here shortly after the close of the War of Independence, when this point was near the center of population of the country; but now the center of population is far to the west of Washington.

Review Questions

1. Compare these states with the Northeastern States in area; in population. 2. What about the amount of level land? 3. In what states are there mountains? 4. What about the fitness of the soil and climate for farming? 5. What advantages for farming do these states enjoy over the Northeastern States? 6. Name the three special farm products of the South. Why are they not raised in other parts of the United States? 7. Tell about the cotton. 8. About the sugar cane. 9. The rice. 10. The tobacco. 11. Name other farm products. 12. Where is ranching important? Why? 13. What can you say about the lumbering? 14. What kind of food fish are found here? 15. What are the chief minerals? 16. In what states is coal found? 17. Iron ore? 18. Oil and natural gas? 19. What about other mineral products? 20. What favorable conditions are there for manufacturing in the South? 21. Tell about the cotton manufacturing. 22. Iron and steel manufacturing. 23. Other manufactures. 24. What advantages for transportation have these states? 25. State the principal facts about Baltimore; Richmond; Wilmington; Norfolk. 26. About New Orleans and other cities on the Mississippi River and its tributaries. 27. About other cities east of the Mississippi River. 28. Other cities west of it. 29. Washington and the District of Columbia.

Suggestions

1. Draw the coast line of these states. Add the principal rivers and cities, and the state boundaries. 2. Represent this group of states in sand, showing the mountains and plains. 3. Make a collection of articles manufactured from cotton, and add them to the school collection. 4. Make a collection of different kinds of wood grown in the Southern States. 5. Raise some cotton and rice in the schoolroom. 6. Name other advantages that the mild climate of the South brings; for instance, in regard to clothing; coal for heating houses; and kinds of houses. Do you see any disadvantages in such a climate? 7. How are the people of New England and those of the South dependent upon each other in the work that they do? 8. What two letters stand for *District of Columbia?* 9. Name and locate the capital of each state in the Southern group. 10. Write the abbreviations for each of these states.

VI. THE CENTRAL STATES

1. Name the states in this group.   2. Which of them border on the Great Lakes?   3. Name

Map study   the Great Lakes.   4. Which of these lakes is highest above the level of the ocean?   How can you tell?   How does the name of this lake suggest that it lies highest?   5. By what river do the waters of these lakes reach the ocean (Fig. 133)?   6. Remembering what was said about the Erie Canal (p. 117), show how goods can be shipped by water from Duluth and Chicago to New York City.   7. Name the three principal rivers in the Central States.   Trace each.   8. Trace the divide between the Mississippi Valley and the valley of the Great Lakes.   9. Which state

than live in either the Northeastern or the Southern States.   There are also many large cities, including Chicago, the second largest in the United States, and St. Louis, the fourth in size.

Let us see what has attracted so many people here, what their chief occupations are, and how these compare with the occupations in the sections already studied.

Agriculture is the most important of these occupations.   Indeed, **Agriculture** this is one of the best farming sections in all the world.

Fig. 168. — The deep, rich soil of the very level plain in the Red River Valley of North Dakota makes this one of the finest wheat regions in the world.

drains entirely into the Great Lakes?   10. Which states drain mainly into the Ohio River?   Into the Mississippi River?   Into the Missouri River?   11. Which state drains partly into the Arctic Ocean?

The area of these twelve states is somewhat smaller than that of the six-

Area and population   teen Southern States just studied, but it is over four times that of the Northeastern States.

A century ago there were scarcely any people living here, excepting Indians and a few scattered trappers.   Now there are over thirty million persons, or more

There are several reasons for this. In the first place, throughout almost the entire section the land is a level plain, or, at most, **1. Favorable conditions for farming** gently rolling and hilly. This is very different, as you **(1)** *Great amount of level land* remember, from most of the land of the Northeastern States. The level surface makes possible to cultivate large tracts land easily (Fig. 168), as in the Sou ern States.

The soil is extremely fertile, too, unlike that in many parts of the Nor

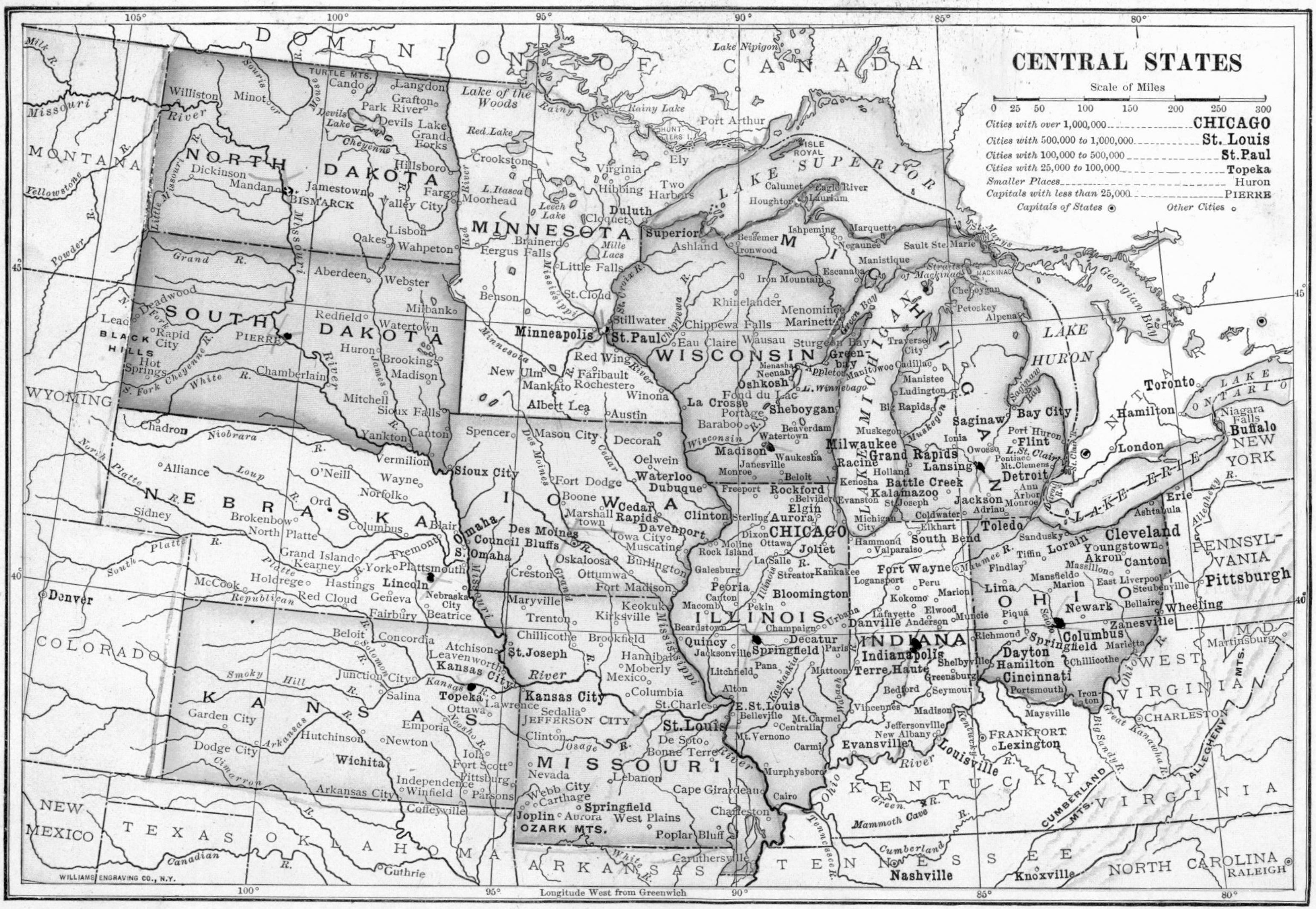

CENTRAL STATES

Scale of Miles

Cities with over 1,000,000........ **CHICAGO**
Cities with 500,000 to 1,000,000.... **St. Louis**
Cities with 100,000 to 500,000...... **St. Paul**
Cities with 25,000 to 100,000....... Topeka
Smaller Places.......................... Huron
Capitals of States...................... PIERRE ○
Other Cities ○

FIG. 169.

WILLIAMS ENGRAVING CO., N.Y.

eastern States, it is also very deep. The absence of steep slopes is one im- **(2)** *A deep, rich soil* portant reason for the deep soil, for the heavy rains cannot easily wash the soil away from level land.

In most parts of the Northeastern and Southern States forests were once **(3)** *Absence of forests* extensive; indeed, there is still much forest left, as we have seen. It required a great amount of labor for the early settlers to cut down the trees and clear the land, in order that the soil might be cultivated.

Over a large part of the Central States, however, such work was unnecessary, for there were no trees. It was *prairie* land, covered only with luxuriant grass, and ready for plowing and planting. A good crop could be raised the first season. This has been a fact of much importance in explaining the rapid settlement of these states.

While this section lies north of the states last studied, and has a **(4)** *Sufficient heat and rain* more severe climate, the summers are long and hot enough to raise many kinds of crops. Also, while the rainfall is less than that farther south (Fig. 205), it is sufficient for farming throughout almost the entire section.

Only on the very western border is there too little rain for agriculture without irrigation. The reason for this lack of rain in the extreme West is that the winds lose most of their moisture by the time they reach the western part of North and South Dakota, Nebraska, and Kansas. There is, however, enough rain for the growth of nourishing grass, and here great numbers of cattle, sheep, and horses are raised.

A very large portion of the Central States is now devoted to **2. Principal farm products** farming. Many kinds of crops are raised, but the **(1)** *Grains* most important are the *grains*.

This is one of the leading *wheat*-pro-

Fig. 170.— A corn field in Kansas. Note how high the stalks grow, and how large the ears of corn are.

ducing regions in the world. It not only supplies wheat to people in the Central and Northeastern States, but ships enormous quantities to Europe and other parts of the world. There are tens of thousands of square miles of land given up entirely to wheat raising (Fig. 168).

Much *corn* (Fig. 170) is raised in the Northeastern and Southern States, but the Central States are the greatest

Fig. 171.—Sheep grazing in a pasture in a hilly part of the Central States, in Missouri.

corn-producing section in the world. Corn requires longer and warmer summers than wheat; for this reason the principal corn belt lies a little south of the principal wheat belt, as you can see by comparing Figures 206 and 207.

Other important kinds of grain are oats, rye, and barley. It is interesting, in traveling across this vast farming country in early summer, to see the broad fields of wheat, corn, and other grains. In some sections, wheat extends as far as the eye can reach; in others, corn; and here and there oats, rye, and barley occupy a portion of the ground. These fields of grain, waving in the breeze, make a beautiful sight.

As in the other groups of states, hay is a very valuable crop, being used as **(2)** *Other crops* feed for animals, especially in winter. Vegetables of many kinds are raised everywhere, but in greatest amounts near the cities; small fruits, such as berries, are abundant; and vineyards and orchards of apples, pears, peaches, and other fruits are common. Among other valuable crops is the sugar beet, from which beet sugar is made; another is tobacco, which

is raised in all these states, but in greatest quantities in the southern portion.

A great amount of stock is to be seen throughout this entire region, for each farmer usually keeps a few **(3)** *Animals* horses, cattle, and hogs. He has chickens, also, and probably ducks, turkeys, or geese. From these facts it is plain that meat, milk, butter, cheese, eggs, and poultry are among the important farm products of this region. In some of the more hilly sections, as in parts of Ohio and Missouri, dairying and sheep raising are the principal farming occupations (Fig. 171).

In the extreme western part of the Central States, where the rainfall is light, grazing is almost the only occupation, except where irrigation is possible. This region reminds us of western Texas.

Before white men settled on these Western plains, vast herds of bison ranged over that great natural pasture; but they have now been killed, and their place is taken by cattle and sheep. These states, therefore, produce large quantities of meat, hides, and wool.

The full-grown cattle and sheep are fattened either on the irrigated farms along the streams or else in the farming country farther east. They are shipped to the meat-packing houses of CHICAGO, KANSAS CITY, OMAHA, or other cities to be slaughtered.

A large portion of the Central States is not noted for its lumber: first, because much of the land never had any forest; and second, because much land that was once wooded has now been cleared. The timber cut from it has been used for building, or other purposes, and the cleared sections have become productive farm land.

Lumbering

The largest area that was covered with timber, when first discovered, was

FIG. 172. — A sawmill in Wisconsin. The logs are floated from the forest by the river, and sawed into lumber in the mill.

in Michigan, Wisconsin, and Minnesota, near the Great Lakes. Here the land is more hilly than in most parts of the Central States, and it was covered with dense forests. Although much of the timber has been removed (Fig. 172), lumbering is still carried on in this section, as well as in some other parts of the Central States. Lumbering is, however, a far less important industry than agriculture.

Having no seacoast, these states do not take part in ocean fishing, but there is fishing in many of the rivers, and several kinds of food fish are found in the Great Lakes. There is, therefore, a small amount of fishing in the Central States, but this is the least important of the great industries.

Fishing

Some of the most useful minerals are found here in large quantities, and mining is second in importance to farming among the industries connected with raw products.

Mining

The country near the western end of Lake Superior, in Michigan, Wisconsin, and Minnesota, is a very rich mineral region. In this district, on the peninsula that extends from Michigan into Lake Superior, there are immense deposits of pure copper. This is one of the leading copper-producing sections in the world.

1. Copper and iron ore

Even far more valuable than the copper is the iron which comes from the Lake Superior district. In some places it is quarried as stone is; in others it is dug out with large steam shovels, as sand may be taken from a sand bank; in still other places it is mined from underground (Fig. 173). No other part of the world produces so great an amount of iron ore as the Lake Superior district.

You have already learned that coal is necessary in order to get the iron from the ore. There is no coal near the Lake Superior mines, but there is an abundance of bituminous coal in the states farther south.

2. Coal

This you can see by examining Figure 211. How far is it from the iron district to the nearest coal fields, as shown on this map? In which of the Central States is the coal found?

The coal of the Central States is used in smelting iron, in heating houses, and in running factories, locomotives, and steamboats. Thus the mineral fuel which lies beneath the soil of so many of these states, is one of the most valuable raw products in this section. It is especially important in Illinois, Ohio, and Indiana, although coal mining is carried on extensively in several of the other states.

3. Oil and gas
After natural gas and petroleum were found in New York and Pennsylvania, borings were made in the rocks of other states, and it was discovered that both oil and gas were imprisoned in some of the rocks of the Mississippi Valley. Indeed, this section has become even more important than the Northeastern States in the production of these valuable substances.

Petroleum and natural gas are found in many places, and have helped greatly in the development of the region. The petroleum is refined and used as already described on page 112. The natural gas, which makes an excellent and cheap fuel, is used in cities and factories; it is often piped into the houses for lighting, and into stoves and furnaces for cooking and heating.

4. Other minerals
There is a variety of other minerals in the Central States. For instance, gold is mined in the Black Hills of western South Dakota; lead and zinc in several of the states, from Wisconsin to southern Missouri; and salt in a number of states, especially Michigan and Kansas. Throughout the entire region, there is an abundance of limestone for cement, and of clay for making tiles, bricks, and pottery. There are also many excellent building stones, especially sandstone and limestone.

There are two conditions that favor manufacturing in any place: the first is

FIG. 173. — Miners at work digging out iron ore from underground in the Lake Superior district.

an abundance of valuable raw materials easy to obtain; the second is either plenty of coal for furnishing heat and power, or else good water power.

Manufacturing
1. Conditions favorable to manufacturing

This section, unlike the Northeastern States, has little water power, with the exception of Minnesota and Wisconsin. On the other hand, coal, oil, and gas are abundant and widely distributed. Most of the Central States are well supplied with coal (Fig. 211). Raw materials of many kinds are certainly very abundant and valuable in the Central States. Name those that come from the farm; from the forest; from underground. With so many raw products and so much fuel for power, there has naturally been great development of manufacturing along various lines.

Since this is our leading wheat-producing section, the greatest flour mills in the country are located here. **2. Manufactures from farm products** On account of the wheat and other grains, breakfast foods are made in enormous quantities, and there are many distilleries and breweries.

The small fruits and vegetables, such as berries, beans, peas, tomatoes, and sweet corn give rise to a great canning industry. Tobacco adds another kind of manufacturing, and the sugar beet still another.

A very important industry is the production of meat. Cattle, sheep, and hogs are slaughtered by the tens of thousands, and the meat and other animal products are shipped to all parts of the country, as well as to Europe. Butter, cheese, lard, soap, hides, wool, and other animal products besides meat are prepared in this section.

While many of these farm products are shipped to other sections for manufacture, much is manufactured in the Central States. For example, there are large woolen mills and shoe factories here, as well as in New England.

There is still much lumber produced here, and it is used not only **3. Manufactures from lumber** for building purposes, but for the manufacture of paper, furniture, and farm implements. On all sides there is a demand for large numbers of wagons, buggies, plows, mowing machines, threshing machines, and other farm implements. Therefore, they are manufactured extensively in this section. Chairs, tables, desks, bedsteads, and hundreds of other articles of wood are also made in these states. Quite possibly, the desk that you use in school came from Michigan.

With so much iron ore on the one hand, and fuel on the other, iron and steel manufactures are very extensive, as might be expected. **4. Manufactures from minerals** To be sure, the iron ore and coal are much farther apart than they are in Alabama; but the ore lies so near the Great Lakes that it is easily and cheaply shipped by boat to lake ports, where coal is readily obtained. There the ore is smelted, and the iron and steel are made into thousands of articles, such as iron ships, locomotives, rails, and the iron parts of farm machinery.

Although far from the ocean, these states are connected with **Transportation** one another, and with the ocean, by excellent highways. Thus the

Fig. 174. — The "Soo" Canal, between Lakes Superior and Huron, dug so that lake boats can go from one lake to another, past the dangerous rapids at Sault Ste. Marie.

products of the region can easily be shipped to any point at home or abroad. These highways are of two kinds —

(1) those that are natural to the country, and (2) those that have been made by man. The first may be called *natural*, the second *artificial*.

Of the natural highways, the Great Lakes are far the best, being so large **1. By lake** that they are properly called *inland seas*. They form, in fact, the most remarkable inland waterway in the world, for the largest vessels can sail upon them, and they reach into the very heart of a fertile and productive country. They connect parts of the Central States not only with one another, but, by short canals around two or three rapids and ·falls (Fig. 174), even with the ocean.

2. By river While the Great Lakes lead toward the east, the Mississippi River and its two large tributaries, the Missouri and Ohio, lead toward the south. These extensive waterways are highways of travel for river boats. Thus every one of the Central States is reached either by a lake or by a river highway.

Among the artificial highways are the roads and short canals; but the **3. By rail** railroads are especially to be noted. The surface of the land is usually so level that railway lines can be laid almost anywhere; and the country is so fertile, and it has become so fully settled, that it is crossed by railroads in all directions.

Of the twenty-six largest cities in the United States, ten are **Principal centers of manufacturing and commerce** found in the Central States alone. These are CHICAGO, ST. LOUIS, CLEVELAND, DETROIT, MILWAUKEE, CINCINNATI, MIN-

NEAPOLIS, KANSAS CITY, INDIANAPOLIS, and ST. PAUL. Where is each located? We have thus far found the *great* cities along the natural transportation routes, where goods can be shipped by water. Is that true of these cities also?

Taking the lake cities first, we find that CHICAGO (Fig. 175), the largest

FIG. 175. — A busy Chicago street crowded with wagons.

city in the Central States, and the second in size in our country, is situated near the south-**1. On the shores of the Great Lakes** ern end of Lake Michigan. It is near this point that the **(1) *Chicago and Milwaukee*** lake reaches farthest south into the fertile farming country of Illinois and Indiana.

It is possible to bring products to Chicago by water even from Europe, for, as you know, Chicago is connected with New York City by lake, canal, and river. There is also a canal in Canada, around Niagara Falls, connecting Lake Erie and Lake Ontario. By this water route, goods may be shipped from Chicago to the ocean along the St. Lawrence River. The Mississippi River furnishes another water highway to the ocean.

Lake Michigan extends so far south that the railways running between the Northwestern and the Northeastern States swing around the lake at this point. This makes Chicago one of the leading railway centers in the country.

Chicago stock yards (Fig. 176). The business of packing, canning, and shipping meat employs thousands of workmen, and many others are employed in tanning the hides to make leather. Much of the tanning is done in Milwaukee.

Much of the wheat from the farming country is sent to Chicago and Milwaukee, either to be shipped farther by boat, or to be ground into flour for

FIG. 176. — A view of the stock yards at Chicago, in which vast quantities of meat and other animal products are prepared every day.

Thus it is well provided with means for transportation both by rail and by water.

Not far north of Chicago, on the western shore of Lake Michigan, is MILWAUKEE, which shares some of the advantages of Chicago. It is much smaller, to be sure, but is larger than New Orleans.

Quantities of raw products from the surrounding country are sent to these two cities. For example, Chicago is the leading meat market in the world. Cattle, sheep, and hogs from the western plains, as well as from the farms of the Central States, are shipped to the

bread. The latter city has long been noted for its great flour mills and breweries. Another important product shipped to these cities is corn, some to be ground into corn meal or made into hominy, starch, cereals, and other things; some to be shipped East. So much corn and wheat are carried to Chicago that it is a noted grain as well as meat market.

Not far from Chicago are extensive coal fields, and since this city has no water power for manufacturing, coal is sent to it, in large quantities, for use in the factories. The ease with which iron ore from the Lake Superior mines can reach Chicago by boat makes this city a manufacturing center for many kinds of iron goods. It is also an important furniture manufacturing city, using much lumber brought by boat.

There are several other prosperous lake cities. The most western of these **(2)** *Other lake* are DULUTH and SUPERIOR, *ports* at the western end of Lake Superior. They are the nearest lake ports to Minnesota and North Dakota, and therefore ship much wheat. Their location near the forests and iron mines around the western end of Lake Superior leads to the shipment of large quantities of iron ore and lumber.

Farther to the east are DETROIT, TOLEDO, and CLEVELAND, which are so near the coal fields that iron manufacturing is very important. In fact, Cleveland is one of the principal iron manufacturing cities in the country; it lies not far from the coal fields, and iron ore is easily brought to it by water. Each of these cities is engaged in other kinds of manufacturing, obtaining raw products, either by water or by rail, from the surrounding country.

Locate the principal cities of these states that are situated on or near the Great Lakes. Named in order of size, they are Chicago, Cleveland, Detroit, Milwaukee, Toledo, Duluth, and Superior. In what state is each of them? On which lake? Through what lakes would one go in passing from Cleveland to Chicago? From Cleveland to Duluth? Find SAGINAW and GRAND RAPIDS, two important centers for lumber and furniture manufacturing.

The greatest river cities are naturally those on the largest rivers; namely, the **2. Along the** Mississippi, Missouri, and **great rivers** Ohio. The most important **(1)** *St. Louis* of these cities is ST. LOUIS, which ranks fourth in size among the cities of the United States. It is located on the Mississippi River (Fig. 177), almost at its junction with its largest tributary, the Missouri.

FIG. 177. — A great bridge across the Mississippi River at St. Louis.

Its central location opens up to St. Louis a river highway of the greatest importance. Boats can go from this city far to the northwest, by way of the Missouri River; as far as St. Paul, by way of the Mississippi; and to Pittsburgh, along the Ohio. Toward the south there is water connection with Memphis, New Orleans, and the ocean.

As people settled at this point, railways were built until, like Chicago, St. Louis has become one of our principal railway centers, and it draws to itself all the products that have been named in connection with Chicago. It is a great meat market, a noted grain market, and is engaged in manufacturing of many kinds. It is the metropolis of the Mississippi Valley, as Chicago is of the Great Lakes region, and New York of the eastern seacoast.

Although large numbers of cattle and

sheep reach St. Louis and Chicago, many of these animals are slaughtered near **(2)** *Kansas City, Omaha, St. Joseph, and Des Moines* the plains on which they are raised. That fact helps to explain the importance of KANSAS CITY, in Missouri, and OMAHA, in Nebraska. Both of these noted meat markets are on the Missouri River. Each has other manufacturing industries, also. Another important city on the Missouri River is ST. JOSEPH, in

York, water power has given rise to an important flour-manufacturing industry. There are scores of grain elevators and flour mills at Minneapolis, some of them of enormous size. Minneapolis is one of the leading flour-producing centers in the world.

Only a few miles away, at the head of navigation on the Mississippi River, is ST. PAUL (Fig. 178). It is the capital of Minnesota, but it owes its growth

Copyright by Sweet, 1905.

FIG. 178. — A general view of St. Paul, with the Mississippi River in the foreground. The state capitol of Minnesota is on the hill at the left.

Missouri, a short distance above Kansas City. Other important cities in this region are DES MOINES, in Iowa, and TOPEKA, in Kansas.

Much of the wheat of the Central States goes to the cities already mentioned, but one of the prin- **(3)** *Minneapolis and St. Paul* cipal grain centers is MINNEAPOLIS, which is near the heart of the wheat region of the Northwest. This city is situated on the banks of the Mississippi River, at a point where the St. Anthony Falls furnish excellent water power. Here, as at Rochester, New

partly to the fact that it is a center for the sale of machinery, clothing, and other articles wanted by farmers. Name some of the other articles that they would need to buy. Minneapolis and St. Paul are so near together that they are sometimes called the "Twin Cities."

In southwestern Ohio, on the Ohio River, is CINCINNATI, which is engaged in the manufacture of cloth- **(4)** *Cincinnati* ing, machinery, and a great variety of other articles. There is coal near at hand, so that power is easily obtained, and there is an abundance of raw products from the surrounding country. Much of the iron used comes from Pennsylvania and West Virginia. Why from these states rather than from the Lake Superior region? What large river city is situated ın Kentucky, farther down the Ohio River?

Locate the principal cities on the large rivers, and tell for what each is important. In order of size, they are St. Louis, Cincinnati, Minneapolis, Kansas City, Louisville, St. Paul, Omaha, and St. Joseph. In which state, and on what river, is each of these? How could you go by boat from Cincinnati to St. Paul? From Cincinnati to Omaha? On what rivers would you travel in each case, and through, or on the border of, what states? Past what cities?

Two of the large cities in these states, like Atlanta in Georgia, are not located **3. Indianapolis and Columbus** upon important waterways. These are INDIANAPOLIS, the capital of Indiana, and COLUMBUS, the capital of Ohio. The chief reason for their rapid growth is the fact that each is situated in the central part of a very fertile state. Also, since the country is a plain, railroads enter them from all directions, making each a center of trade and manufacturing.

There are many other important cities in the Central States, about which you **4. Other cities** will learn later. These include the capitals of the states. Name and locate each of the capitals. There are also many busy manufacturing and trade centers. The largest of these are DAYTON, YOUNGSTOWN, and AKRON, Ohio; PEORIA, Illinois; and EVANS-

VILLE, TERRE HAUTE, and FORT WAYNE, Indiana. Locate each of these.

1. How do these states compare in area with the two groups already studied? In population? 2. What is the leading occupation? Which of the great **Review Questions** occupations is least important here? 3. What conditions have greatly favored farming? 4. Why is there so little rain in the western part of this section? 5. What grains and other farm crops are raised? 6. What can you tell about each? 7. What animals are raised? 8. What can you tell about the grazing in the western part? 9. State the principal facts about lumbering. 10. About fishing. 11. Name the chief mineral products and tell what you can about each. 12. What conditions have greatly favored manufacturing? 13. What are the chief manufactures from farm products? 14. From lumber? 15. From minerals? 16. What do you know about the transportation routes (a) by lake, (b) by river, and (c) by rail? 17. Name the dozen chief cities

FIG. 179. — A crowd of workmen leaving a factory at the close of the day, at Dayton, Ohio.

in this group of states. 18. Which of these are lake ports? 19. Which are on the rivers? 20. What two large cities are not on important waterways? 21. Name and locate the capital of each state. 22. Name and locate the other cities mentioned. 23. State the principal facts

New Jersey

Kenebeck

Nigra

Pitsburg

Rotchers

Pennslvania

New York

New Jersey

Deleware

Mississippi R

Genesee R

Massas

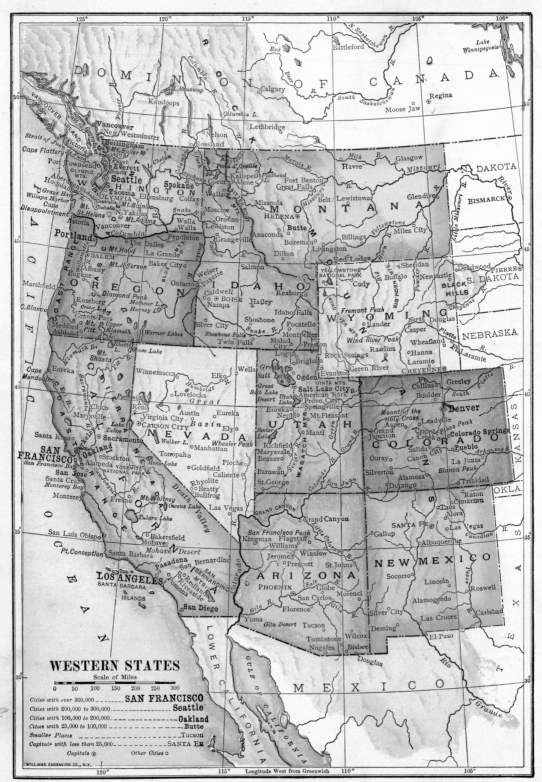

WESTERN STATES

Scale of Miles

Cities with over 300,000 ____ SAN FRANCISCO
Cities with 200,000 to 300,000 _____ Seattle
Cities with 100,000 to 200,000 _ _ _ _ Oakland
Cities with 25,000 to 100,000 _ _ _ _ _ _ Butte
Smaller Places _____ Tucson
Capitals with less than 25,000 __ SANTA FE
Capitals ◉   Other Cities ◦

WILLIAMS ENGRAVING CO., N.Y.

Longitude West from Greenwich

FIG. 180.

about Chicago and Milwaukee. 24. About each of the other Great Lake ports. 25. About St. Louis. 26. Kansas City and Omaha. 27. Minneapolis and St. Paul. 28. Cincinnati. 29. Indianapolis and Columbus.

Suggestions 1. Make a sketch of the Mississippi River with its two main tributaries. 2. Of the Great Lakes. 3. Upon these drawings show, by a cross, the location of each of the great cities. 4. Add some wheat, corn, and other grains to the school collection. 5. Find drawings, or pictures, of the principal fresh-water fish that are caught in the Great Lakes and the large rivers. 6. From what animals do wool, beef, veal, pork, mutton, lard, tallow, and leather, come? 7. Draw a map of the Central States, putting in lakes, large rivers, capitals and other principal cities.

VII. THE WESTERN STATES

Map study 1. Name the states in this group. Write the names. 2. In what direction do the mountain ranges cross them? 3. Name the principal ranges. 4. Name and trace the chief rivers. 5. In what section do you find very few rivers? What does that suggest about the rainfall? 6. Find some rivers emptying into lakes with no outlet. Are those salt- or fresh-water lakes? Why? 7. How far is it across these states, measuring from the northern to the southern boundary of the United States? 8. How far is it from New York City to San Francisco? 9. Measure the length of California. Compare its length with that of Pennsylvania. 10. How does the Pacific coast line compare in regularity with that of the Northeastern States (Fig. 140)? 11. On Figure 136 note whether San Francisco is farther north or south than New York City. 12. On the same map find out, at nearly as you can, the point that is midway between New York City and San Francisco.

Area and population Each of these eleven states is larger than the whole of New England. Together they are larger than the Northeastern and Southern States combined. Indeed, they make up much more than one third of the entire area of the United States.

Yet the population of these states is more than twelve million, while that of the Northeastern and Southern States together is more than fifty-five million.

Reasons for small population This means that the Western States are very thinly settled; in fact, this is by far the most thinly settled part of our country. Let us find some of the reasons for this fact.

1. Their position so far west One reason is their far western position. Most of the early settlers in this country came from Europe, as you know (p. 101), and settlements were first made along the eastern coast. It was a long distance from there to the Mississippi River, and it was only after the Eastern States were fairly well occupied, that many people crossed the Mississippi to go farther west. Now that the East is so fully settled, more and more people go to live in the Far West.

2. Their many mountains and plateaus Another important reason why there are so few people is the mountainous condition of the country. We have already learned (p. 104) that the Appalachian Mountains greatly hindered early settlers from reaching the fertile valley of the Mississippi. The mountains of the West are far more extensive, and more difficult to cross, than the Appalachians (Fig. 181). Instead of one mountain chain, there are four great mountain systems extending north and south, and between them are broad plateaus, some of which are more than a mile above the level of the sea. A large portion of the Western States is plateau country.

In traveling westward from the Mississippi, one passes first over the Great Plains, whose height above the level of the sea gradually increases to about a mile. Then come the *Rocky Mountains*, which rise five or ten thousand feet higher. Note the states that they cross. The name *Rocky* suggests how difficult it is to travel over them, for they are very rough, as well as high.

FIG. 181. — A lake in the picturesque Rocky Mountains of Montana.

For nearly a thousand miles to the west is a broad plateau with one part, called the *Great Basin*, lower than the rest. In this basin are numerous lower, short mountain ranges, called the *Basin Ranges*. On the western side of the Great Basin, in California, are the *Sierra Nevada* ranges; and farther north, in Oregon and Washington, are the *Cascade Ranges*. Before the Pacific is reached, still a fourth system of mountains, called the *Coast Ranges*, must be crossed. They are separated from the Sierra Nevada by a broad valley. All these Western mountains together are known as the *Western Cordillera*.

A third reason for so sparse a population is the lack of rain. We have already learned that the western parts of Texas (p. 122) and the states **3. Their lack** farther north (p. 133) re- **of rain** ceive too little rain for agriculture.

There are two reasons for this dryness. In the first place, in the southern portion the winds blow from the land, not from the ocean. They cannot, therefore, carry much vapor, and part of the country is a true desert (Fig. 182).

In the second place, although the winds farther north blow from the Pacific Ocean, they soon lose their moisture. They have plenty of vapor when they reach the coast, but as they rise over the mountains, much of

FIG. 182. — Desert landscape in southwestern United States. Only scattered bushes grow in this sandy waste.

this falls as rain or snow. The rainfall is therefore very heavy on and near the Coast Ranges. Continuing eastward, the winds blow over the Sierra Nevada and Cascade ranges, and are there robbed

Fig. 183. — Cutting wheat in the fertile wheat region of eastern Washington. By this large machine, drawn by thirty-two mules and horses, the wheat is cut, threshed, and put into sacks ready for shipment.

of more moisture. The air then becomes so dry that a large part of the country farther east, as far as the Rocky Mountains, receives very little rain.

Again, on crossing the lofty Rocky Mountains, these west winds lose still more of their moisture. This is suggested, on the map, by the number of large rivers that find their sources in these mountains. Name and trace some of them. As a result, if winds from the Gulf of Mexico and the Atlantic Ocean did not bring some vapor for rain, the country east of the Rockies might be as dry as the Sahara Desert. As it is, some rain falls even close to the eastern base of the Rocky Mountains, so that this region, though arid, is not a true desert. Farther east the rainfall increases, until in central Kansas, Nebraska, Oklahoma, and the Dakotas there is enough for agriculture.

In the plateau and Great Basin region, which lies between the Sierra Nevada-Cascade System and the Rocky Mountains, the climate is, for the most part, dry or arid. Note the states that are included. In places, even, the climate is so dry that the country is a real desert.

On these deserts one may travel for scores of miles without seeing vegetation of any kind excepting cactus, scattered blades of grass, and such other plants as grow in dry soil. There are no trees, because of lack of water; and there is little to be seen except sand and rock. It was very difficult for early settlers to cross these arid and desert regions, for there was often no water to drink, and there was little game for food. Even to-day there are large areas where no one lives.

Some parts of this section, however, are well watered. On many of the mountain slopes, and on some of the plateaus, there is an abundance of rain for farming.

Agriculture

1. The best-watered section and its products

Along the Pacific coast, in particular, from central California to Canada, there

L

is plenty of rain (Fig. 205). Measure this distance. It is here, in western Washington, where the west winds rise to pass over the mountains, that the heaviest rainfall in the United States occurs.

This rainy region has also a mild climate and fertile soil, and is, therefore, a very rich farming country. Fruits of many kinds are raised, such, for instance, as peaches, plums, apricots, pears, apples,

ing the winter season the rain often pours down, until rushing torrents are formed among the hills and mountains. In the summer season, however, when plants most need moisture, the winds no longer blow from the ocean. On that account, no rain falls in summer, and the southern part of California is then a true desert. This is the case

2. Irrigated sections and their products

(1) *Southern California*

FIG. 184. — Picking oranges in the irrigated country of southern California, near Pasadena.

grapes, and berries; and farther south, in California, oranges, lemons, grapefruit, and figs thrive. In Washington (Fig. 183) and Oregon, east of the mountains, and in the Great Valley district of California, wheat growing is an important industry.

The southern half of California, being near the ocean, might be expected to receive abundant rainfall. Indeed, dur-

even within sight of the ocean, and where the soil is very fertile.

Why could not some of the rain that falls in winter be stored up then for use in summer, when wanted? That was the question that men asked, and they set to work to store up the water.

Dams were built among the hills and mountains, collecting the winter's floods into ponds and lakes, and holding the water there till summer came. Then ditches many miles long were dug, or pipes were laid, leading the water down from these reservoirs to the fertile plains. Smaller ditches were dug from the main ones, leading to the farms in various directions. From these each farmer could turn the water into still smaller ditches on his own land, and, when he wished to do so, could flood his fields. Thus, as often as was necessary during the long, dry summer, the crops could be given the water that they needed.

This is what is meant by *irrigation*. It is quite expensive, but it is even better than rain, because it supplies the exact quantity of water that is needed, and at the time that it is wanted.

Irrigation has changed much of southern and central California from a barren desert into a paradise of flowers, fruit trees, and beautiful homes. This is the land from which many of our oranges (Fig. 184) and lemons now come, the other important source being Florida. Also, quantities of peaches, grapes, figs, olives, and nuts are raised here, as well as grain, vegetables, and other crops.

The climate is delightful, and many people go there to spend the winter. In the midst of a great irrigated garden in southern California is the large city of LOS ANGELES, surrounded by orange groves and thriving towns.

The region around SALT LAKE CITY, in Utah, is another irrigated section **(2)** *Salt Lake City and vicinity* similar to that just described. The Mormons, who first settled there, have changed that part of the desert also into a magnificent garden. The mountains, not far away, supply water for irrigation, and fruits, alfalfa, and many other farm products are produced in abundance.

Near by is the Great Salt Lake, the largest lake in the Great Basin. Although many streams descend from the neighboring mountains, so much water evaporates in this arid region that the lake does not rise high enough to overflow. It has therefore grown more and more salt, until now its water is even much salter than the ocean itself. It is so salt, and on that account so dense, that a person cannot sink in it.

Central Colorado, in the neighborhood of DENVER, is a third important irrigated section. There are **(3)** *Other irrigation districts* many extensive irrigation works in Idaho and Wyoming, and, indeed, all along the eastern base of the Rocky Mountains, from Mexico to Canada, as well as in the larger valleys among the mountains.

Near Denver, for example, there is a large irrigation ditch, which supplies water to hundreds of farms. It is interesting to know that in each case, while land that is low enough to be watered from the ditches is very valuable, the land that is higher than the ditches is almost worthless. Fruits, garden truck, grain, alfalfa, grass, sugar beets, and other farm products are extensively grown on these irrigated farms.

Among the Western mountains, and along the rivers, there are many other irrigated sections, as in New Mexico and Arizona. Yet the amount of irrigated land **(4)** *Work of the United States government in irrigation.* in the West is small compared with the amount that is still either desert or dry enough to be called *arid*. Much of this land will probably always remain arid, because no water can be obtained for it

There is, however, much land, now almost useless, that might be irrigated if the expense could be met. Most of this land still belongs to the United States government, and it is very important that water be brought to it, so that settlers may occupy it and make it produce valuable crops. For these reasons the United States government is now spending millions of dollars in building extensive irrigation works in the West. Some of the largest of these works are in Idaho and Arizona.

While the greater part of the arid lands is without irrigation, and for that reason is not cultivated, it is by no means entirely useless. Most of it receives rainfall enough for a crop of nourishing grass. This vast arid section, therefore, is valuable for grazing. It is the land of the cattle ranch (Fig. 185) and of the cowboy, who

3. Ranching

In many parts of the West one can travel on horseback for days without seeing any trees, excepting, perhaps, some cottonwoods growing along a stream. Yet this is not true of all parts, for there are extensive forests on the mountains and plateaus, and the Pacific coast is the land of the *big trees*. The largest trees in the

Lumbering

Fig. 185. — Cattle drinking in the ranch country of western North Dakota.

spends most of his time in the saddle looking after his herds. Besides cattle many sheep and horses are also raised.

The sheep are driven in flocks from place to place for feeding, but the cattle and horses are often allowed to roam about almost like wild animals. Many single ranchmen own thousands of sheep or cattle. Since the grass on which they feed grows in scattered tufts, the animals must wander over much land in feeding. It is plain, therefore, that the ranchmen must live far apart, and that a grazing country has very few people.

The cattle and sheep are shipped eastward in great numbers, even to Europe, to furnish meat, leather, and wool.

world grow here, and some of them have been growing for a thousand years or more.

Many of the trees are as large round as an ordinary living room, and several have been found to be over ninety feet in circumference, which is as much as the distance around many a schoolroom. The main limb on one of these trees, called the Grizzly Giant (Fig. 186), starts from the trunk two hundred feet above ground, and measures six and one half feet in diameter, or more than most large trees in the East. A single giant tree will supply lumber enough to build a whole house.

In such a region lumbering is naturally a flourishing industry, and the forests are being cut down very rapidly. This is true especially of Washington and Oregon and California, and there are many lumber mills on the lower

by far the most prominent. The salmon spends most of its life in the ocean, but "runs" up **Fishing** the rivers in order to lay its eggs in fresh water. These fish go up many streams, from California northward, and are caught in immense quantities. Great numbers, for example, run up the Columbia River, so that salmon fishing is very important there (Fig. 187). Trace this river.

FIG. 186. — The huge trunk of the Grizzly Giant, in the redwood forest of California.

Most of the salmon caught are canned, though some are sent away on ice as fresh fish. Probably much of the canned salmon that you have seen has come from the canneries either near PORTLAND, Oregon, or Puget Sound, or else along the coast farther north. ASTORIA, on the lower Columbia, and BEL-

Columbia River, and along the shores of Puget Sound. Find this sound on Figure 180. The mountains and high plateaus in other parts of the Western States also bear extensive forests, and here, too, lumbering is an important industry.

While there is fishing of various kinds along the Pacific coast, salmon fishing is

LINGHAM, on Puget Sound, are especially noted for the salmon industry.

Although agriculture, lumbering, and fishing are important, it is for mining that the Western States are most noted. Among the **Mining** minerals, gold and silver, called the *precious metals*, are especially prominent.

FIG. 187. — Salmon fishermen in the Columbia River, near Astoria, showing the large salmon caught in their nets.

Gold is the most valuable of all. When gold was first discovered in the stream gravels of California, in 1848, thousands of persons, in the East and in Europe, made a mad rush to the new gold fields.

1. Gold

At that time the journey to the Pacific coast required many weeks of steady travel. Some went on ships, going by way of the Isthmus of Panama, or even sailing completely around South America; but great numbers traveled directly across the continent in wagons, toiling slowly across the plains, mountains, and plateaus, accompanied by their families. Some used oxen, others horses. The journey overland was difficult and dangerous, for there were bands of roaming Indians (Fig. 189); the trails were poorly marked, so that one might easily lose his way; and in the desert one might even die of thirst. Hundreds of people perished on the way.

Later, gold was found in the midst of the solid rock among the mountains. Such rock, with gold in it, is called *gold ore*, and this must be crushed into fine bits before the gold can be collected. This requires much machinery, and is one of the important parts of mining.

Gold is now mined in several states besides California. Indeed, more gold now comes from Colorado than from California. DENVER, the largest city in Colorado, and PUEBLO, not far distant, owe their growth in large part to the gold and other minerals mined near them. Find these cities on the map.

Silver is another precious metal found in the West. Nevada produces more silver than any other state in the Union, but much is

2. Silver

obtained in Montana, Utah, Colorado, and Idaho (Fig. 188). Each of these states also produces large quantities of gold.

Copper is a third valuable metal. The greatest copper mines in the world are situated in and near BUTTE, in Montana. More copper has come from Montana than from any other state; but Arizona now produces even more than Montana, and BISBEE in Arizona is a great mining camp.

3. Copper and lead

Lead is a fourth metal mined in the West. Idaho produces the largest amount, but much comes also from Colorado and Utah. What are some of the uses of copper and lead?

Iron ore is found in many of the Western States, but little is mined as yet, except in Colorado. Most of the Western States produce some coal, Colorado and Wyoming being in the lead. Coal mining in the West is rapidly increasing, for there is much excellent coal there.

4. Iron, coal, and petroleum

Petroleum has been found in many of the Western States, especially in California. In fact, this state produces more oil than any other

FIG. 188.—Miners at work underground in one of the silver-lead mines of the famous Cœur d'Alene district of Idaho.

state in the Union. So much petroleum is found there that it is even used as fuel on railway engines.

Western United States is the leading metal-producing section in the world, and every year new mines are discovered. Much of the land

FIG. 189. — An Indian Chief.

belongs to the government, and when a person finds a valuable deposit of metal, he can obtain a title to the land from the government. This has led many men, called *prospectors* (Fig. 190), to spend their lives roaming about over the

5. The prospector

FIG. 190. — A prospector with his burros, loaded with tools and supplies. In the mountains of Arizona.

Western plateaus and mountains seeking, or *prospecting for*, deposits of metal.

In some parts of the West travelers can see, even from the car windows, scores of little tunnels dug into the sides of the mountains by prospectors who have been hunting for ore. It is a hard, lonely life that such men lead, and is often full of danger. Most of them fail to find valuable deposits, but once in a while a prospector discovers a rich vein, and suddenly finds himself a wealthy man.

Knowing the raw products of the Western States, we can tell what the principal kinds of manufacturing are likely to be. Name the chief raw products.

Manufacturing

Wheat is ground into flour in many places, partly by means of water power. Quantities of grapes, peaches, apples, and other fruits are either canned or dried, and many grapes are made into wine, especially in California.

1. Manufactures from farm, forest, and ranch products

Lumbering gives rise to much manufacture of boards, shingles, furniture, and other articles. In some of the larger cities, the hides of cattle and sheep are manufactured into boots, shoes, and gloves, and the wool of sheep into woolen cloth; but still greater quantities of these raw materials are sent East for manufacture.

Many iron and steel goods are made along the Pacific coast and in Colorado, as well as at some other points. The ores of gold, silver, copper, and lead are too heavy to haul far. Therefore, in order to get the metals from the ores, they are crushed and melted at many points. The buildings in which the crushing is done are called *stamp mills*, and those where the ore is melted are called *smelters* (Fig. 191). Since mining is so promi-

2. Manufactures from the products of the mines

FIG. 191. — A smelter at Pueblo, Colorado, where the metal is obtained from the ore.

nent in the West, this kind of manufacturing is carried on very extensively.

On the whole, manufacturing has not been so greatly developed in these states as in those farther east. **3. The future of manufacturing in the West** It is rapidly increasing, however; and, since there is much water power and coal in the West, it will doubtless continue to increase. Indeed, it seems probable that parts of this region, especially along the coast, will, at no very distant time, rank high among the manufacturing districts of the country.

Transportation of goods to and from the Far West was at first provided by **Transportation and trade** means of wagons, slowly toiling across the country, or else by ships that sailed around South America. Since then, railroads running east and west have been built.

There are several of these railways now, and they carry an enormous **1. Transcontinental railroads** amount of freight. Since they cross the continent, they are called *transcontinental* lines (*trans* = across). With the opening of a short water-route, by way of the Panama Canal, ocean commerce between the East and West will, no doubt, be cheapened and greatly increased.

In recent years, an extensive trade has sprung up with other parts of the **2. Trade with Alaska and Asia** world besides the Eastern States. One of these sections is Alaska. Thousands of persons have gone to this northern land, and for supplies they depend mainly upon the seaports of our western coast.

The trade with Asia has also been rapidly increasing. It seems probable that, in the future, trade with Asia will have much the same importance for cities on the Pacific coast that trade with Europe has had for cities on the Atlantic coast. The harbors along the western coast, that make such ocean transportation possible, are not numerous, but several of them are excellent.

One of the best of these harbors is that of SAN FRANCISCO. It has much the same importance on the **3. Principal harbors** Pacific coast that New York harbor has on the Atlantic. Southeast of this there is no very good natural harbor until SAN DIEGO is reached. How many hundred miles is that? North of San Francisco there is no very good harbor until the Columbia River is reached. Here is located PORTLAND, a hundred miles upstream on the Willamette River, near its junction with the Columbia. Farther north still, in Washington, is Puget Sound, with many fine harbors. Here are found SEATTLE and TACOMA.

The largest city in the Western States is San Francisco (Fig. 192), which is the eleventh city in size in the country. It is located on **Leading centers of manufacturing and commerce** San Francisco Bay, which is **1. Cities of Pacific slope** the natural outlet of the Valley of California, that **(1) San Francisco and vicinity** lies between the Sierra Nevada and Coast Ranges. This fertile section is one of the finest and most productive agricultural regions in the country. San Francisco Bay is the natural outlet, also, of the gold mines of California. Railroads extend from this point north, east, and south, and ships sail from it to all parts of the Pacific Ocean, and even to Europe. It has an extensive and growing trade with the Orient, particularly with China and Japan.

FIG. 192.—A part of the water front of San Francisco, where the ferries from Oakland are all the time going and coming.

As in the case of other cities on fine, large harbors, there is one main city, with other important ones near by. San Francisco is far the largest, but OAKLAND, BERKELEY and ALAMEDA are just across the Bay from it. SACRAMENTO, the capital of the state, lies a short distance northeast, STOCKTON east, FRESNO and SAN JOSÉ south, of San Francisco.

San Francisco and Oakland are busy manufacturing centers, having foundries, machine shops, flour and woolen mills, many other factories, and shipyards. The fire that followed the earthquake of 1906 destroyed many of the best buildings in the city, and for a short time greatly checked its growth. It is wonderful how rapidly San Francisco recovered from that severe blow. In rebuilding it, the people have made even a finer city than before, with many large, modern buildings.

(2) *Los Angeles*

LOS ANGELES, far southeast of San Francisco, is the principal city in southern California. It lies twenty-five miles from the coast in the midst of a remarkable fruit region, from which vast quantities of fresh, dried, and canned fruits are shipped, mainly by rail. What has already been said about this city (p. 147)?

(3) *Portland*

PORTLAND (Fig. 193) is the chief city of Oregon, having extensive manufactories of

FIG. 193.—The city of Portland, with the lofty and beautiful snow-covered peak of the volcano, Mt. Hood, in the distance.

woolen goods, flour, and furniture. It is a distributing point for the fertile country round about, and is reached by several of the transcontinental railroads. It has much trade with Alaska and Asia, and is growing very rapidly.

On the shores of Puget Sound are SEATTLE and TACOMA, as well as Bellingham and Everett and several smaller cities and towns. Transcontinental lines extend to

(4) *Cities on Puget Sound*

SPOKANE, in eastern Washington, is situated in the midst of a fertile wheat and fruit region, for which it is the principal trade center. Being located on the Spokane River, at a point where falls supply an abundance of water power (Fig. 194), extensive manufacturing has developed, especially lumber and flour mills. Three transcontinental lines enter Spokane, and it has grown very rapidly. It is

(1) *Spokane*

FIG. 194. — The falls in the Spokane River, around which the city of Spokane has grown.

these two cities, which are also connected by rail with Portland and San Francisco to the south, and Vancouver to the north. These cities are centers for lumber, and also for the distribution of such goods as are needed in the farming country.

Seattle, being the farthest north of the west coast cities, has the most extensive trade with Alaska. There is also a great and growing trade with the countries of Asia. As in the case of Portland, the recent growth of this city has been remarkable.

The inland cities are of several kinds. Some are largely manufacturing cities; others are mainly centers of trade; while many are almost wholly mining cities.

2. Inland cities

the trade center for the famous Cœur d'Alêne mining regions of Idaho, from which come great quantities of silver and lead.

DENVER, the largest city in the interior, is mainly a manufacturing and trading center. It lies out on the plains, close to the eastern base of the Rocky Mountains. Being a railroad center, goods are easily shipped to and from the surrounding farming and ranching country. There are no mines close by, but in the mountains, at no great distance, are valuable mines of gold, silver, and lead, as at CRIPPLE CREEK and LEADVILLE. Much of the ore from these places is shipped to Denver for smelting.

(2) *Denver, Pueblo, and Salt Lake City*

Pueblo, farther south, has much the same relation to the surrounding country that Denver has. Ores are shipped to Pueblo for smelting, and since both coal and iron ore are found not far distant, iron smelting (Fig. 191) and manufacturing have developed.

Salt Lake City, in the midst of an oasis due to irrigation, is mainly a trade

Arizona, thriving cities in the midst of fertile irrigated regions.

Many smaller cities and towns in the West, about some of which you will learn later, are important trade centers in the farming or ranching country.

Butte, in Montana, may be taken as a good example of a flourishing *mining center*. **(3)** *Butte*

Fig. 195. — The Canyon of the Colorado, a gash of over a mile in depth cut by the river in the solid rock.

When a vein of metal that some prospector discovers turns out to be very rich, many men are needed in obtaining the metal. Some are employed to dig out the ore, others to crush it in the stamp mills, and still others to work in the smelters. Thus a good-sized town may quickly spring up about a single rich vein. Very often, too, where there is one rich mineral vein, there are others close by, so that a group of mines may be opened near together. Then a mere mining camp may quickly become a large city. That is what happened in the case of Butte. It is a great copper-mining center, and, since the ore contains some silver, this precious metal is also produced.

There are many mines at Butte, even within the city limits. Some of the shafts reach thousands of feet down into the earth, and the tunnels that are left underground when the ore has been removed are, taken together, hundreds of miles in length. Hundreds of men there spend most of their lives far underground, coming up to the surface only to eat and sleep. Many men are also employed in the smelters. There are scores of such mining centers in the West, although most of them are only small towns, or "camps."

center. The products of the farms find their way to the city for sale, and, in return, the city supplies the farmers with articles that they need. It also supplies goods to the mining towns in the neighboring mountains. The same is true of Boise, Idaho, and Tucson and Phoenix,

Besides such cities as have just been mentioned, there is one other important kind; that is, the pleasure and health resort. The dry, sunny climate of much of the West is **Pleasure and health resorts** favorable to invalids, and pleasant for any one. For this reason great numbers

1. Health resorts of people go for their health to COLORADO SPRINGS, in Colorado, to LOS ANGELES, in California, and to other parts of the Southwest. Many also go to the seacoast, as to SAN DIEGO, for a winter resort, since the climate there is warm throughout the winter.

Many other people visit the West as tourists, for western

2. The lofty mountains United States has some of the finest scenery in the world. There are vast plateaus and rugged mountain ranges, on some of which snow and glaciers are always present. Among them are deep valleys, shut in by lofty mountains; beautiful lakes, like Lake Tahoe in California and Crater Lake in Oregon; and wonderful waterfalls, like the Yosemite Falls in California and the Shoshone Falls in Idaho. There are also finely shaped volcanic cones, such as Mt. Rainier, Mt. Hood, and Mt. Shasta, more than fourteen thousand feet high. Locate these volcanoes.

In addition to such scenery, there are many deep, narrow

3. Grand Canyon of the Colorado valleys, or *canyons*, the largest of which is the *Grand Canyon of the Colorado River* (Fig. 195), in Arizona. This is a mighty gash cut into the earth by the Colorado River, which flows along its bottom a mile below the surface of the plateau. This canyon has been cut through rock layers that are brightly colored, and that are gullied into many

odd shapes. It is one of the grandest scenes on the earth.

North of this, in the northwest corner of Wyoming, there is a sec- **4. Yellowstone National Park** tion that has no equal among all the wonders of the world. This,

FIG. 196. — The Giant Geyser in eruption, one of the many geysers in the Yellowstone National Park.

known as the *Yellowstone National Park*, is so wonderful that it has been set apart by the government as a national park, to which people are freely admitted.

Here are hundreds of springs from which boiling hot water pours forth. In some places, the boiling water and steam now and then shoot upward with a roar, rising to a height of from one hundred to two hundred feet. These springs are called *geysers* (Fig. 196), and there are scores of them in the Park.

Here, too, is the Yellowstone River, whose waters tumble three hundred and eight feet in

Fig. 197. — A grizzly bear in the Yellowstone National Park.

a single fall. In the deep canyon, which the river has cut below the Yellowstone Falls, the rocky banks are, in places, a quarter of a mile high, and beautifully colored. It is truly called a "Wonderland."

The law allows no wild animals to be killed in the National Park. For this reason they have thrived here, and as one goes through the Park, he can sometimes see them in the woods by the roadside. Among the large animals are the elk, the black bear, the grizzly bear (Fig. 197), and the buffalo or bison. This is now the only place in the United States where the bison is found in a wild state, although there were tens of thousands of them when the Western country was first visited by white men.

Review Questions

1. What have you learned about the area and population of these states? 2. Give three reasons for so small a population. 3. What mountains are included in the Western Cordillera? 4. Why is there so little rain in most of these states? 5. Locate the best-watered section, and name its farm products. 6. What are the farm products of California? 7. Explain how land is irrigated. 8. Tell about Salt Lake City and vicinity. 9. About Denver and vicinity. 10. What is the United States government doing for irrigation? 11. Tell about ranching in the West. 12. What about lumbering? 13. Fishing? 14. What minerals are extensively mined in these states? 15. State the principal facts about gold mining. 16. About silver. 17. About copper and lead. 18. About iron, coal, and petroleum. 19. What do prospectors do? 20. What about the importance of mining in these states? 21. What about the manufacturing? 22. How are trade and transportation provided for? 23. State the principal facts about San Francisco and vicinity. 24. Los Angeles. 25. Portland. 26. Cities on Puget Sound. 27. What different kinds of inland cities are there? 28. Tell about Spokane. 29. Denver, Pueblo, and Salt Lake City. 30. Butte. 31. Name and locate the principal cities in these states. 32. Why are there many pleasure and health resorts in the West? Name the principal ones. 33. Tell about the mountain scenery. 34. Describe the Grand Canyon of the Colorado. 35. What is there of interest in the Yellowstone National Park?

Suggestions

1. Describe an imaginary overland journey to California in the early days. 2. Make a list of articles made of gold; of silver; of copper; of lead. 3. Obtain some of these ores for the school collection. 4. Ask some grocer what California fruits he keeps. 5. Visit a fish market to see some salmon. Find the picture of one in the dictionary. Make a drawing of it. 6. Show how you might irrigate a certain piece of land near you. 7. Write to some Western railway asking for their illustrated circulars, in which are many views of Western scenery. 8. Through what states must the waters of the Yellowstone River flow in reaching the Gulf of Mexico? 9. Past what cities? 10. Make a drawing of the Western States, showing the principal

mountain ranges, rivers, and cities. 11. Make a sand map of the same. 12. Name and locate the capital of each state. 13. Write the abbreviation used for each state.

VIII. DEPENDENCIES OF THE UNITED STATES

Map study 1. On the map of the world (Fig. 106) locate (*a*) Alaska; (*b*) Porto Rico; (*c*) The Philippine Islands; (*d*) The Hawaiian Islands. 2. On the map of North America (Fig. 133) locate Alaska, and Porto Rico. 3. Bound Alaska. 4. What large river crosses Alaska? 5. Name the largest islands in the Philippines (Fig. 272).

A good part of Alaska is mountainous (Fig. 198), and much of it is in the frigid zone, as you can see. About how much of it? In addition, at that time we already had more land than we knew what to do with. For these reasons, most persons thought that the purchase of Alaska was very unwise. They even called it "Seward's folly," because Secretary Seward, who was in President Lincoln's cabinet, was the one who chiefly urged the purchase.

Reasons why it was a wise purchase It has turned out, however, to be a wise purchase, indeed, for Alaska has come to be an important part of the United States, and is developing rapidly.

Fig. 198. — The snow-covered mountains of the St. Elias chain, Alaska.

1. Alaska

Purchase of Alaska, and why it at first seemed unwise Alaska (Fig. 133), which was purchased from Russia in 1867 (for $7,200,000), is almost one fifth as large as the United States. Measure to see how far this territory is from our nearest ports, on Puget Sound. Most people thought it very foolish to buy a territory so far away and so far north.

Most of Alaska is too mountainous and cold for agriculture. Yet the summers are warmer than one might expect, and some parts of the country are level enough for farming. Already some crops are raised there, and, doubtless, portions of Alaska will some day produce the more hardy grains and vegetables. Doubtless, also, grazing will become important, for there are extensive natural pastures on which sheep and cattle can feed. In addition, the forests will some day be of value, for there are large areas covered with timber.

1. Agriculture and lumbering

2. Fishing At present the fishing proves the wisdom of the purchase of Alaska much more than the industries just mentioned.

The catching of seals was the first industry of importance there. One kind **(1) Sealing** of Alaskan seal, called the *fur seal*, has a very fine fur, which is highly prized for making muffs and coats. Already seven times as much money has come from sealing as was paid for the entire territory of Alaska. The skins are especially valued because

FIG. 199. — One of the fiords of the narrow " Inside Passage " to Alaska.

of their warmth and beauty; and as there is no great number of them, they are very expensive. A woman must pay several hundred dollars for a seal-skin coat.

More recently the salmon has come to be of great value. Here, as in the **(2) Catching of salmon and other fish** Columbia River (p. 149), tens of thousands of salmon go up the streams every summer, in order to lay their eggs in fresh water. Indeed, explorers in that country, when wanting salmon for food, often kick them out of the small streams, instead of catching them in the usual way.

These fish are caught and taken to the canneries, where they are cooked and placed in cans, for shipment to all parts of the world. Already, the salmon taken from the Alaskan streams have yielded ten times as much money as Alaska cost us.

Among other fish, halibut and codfish are common on the shallow banks along the Alaskan coast, and vessels from our Western States now go there to catch them.

It is, however, the gold that has attracted most attention to this territory. The famous *Klondike* re- **3. Mining** gion, in northwestern Canada, first drew large numbers of men to Alaska; for the easiest route to the Klondike was across Alaska. Thousands of prospectors rushed there in 1896 and 1897, just as they did to California in 1849.

Valuable deposits of gold have since been found at NOME and other places in Alaska. Already more than twenty times as much gold has been mined as we paid for the entire territory, and Alaska now produces two or three times as much gold each year as we paid to Russia.

There are also very extensive deposits of copper and coal, but as yet these minerals have not been mined to any great extent.

So many persons go to Alaska for the mining and fishing, or for the scenery, that steamships, chiefly from Seattle, now make regular trips up the Alaskan **Transportation** coast. It is one of the most wonderful voyages in the world. For a thousand miles, from Seattle northward, the steamer threads its way through a narrow passage, bordered on either side by lofty mountains (Fig. 199). Precipices and wooded slopes come down to the very sea, and in the background are snow-capped mountains, with glaciers in their valleys.

The mountains make it very difficult to build railways; yet a short road leads inland over one of the passes, called White Pass, and others are now being built. One of the principal routes to the interior is up the Yukon River by steamboat; but in most parts of Alaska travel is still very slow and difficult. In most sections there are not even trails as yet.

Towns There are only a few towns in Alaska, and most of these vary greatly in size from year to year. Many of the people spend only the warmer season there, going in the spring and returning to the states in the autumn. JUNEAU is now the capital, but SITKA was formerly the capital.

2. Cuba and Porto Rico

On his first voyage, Columbus discovered some islands southeast of the United States (Fig. 133). These were later called the West Indies, because, as you remember (p. 86), Columbus thought he had reached India.

How these islands happen to be under our guidance The Spaniards took possession of these islands, and long held the larger ones as colonies. The people were not content under Spanish rule, and there was much trouble and bloodshed. Yet Spain held Cuba and Porto Rico until 1898. At that time the Cubans were fighting a war for independence, and the United States went to their aid. This quickly brought on a war between our country and Spain, called the Spanish-American War. Spain gave up Cuba and Porto Rico at the end of the war. Our government then took control of Porto Rico, and holds it still; but Cuba was allowed its independence, under our

protection. It is not, therefore, really a part of our territory, as Porto Rico is.

Spanish is the language spoken on both of these islands, and many of the people are Spaniards; but there are also many negroes and half-breeds.

Their chief products In what zone do these islands lie? That fact alone tells you that they are very different from Alaska. Not only is the climate warm (Fig. 200), but there is an abun-

FIG. 200. — Palm trees in Havana. Examples of tropical vegetation.

dance of rain, and a very fertile soil. Their products, therefore, are partly the same as those that were found peculiar to the Southern States. What were those (p. 122)?

In both islands the principal product is sugar cane, from which great quantities of sugar are made. Much tobacco and coffee are also grown, as well as oranges, bananas, pineapples, and other tropical fruits. From the forests valuable tropical woods are obtained.

Much of the trade of both islands is with the United States. The largest Chief cities city is HAVANA, in Cuba, which is as large as Minneapolis. Locate this city. The chief city of Porto Rico is PONCE, but SAN JUAN is nearly as large.

FIG. 201. — A native Philippine girl.

3. The Philippine Islands

The Philippine Islands (Fig. 106) were also obtained as a result of the Spanish-American War. At first How these islands came into they were governed entirely our possession by the United States, but now they have their own legislature, and partly govern themselves.

M

Find these islands on Figure 272; also on a globe. Name and locate the larger islands (Fig. 301). How would you reach them from San Francisco? From New York? Through what waters would you pass?

There is a great mixture of people in the Philippine Islands. There are some Spanish, some Americans, Kinds of and many Japanese and people Chinese, but most of the inhabitants are natives (Fig. 201).

There are several races among the natives, most of whom are partly or wholly civilized. Of these the *Tagalogs* are most advanced, having learned the arts of civilization from the Spaniards. A number of small islands in the southwestern part of the main group are occupied by Mohammedans, called *Moros*. Among the mountainous parts of the other islands, real savages live in the dense forests of the interior. Some of these savages, called *Negritos*, or little negroes, are a race of very small, black people.

The United States has the difficult task of governing and teaching these people until they become able to look after themselves. While the natives speak different languages, Spanish is the most common one, as in Cuba and Porto Rico. The use of the English language, however, is rapidly increasing.

There are more than three thousand islands, large and small, in the whole group, and all of them lie Products of in the tropical zone. Some the islands of their products, therefore, are sugar, coffee, rice, tobacco, and tropical fruits. One of the most valuable of all the products is hemp, large quantities of which are shipped abroad. This hemp is used in making a fine quality of rope, called Manila rope.

The dense tropical forests, which cover parts of the islands, contain valuable kinds of hardwood. There are some minerals, but thus far there has been little mining.

The two largest islands are *Luzon*, which is nearly as large as Pennsylvania,

Area, population, and chief city

and *Mindanao*, which is a little smaller than Luzon. How far apart are they? The area of all the islands together is about three times that of Pennsylvania.

Luzon has about half as many people as Pennsylvania, and all the islands together have about eight million inhabitants. There are, therefore, many towns and some large cities. The principal city is MANILA, situated on a fine harbor in Luzon. It has an extensive trade with the United States and Europe.

Every few years one of these bursts forth in eruption, and then vast quantities of melted rock, or *lava*, pour down the slopes toward the sea.

FIG. 202. — A house in the Philippines, built of bamboo and covered with thatch. The house is raised above the ground because of the dampness.

4. The Hawaiian Islands

Far out in the Pacific, between the United States and the Philippines

How they came into our possession

(Fig. 106), lies a group of small islands called the Hawaiian Islands. They used to form a little kingdom, but in 1893 the people rebelled and formed a republic. Later they asked to be made a part of the United States, and in 1898 this was done.

These islands are very small, and are scattered over a distance of a thousand

Why they are of special value to us

miles. They are built of lava that has risen from within the earth, and on Hawaii (Fig. 301), the largest island, there are two volcanoes that are still active.

Such islands, so far away, might seem to be of little value. Yet we have many vessels that make the long voyage from our Western seaports to China, Japan, Australia, and the Philippines. They now and then suffer serious accidents on the way, and run the danger of getting out of coal and other supplies. These islands lie on the route that some of these vessels take, and about a third of the way between the United States and Asia. For these reasons the Hawaiian Islands are of great importance to us; they serve as a stopping place, where repairs can be made, and where coal and supplies can be obtained.

You can, perhaps, name the principal products of the Hawaiian Islands, since

they lie in the tropical zone. Sugar
Their products and principal city raising is the chief industry. Other products are rice coffee, wool, and tropical fruits.

HONOLULU is the chief city, and its port is deep enough for the largest vessels.

FIG. 203.— Five native Hawaiian girls.

5. Other Territory

Between the Hawaiian and Philippine Islands are the *Wake Islands* (Fig. 106), and **Small islands** the island of *Guam*, both of which belong to the United States. Far to the southwest of Hawaii, in the southern hemisphere, are the *Samoa Islands*, one of which, called *Tutuila*, belongs to us (Fig. 301).

The United States owns several other small islands in the Pacific Ocean. All of these islands are too small to have products of much value, but some of them are important as stopping points and coaling stations.

The small Republic of Panama (Fig. 133) owns the narrow strip of land, or **The Panama Canal Zone** *isthmus*, that connects North and South America. Across this Isthmus of Panama the United States government is now digging the

Panama Canal, through which even the largest ocean vessels will be able to pass.

By an agreement with the Republic of Panama, and by the payment of $10,000,000, our government has obtained control of the country for five miles on each side of the Canal. This is called the *Panama Canal Zone*. It is quite necessary that our government should control this strip of land, so as to protect its ships and the Canal.

Review Questions
1. Why did the purchase of Alaska seem unwise at first? 2. Show that it has already proved a wise purchase. 3. What about transportation there? 4. Name and locate the principal towns. Which is the capital? 5. Explain how Cuba and Porto Rico came under our guidance. 6. Name their chief products. 7. Name and locate the principal cities. 8. How did the Philippine Islands come into our possession? 9. Tell about their inhabitants. 10. What are their products? 11. What about their area, population, and principal city? 12. How did the Hawaiian Islands come under our control? 13. How are they of special value to us? 14. What are the products? 15. Name and locate the principal city. 16. What other distant islands belong to the United States, and how are they of value to us? 17. What is meant by the Panama Canal Zone? 18. Why should this be a dependency of the United States? 19. Name the dependencies of the United States. 20. Locate each on the map (Fig. 106). 21. In what zone is each?

Suggestions
1. Make a drawing of Alaska, and locate the places mentioned. 2. Learn more about the fur seal 3. Why has it probably been wise for the United States to take control of Porto Rico and the Philippines? 4. Which of our dependencies seems to you most valuable? Why?

IX. REVIEW OF THE UNITED STATES, WITH COMPARISONS

We have seen that the forty-eight states in our Union have been settled by people **Distribution of** who came from the East. **population** First, the Atlantic coast was settled by immigrants from England and other countries of Europe. Then there was a movement of pioneers westward across the Appalachian Mountains and

and most of our twenty-five largest cities, would be found *east* of this line.

While this line would pass through the middle of the country, the *center of population* would be to the east of it. It is a long distance east, too. You will find this point, in southeastern Indiana, marked by a star on the map (Fig. 204). There are just about as many persons in the United States living east of this star as west of it, and as many north of it as south. That is what is meant by the center of population. How far do you live from this point?

From the map (Fig. 204) you can tell what parts of the country are most densely settled. Where are they? What parts are least densely settled? From what you have learned, can you give the reasons in each case?

Of the great occupations in the United

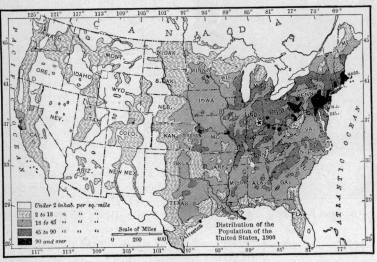

Fig. 204. — Distribution of population in the United States, 1900.

the Mississippi Valley. Finally, settlers pushed across the Western mountains, until the Pacific coast was reached. Now the ninety-two million persons in the United States are distributed over all parts of the country.

They are by no means evenly distributed. On Figure 204, if you drew a line from Galveston, Texas, directly northward, past Kansas City, Missouri, to our northern boundary, you would divide the United States into two nearly equal parts. But the number of people would not be divided equally, by any means. Far the greater number of them,

States, that of agriculture is **Agriculture** most important. More than one third of all the workers in our country are engaged in that one branch of industry.

Conditions in the United States are very favorable to agriculture. In no part, except on the highest **1. Climate** mountains, is it too cold to **and soil** raise valuable crops; and in most parts the soil is fertile. Name some states that have very fertile soil (pp. 122, 133). Name a section where the soil is not so good (p. 109). Why is hilly and mountainous country not well suited to farming (p. 109)?

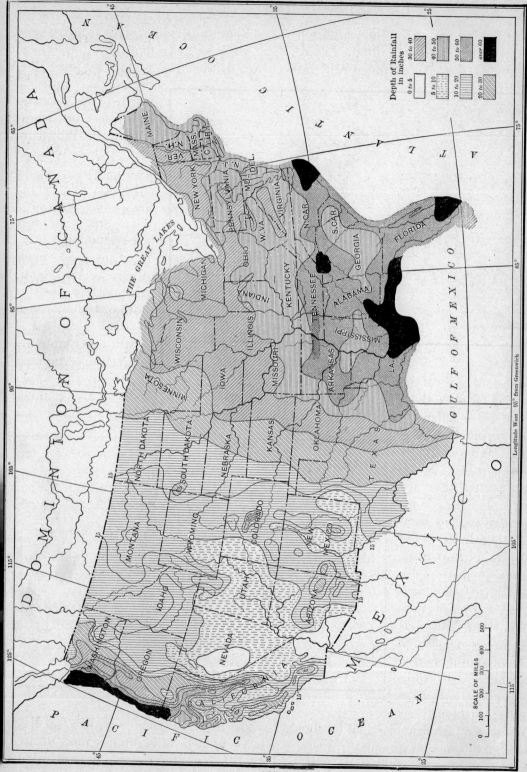

Fig. 205.— Rainfall map of the United States.

165

The lack of rain is the chief hindrance to farming in several of the states. Figure 205 shows how much rain falls

Other important products are raised in some sections more than in others. One of these is wheat. Figure 206 shows the states in which the largest quantities of wheat are grown. Which are they? For what is wheat used?

Figure 207 shows the same for corn. What states produce large amounts of it? What uses are made of corn? Why is the principal corn section south of that of wheat (p. 134)?

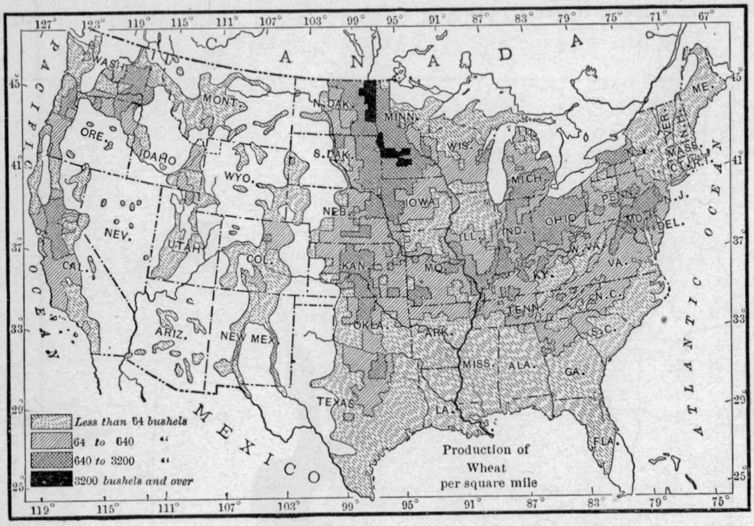

FIG. 206. — The wheat regions of the United States.

Still other crops are confined to certain sections of the country. What three very important farm products are confined to our Southern States? Name the

in different parts of our country. Which section receives the greatest amount? What states suffer for want of it? In what sections is irrigation extensively developed (p. 146)? Name some states that are partly deserts. Why do these regions have so little rain (p. 144)?

Certain important farm products are 2. Farm products found in almost every place where there is farming. One of these is hay; another cattle, together with milk and butter; a third is poultry; a fourth is potatoes; a fifth is apples. Why should these products be so common? Where is dairying prominent? Why there (p. 109)?

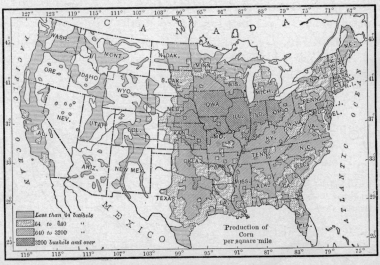

FIG. 207. — The corn regions of the United States.

states in which each is grown (pp. 122, 123). Which states produce most tobacco (p. 123)? Where else is it cultivated?

While fruits are common in all parts of the country, there are different kinds in different sections. Show, on Figure 208, what two states grow oranges, lemons, and other semitropical fruits, very extensively. What states grow large quantities of grapes?

The greatest number of hogs are raised in the states where there is much corn. Do you see the reason for this? What states, therefore, produce most hogs?

While cattle are found in very many states, Texas has a third more than Iowa, which ranks second in this respect; New York ranks third, and Kansas fourth. From what has been said, can you explain why these states raise so many cattle (p. 148)?

Sheep are likewise raised in many sections. The state that produces the greatest number is Wyoming, followed by Montana and Idaho. Why are there so many sheep in these states (p. 148)?

Although farming is by far our greatest industry, it is surprising what a small part of all our land is now really under cultivation.

3. Proportion of land that is cultivated

Figure 209 makes this clear by the use of a circle. The circle represents all the land in the United States, and the portion marked *improved* shows the part that is now used to produce crops. The part of the circle marked *unimproved* shows the proportion that has not yet been plowed, or otherwise improved, so as to raise crops. Some of it is swamp land, some is covered with forest or underbrush, some is used for grazing. From this figure it is plain that less than *one fourth* of all the land in our country is now really cultivated; and more than *one half* is not even in farms.

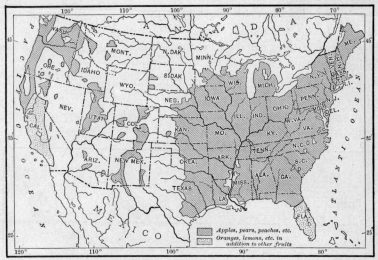

Fig. 208. — Map showing the sections of the country where fruit raising is extensively carried on.

One reason why there is so little cultivated land is that, as yet, only the best has been farmed. When there is more need of farms, some of the poorer land

4. Why so little land is under cultivation

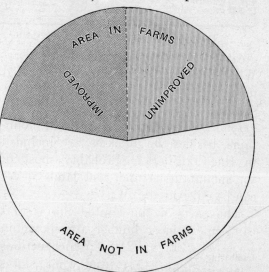

Fig. 209. — Extent of farming in the United States.

will be made to yield crops. There are two great difficulties, however. A large part of the portion of the circle marked *not in farms* represents the arid lands of the Western States. Locate these (p. 145). People will not be eager to receive farms there, even as a gift from the government, until they are able to irrigate them. What is the government now doing to make some of this land more attractive to settlers (p. 147)?

A second reason why much land must remain uncultivated is that there is a

country are furnishing the largest amount of lumber at the present time (pp. 110, 125, 135, 148)? What portions furnish little or none? Why?

In what sections of the United States is fishing an important industry (pp. 110, 125, 149)? What kinds of fish are caught in the different sections? What **Fishing** cities are extensively engaged in fishing? More persons are employed in this industry in Maryland and Virginia than in any other states. How can you explain that fact (p. 125)? There are only about one hundred and forty-three thousand people engaged in fishing in the country, while there are over ten million engaged in farming.

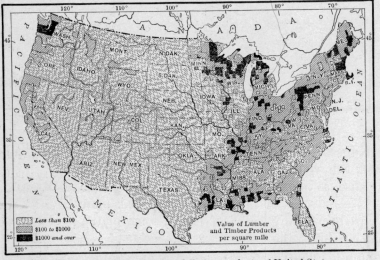

FIG. 210. — Value of lumber and timber products of United States.

great deal of mountainous country. What are the names of our principal mountain systems? Through what states do the Appalachian Mountains extend? The Cordillera? What mountains, besides the Rockies, are included in the Cordillera? Probably most of the mountainous and arid lands never can be cultivated. Why?

The parts of the United States that can supply most lumber are shown in **Lumbering** Figure 210. Which sections are they, and what states are included? What portions of the

Coal is the most important mineral found in the United **Mining** States. Of the two main kinds, far more of the bituminous coal is produced than of the anthracite. Figure 211 shows where coal is mined. In which state is the anthracite found? What important cities are in that vicinity? What states produce much soft coal? Why is coal of so great importance?

Iron ore is the mineral that ranks second in value. From Figure 211 tell in which states it is chiefly found. Name cities that depend very much upon coal and iron ore for their importance.

Copper ranks third in value. In what states is it mined in large quantities? Which city in Montana is a noted copper-mining center (p. 155)?

Gold ranks next to copper, and then comes silver. In what states are these precious metals chiefly found (p. 150)?

Fig. 211. — Distribution of coal and iron in the United States.

is it chiefly carried on? In what states is there extensive cotton manufacturing? What cities are noted for their flour mills?

Much the greater part of our ocean trade is Transportation and trade carried on with Europe. For this purpose good harbors are necessary along our eastern coast. Fortunately, that coast is well supplied with fine harbors. Name several of them (pp. 116–120 and 128–130).

The Pacific coast has few bays, and in many places the Coast Ranges rise directly from the water's edge. Thus, good harbors are few and widely scattered. There are several excellent ones, however. Name them (p. 152).

The amount of petroleum produced in the United States each year is valued at more than the gold, and the natural gas at more than the silver. Clay products are worth more than the gold and silver together, and the building stones and cement more than all the gold. Tell what you can about each of these mineral products.

Manufacturing ranks second among the great industries in the number of persons employed. In Figure 212 are shown the parts of the country that do a large amount of manufacturing. What sections do most of it? What can you tell about the manufacturing in the Northeastern States (p. 112)? In the Southern States (p. 126)? In the Central States (p. 136)? In the Western States (p. 151)?

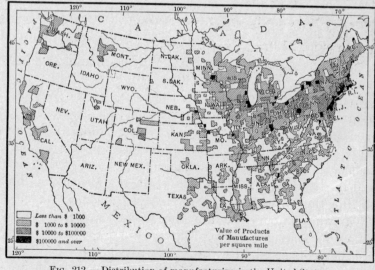

Fig. 212. — Distribution of manufacturing in the United States.

The greatest manufacturing industry is that of iron and steel. In what cities

Named in the order of their commerce, the seven principal ocean ports of the

United States are as follows: (1) New York; (2) Galveston; (3) Boston; (4) Philadelphia; (5) New Orleans; (6) Baltimore; (7) San Francisco. Locate each of these. The two Puget Sound ports together rank higher than Baltimore. What are their names?

Most of the rivers of the Northeastern States are not of much value for navi-

FIG. 213. — Map to show the navigable interior water routes of the United States.

gation (Fig. 213). Why (p. 116)? Yet there is one notable exception. Which is it?

Which river in the United States is of greatest importance for navigation? About how long is it (p. 258)? What large tributaries has it? What important cities are located on the main river and its tributaries? In which state is each of these cities?

Of what importance are the Great Lakes for navigation (p. 138)? How are they connected with New York City by water? What important cities are located on these lakes? Trace the water route from Duluth, or Chicago, to New York City.

In what ways will the Panama Canal be of importance to the United States (p. 152)?

From Figure 214 what do you observe about the number of railroads in the East? In the South? In the Central States? What great railroad centers can you find on this map?

The ten largest cities in the United States, named in order of their size, are as follows: (1) New York; (2) Chicago; (3) Philadelphia; (4) St. Louis; (5) Boston; (6) Cleveland; (7) Baltimore; (8) Pittsburgh; (9) Detroit; (10) Buffalo. Locate each of these. Give some reason why each has become so important.

Leading centers of manufacture and commerce

Name and locate other important centers of manufacturing in the Northeastern States; in the Southern States; in the Central States; in the Western States.

Name the dependencies of the United States. Locate each on the map (Fig. 106); on a globe. What important products are furnished by them? What products do some of them supply, which cannot be raised in large quantities in our own country? Give other reasons why these dependencies are of value to us. Which are in the Torrid Zone?

Dependencies

Write the names of our dependencies, arranging them, as nearly as you can, in the order of their importance.

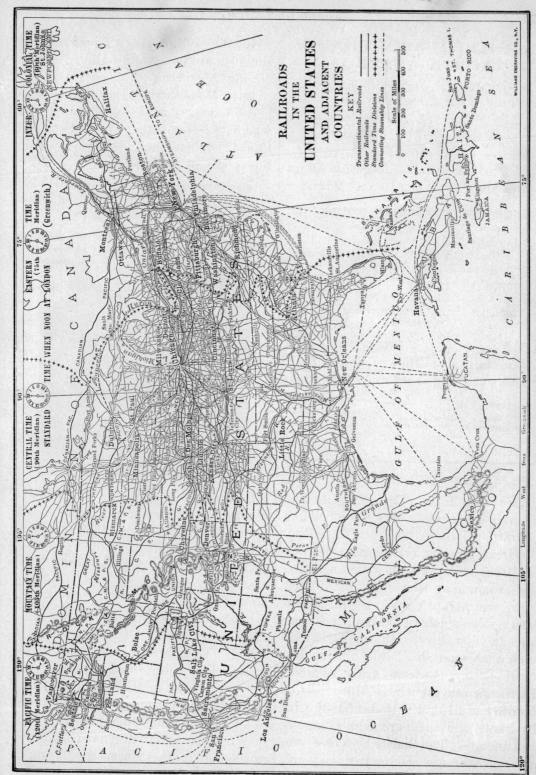

FIG. 214. — Map showing the railroads of the United States.

X. OTHER COUNTRIES OF NORTH AMERICA

1. Canada, and Other Countries North of Us

1. What parts of the boundary line between the United States and Canada are natural (Fig. 133)? **Map study** 2. In what zones does Canada lie? What can you say about its climate? 3. What can you tell from the map about its rivers and lakes? About its mountains? 4. Into what large river do the Great Lakes empty? 5. What Falls are in the river between Lake Erie and Lake Ontario (Fig. 136)? 6. How must these Falls hinder shipping? 7. Which one of the Great Lakes lies wholly within the United States? 8. How near are Detroit and Buffalo to Canada? 9. Locate Newfoundland. 10. Locate Greenland.

(1) *Canada*

Canada is about the size of the United States, including Alaska; yet its population is less than eight **Area, population, and government** million, or not so large as that of our single state of Pennsylvania.

Canada includes nine provinces that correspond, in a way, to our states. Together they form a Union, called the *Dominion of Canada*, which is much like our own Union. Although it is a *colony* of Great Britain, as you have learned (p. 102), the people make their own laws, and are quite as independent as we are.

A large part of Canada is really waste land. The northern portion, including many islands in the Arctic **Why settled chiefly in the southern part** zone, has hardly any inhabitants except a few Eskimos. Farther south there is a broad belt of forest (Fig. 215). This also has few inhabitants, and these are mainly hunters and Indians. The climate here is severe, and much of the soil is too rocky and sterile for agriculture

In the southern part, however, the summers are long and warm, like those of our Northern States. As in our country, too, there is much good soil here, and there is plenty of rain everywhere except in the west. Southern Canada is, therefore, the section in which the people are mainly found.

FIG. 215. — A moose in the woods of Canada.

Since southern Canada is so much like our Northern States, the same products are found in the two regions. For example, in the **Agriculture** east, as in New England, much of the land is not suited to farming. Yet there is good soil in many places, where fruits, vegetables, and other farm products are raised. There is also much dairying, as in New England.

Farther west, in the province of Ontario, the farm products resemble those of New York and Ohio. There is extensive fruit raising; also dairying, grain raising, and other forms of farming. This is one of the most fertile parts of

FIG. 216. — Farmers at work in the fertile wheat fields of western Canada, near Winnipeg.

Canada, and one of the most densely settled.

Still farther west, the great open plains of the Red River Valley extend northward into Canada. This section, like North Dakota and Minnesota (p. 133), has come to be one of the best wheat-producing regions in the world (Fig. 216). West of this is the region of dry plains. Here, as in Montana (p. 148), cattle and sheep raising are important industries.

The forest that we found covering much of northern New England, extends into **Lumbering** Canada, and, stretching westward north of the Great Lakes, forms one of the greatest forests in the world. Altogether about one third of the surface of Canada is covered with timber. Lumbering is, therefore, a very important industry.

In eastern Canada, as in New England, many men engage in fishing, catching **Fishing** codfish, halibut, mackerel, and other fish. On the Pacific coast the catching of salmon is the leading fishing industry, as in Oregon, Washington (p. 149), and Alaska (p. 159).

Mining is less extensive in Canada **Mining and** than in the United States, **manufacturing** although many valuable minerals are found there. Gold, silver, and other minerals are mined in the western mountains, as they are farther south in the United States. This mineral belt extends far north, too, for you will remember that the Klondike region is in Canada (p. 159).

The section north of Lake Superior contains valuable minerals, like that south of it (p. 135). Some very rich silver mines have been discovered in central Canada north of the Great Lakes. Iron ore is also found in this region and in eastern Canada.

There is good coal in Nova Scotia, on the Atlantic coast, and coal is also found in the western mountains; but it is wanting in the central part of Canada. This lack of coal in central Canada interferes somewhat with manufacturing there. Yet there is much water power, and coal can be obtained either from the United States or from Nova Scotia by way of the St. Lawrence River. The chief manufacturing section is in the southeast, from Lake Huron eastward.

You have already learned how important the Great Lakes are to the commerce of the United States. They **Transporta-** are of equal value to Canada, **tion** but Canada has one advantage over us. It has connection with the sea by way of the St. Lawrence River. This water route is of so great importance that the Canadian government has built ship railways in the more settled parts, including the Grand Trunk line and the Canadian Pacific (Fig. 214).

Copyright, 1906, by Wm. Notman & Son, Montreal.

FIG. 217. — A steamer going down the Lachine Rapids just above Montreal. It must take the canal around these rapids in going upstream.

canals around the rapids (Fig. 217) in the rivers. Thus, by river, canal, and lake, large vessels can go from the Atlantic Ocean all the way to the western end of Lake Superior.

Canada has an excellent system of

FIG. 218. — A view over the city of Montreal, with the broad St. Lawrence River in the distance.

The largest city of Canada is MONTREAL (Fig. 218), on the St. Lawrence River. Large ocean vessels can go up the river to Montreal, but because of rapids (Fig. 217) they can get no farther. Only lake vessels, and such others as are small enough to pass through the canals, can go above that point. This makes Montreal, like Buffalo, a place where goods must be transferred from one kind of boat to another. It is also a place to which raw products can be easily brought, and

Principal centers of manufacture and commerce

1. On the interior waterways

from which manufactured goods can be shipped. Montreal is, therefore, a very busy city, with much manufacturing and commerce.

A short distance west of Montreal, on the Ottawa River, is the city of OTTAWA, the capital of Canada. It is located at a point on the river where there is a large fall, supplying water power for use in sawmills and other factories.

On the St. Lawrence River below Montreal is QUEBEC, one of the most quaint cities on the continent. It was founded many years ago by the French, and the French language is still in common use there.

Another large city on the great interior waterway is TORONTO, which lies on the northern shore of Lake Ontario, opposite the mouth of the Niagara River. It is a busy manufacturing and shipping center.

On the Atlantic coast are the two seaports of HALIFAX and ST. JOHN, **2. Other cities** and on the Pacific coast, VICTORIA and VANCOUVER. Locate these cities. Each of them has extensive commerce. WINNIPEG, far in the interior, and away from the Great Lakes waterway, reminds us of Minneapolis, for it is in the midst of the Red River Valley wheat region, and is an important flour-milling center.

(2) Newfoundland

Only one part of the British territory to the north of us has refused to join the Dominion of Canada. This is Newfoundland, including the island by that name and a narrow strip of the Labrador coast.

The capital of the colony is ST. JOHN'S, and the principal industry is fishing. Near the island of Newfoundland, and along the Labrador coast, there are extensive shallows, called *banks*, on which cod, halibut, and other fish live.

To these fishing banks vessels come from Europe, and from the fishing ports of eastern United States and Canada, as well as from Newfoundland.

(3) Greenland

There are a number of islands north of Canada in the Arctic zone. They are, for the most part, desert lands, and almost uninhabited.

Even in summer, floating ice is usually in sight. Some of the ice is that which has formed on the surface of the sea during the winter. There are also much larger masses, called *icebergs* (Fig. 219), which sometimes rise as much as two or three hundred feet above the

FIG. 219. — An iceberg floating in the Arctic Ocean. This huge mass of ice rises nearly two hundred feet above the water.

surface of the water. These icebergs have broken off from the vast masses of ice, called *glaciers*, that move down to the sea from the frozen lands of the North.

Most of the large icebergs come from the immense island of Greenland, which is almost entirely covered by a thick ice sheet. No land can be seen anywhere excepting along the coast, all the rest being buried beneath the vast glacier. A few Eskimos live along the coast, and also a few Europeans, called Danes, who have come from Denmark, a country in Europe which owns Greenland.

2. Mexico, and Other Countries South of Us

1. What does Figure 134 tell you about the highlands and lowlands of Mexico? (Notice the rivers.) 2. Find the capital of Mexico (Fig. 133). 3. In what **Map study** zones does the country lie? 4. Does its coast line suggest few or many good harbors? Why? 5. What is the distance across the central part of the country from east to west? 6. What

water lies south of Mexico? What land southeast? 7. Name the four largest islands in the West Indies.

(1) *Mexico*

Mexico is about one fourth as large as the United States, and has less than one

Area, population, and government

sixth as many inhabitants. Like the United States, it is an independent country and a republic. It consists of nearly thirty states that form a union similar to ours.

FIG. 220. — Colima, one of the Mexican volcanoes, in eruption. The column of steam and ashes is two or three miles high. The white patch on the side of the mountain is a lava flow.

The Tropic of Cancer crosses Mexico north of its central part, showing that

Why much of the country has not a tropical climate

a large portion of the country is in the tropical zone. Yet Mexico has a much cooler climate than this fact

suggests. The reason is that much of the country is very high land; and, as you have learned (p. 25), the climate is cooler on such land.

The Cordillera of western United States extend into Mexico, and there are broad plateaus, often over a mile in height, crossed by mountain ranges which rise even more than another mile. Several of the loftiest peaks are volcanoes, made of lava (Fig. 220); and some of the peaks are so high that they are always covered with snow, in spite of the fact that they lie in the torrid zone. From these facts it is plain that the climate of Mexico is tropical only along the lowlands near the coast.

There is heavy rainfall along the eastern coast, and in the southern part. In the central and western

The wet and dry parts

parts, on the other hand, the land is drier, and in places even a desert. This is an extension of the arid belt of western United States.

With such differences in temperature and rainfall, we may expect a variety of products from the soil.

Products

1. Agricultural products and lumber

A journey from the east coast of Mexico to the interior shows this variety. Starting on the lowland, where it is very hot and damp, tropical crops are found. Here also are dense tropical forests containing such valuable woods as rosewood, ebony, and mahogany.

Passing up the slopes of the plateau, one reaches a cooler climate where extensive coffee plantations are found (Fig. 221); and there, also, sugar cane, cotton, and tobacco are raised. Farther westward, and higher up on the plateau, only the crops of the warm temperate climate, such as wheat, corn, and grapes are cultivated.

Still farther on, the climate becomes so dry that even these cannot be raised without irrigation. After that, until the mountains are reached, the country is mainly arid, being fit only for cattle, horses, and sheep, and having few inhabitants except on the oases.

Much of the mountain region is too cold and rocky for farming; but, as in

Fig. 221. — Mexicans spreading out coffee to dry. The entire ground is covered with the coffee berries.

our Western States, these moun

2. **Minerals** tains yield valuable metals, especially silver. Indeed, Mexico produces more silver than any other country in the world, except the United States. There are also gold, copper, and lead mines.

There is not much manufacturing in Mexico, for two rea

3. **Manufactures** sons. One is that good coal is not abundant. A second is that many of the people are too ignorant and lazy to manage machinery.

This country was once owned by Spain, as you know (p. 101); but only one person in five is a Spaniard. The rest of the people are either Indians and Negroes, or else Spaniards with Indian or Negro blood in their veins, called *half-breeds*. Very few of the Indians are civilized,

and many of the half-breeds are uneducated, and cannot be trusted to handle machinery. Mexico is, however, advancing very rapidly.

The capital and largest city of the republic is MEXICO, located in the central part of the country. How **Chief cities** does it differ in its location from most of the large cities so far studied?

On the eastern side the coast is regular, as you can see on the map, so that there are few harbors. VERA CRUZ is the chief seaport, but its harbor is poor.

(2) Central America

The region southeast of Mexico is divided into several small

Fig. 222. — Bunches of bananas piled by the side of the railroad, awaiting shipment.

countries, called the countries of Central America (Fig. 133). Their **The countries** names are British Hondu- **and their forms** ras, Guatemala, Honduras, **of government** Salvador, Nicaragua, Costa Rica, and Panama.

What have you already learned about

N

Panama (p. 163)? British Honduras is a colony of Great Britain. The others are republics, each having a government and capital of its own.

Neither the countries nor the cities are of much importance. Spanish is the *The inhabitants and products* language spoken in all of them, and, as in Mexico, the people are mainly Indians, Negroes, and half-breeds.

islands, at some distance from the coast, which form a group, or *archipelago*, called the West Indies.

The four largest islands are sometimes called the *Greater Antilles*. What is the name of each (Fig. 133)? *The three groups of islands* What have you already learned about two of these (p. 160)? A third, Haiti, is divided into two independent Negro republics, while

FIG. 223. — Native women of Jamaica going to market, each with a burro, or small donkey, loaded with baskets of vegetables and fruits.

The main products are tropical fruits (Fig. 222), sugar cane, coffee, and tobacco. Large sections are covered by tropical forests from which valuable hard woods, dyes, and rubber are obtained.

(3) *The West Indies*

Besides the countries on the mainland of the continent, there are numerous

Jamaica, the fourth, is a colony belonging to Great Britain.

North of the Greater Antilles lies a group of low coral islands, called the *Bahamas*, which also belong to Great Britain. From Porto Rico southward to South America is a chain of small islands, known as the *Lesser Antilles*, which belong to Great Britain, France, and other countries of Europe.

FIG. 224.

The boundary of Ecuador is in dispute.

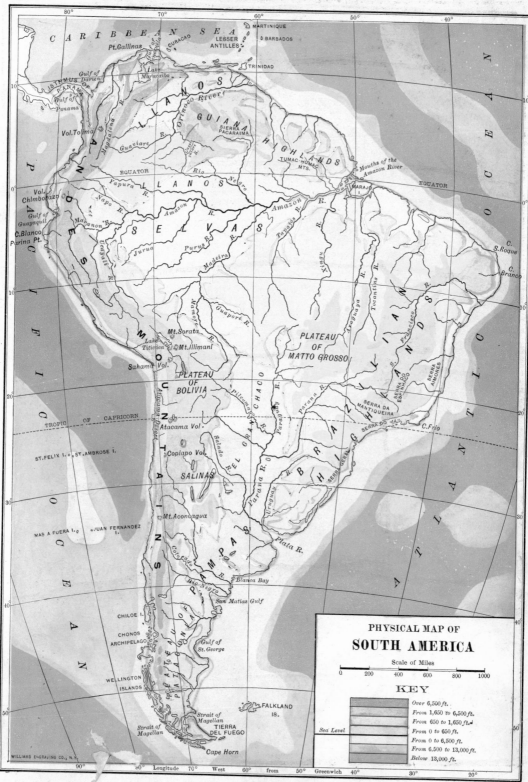

PHYSICAL MAP OF
SOUTH AMERICA
Scale of Miles

0   200   400   600   800   1000

KEY

	Over 6,500 ft.
	From 1,650 to 6,500 ft.
	From 650 to 1,650 ft.
	From 0 to 650 ft.
Sea Level	From 0 to 6,500 ft.
	From 6,500 to 13,000 ft.
	Below 13,000 ft.

WILLIAMS ENGRAVING CO., N.Y.

FIG. 225.

Like the Hawaiian Islands, the Lesser Antilles are mostly volcanoes rising above the water. In 1902, one of these volcanoes, Mt. Pelé, on the island of Martinique, burst forth in a terrible eruption which killed over twenty-five thousand people. In a few seconds the beautiful city of St. Pierre was completely destroyed, and only one person escaped almost instant death.

The principal product of the West Indies is sugar cane; but tobacco, coffee, cocoa, spices, and fruits —

Their products especially bananas, oranges, and pineapples — are also grown in abundance. Valuable tropical woods are supplied by the forests. There is very little manufacturing, and, with the exception of Havana, in Cuba, there is no very large city.

3. The Bermuda Islands

Far out in the open ocean, east of North Carolina, is a group of very small coral islands, called the *Bermuda Islands*, which belong to Great Britain (Fig. 133). They produce early vegetables and flowers, such as Easter lilies, most of which are shipped to New York.

The climate is so mild that these islands are visited every winter by large numbers of people from the United States who wish to escape the cold of our Northern winter.

Review Questions 1. Compare Canada with the United States in area and population. 2. What about its government? 3. Why is it settled chiefly in the southern part? 4. Tell about its agriculture. 5. About the lumber industry. 6. The fishing. 7. Mining and manufacturing. 8. What about transportation? 9. Name, locate, and tell the chief facts about each of the large cities. 10. State the principal facts about Newfoundland. 11. About Greenland. 12. How does Mexico compare with the United States in area and population? 13. What kind of government has it? 14. Why is it not a very hot country in most parts? What about its rainfall? 15. Tell about its agricultural products and lumber. 16. What minerals does it produce? 17. Why has it little manufacturing? 18. Name and locate the principal cities. 19. Name the countries of Central America. 20. What are their forms of government? 21. Tell about the inhabitants. 22. What are the products? 23. What three groups of islands make up the West Indies? 24. Locate each group. 25. What are the principal products of these islands? 26. Give some facts about the Bermuda Islands.

Suggestions 1. What difficulty had to be met in building the Welland Canal between Lakes Erie and Ontario? How was it overcome? 2. What difficulties must the Canadian Pacific Railway meet in running its trains in winter? 3. How can you explain the fact that there are no large cities along the great Mackenzie River in Canada? 4. Read Longfellow's poem, "Evangeline"; the scene of the story is in Nova Scotia. 5. Why are there no large rivers in Mexico? 6. Name three or four large cities in the United States that, like Mexico City, are not located on any important water route.

XI. SOUTH AMERICA

Map study 1. Compare South America with North America in shape. 2. What great mountain range extends along the western side? 3. Name the countries of South America. 4. Which one is largest? 5. Which is second in size? 6. What is the coldest part of South America? 7. Which part of the continent lies in the tropical zone? 8. Which part has a climate very much like our own? 9. When does Argentina have winter (p. 92)? 10. Name the three principal rivers. Locate each.

South America is nearly as large as North America, and has been known **Area and population** quite as long; for it was discovered by Columbus on his third voyage, and one of its northern countries is named after him. Find it on the map. Yet South America has only about one third as many inhabitants as North America.

There was no way of knowing, at first, which of the two continents in the

New World would be settled the more rapidly. Yet there are several reasons why South America might have been expected to develop as rapidly as North America.

Why more rapid settlement might have been expected

One reason is the fact that the two are similar in several important respects: (1) they have the same general shape; (2) each has its highest mountains on the western side; (3) each has broad, fertile plains; and (4) in each there are large,

1. Resemblance to North America

FIG. 226. — A view in Ecuador, showing tropical foliage.

navigable rivers reaching into the very heart of the continent.

In some respects South America has important advantages over North America. No part of South America extends into the frigid zone; but a large part of Canada, the largest country in North America, is so cold that no crops can be raised.

2. Advantages over North America

Second, the rain-bearing winds, which blow mainly from the Atlantic, water most of South America abundantly. A narrow strip on the western side of the Andes Mountains, and a part of Argentina, where west winds blow, are the only arid and desert sections. This is very different from North America, where, as you remember, a large portion of the West is arid.

In addition, large quantities of gold and silver were discovered in South America much earlier than in North America. Adventurers in search of the precious metals thronged into South America hundreds of years before the rush for California gold took place. That gave an early start to immigration.

In spite of these facts, the settlement of South America has been very slow, compared with that of North America.

Why settlement has not been rapid

1. Because of the climate

One of the most important reasons is the climate. While no part of the continent lies in the very cold belt, much more than half of it is in the torrid zone (Fig. 226). Note where the equator and the Tropic of Capricorn cross the continent. What does the latter line tell you (p. 91)? Where must the Tropic of Cancer be?

Although vegetation thrives in the torrid zone, it is not a good place for people to live. The dampness and heat make it difficult for people to work, and even cause serious sickness. There is, however, little need for work, for it is easy to get food, clothing, and shelter where vegetation is so abundant. This tends to make men lazy. That kind of climate is certainly not attractive, especially to people from countries, such as those of Europe, which have a temperate climate; yet European countries are the ones from which immigrants would have come.

The most prosperous countries in the

Fig. 227. — A view in the lofty Andes Mountains of Chile. Here the surface is very rough and rocky, and snow remains all the year round.

world are in the temperate zone, but only the smaller part of South America lies in that zone, as you can see (Fig. 116). What countries are included in it? Most of the people of South America live either in these countries or else on the plateaus and mountain slopes, which, as you know, have a cool climate, even though in the tropical zone.

A second reason for the slow settlement is the lack of coal. Some coal is found there, it is true, but very little is **2. Because of the lack of coal** mined. The importance of coal for manufacturing has already been seen in our study of the United States. Without that mineral our country would not have developed so many industries, nor have attracted such great numbers of immigrants.

Most of the coast of South America is very straight, so that there are few **3. Because of the lack of harbors** bays and harbors. Compare North and South America in this respect. The western coast is especially straight, and for long distances there are no harbors at all. Moreover, the lofty Andes rise, like a great wall, almost out of the ocean, so

that it is very difficult to carry goods from the western seacoast to the interior (Fig. 227).

Thus the scarcity of good harbors, as well as the lack of coal, is unfavorable to manufacturing and commerce. Yet these are two occupations that attract and support large numbers of people.

A fourth reason for the small population of South America is the kind of people who live there. All of the continent was once **4. Because of the kind of people there** owned by Spain and Portugal, and the languages of these countries are still spoken there, Portuguese being used only in Brazil. Like Mexico and Central America, the South American countries have rebelled, and now all but the Guianas are independent republics.

Some of the people are Spanish or Portuguese, but far more are Negroes, Indians, and half-breeds. More than half of all the South American people can neither read nor write. In some of the countries, too, the people have been very quarrelsome, and have spent much of their time in fighting instead of developing industries. On account of so much ignorance, and so many rebellions, Europeans have not been so attracted to South America as to North America. Of late, however, there has been great improvement, and some of the countries have developed very rapidly.

1. Argentina, Uruguay, and Paraguay

From what has been said you can, perhaps, pick out the most progressive countries of South America. They lie in the temperate zone.

Argentina, the leading one, is the nation of South America that most reminds us of our own. It is only about one third as large as the United States, to be sure, but it has the same variety of climate from east to west. There is plenty of rain in the northeast, while in the interior there are broad stretches of arid plains. From north to south there is a great difference in temperature, even greater than in our country. As in the United States, much of Argentina consists of plains, with lofty mountains in the west.

Comparison of Argentina with United States

Argentina is one of the greatest wheat-producing countries in the world, and other grains are common. In the north the climate is so warm that tobacco, sugar cane, cotton, and tropical fruits are raised.

Its products

On the treeless plains of the interior, called *pampas*, there is excellent grass, and one of the chief industries there is cattle and sheep raising. This reminds us of the arid parts of western United States. Argentina is also one of the leading cattle and sheep countries of the world.

Paraguay and Uruguay have much the same products as Argentina, being especially noted for their cattle and sheep. Paraguay also has a number of tropical products, as you might expect. Why?

Paraguay and Uruguay

The Parana River and its tributaries form excellent highways for commerce with the interior, as do the Mississippi and its tributaries in North America. BUENOS AIRES, at its mouth, is the largest city in South America, having over a million inhabitants. MONTEVIDEO, in Uruguay, is about the size of Pittsburgh.

Transportation and centers of commerce

Both of these cities are important seaports, exporting the products of the region to Europe and North America. Buenos Aires is a busy, modern city, with many fine buildings, quite like some of our best American cities. It has much manufacturing as well as commerce.

2. Brazil

Brazil is the one country in South America that formerly belonged to Portugal, and the Portuguese language is still spoken there.

It is a much larger country than Argentina, being even larger than the United States. Yet it has less than one fifth as many inhabitants as our country, and of these, less than one half are white men.

Area and population

A large part of Brazil, including much of the valley of the Amazon and its tributaries, is covered with dense tropical forests, through which one can scarcely make his way without first cutting a path. Few people except Indians live here, and, although large boats can go far up the Amazon and its tribu-

The tropical forest and its products

taries, there is not a single large city in this entire valley. How different it is in the valley of the Mississippi!

The Indians live mainly by hunting and fishing, or by picking the tropical fruits from the trees and bushes. The rubber tree grows

FIG. 228. — A view of the city and harbor of Rio de Janeiro.

in the tropical forest, and also the cocoa tree, from whose seed chocolate is made. Great quantities of rubber are shipped from PARA, at the mouth of the Amazon.

Most of the inhabitants of Brazil live in the eastern and southern parts.

The more settled part and its products Much of this section is a plateau, crossed by low mountains. Because of the elevation the temperature is much more agreeable than in the Amazon Valley; and, as you will see from the map, the very southern portion lies in the temperate zone.

The chief industry is farming. Besides grain, the crops of the warm temperate and tropical climates thrive, especially tropical fruits, cotton, sugar cane, tobacco, and coffee. The last is most important. Many cattle are raised.

Valuable minerals, including gold, diamonds, and some coal, are found in the plateau region of Brazil. Indeed, this is one of the principal diamond-producing countries in the world. Manufacturing is rapidly developing in eastern and southern Brazil.

Centers of commerce The most important cities are on the coast, by far the largest being RIO DE JANEIRO, the capital (Fig. 228). SÃO PAULO, which lies to the southwest, back from the coast, is second in size among the cities of Brazil. BAHIA and PERNAMBUCO, farther north on the coast, are third and fourth. Rio de Janeiro is the second city in size in South America. Which is the first? It has a splendid harbor, and is a very busy seaport.

3. The Andean Countries

The countries in the western part of South America are very mountainous,

FIG. 229. — A group of llamas, the beasts of burden of the lofty Andes.

for the Andes rise from the seacoast and extend all the way from Panama to Cape Horn. Which **Facts about the Andes Mountains** country stretches fully half of this distance? Which is next longest?

Although these mountains are not so broad as the Cordillera of North America, they form one of the longest and highest mountain chains in the world. The loftiest peak is Aconcagua in Argentina, which rises 22,860 feet above sea level. The loftiest in North America is Mt. McKinley in Alaska, which is almost half a mile lower (20,460 ft.), or about the height of Mt. Chimborazo in Ecuador.

These lofty mountains are even now growing higher. Now and then, as they are slowly pushed upward, the rocks break apart and severe earthquakes result. This region has been visited by some of the most terrible earthquakes in the world's history, destroying many lives and buildings. Besides that, some of the

Fig. 230. — A view of Arequipa in Peru, at the base of one of the volcanic cones of the Andes.

highest peaks are volcanoes (Fig. 230) from which lava and ash are at times sent forth.

Rich deposits of precious metal were found in the Andes soon after the dis-**Valuable minerals** covery of South America, and this was the principal reason why the Spaniards took possession of so much of the continent. Hundreds of millions of dollars' worth of gold and silver have been taken out of the rocks of the Andean chain, and every year large quantities are still mined.

You will notice that one of the Andean countries lies mainly in the south tem-

perate zone, as Argentina does. Which one is it? You will readily understand, therefore, why *Chile* is the **The leading country and its products** most progressive country on the west coast. How long is this country? About how wide?

Although it is so long and narrow, and so mountainous, Chile has much good farm land. The crops range from the grains of the cold temperate climate to the products of the tropical zone. There is also much grazing land. The cool climate of the southern part is favorable to work, and the people of Chile, like those of Argentina, are engaged in various kinds of manufacturing.

Name the other countries in western South America. Which has sea-**Other countries and their products** coast on both oceans? Which has no seacoast? Which is crossed by the equator? (*Ecuador* is a Spanish word for equator.) Which countries in South America lie entirely in the tropical zone? Which lie partly in this zone?

In southern Peru and northern Chile, the climate is so arid that there are extensive deserts; but elsewhere an abundance of rain falls. There are also great differences in temperature. For example, in central Peru the lower lands, near the coast, are very hot and damp; but as one climbs the mountain slopes, it rapidly becomes cooler. Only tropical plants grow near the coast, producing tropical woods, rubber, cocoa, coffee, and sugar; but grains and other crops of temperate climates are raised higher up the mountain sides.

Since Chile is the leading Andean country, it is natural that it should have **The principal cities** the largest city on the Pacific coast. SANTIAGO is that city, being the capital of Chile, and having a population of one third of a million. It is situated fifty miles inland, and half a mile above the level of the sea. VAL-PARAISO, the largest and busiest port on the Pacific coast, is also in Chile. It is about half the size of Santiago. Name the capitals and chief seaports of the other Andean countries.

4. Venezuela and Guiana

North of Brazil is Venezuela, which includes most of the Orinoco Valley. Here are broad plains, called *llanos*, which produce excellent grass, so that cattle raising is one of the leading industries. Coffee and cocoa are also raised. Tropical woods and rubber, as well as minerals, are other products of this country. What is the capital?

Just north of the mouth of the Orinoco River is Trinidad Island, which belongs to Great Britain. On that island is a pitch lake, from which much of the asphalt used in our street pavements is obtained.

Guiana is divided into three parts, which are colonies of three nations of Europe. What are the names of the parts? What are the names of the countries that own them? The products of these regions are similar to those of Venezuela.

1. Compare North and South America in area and population. 2. Why might South America have been expected to have been settled as rapidly as North America? 3. Give several reasons why it has not been settled so rapidly. 4. Compare Argentina with the United States as to area, climate, and surface features. **Review Questions**

5. What are its principal products? 6. What are the conveniences for transportation? 7. What large cities are located here? 8. Tell about Paraguay and Uruguay. 9. Compare Brazil with the United States in area and population. 10. Give some facts about the tropical forest and its products. 11. About the more settled part and its products. 12. Name and locate the chief centers of commerce. 13. What can you tell about the Andes Mountains? 14. About their minerals? 15. Name the leading Andean country and its products. 16. What about the other Andean countries and their products? 17 Name and locate the principal cities in western South America. 18. State some facts about Venezuela. 19. About Trinidad Island. 20. Guiana.

1. Make a sand model of South America, showing the highlands and lowlands. 2. Read about Pizarro's conquest of Peru. 3. Find out something about the **Suggestions** Inca Indians. 4. What are the five leading

FIG. 231.—Native women of Venezuela washing clothes along the water front.

cities of South America? 5. Compare South America with North America in regard to distance from Europe. Which has the advantage in this respect for immigration? 6. Will the Panama Canal be of importance to us in our trade with any part of South America? Examine a globe to see. 7. If the southern end of Chile were placed at San Diego in California, where in North America would the northern end reach? 8. Draw an outline map of South America, putting in the mountain ranges, chief

...ers, and cities. Add the boundaries and names of the several countries. 9. Name and locate the capital of each South American country.

XII. EUROPE

1. Trace the boundary line between Europe and Asia, naming the mountains and waters **Map study** that help to form it. 2. How does the coast line of Europe compare in regularity with that of South America? Of North America? 3. Name the largest peninsulas, and draw an outline map to show them. 4. Where are the highest mountains? 5. Where are the plains? Which very large country is made up mainly of plains? 6. In what zones is Europe? 7. Point out those countries of Europe in which some of the people that you know used to live. 8. What route did they probably take in order to reach America? 9. Walk toward Europe.

1. General Facts about Europe

You have already learned (p. 95) that Eurasia is the largest land mass on **Eurasia** the earth. It extends northward far within the Arctic Circle, and southward almost to the equator. From east to west it reaches nearly halfway around the earth. Show this on a globe. It is much larger than North and South America together.

Eurasia is the most irregular of all the lands, having many large peninsulas. **The peninsula** Name four or five of these. **called *Europe*** The largest of all is the one we call *Europe*. Notice on the map (Fig. 232) that water borders Europe on the southern, western, and northern sides, making it a peninsula. What are the names of the bodies of water that so nearly surround Europe?

It is not easy to tell just where to draw the boundary between Europe and Asia. Indeed, some maps show one boundary line, some another. Trace the boundary, and tell what parts are natural (p. 102), and what parts artificial. Although joined to Asia on the east, it is common to class the peninsula of Europe as one of the continents.

Make a list of the different countries that you find on the map of Europe. How many are there? Each **Why so many** of these has its own lan- **countries, with** guage, so that a person **different languages** living in one country cannot understand what is said in another, unless he has learned its language.

Some of the reasons for so many countries and languages are easy to understand. For instance, it is plain why the British **1. Because** **the water** Isles should form a separate **often separates** nation. Being surrounded **the people** by water, and thus cut off from other people, the British have remained independent, and formed a language of their own.

Italy is *nearly* surrounded by water; and on the north, where there is no water, the Alps Mountains **2. Or water and** rise, like a great wall, shut- **mountains sepa-** ting out people on that side. **rate them** Italy has, therefore, developed a government and language of its own. Note how many other countries of Europe are on peninsulas. Name them.

The water and mountains have had much influence in breaking Europe up into so many countries with different languages. In times past, when there were no railroads, and there was little travel, each lot of people, thus separated from others, learned to govern themselves and speak a separate language.

There is a third important reason for so many countries and languages. Hun-

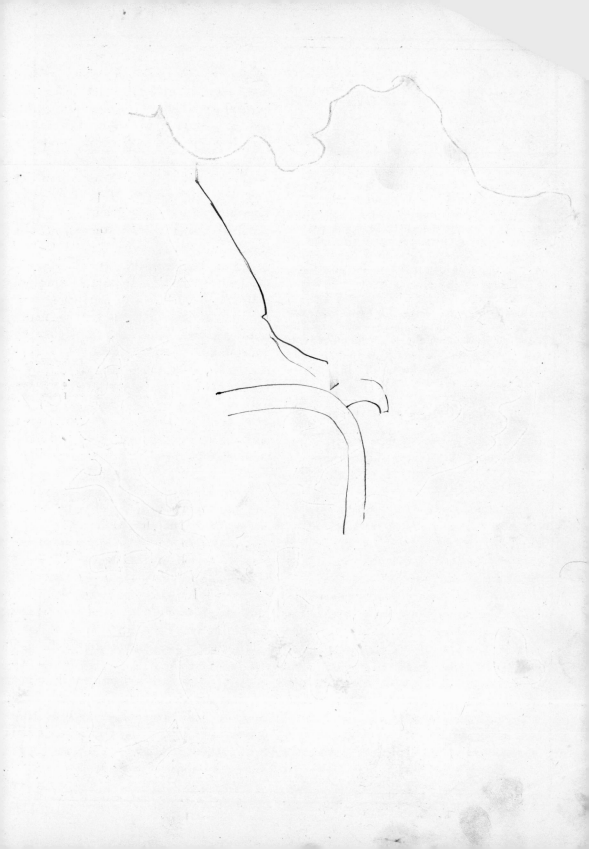

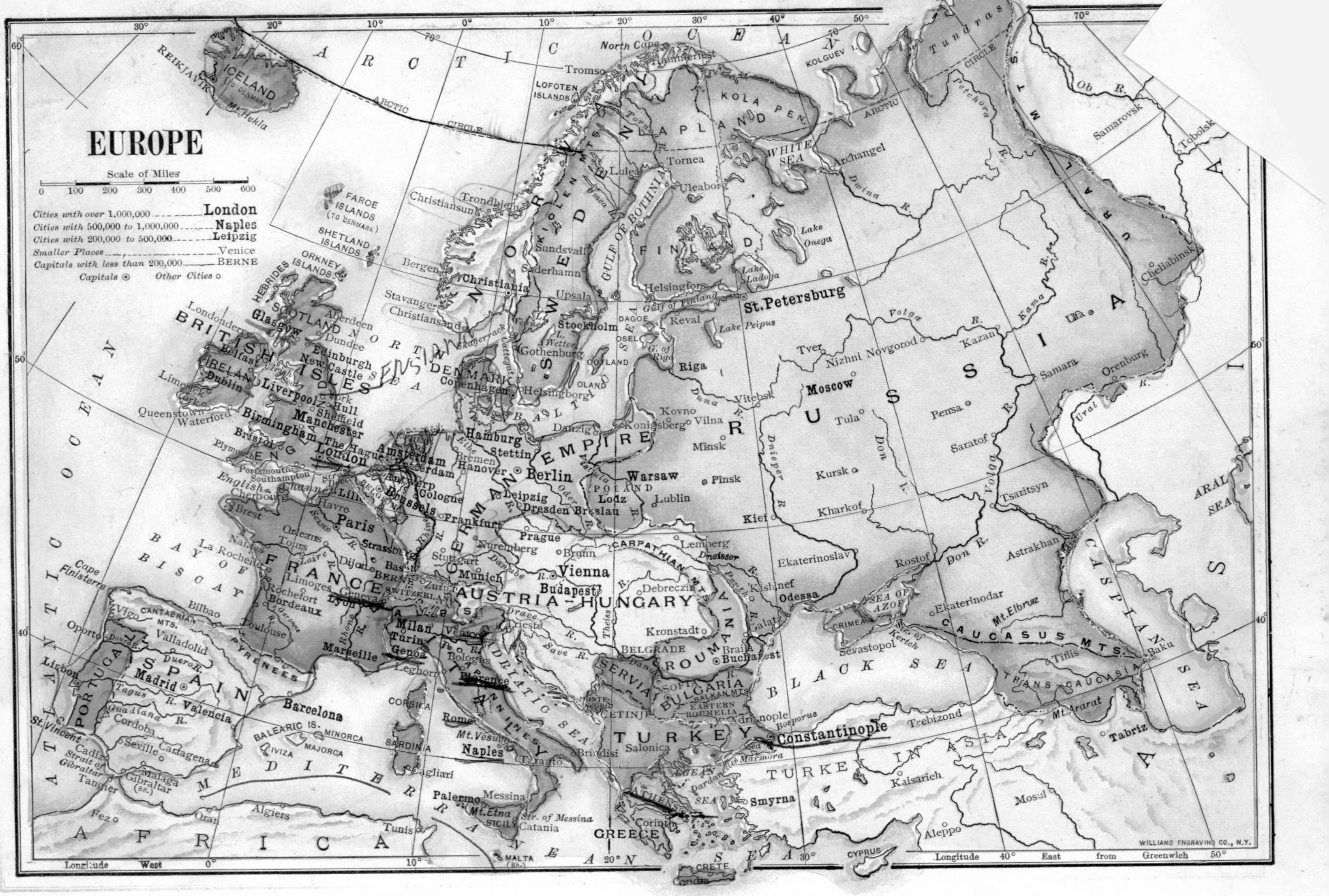

EUROPE

Scale of Miles

Cities with over 1,000,000 ————— London
Cities with 500,000 to 1,000,000 ————— Naples
Cities with 200,000 to 500,000 ————— Leipzig
Smaller Places ————— Venice
Capitals with less than 200,000) —— BERNE
Capitals ⊙ Other Cities ⊙

FIG. 232.

ARCTIC OCEAN

ATLANTIC OCEAN

MEDITERRANEAN SEA

AFRICA

RUSSIA

CASPIAN SEA

BLACK SEA

CAUCASUS MTS.

TRANS CAUCASIA

GERMAN EMPIRE

AUSTRIA-HUNGARY

FRANCE

SPAIN

PORTUGAL

ITALY

TURKEY

GREECE

SERVIA

ROUMANIA

BULGARIA

BRITISH ISLES

SCOTLAND

IRELAND

ENGLAND

NORWAY

SWEDEN

FINLAND

DENMARK

ICELAND

REIKJAVIK

London · Paris · Berlin · Vienna · Rome · Madrid · Lisbon

Moscow · St. Petersburg · Warsaw · Budapest · Constantinople

Stockholm · Christiania · Copenhagen · Hamburg · Munich

Naples · Palermo · Marseille · Barcelona · Smyrna · Odessa · Kiev

GULF OF BOTHNIA

WHITE SEA

NORTH SEA

ADRIATIC SEA

AEGEAN SEA

BAY OF BISCAY

URAL MTS.

CARPATHIAN MTS.

PYRENEES

ALPS

APENNINES

CRETE

CYPRUS

SARDINIA

CORSICA

SICILY

FAROE ISLANDS

SHETLAND ISLANDS

ORKNEY ISLANDS

HEBRIDES

BALEARIC IS.

Longitude West 0 East from Greenwich

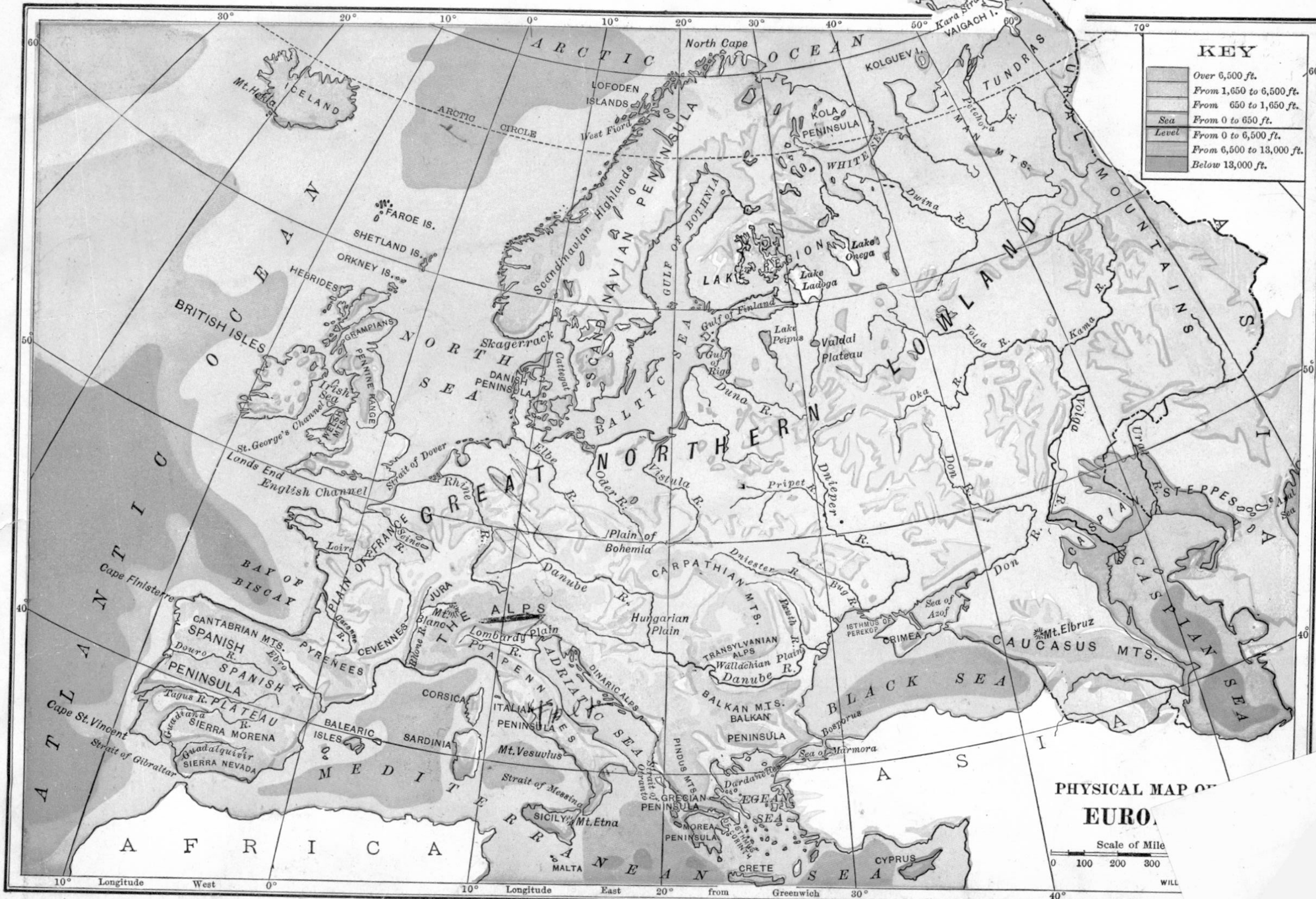
PHYSICAL MAP OF
EUROPE
Scale of Miles
0 100 200 300
KEY
Over 6,500 ft.
From 1,650 to 6,500 ft.
From 650 to 1,650 ft.
From 0 to 650 ft.
Sea Level
From 0 to 6,500 ft.
From 6,500 to 13,000 ft.
Below 13,000 ft.
ARCTIC OCEAN
ATLANTIC OCEAN
NORTH SEA
BALTIC SEA
BLACK SEA
CASPIAN SEA
MEDITERRANEAN SEA
ADRIATIC SEA
AEGEAN SEA
WHITE SEA
ASIA
AFRICA
GREAT NORTHERN LOWLAND
SCANDINAVIAN PENINSULA
Scandinavian Highlands
URAL MOUNTAINS
TUNDRAS
TIMAN MTS.
STEPPES
CAUCASUS MTS.
Mt. Elbruz
CARPATHIAN MTS.
TRANSYLVANIAN ALPS
Wallachian Plain
Hungarian Plain
Plain of Bohemia
THE ALPS
JURA
Mt. Blanc
Lombardy Plain
APENNINES
ITALIAN PENINSULA
DINARIC ALPS
BALKAN MTS.
BALKAN PENINSULA
PINDUS MTS.
GRECIAN PENINSULA
MOREA PENINSULA
ISTHMUS OF CORINTH
SPANISH PENINSULA
SPANISH PLATEAU
CANTABRIAN MTS.
PYRENEES
SIERRA MORENA
SIERRA NEVADA
CEVENNES
PLAIN OF FRANCE
DANISH PENINSULA
KOLA PENINSULA
LAKE REGION
Lake Ladoga
Lake Onega
Lake Peipus
Valdai Plateau
CRIMEA
ISTHMUS OF PEREKOP
Sea of Azof
Bosporus
Sea of Marmora
Dardanelles
Strait of Otranto
Strait of Messina
Strait of Gibraltar
Strait of Dover
English Channel
St. George's Channel
Irish Sea
Skagerrack
Cattegat
Gulf of Bothnia
Gulf of Finland
Gulf of Riga
BAY OF BISCAY
West Fiord
North Cape
Cape Finisterre
Cape St. Vincent
Lands End
BRITISH ISLES
GRAMPIANS
PENNINE RANGE
WELSH MTS.
HEBRIDES
ORKNEY IS.
SHETLAND IS.
FAROE IS.
ICELAND
Mt. Hekla
LOFODEN ISLANDS
KOLGUEV I.
VAIGACH I.
Kara Strait
ARCTIC CIRCLE
Dwina R.
Petchora R.
Volga R.
Kama R.
Oka R.
Ural R.
Don R.
Dnieper R.
Pripet R.
Bug R.
Dniester R.
Pruth R.
Danube R.
Duna R.
Vistula R.
Oder R.
Elbe R.
Rhine R.
Seine R.
Loire R.
Garonne R.
Rhone R.
Po R.
Ebro R.
Douro R.
Tagus R.
Guadiana R.
Guadalquivir R.
CORSICA
SARDINIA
BALEARIC ISLES
SICILY
Mt. Etna
Mt. Vesuvius
MALTA
CRETE
CYPRUS
Longitude West 0° Longitude East from Greenwich

FIG. 233

dreds of years ago wars were very frequent, — much more so than now. People, **3. Or their quarrels separate them** especially those who were not separated either by water or by mountains, often quarreled with one another, went to war, and finally set up different governments. What countries do you find on the map that do not seem to be cut off from their neighbors, on all sides, either by water or by mountains?

Australia, it is the smallest of all the continents. The whole of Europe is only a little larger than the United States, including Alaska. Yet it contains five times as many inhabitants as our country. This makes it plain that Europe is much more thickly settled than the United States.

In spite of the fact that **How Europe is the leading continent** Europe is so small, it is really the most important of all the continents.

FIG. 234. — The lofty Alps, from whose summits the snow never melts. Many people visit this place every summer because of the grand scenery.

There was a time when there were many more countries in Europe than now, but in recent years many of the smaller divisions have been united. This shows that people are learning to live together more peaceably than they once did.

Area and population of Europe . Although Europe is called a continent, it is really very small to be given that name. Next to

In the first place, it is the mother continent for the New World, because America has been settled by **1. The mother continent** immigrants from Europe (Fig. 235). What different countries of Europe first settled North America (p. 101)? South America (p. 181)? Point out these countries on the map of Europe. What country of Europe still holds about half of North America as its colony. Europe is the mother continent for other parts of the world, also, as you will learn later.

While Europe is the *mother* continent for much of the world, she is also the **2. The teacher of the world** *teacher* of most of it. Her children, who are scattered over the New World and elsewhere, naturally look to her for instruction. Other

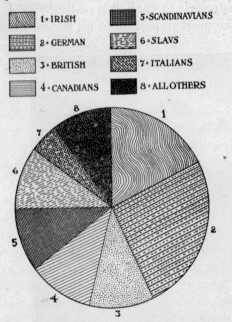

1 = IRISH   5 = SCANDINAVIANS
2 = GERMAN   6 = SLAVS
3 = BRITISH   7 = ITALIANS
4 = CANADIANS   8 = ALL OTHERS

FIG. 235. — A comparison of the foreign-born residents of the United States, according to the nations from which they come. In this figure the space marked 1 represents the native-born Irish living in the United States in 1900; the space marked 2 represents the Germans, etc.

parts of the world, such as China and Japan, look to her, too.

The countries of Europe, being so much older and so much more progressive than many other countries, have long taken the lead in discovering the best ways of carrying on agriculture, mining, manufacturing, and commerce. Most of the best books, also, and of the best music, paintings, and sculpture have come from Europe. For these reasons

people from all parts of the world look to Europe for the best thoughts on most subjects, and they often go there to study.

Some of the countries of Europe have been far more active than others as world leaders. There are **Europe's** six that are now especially **World Powers** prominent; namely, The British Isles, Germany, France, Italy, Austria-Hungary, and Russia. Locate each of these.

They are called the *Great Powers of Europe*, because they are the most powerful countries on that continent. They are also known as *World Powers*, because they are among the most powerful nations of the world. The United States and Japan are the only other World Powers. The remaining countries of Europe are called the *Lesser Powers*.

2. The Great Powers of Europe

(1) *The British Isles*

Of all the European countries, the one most nearly related to us is the *United Kingdom* of Great Britain **Why most** and Ireland. It is from **truly our** these two islands, called the **mother country** *British Isles*, that we have obtained our English language; and from them, too, a larger number of settlers have come to our shores than from any other country in the world (Fig. 235). Moreover, we carry on more commerce with the United Kingdom than with any other nation.

While, therefore, many of the European countries have some claim to be called mother countries to us, — since they have sent so many settlers here, — the United Kingdom is most truly of all our *Mother Country*.

Fig. 236. — Sheep grazing in a pasture in England.

The United Kingdom consists of two islands, *Great Britain* and *Ireland*. The **The smallness of this kingdom** larger of these, Great Britain, is made up of three parts — *England, Scotland,* and *Wales.* The two islands together are much smaller than our one state of California, but there are nearly half as many people living in them as live in the entire United States. This shows that the British Isles are very densely settled.

Notwithstanding its small size, the United Kingdom is in many respects **Its importance** the most powerful and the most important country in the world. It carries on more foreign commerce than any other nation; it has more and larger colonies; and in it is London, the largest city in the world.

There are, of course, excellent reasons why so small a country should have become so important. Let us see what they are.

It is certainly not agriculture that **Why agriculture is not especially important** has given the United Kingdom its rank. Indeed, in so small a country, one would hardly expect it to be. Even aside from its size, however, there are two reasons why agriculture is not of great importance here. In the first place, much of the land is too hilly and rocky for farming. In the second place, the islands are so far north that the summer climate is too cool. It is too cool even for wheat raising in the larger part of the two islands. Indian corn cannot be grown in any part, nor is grape culture general. Of course, then, such products as cotton, tobacco, and sugar cane are quite out of the question.

However, it is possible to raise the grains and vegetables of cool temperate climates, such as oats, barley, cab-**The farm products** bages, turnips, and potatoes. Another crop that thrives here is grass. The winds come mainly from the west, causing a damp climate; and since they blow from the warm ocean, the winters are not severe. Therefore, grass remains green throughout most of the year. It is because of its green grass that Ireland is often called the green, or Emerald Isle.

Largely on account of the fine grass, the principal agricultural industry of the British Isles is grazing (Fig. 236).

There are large numbers of horses and cattle, and still greater numbers of sheep. There are almost as many sheep in the British Isles as there are people, and in Scotland there are five times as many. These animals, of course, supply many important products, such as milk, butter, meat, hides, and wool. Yet far too little food is produced in these islands to feed the people.

States and Germany, produce more iron ore. There are also clays, building stones, and other valuable minerals.

With plenty of coal and iron, Great Britain has become one of the leading iron and steel manufacturing **Manufacturing** centers in the world. The **1. Iron and steel** products of the factories are **goods** used not only at home, but are sent abroad in great quantities.

FIG. 237. — Shipping in the busy harbor of Glasgow.

There is almost no lumbering, for there is scarcely any forest except that in parks. Almost all the wood used in the **Lumbering** British Isles has to be brought **and fishing** from abroad.

Fishing is a very important industry along the coast, and on the fishing banks, where fish are abundant. These salt-water fish are much used as food by the British people.

The key to the greatness of these islands is found largely in the minerals that lie buried in the rocks. **Mining** The most valuable of these are coal and iron ore, which are widely scattered. The United Kingdom is the second greatest coal-producing country in the world, ranking next to the United States. Only two nations, the United

The leading center for the manufacture of iron and steel is BIRMINGHAM, in England. The next center is in and near Glasgow, in Scotland. The two cities, GLASGOW (Fig. 237) and EDINBURGH, lie in the *Lowlands of Scotland,* a fertile agricultural region, rich in coal and iron. Glasgow is the principal city for steel shipbuilding in the world. Coal and iron from England and Scotland are easily sent by boat across the Irish Sea to the coast of Ireland. Largely for this reason the city of BELFAST is also noted for its iron manufacturing, especially for shipbuilding.

The United Kingdom is noted for many other kinds of manufacturing.

Fig. 238. — Loch Achray, in the Scottish Highlands.

FIG. 239. — St. Paul's Cathedral, London, from the Thames.

Wool, for example, is made into woolen cloth; and cotton, imported from the **2. Woolen and cotton goods** United States, and other parts of the world, is manufactured into cotton goods.

The center for this work is MAN-CHESTER, together with a number of smaller cities near by. LIVERPOOL, on the western seacoast, about thirty-five miles from Manchester, is the seaport for this region, and is itself a great manufacturing city.

The largest city in Ireland, BELFAST, is noted for its linen manufacture. The **3. Linen** linen is made of flax that thrives in the cool, damp climate of the Emerald Isle. DUBLIN, the capital of Ireland, also has important manufactures.

Great numbers of people are employed in all this manufacturing. They pro-**Commerce** duce so much cloth, steel, and iron goods, and so many other articles, that the British people could not possibly use all of them. They must find a market for them in other countries.

On the other hand, it is necessary for the British people to import much of the food that they eat. It is impossible to raise it all on these two small islands, just as it would be impossible to raise enough for the people of a city within the city limits. Besides food they must also import much wool, cotton, and other raw products for manufacturing.

The export of so many goods, and the import of so many others, gives rise to an enormous amount of trade, and makes the transportation of goods of the greatest importance. Partly for these reasons the United Kingdom has more ships than any other nation in the world, and they sail to every important port on the earth.

Having many ships, it has been easy for the British people to explore all parts of the earth. Also, having **British colonies** to sell so many goods abroad, and to buy so much food abroad, it has been natural for the British nation to take possession of newly discovered lands.

In this way the United Kingdom has come into possession of Canada, Australia, India, several large countries in Africa, and scores of islands and smaller possessions. These are called *colonies*, and the British have more of them than any other nation in the world. You will remember that our own country was an English colony before our War for Independence.

The British colonies cover one hundred times as much surface as the British Isles themselves, and have nine times as many inhabitants. These colonies help greatly to make the United Kingdom a World Power, both by their trade, and by their support in times of danger.

The commerce of the United Kingdom is centered largely in the principal seaports, especially LONDON, LIVERPOOL, and GLASGOW. **Great centers of manufacturing and commerce**

London, the largest city in the world, is situated on the short Thames River, as far up as ocean vessels can go. It is the capital of the country, is engaged in manufacturing of almost every kind, and has the most important shipping interests of any city in the Kingdom.

Locate Liverpool, Glasgow, Edinburgh, Birmingham, and Manchester. What has been said about each? Name the two principal cities of Ireland. For what is each important?

Great Britain and Ireland, together with the colonies, form the *British Empire.* Its government, unlike our own, is a monarchy, and the name of the present king is George V (Fig. 240). This is not an absolute monarchy, however, for the people have an important share in making the laws, as in our own country. They elect representatives to *Parliament,* which corresponds to our Congress at Wash-

The British Empire and its form of government

Fig. 240. — George V, King of England.

ington, and meets in London (Fig. 241).

(2) *German Empire*

Until the year 1871, the country marked *German Empire* on the map was divided among a large number of small independent governments. In that year they all united to form the German Empire. The government is a monarchy, the present ruler, called the *Kaiser,* being Emperor William II (Fig. 242).

Form of government

Fig. 241. — The Parliament building in London, with the Thames River in front.

Germany is a better agricultural country than the United Kingdom, for two

Why agriculture is prominent here

reasons. In the first place there is a much larger area of level land. The northern half of the country is a plain, and although the southern half is hilly, and in places mountainous, there is much good farming land there.

FIG. 242.—William II, the Emperor of Germany.

The second reason is the warmer summer climate in a part of Germany, for Germany lies farther from the sea than the British Isles, and a part of it is also farther south. A large portion of the Empire is south of the southern part of England, and no portion extends so far north as northern England.

Among the chief farm products are

o

rye, oats, barley, and wheat. Little corn is raised, but potatoes,

Farm products

which were introduced into Europe from America, are a very valuable crop.

The Germans have so improved the beet as to produce the new kind, known as the *sugar beet*, from which sugar is made. Hops, used in the manufacture of beer, and grapes for use in making wine, are grown in great quantities (Fig. 243). There is also much graz-

FIG. 243.— German peasants carrying grapes from a vineyard.

ing, especially on the poorer soils and uplands, and there are great numbers of cattle, sheep, hogs, and goats.

There is much more forest land in Germany than in Great Britain, about one fourth of the Empire being wooded. The Germans take great care of their

Lumbering and fishing

forests, and even plant trees on land that is not especially valuable for farming. When wood is needed, certain trees are selected for cutting, while the others are left to grow. Such care of the forests is called *forestry*, and the forest lands of Germany are as carefully attended to as are many farms. The Germans are the leading foresters of the world.

Along the seacoast there is much fishing, but this is less important than the other industries.

As in Great Britain, minerals are among the leading resources of this **Mining and manufacturing** country. Coal beds exist at several points, and there are also valuable deposits of iron ore, gold, silver, copper, lead, zinc, salt, and other minerals.

With abundant coal and iron ore, Germany has become a great manufactur-

FIG. 244. — The Rhine River in Germany. Notice the castle perched on the hilltop on the left, and the vineyard in the front of the picture.

ing country, making all kinds of iron and steel goods, as well as woolen, cotton, and linen goods. There are many other kinds of manufacturing, such as the making of sugar from sugar beets, the brewing of beer, and the manufacture of wine from grapes. Germany ranks next to Great Britain among the manufacturing countries of Europe.

Germany exports a great amount of **Commerce** sugar, wine, beer, textile goods, and iron and steel goods. Like Great Britain, however, she must import all of her cotton, much of her wool, and much of her food. What countries that you have studied might send these products to Germany?

Like the United Kingdom, Germany has important colonies, although they are not nearly so extensive as the British colonies. Her trade with these colonies, which are mainly in Africa, is of considerable value; but commerce with other countries is far more important.

For transportation of goods from one part of the Empire to another, Germany is greatly favored by her rivers. From the map, you will see that the principal ones flow northward. What rivers do you find? Trace their courses.

Navigation is possible upon all of these, but it is most extensive on the Rhine (Fig. 244). Boats can ascend this stream all the way from the sea to the boundary of Switzerland. How far is that? You can see how very important this must be in carrying goods across the Empire.

The chief seaport of Germany is HAMBURG, on the Elbe River. BREMEN, west **Great centers** of Hamburg, is another im- **of population** portant port. Why are these cities more favorably situated than those farther east on the Baltic Sea? There is now a ship canal across the peninsula south of Denmark. How is that an advantage to Germany?

There are many other large cities in Germany. The greatest of all is BERLIN, the capital and largest city of the Empire. Here are located the palaces of the Emperor and many government buildings. Berlin has also many museums, noted picture galleries, and a large university. In addition, it is a great manufacturing center.

FIG. 245. — A street in Frankfurt, with quaint old German houses.

LEIPZIG is well known for its trade in books, while DRESDEN and MUNICH, like Berlin, have wonderful collections of pictures. The schools, universities, and museums of Germany are among the best in the world, and many Americans go there each year to study. COLOGNE has an old cathedral of note, and FRANKFURT is an important center of commerce. Locate each of these cities on the map.

(3) *France*

France is one of the few countries in Europe, and the only large one, that has **Its form of government** a republican form of government. For many centuries it was a monarchy, but now the people elect a president and representatives, just as we do. The President of the Republic from January 1906 to 1913 was Armand Fallières (Fig. 246).

Agriculture
1. Comparison with England and Germany By looking at the map, you will see that France lies farther south than England, and that fully half of it lies farther south than the southern part

of Germany. Its climate is therefore warmer than that of either of those countries, and this makes it possible to produce a greater variety of crops. Farming is especially favored, too, by the fact that a large part of the surface is made up of plains.

One of the principal products is wheat (Fig. 247), which can be raised through- **2. The farm products** out the entire country. All the other crops of Germany can also be produced in France. Name several. France is even more noted than Germany for its grapes, which can be grown everywhere except in the northern third of the country. One of the principal grape-producing districts is that about BORDEAUX.

FIG. 246. — Armand Fallières, President of France.

In southern France there is an industry that we have not studied before; namely, the production of raw *silk*. This valuable substance is obtained from cocoons spun by a caterpillar, called the silkworm. Each of the cocoons is made of a fine, silky thread several thousand yards long, looking somewhat like the thread in a spider's web.

The silk industry, therefore, depends upon these worms, and much care must be given to them. Their principal food is the leaf of the

FIG. 247. — A scene in a wheat field in central France. Notice that the women, as well as the men, work in the field.

mulberry tree, which is cultivated in large groves in the Rhone Valley. The leaves are plucked from the trees and fed to the silkworms; and when these caterpillars reach the right stage, they spin the cocoons which are of so much value.

Neither lumbering nor fishing is of very great importance in France. Yet,

Lumbering and fishing as in Germany, the French carry on forestry on the poorer lands. There is some fishing along the coast, and many vessels go to the fishing banks of the North Sea.

There is some coal, especially near the boundary of Belgium, but France has no

Mining such important coal beds as are found in both Germany and England. It is necessary, therefore, to import some from Germany, Belgium, and Great Britain. Neither is there so much iron ore in France as in these other countries, although there is some.

For these reasons the manufacture of iron goods is far less extensive in France than in Germany **Manufacturing** and Great Britain.

There is, however, much textile manufacturing, one of the principal kinds being silk making. After the cocoons have been softened in hot water, the threads are unwound, and then wound upon spools. They are later made into silk thread, which is then woven into cloth, ribbons, and other silk goods.

The manufacture of silk goods is one of the principal industries of France, and the products of the silk factories are sent to all parts of the world. The center of the industry is LYON, the leading silk-manufacturing city in the world.

Other textiles made in France are linen, cotton, and woolen goods. The French are very skillful and artistic people, and the French cloths are among the finest that are made. The making of shoes, gloves, wine, and beet sugar are also important industries.

France exports large quantities of textile goods, wine, and leather goods. She imports coal, iron, wool, cot- **Commerce** ton, raw silk, and many articles of food. Thus she has a very extensive commerce with foreign countries. The republic has a number of colonies — mainly in Africa and Asia — whose combined area is many times that of France itself. As is the case with the United Kingdom, these colonies greatly increase the trade of France.

For the transportation of goods abroad, France has the advantage of facing both the Atlantic Ocean and the Mediterranean Sea; and there are good seaports on both coasts. What ports do you find on the map? What rivers connect these

been dredged so that small ocean vessels can ascend it as far as Paris, while still smaller boats can go much farther up the river.

Paris is, perhaps, the most beautiful city in the world (Fig. 248), with magnificent avenues and buildings. It has noted picture galleries and museums,

FIG. 248. — A view along the finest street of Paris.

ports with the interior? Trace each. Boats pass freely up these rivers, except the Loire, which is too shallow for navigation.

The largest and most important city in France is PARIS, on the Seine River.

Great centers of population It is the capital of France and the third city in size in the world. What two are larger pp. 118 and 191)? As in other large cities, there is much manufacturing here. Its seaport is HAVRE; but the Seine has

and many foreigners go there to study painting, music, architecture, and other subjects.

The leading seaport of France is MARSEILLE, the second city in size in the country. It has especially important trade with the countries bordering the Mediterranean, including Algeria and Tunis, in northern Africa, which are French colonies. It is the port for LYON, the third city in size in France. BORDEAUX, on the Garonne River, in the midst of the grape district, is the principal shipping point for wines.

(4) *Italy*

This country is mainly a long peninsula, shaped like a boot, which extends down into the Mediterranean Sea. What sea lies to the east of it? The island of Sicily, on the south, and also Sardinia on the west, both belong to Italy.

The parts of the country

Like Germany, Italy was for a long time divided into several independent countries. Now, however, these are all united under a single government, the king at the present time being Victor Emanuel III (Fig. 249).

Its government

Much of the surface of Italy is mountainous, as you can see on the map. The lofty Alps form the northern part, and the Apennines extend, like a backbone, down the center of the peninsula. There is, therefore, much rugged land that is unsuited to agriculture.

Hindrances to agriculture

A second drawback to farming is the fact that in most parts of the country the rainfall in summer is so light that irrigation is necessary.

In spite of these hindrances, agriculture is by far the leading industry of Italy, while mining and manufacturing are much less important than in the three

Why agriculture is the leading industry

FIG. 249. — Victor Emanuel III, King of Italy.

countries already studied. One of the principal reasons for this difference is that there is scarcely any coal in Italy, and very little iron. It is true that there are many mountain streams, with excellent water power; and these are used to some extent for manufacturing; but because coal and iron are lacking, Italy has not become a *great* manufacturing country.

The mountain streams, however, are of great value for irrigation, and have long been used for that purpose. Among the mountains are many fertile valleys, and there are also some plains with very rich soil. The largest and best of these plains is the Po River Valley in the northern part of the country. It is one of the finest farming sections in the world. Locate the Po River (Fig. 233).

The warm climate of Italy gives it a great advantage for agriculture over most of the countries of Europe. Although Rome, in the central part, lies in about the same latitude as New York and Chicago, the winters of Italy are everywhere mild. Along the seacoast there is scarcely any frost, and snow rarely falls; but it is colder farther inland and among the mountains. Thus, even though Italy lies so far north, it is able to produce the crops of warm countries.

Among the principal agricultural products are oranges, lemons, grapes, and

FIG. 250. — The castle of St. Angelo, one of the ancient buildings of Rome.

FIG. 251. — A street scene in Florence, Italy, the Duomo, or cathedral, in the background.

rice. Where in eastern United States are these crops produced (pp. 123, 124)? How **Agricultural products** much farther south is that? The mulberry tree thrives here as in France, and silk culture is one of the leading industries. Besides these special crops, wheat, maize, vegetables, grapes, and olives are grown in large quantities; and many cattle, sheep, and goats are raised, as well as much poultry.

The capital of the kingdom is ROME, a city not quite so large as Detroit. **Centers of population** In it are the palace of the king, and many government **1. Rome** buildings. Here also resides the Pope, the head of the Roman Catholic Church. He lives in a palace, called the Vatican, close by the great St. Peter's Cathedral.

Although Italy still ranks as one of the World Powers, there was a time when this peninsula was far more important, in comparison with other countries, than at present. Nearly two thousand years ago, for instance, at the time of Christ, the city of Rome was the center of the mighty Roman Empire, which controlled most of the world that was then known.

Rome was much larger then, and had many magnificent buildings and works of art. For hundreds of years after that, these buildings were allowed to decay; some were destroyed during the wars, and most of them became ruins, or were covered up entirely by sand, dust, and débris of various kinds. Recently, however, the débris has been dug away from around them, and parts of them can now be seen as they stood when Julius Cæsar lived there (Fig. 252). These ruins are among the most interesting sights in the city.

The largest city in Italy to-day is NAPLES, at the head of the beautiful Bay of Naples, and near the foot of Mount Vesuvius. **2. Naples** There is much shipping from this port, which is situated in the midst of a very fertile farming region.

Mount Vesuvius can be plainly seen from Naples, and when it is in eruption, ashes hurled from it often settle in the streets of the city. Over eighteen hundred years ago, there was a terrible eruption of Vesuvius, during which vast quantities of ashes were thrown into the air. Settling on the surrounding country, the ashes formed a layer deep enough to bury towns near the slopes of the volcano.

FIG. 252. — Ruins of some of the fine old buildings of ancient Rome, which for centuries were buried beneath rubbish.

Among these was POMPEII, which was completely destroyed. The ashes have been dug away from much of this city, and now one can see the streets just as they formerly were, (Fig. 253). The houses also are partly preserved, and, in some cases, even the decorations on their walls.

FLORENCE, northwest of Rome, is noted for its fine picture galleries and other works of art. Farther **3. Cities of** north, on the western coast, **northern Italy** is GENOA, the chief seaport of Italy.

It was here that Christopher Columbus was born. In the Po Valley are MILAN and TURIN, both important manufactur-

FIG. 253. — A general view of Pompeii, which was buried beneath ashes erupted from Vesuvius (seen in the background) over eighteen hundred years ago. During the last century the ashes were dug away, so that one can now walk around among the ruins of the buildings and through the streets.

ing centers. Milan is further noted for its beautiful cathedral.

An especially interesting city is VENICE, at the head of the Adriatic Sea. It is built upon a marsh, being surrounded by water and having canals for streets. Instead of driving about the city, one rides in boats, called *gondolas* (Fig. 254), which also serve to carry goods from point to point. Many bridges cross the canals, while footpaths extend along their margins, so that one can walk about if he chooses; but there are no wagon roads nor horses.

(5) *Austria-Hungary*

This Empire is larger than any other country in Europe except Russia; yet Area and parts it is not so of the country large as our state of Texas. It is made up of two main parts: (1) *Austria*, on the west, where many of the people are of the same race as the Germans, and where German is the principal language; and (2) *Hungary*, where entirely different languages are spoken, and

FIG. 254. — A gondola on one of the canals in Venice.

where the people are of very different races, some having come from Asia.

Austria and Hungary are united to form a monarchy under a single ruler;

yet each is independent of the other in some respects, and each has its own capital. The present emperor is Francis Joseph I (Fig. 255).

Government

Fig. 255. — Francis Joseph, Emperor of Austria-Hungary.

Turkey. Still other ranges, called the Carpathian Mountains, swing along the northern and eastern boundary of the Empire. Yet, again as in Italy, there are many fertile valleys in this mountainous country, and agriculture is by far the most important occupation.

The best farming section is the vast plain in the middle part, inclosed by mountains. This is one of the principal grain-producing sections of Europe. Among the products of Austria-Hungary are silk, and the crops that were found in Germany and northern Italy. Name several of these crops. There is also much grazing land on the mountain slopes.

A large part of the land is too rough and mountainous for either farming or grazing (Fig. 256). On that account there is more forest than in any of the other European countries we have studied.

There are many valuable minerals in the mountain rocks, including iron,

Agriculture and lumbering

As you can see from the map, Austria-Hungary is in the same latitude as southern Germany and northern Italy. The climate is therefore about the same as in those countries. Trace the boundary of the Empire.

As in Italy, a large part of Austria-Hungary is mountainous (Fig. 256). Notice on the map that the Alps extend into this country; also that mountain ranges branch from the eastern end of the Alps southeast toward

Fig. 256. — A street in Innsbruck in Austria, with the snow-covered Alps rising steeply in the distance

gold, silver, copper, lead, and quicksilver; but since there is little coal, manufactur-
Mining and manufacturing ing is not highly developed. Another reason for the small amount of manufacturing is the fact that many of the people are not progressive, and lack skill in handling machinery. Most of the manufacturing is carried on near the German border, where the people are like the Germans, and where it is possible to obtain coal from Germany.

By far the largest city is VIENNA, the fourth in size in Europe; only London, Paris, and Berlin are larger. **Centers of population** It is the capital of Austria, a manufacturing center, and a beautiful city, being often classed with Paris in this respect.

BUDAPEST (Fig. 257), the capital of Hungary, farther down the Danube, is less than half the size of Vienna. Like Minneapolis, it is surrounded by wheat farms and is a noted flour-milling center.

PRAGUE, in the northwest, near Germany, is the principal manufacturing city. The chief seaport is TRIESTE, at the head of the Adriatic. Look in the table on page 258 to find how it compares in size with Liverpool, Hamburg, Genoa, and other seaports already studied. Can you give reasons for its small size?

FIG. 257. — A view of the Danube River at Budapest.

A third reason for the small amount of manufacturing is the difficulty of transporting goods. You will notice that Aus-
Commerce tria-Hungary has no coast line on the Atlantic Ocean. The strip of coast along the Adriatic Sea is far away from the Atlantic, and is separated from the interior of the country by mountains that are difficult to cross. It is true that the central part of the country can be reached by river boats, for the Danube River crosses Austria-Hungary in its course to the Black Sea. Goods from the Atlantic Ocean can reach Vienna, therefore, by being carried into the Black Sea from the Mediterranean, and thence up the Danube. However, this is a very roundabout route. Trace it on the map.

For all these reasons Austria-Hungary has little foreign commerce, and a large part of what it has is carried on through German ports. From these facts can you see some reasons why this Empire has no colonies?

(6) *Russia*

Russia is larger than all the other countries of Europe combined, but only about **Area and population** one-half the size of the United States. Its population, however, is considerably larger than ours, and about twice that of any other European country.

The Ural Mountains form a part of the eastern boundary of European Russia. The Russian Empire, however, extends thousands of miles farther east, reaching across Asia even to the Pacific Ocean. The part of the Empire beyond the Urals is called Siberia. Including Siberia, and other Russian possessions in Asia, the area of the whole Empire is greater than that of all North America. Only the European part is now to be studied.

The government of Russia is different from any thus far studied. France is a republic, and the four other Great Powers of Europe are called *limited monarchies;* but the Rus-

Government

sian government is an *absolute monarchy,* or *despotism.* This means that the ruler, who is called the *Czar,* can do more nearly as he pleases than can the other rulers of Europe. The name of the present Czar is Nicholas II (Fig. 258).

FIG. 258. — Nicholas II, Czar of Russia.

In recent years the people have been allowed to elect representatives to the *Duma,* which somewhat resembles our Congress. Yet even in the Duma, the representatives are not free to speak and vote as they choose.

Russia is chiefly an agricultural country. As in the United States, the great

Advantages for agriculture

variety of temperature is an advantage for agriculture, for it makes many different crops possible. Observe on Figure 232 that Russia extends almost as far south as Italy does, while in the north it reaches into

the Arctic zone. About how many miles is it from the most southern to the most northern point?

It is a very level country, too, with much fertile soil. While there are mountains along a part of the boundary, Russia is mainly a vast plain, like the plains of the Mississippi Valley.

In some parts of Russia the climate is unsuited to agriculture. In the northern part, for instance, the plains, called *tundras,* are always frozen. Even

Sections unsuited to agriculture

in summer they thaw out only at the surface, and trees cannot grow upon them. Mosses and grasses are the chief plants there, and the reindeer, which feeds upon them, is the principal domestic animal (Fig. 259). It is the main support of the few people who live on the tundras.

Southeastern Russia, on the other hand, is too dry for agriculture without irrigation. This is the region of the *steppes,* which resemble the arid lands in our Western States; here grazing is the leading industry.

In central and southern Russia wheat, rye, oats, and other grains are common. Indeed, this is one of the

Agricultural products

leading grain-growing sections of the world. Other important products are potatoes, hay, flax, and hemp. In the extreme southern part the climate is so mild that such crops as cotton and tobacco are produced.

More than one third of

Lumbering, mining, and manufacturing

Russia is covered with forest, so that lumbering is a very important industry.

Russia is also a noted mining country. It is one of the leading gold-producing nations, and so much petroleum is found here that it is used as a fuel in factories, steamboats, and railway engines. There is, however, little iron and coal mining, and partly on this account manufacturing is not greatly developed.

FIG. 259. — Reindeer used in winter for drawing sleds over the snow-covered ground of northern Russia.

One reason why all the industries of Russia, including manufacturing, are very backward, is the condition of the people. Until a few years ago, the great mass of the common people, or *peasants*, were really slaves. These peasants, called *serfs*, had hardly any education, and were treated much as dogs and horses are treated.

The serfs have now been freed, but they are still very ignorant, and are not allowed to take any real part in the government. Few of them can read and write, and few know what other people in the world are doing. Such people lack the knowledge and ability necessary for manufacturing and other industries.

Since Russia is mainly an agricultural country, its exports are largely food products and raw materials for manufacture, and its imports are chiefly manufactured goods. How different this is from England, Germany, and France!

Commerce

Russia is unfortunate in lacking good seaports. A part of the seacoast is on the Arctic Ocean, where the harbors are icebound most of the year. A part is on the Baltic Sea, and there, also, the harbors are frozen over in winter. The Caspian Sea has no outlet, so that vessels cannot get out of it.

The best seacoast is on the Black Sea, but to get from this to the Atlantic Ocean, it is necessary to pass through a narrow strait, called the Bosporus, and then through the Mediterranean Sea. This is a very long journey. Russia therefore resembles Austria in its lack of good and convenient seaports.

On the other hand, the interior of Russia is so level that it is easy to build railroads there. Water transportation is easy, too, because there are several large rivers. Name them, and trace each one on the map. Into what water does each empty? The largest is the Volga, the greatest river in Europe, but it is unfortunate that it flows into the Caspian Sea. Why unfortunate?

The value of these rivers is greatly increased by means of canals, which, like railroads, are easily built across the plains. It is possible to go by river and canal, from both the Caspian and Black seas to the Baltic sea. On what rivers might one travel in making each of these journeys?

The largest city and capital of Russia is ST. PETERSBURG, a seaport at the head of the Gulf of Finland. This is the city in which the Czar lives and the Duma meets, and is larger than Philadelphia. It is not noted

Great centers of population

either for its manufacturing or commerce, being chiefly a government center. Find some point in North America that is in the same latitude as St. Petersburg.

RIGA is another seaport farther south. Locate it. Russian commerce on the Black Sea is more important than that on the Baltic. The leading seaport there is ODESSA, which is the nearest port to the fertile wheat region of central and southern Russia. Great quantities of wheat are exported from Odessa, which also has many flour mills.

In the center of the country is Moscow (Fig. 260), which in size is next to St. Petersburg. It is the leading railroad center in the Empire. WARSAW, in Poland, is another large interior city. It has much manufacturing.

FIG. 260.—A church in the Russian city of Moscow.

A second reason for the small number of inhabitants is the ruggedness of the land. The surface is so mountainous that farming is impossible over the greater part of the peninsula. Most of the people are found in the southern and eastern parts, where the climate is milder and the land more level.

The hardy grains and vegetables are the principal farm crops, and many cattle and sheep are raised on the mountain pastures. Why would you not expect to find cotton, grapes, and tobacco growing here?

Agriculture, lumbering, and fishing

Where the mountain slopes are too rugged for farming, there are extensive forests. About one fourth of Norway and much of Sweden is covered with forest. Therefore, lumber is one of the leading products of both countries.

Since crops are not extensively raised, fish are much used for food. There are

3. The Lesser Powers of Europe

(1) *Norway and Sweden*

The two kingdoms of Norway and Sweden, occupying the Scandinavian Peninsula, are each larger than the British Isles. Yet both together have a very much smaller population.

Why thinly settled

One reason for the sparse population is the latitude. Look upon a globe to see what part of North America is in the same latitude. It would not be possible for the few million inhabitants of these two countries to live there if it were not for the warm west winds, which blow from the ocean. Even with that help, most of the region has a very cold climate.

FIG. 261. — A view in one of the deep, grand fiords on the coast of Norway.

the heavens and does not set even in the middle of the night. For this reason the northern part of the peninsula is sometimes called "the land of the midnight sun."

The fiords of Norway and the protected bays of Sweden form excellent Transporta-harbors, and for tion of goods this reason the Scandinavian people have become skillful sailors. In fact, in some of the Norwegian fiords, the only way to get from one point to another is by boat. The need of obtaining fish for food has also helped to make the people skillful in handling vessels, while the abundance of lumber has made it possible for them to build vessels very cheaply.

many of these, especially cod and herring, in the shallow waters near the coast.

Some valuable minerals are found in Scandinavia, notably iron in Sweden; Mining and but there is no coal. The manufacturing mountain streams, however, furnish much water power, some of which is used in manufacturing. Most of the manufacturing is in the southern part of the peninsula, where it is not difficult to import coal for fuel.

On the map you will notice that the coast of Scandinavia is very irregular, especially in Norway. Here the sea enters the Scenery deep mountain valleys, forming long, narrow bays, with steep walls. Some of these inlets, called *fiords* (Fig. 261), reach many miles into the land. They make excellent harbors and form some of the grandest scenery in Europe.

Many tourists go up the coast of Norway every summer in order to enjoy the scenery of the fiords, and to see the great glaciers that descend from the high mountains at their heads. The tourist steamers cross the Arctic Circle and go as far as North Cape, where in summer one is able to see the midnight sun. During several weeks of summer, here, the sun circles around

FIG. 262. — A Lapland boy, whose home is in northern Norway.

Largely for these reasons, the Norwegians and Swedes are extensively engaged in shipping. They build boats, and man them with sailors for use both in fishing and in carrying goods. Navigation is one of their leading industries, especially the carrying of goods for people of other countries.

The chief cities are in the south. STOCKHOLM, the largest, is the capital Chief cities and of Sweden. CHRISTIANIA is government the capital and principal city of Norway. Each of these countries is a limited monarchy, with a king who lives in the capital.

(2) *Denmark*

Just south of Scandinavia is a very small peninsula pointing northward. On Its relation to its northern end is the little Scandinavia country of Denmark, a limited monarchy, which also includes several small islands near by. The people of Denmark are closely related to the Scandinavians in language and customs, and at one time all three were united in one nation. In fact, these three countries are often called the *Norse* nations, or the countries of the Norsemen, or Northmen.

Denmark is quite unlike Scandinavia in one respect; that is, it has Industries no mountains. Everywhere the surface is low, but much of the land is either sandy or swampy, so that there is less farming than one might expect. However, agriculture is the occupation of about half the people, and one of the principal industries is dairying. There is also much manufacturing and commerce.

You have already learned that Greenland is a Danish possession (p. 175). The Danes also own the Colonies and Faroe Islands and Iceland, chief city as well as some small islands in the West Indies.

The capital and largest city is COPENHAGEN, situated on an island east of the peninsula.

(3) *The Netherlands*

This little country is often called *Holland ;* but the nature of the country is more clearly shown in its Nature of the other name, *The Nether-* country *lands,* which means *low lands.* Almost all of this country is a low plain, partly the delta of the Rhine. Indeed, much

FIG. 263. — A windmill in The Netherlands, used for pumping out the water from the land inclosed in dikes.

of it is even lower than the surface of the sea.

In order to live on this very low part, the inhabitants have built embankments, called *dikes,* to keep the sea out, and have dug canals to drain the land. The water that collects inside the dikes is pumped out by windmills (Fig. 263), or by steam. Canals extend in all directions, and furnish excellent highways for travel. They are, in fact, among the most important highways (Fig. 264), being used in summer for boats, and in winter for skating and sledding.

The damp, level land is well suited to agriculture, and this is the principal industry. Cattle raising and dairying are most important. **Agriculture** The dairy products, especially butter and cheese, are shipped to other countries,

The Netherlands is a limited monarchy. The monarch resides at THE HAGUE, but the largest city **Principal cities** is AMSTERDAM. Another large city is ROTTERDAM, a noted seaport.

(4) *Belgium*

Holland is smaller than Denmark, but Belgium, another limited monarchy, is even smaller than Holland. **Area and population** Yet it contains more people than the Netherlands, and is, in fact, the most densely settled country in Europe. Find its area and population in the table on page 255, and compare it in these respects with some of our states.

The northern part of Belgium is a low plain, but the southern half is **Agriculture** much higher, and in places is quite hilly. Most of the kingdom is well suited to agriculture, and produces the same crops as Holland and Germany. What are these? One

FIG. 265. — Women in Belgium taking milk to market in a cart drawn by dogs.

some of the cheese — called Dutch cheese — being sent to the United States.

The Hollanders, or Dutch, as they are usually called, have been great explorers. They once had **Navigation and commerce** possession of the Hudson Valley, even the part where New York City now stands; and they still own some of the richest islands in the East Indies. They have much commerce with the colonies, as well as with other parts of the world.

very valuable product is flax.

The Belgians have long been skillful in the manufacture of linen and fine lace from flax, and also in **Manufacturing** weaving cloth from wool. In fact, it was from them that the English received some of their first lessons in manufacturing. BRUSSELS, the largest city, is famous for its beautiful lace, linen, and Brussels carpets. The latter are made of wool on a mat of linen.

FIG. 264. — A canal at Middleburg in Holland.

Besides such work, Belgium is noted for its manufacture of iron. This is because of the abundance of excellent coal, and of valuable iron deposits. Although so very small, Belgium may be compared with Germany and Great Britain as a manufacturing center.

BRUSSELS, the capital, is a city about the size of Boston. The principal seaport, ANTWERP, is half as large.

Principal cities

(5) *Spain and Portugal*

There are several important facts which have prevented Spain from hold-ing a high rank among the nations of Europe. One of these is the fact that a large part of the Spanish peninsula is too mountain-ous and rugged for agriculture. Most of it is a plateau, or table-land, half a mile or more above the level of the sea; and this is crossed by several mountain ranges. The Pyrenees, which extend along the northern border, are lofty mountains; but a range on the southern side, called the Sierra Nevada, is even higher. It has peaks almost as high as those of the Alps. Only along the coast, and in a few of the river valleys, is there much low land. Name and trace the principal rivers.

Mountains and plateaus

The peninsula lies so far south that its climate might be expected to be warm like that of Italy; but while there are some small sections low enough to have a warm climate, most of the peninsula is so elevated that it has a cooler climate than one might expect from its latitude.

Climate

Lack of rain is an even more serious drawback. The Spanish peninsula lies south of the belt of west winds, so that vapor is not brought from the ocean as freely as it is in the countries farther north. Much of the land, therefore, is arid; only along the northern and western coasts, including much of Portugal, is there enough rainfall for agriculture.

The people of Spain and Portugal have not been progressive, which is the greatest disadvantage of all. At the time of Columbus they were leaders in exploring the

Backwardness of the people

FIG. 266. — Country people, or peasants, of Spain in native costume.

world; but since then they have been very slow to advance. They have lost most of their many colonies, and the chief reason for it was that they were old-fashioned and cruel in their methods of government. Partly for this reason these nations have become of less and less importance. While England, France, and Germany have gone steadily forward, Spain and Portugal have fallen far behind.

P

Cattle and sheep raising are the principal industries on the arid plateau, **Agricultural products** and there is farming in the rainy section, or wherever the mountain streams make irrigation possible. For centuries the Spaniards have made use of irrigation, and they introduced it into the New World. The chief crops are wheat and other grains, but in the warm southern valleys, grapes, olives, lemons, oranges, and figs are raised.

Spain, is the largest city in the peninsula; and the chief Spanish seaport **Principal** is BARCELONA. LISBON, the **cities** capital of Portugal, is another important seaport. Look in the tables on pages 256, 257 to see how these cities compare in size with some of our largest cities.

GIBRALTAR, on the southern tip of Spain, at the entrance to the Mediterranean Sea, is a part of the British Empire, and is strongly fortified. Why is this a good location for a great stronghold?

FIG. 267. — Here a road winds its way across a barren mountain pass, with the lofty, snow-covered Alps towering above it.

Spain is a very important mineral region, producing gold, silver, quick-**Mining and** silver, lead, copper, and iron. **manufacturing** There is no good coal in the country, and most of the iron has to be shipped to other countries for manufacture. There is very little manufacturing on the peninsula, and commerce is not extensive.

Both Spain and Portugal have been limited monarchies; but in 1910 Portugal became a republic. MADRID, the capital of

(6) *Switzerland*

Switzerland is the only country of Europe, thus far studied, that has no seacoast. Neither has it a **Languages and** language of its own. No-**government** tice what countries surround it. Although it is very small, most of the inhabitants of the southern part speak Italian; those in the west, French; and those in the north and east, German. The most common language is German.

Fig. 268.—Cattle grazing in the mountain pastures high up in the Alps near the snow line.

This is the only European country that you have studied, except two, that is not a monarchy. Its people, living among the mountains where they could easily defend themselves, or hide from their enemies, declared themselves independent of kings hundreds of years ago, and the country has long been a republic.

The many lofty mountains seriously interfere with agriculture (Fig. 267). Agriculture The Alps extend completely across the country, and the Jura Mountains skirt the northwestern boundary. These mountains are so rugged that few people live among them, except in the valleys. Between the two mountain districts, however, is a narrow plateau where the surface is much less rugged. It is here that most of the people dwell.

One of the leading farm products is grain, raised mainly on the plateau. On the lower lands, especially near the German border, there are extensive vineyards. There is excellent pasturage for cattle and goats among the mountains, and these animals are raised there in great numbers (Fig. 268). In spring and summer, as the snows melt from the mountain sides, the goats and cattle are pastured higher and higher. Such pasture is called an *alp*, and this is the origin of the name of the range, the Alps.

Where the mountain slopes are too **Lumbering and manufacturing** rugged for farming, there is much forest. Therefore, lumber is an important product of the country.

Although there is no good coal in Switzerland, the Swiss do a large amount of manufacturing. Among their principal products are wine, butter, and cheese. Wood carving is also an industry in which many of the Swiss find employment. During the long winters, the wood from the mountains is shaped into toys, clocks, and other articles. Have you ever seen a Swiss clock?

The Swiss have become widely known for their manufacture of textile goods, such as lace, linen, silk, and cotton goods. They also make much jewelry, especially watches. In some of this work, water power is used, for an abundance of power is supplied by the mountain streams. A great deal of the manufacturing, however, is done by hand in the homes of the workmen, rather than in large factories. From these facts you can readily see that the Swiss people must be very skillful, progressive, and well educated.

In the lofty Alps there is some of the grandest scenery in the world. Their snow-covered **Entertainment of tourists** peaks, their glaciers descending into the valleys, and the lakes in their midst, are wonders that many people like to view. Tens of thousands of people go to Switzerland every summer to enjoy the climate and the scenery, and one of the chief occupations of the Swiss people is to take care of such visitors.

The capital of the Republic is BERNE. **Chief cities** Other important cities are ZÜRICH, BASLE, and GENEVA, three manufacturing centers.

(7) *Greece*

Italy, Spain, and Portugal were once far more important, in comparison with other countries, than at present. The same is true of Greece. **Its former greatness**

The country in Europe that has perhaps had the greatest influence upon the rest of the world is this small one. The Romans received many of their beliefs and customs from Greece, and since many of our customs came from the Romans, we also are greatly in debt to the Greeks.

FIG. 269. — Ruins of ancient Athens. The rocky height in the background is the Acropolis, on which there are some fin ruins of buildings many centuries old.

They were highly cultured people, and some of their sculpture and buildings are the most perfect and beautiful that have ever been made.

The center of this important country was ATHENS, once the most famous city in the world, and still the capital of the **Chief cities** little kingdom of Greece. It was an important place many years later, at the time of Christ. Both ATHENS and CORINTH are mentioned in the Bible. Athens is even now the principal city, and, like Rome, has many interesting ruins (Fig. 269).

The surface of Greece is so mountainous, and the climate so dry, that the farm products are not of great value. **Principal industries** Among the principal crops are currants, grapes, and other fruits. Grazing

Fig. 270. — A street scene in Constantinople.

one of the leading industries, but there is little mining or manufacturing, and the commerce is not extensive.

(8) *Turkey and the Balkan Countries*

Chief city of Turkey The largest city in southeastern Europe is CONSTANTINOPLE, which is not quite so large as Philadelphia. It is situated on the narrow strait of the Bosporus, and guards the entrance to the Black Sea at the point where southern Europe comes nearest to Asia. This city is the capital and largest city of the Turkish Empire, which, like Russia, is a country that lies partly in Europe and partly in Asia. In addition, it has territory in northern Africa.

Character of Turkish government The Turkish government has been the worst in Europe, worse even than that of Russia. The ruler, called the *Sultan*, has been an absolute despot, who governed his people so badly that they have been kept very ignorant and poor. Only recently have the people been given some voice in the government.

One proof that the government has been bad is the fact that the people in many parts of the Empire have rebelled against it and fought for freedom. For example, *Roumania*, east of Austria, used to belong to Turkey, but is now an independent kingdom. The same is true of Greece. *Bulgaria*, *Servia*, and *Montenegro* also used to be a part of the Turkish Empire. Other people,

in sections still belonging to Turkey, would gladly be rid of the rule of the Sultan.

Products of these countries Owing largely to misrule, neither Turkey nor the Balkan countries just named have developed greatly. The main industry is agriculture, although much of the land is too mountainous for that purpose, and the methods of carrying on the industry are very backward. There are, however, broad plains in the Danube Valley, in Bulgaria and Roumania, where much grain is produced. Grapes, other fruits, and vegetables are raised in all of these countries; but one of the chief industries is grazing.

Europe **1. Questions** 1. What is meant by Eurasia? By Europe? 2. Why has Europe so many independent countries with separate languages? 3. What about the area and population of Europe? 4. What reasons are there for regarding Europe as the most important continent? 5. Name and locate the Great Powers of Europe. Why also called World Powers?

2. Suggestions 1. Draw an outline map of Europe. Put in the boundaries of the principal countries. 2. With what part of North America does Europe correspond in latitude? 3. Find out why its climate is so much warmer.

British Isles **1. Questions** 1. Give reasons for regarding the British Isles as our mother country. 2. What are the parts of the United Kingdom? What about their area and population? 3. In what respects is this country especially important? 4. Why is agriculture not very prominent? 5. Name the main farm products. 6. What about lumbering and fishing? 7. Mining? 8. Manufacturing? 9. Commerce? 10. British colonies? 11. Locate and state the principal facts about the chief cities. 12. What is meant

FIG. 271. — A Turkish lady in native costume.

by the British Empire, and what is its form of government?

1. What books have you read whose authors lived in the British Isles? 2. What are the **2. Suggestions** people from each of the four parts of these islands called? 3. What waters surround the British Isles? 4. Make a sketch of the British Isles, putting in the chief cities. 5. Suppose that you are now in London; point to Wales, Scotland, Ireland, the United States.

1. Tell about the founding of the German Empire, and its form of government. 2. Why **Germany** is agriculture more prominent **1. Questions** here than in the British Isles? 3. What are the farm products? 4. State the chief facts about lumbering and fishing. 5. Mining and manufacturing. 6. Commerce. 7. Chief cities.

1. Make a collection of photographs from Germany. 2. Do you know of some noted **2. Suggestions** German paintings? Or of any music written by Germans? 3. What stories do you know about the Rhine River? 4. Make a drawing of Germany, including the principal rivers and cities. 5. What countries surround it?

1. What is the form of government? 2. What advantages for agriculture has it over **France** the British Isles and Germany? **1. Questions** 3. Name its chief farm products. 4. Tell about its lumbering and fishing. 5. Mining. 6. Manufacturing. 7. Commerce. 8. Chief cities.

1. Make a collection of photographs of Paris. 2. Examine a cocoon, and a piece of **2. Suggestions** silk. 3. When a hole is broken into a cocoon, its value for silk is destroyed. Why? 4. Make a drawing of France, including the main rivers and cities. 5. Bound France.

1. Bound Italy, and tell its parts. 2. What is the form of its government? 3. What **Italy** serious hindrances are there to **1. Questions** agriculture? 4. Why is agriculture still the leading industry? 5. What are the chief farm products? 6. State the leading facts about each of the principal cities.

1. Find pictures of some of the ruins in Rome, or elsewhere in Italy. 2. What kinds of work do Italian immigrants to **2. Suggestions** the United States usually undertake? 3. What copies of great paintings from Italy have you seen? 4. Make a drawing of Italy, including the chief cities. 5. Imagine that you are now in Rome; walk toward Naples; Genoa; Paris; Berlin.

1. How large is this country? 2. What about its two parts? 3. What kind of government has it? State the princi- **Austria-Hungary** pal facts about agriculture and **1. Questions** lumbering. 4. Mining and manufacturing. 5. Why is there so little commerce? 6. Name, locate, and state the main facts about the chief cities.

1. How far is Vienna from other leading cities of Europe? 2. Trace the course you would take if you traveled by water from New York to Vienna. 3. Bound **2. Suggestions** Austria-Hungary. 4. Make a drawing of it, including in the sketch the Danube River and the principal cities.

1. What about the area and population of Russia. 2. The government? 3. What conditions favor agriculture? 4. What **Russia** sections are unsuited to agricul- **1. Questions** ture? Why? 5. What are the principal agricultural products? 6. Tell about lumbering, mining, and manufacturing. 7. Commerce. 8. Principal cities.

1. Why would you not expect Russia to have as many skillful sailors as the British Isles? 2. Name some city in the United States that has about the same latitude as Odessa. 3. Show the route a ves- **2. Suggestions** sel might take in going from Odessa to St. Petersburg. 4. Bound Russia. 5. Make a drawing of Russia, putting into it the principal rivers and cities.

1. Why are these countries thinly settled? 2. Tell about their agriculture, lumbering, and fishing. 3. Mining and manu- facturing. 4. Scenery. 5. Why **Norway and** is transportation of goods so im- **Sweden** portant? 6. Locate the chief **1. Questions** cities. What is the kind of government?

1. Sketch the peninsula. Put in the principal cities, and North Cape. 2. What **2. Suggestions** is the latitude of North Cape?

Denmark
1. Questions
1. What is the relation of Denmark to Norway and Sweden? 2. What are the principal industries? 3. Name and locate its colonies. 4. Its chief city.

The Netherlands
1. Questions
1. State the character of the country. 2. Tell about its agriculture. 3. What about navigation and commerce? 4. Name and locate the principal cities.

2. Suggestions
1. Find out something about the Dutch flower gardens where bulbs are raised. 2. Tell what you would expect to see in crossing Holland on a train. 3. What would result, if a dike were to give way? 4. Who is the present monarch?

Belgium
1. Questions
1. What about the size of this country? 2. The population? 3. What crops are raised? 4. Tell about the manufacturing. 5. Name and locate the principal cities.

2. Suggestions
1. Examine some Brussels carpet. 2. Sketch Holland and Belgium together, putting in the chief cities. 3. Make a sand map of them, showing elevation of the land and the position of dikes.

Spain and Portugal
1. Questions
1. What are the surface features of this peninsula? 2. What is the climate? 3. How has the backwardness of the people been a disadvantage? 4. What are the principal agricultural products? 5. What about mining and manufacturing? 6. Name and locate the principal cities.

2. Suggestions
1. Why would you not be able to ascend the rivers of this peninsula a long distance from the coast? 2. Make a sand map of Spain, showing the highlands and lowlands, the cities and rivers. 3. Examine some quicksilver. What are some of its uses? 4. Find out something about the Moors, and the Alhambra, in southern Spain.

Switzerland
1. Questions
1. What languages are spoken? 2. What is the form of government? 3. Tell about the agriculture. 4. Lumbering. 5. What kinds of manufacturing are there? 6. Why are there so many tourists? 7. Locate the chief cities.

2. Suggestions
1. Read the story of William Tell. 2. What disadvantages do you see in having so many languages? 3. What large rivers rise in Switzerland? Describe the course of each to its mouth. Write a story, describing a visit to Switzerland.

Greece
1. Questions
1. Tell about its former greatness. 2. Its principal city. 3. What are the industries?

2. Suggestions
1. Read some stories of the ancient Greeks. One of the most interesting is the Odyssey. 2. Collect photographs of the ruins in Athens.

Turkey and Balkan countries
1. Questions
1. Locate the principal city of Turkey. 2. What is the character of the Turkish government? 3. Name the Balkan countries. 4. What are the principal products?

2. Suggestions
1. What is the boundary between Turkey in Europe and Turkey in Asia? Trace it. 2. Russia would greatly like to get possession of Constantinople. Why? 3. Make an outline sketch of Turkey in Europe.

General Review Questions
1. What countries of Europe suffer, to some extent, for want of rain? 2. What is the largest river of Europe? Is it the most important? Why? 3. What rivers rise in the Alps? 4. Through what countries does each flow? 5. What large cities are located upon each? 6. Make a sketch map of Europe, showing the location of the chief rivers and cities. 7. Name and locate the principal mountain ranges of Europe. Include these in your sketch. 8. On your sketch map, draw the boundaries of the countries. 9. What three countries are republics? 10. What two have a despotic form of government? 11. Which countries border on the Atlantic Ocean? 12. On the Mediterranean Sea? 13. Which have a very good position for commerce? Why? 14. Which have a very poor position for commerce? Why? 15. Name the leading agricultural countries of Europe. 16. Name the leading manufacturing countries. 17. Bound each of the Great Powers of Europe. 18. Name and locate the capital of each of these Great Powers. Put them on your sketch map. 19. Name the capital of each of the Lesser Powers.

XIII. ASIA

1. Through what zones does Asia extend (Fig. 272)? 2. Where are the highest mountains and plateaus? **Map study** 3. What rivers have their sources in that region? 4. What large inland seas do you find? 5. What three large peninsulas are on the southern side? 6. What two are on the eastern side? 7. What islands lie east of Asia? 8. How does Asia compare in size with Europe? 9. Find Asia on a globe. 10. How could you reach it, if you wished to go there?

1. General Facts about Asia

The main part of Eurasia, which we call Asia, is larger than any other conti- **Area and popu- lation** nent. Indeed, it is greater than North and South America together, or Europe and Africa together.

It has more inhabitants, also, than any other continent. More than one

Fig. 274. — A nomad family in camp on the desert of Persia.

half of all the persons on the earth live in Asia; and in the one country of China there are more people than in all the countries of Europe combined.

It might be expected that Asia would **Why little is known of Asia** be one of the best known of the continents; for it has the oldest civilization, and is very near

Europe. Besides that, long before the New World was discovered, a flourishing trade was carried on between Europe and the Indies. The fact is, however, that Asia, next to Africa, is the least known among the continents. Let us find some of the reasons for this.

In the first place, although Europe and Asia are so close together, their leading countries are sepa- **1. Because of arid and desert land in the west** rated by a desert, which is really more difficult to cross than either mountains or the sea.

The two great seas in southwestern Asia, the Caspian and Aral seas, have no outlets and are salt, although large rivers pour volumes of fresh water into them. What are the names of these rivers? How does the area of these lakes compare with that of Lake Superior, the largest of our Great Lakes (p. 258)? While these salt seas are of great size, the fact that they have no outlets tells very clearly that the climate here is dry, for the water evaporates faster than the rivers can pour it in.

Most of the vast region between the Irtish River and Africa is either desert or arid land (Fig. 273). Estimate the distance across this arid country from east to west. When you realize that it is two or three thousand miles, you can see what a barrier this section must always have been to commerce and acquaintance between the people of the two continents.

In the second place, it is easy to see why Siberia — which makes up more

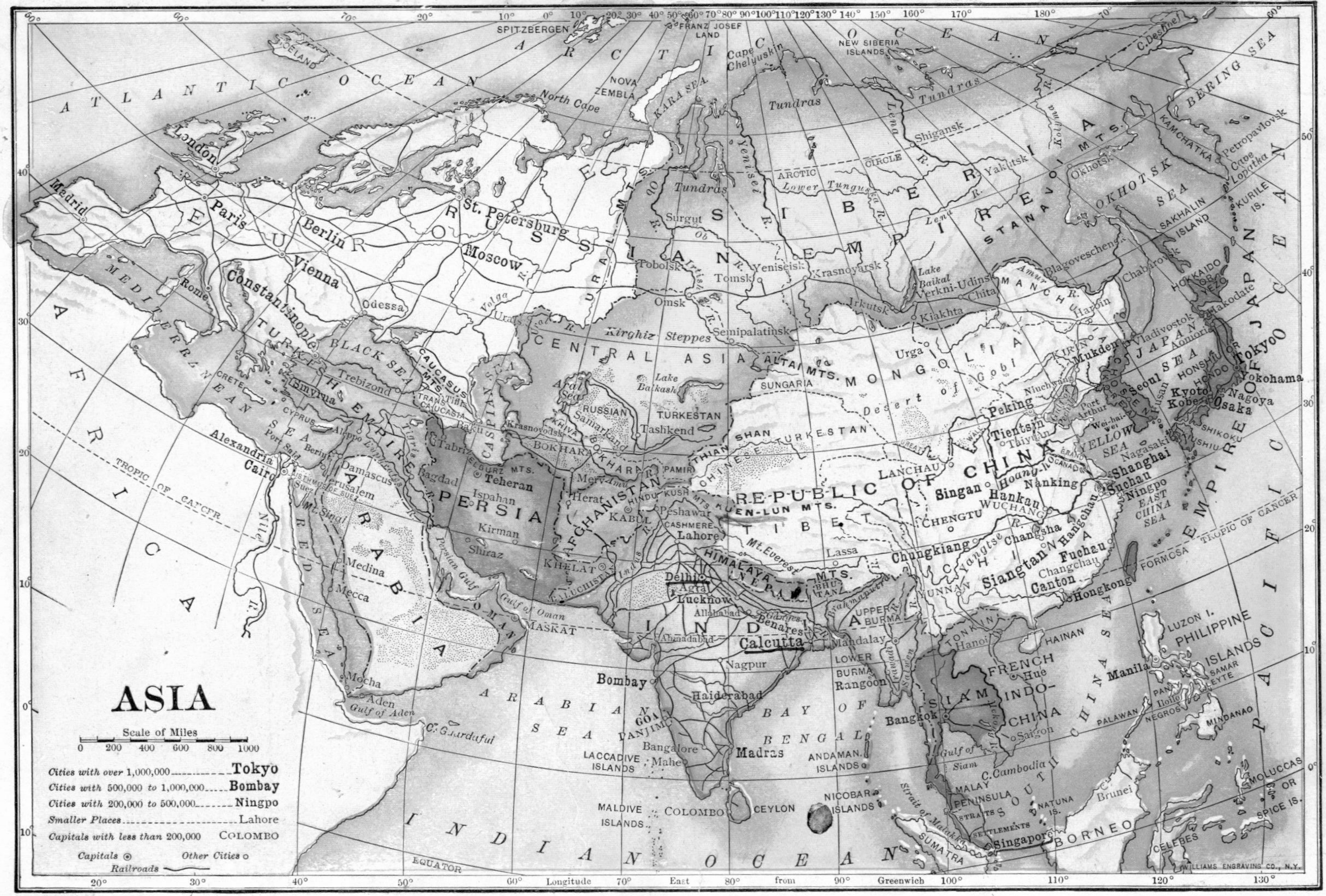

ASIA

Scale of Miles

0 200 400 600 800 1000

Cities with over 1,000,000 .... **Tokyo**
Cities with 500,000 to 1,000,000 .... **Bombay**
Cities with 200,000 to 500,000 .... **Ningpo**
Smaller Places .... Lahore
Capitals with less than 200,000 .... COLOMBO

Capitals ⊛   Other Cities ○
Railroads ......

FIG. 272.

Williams Engraving Co., N.Y.

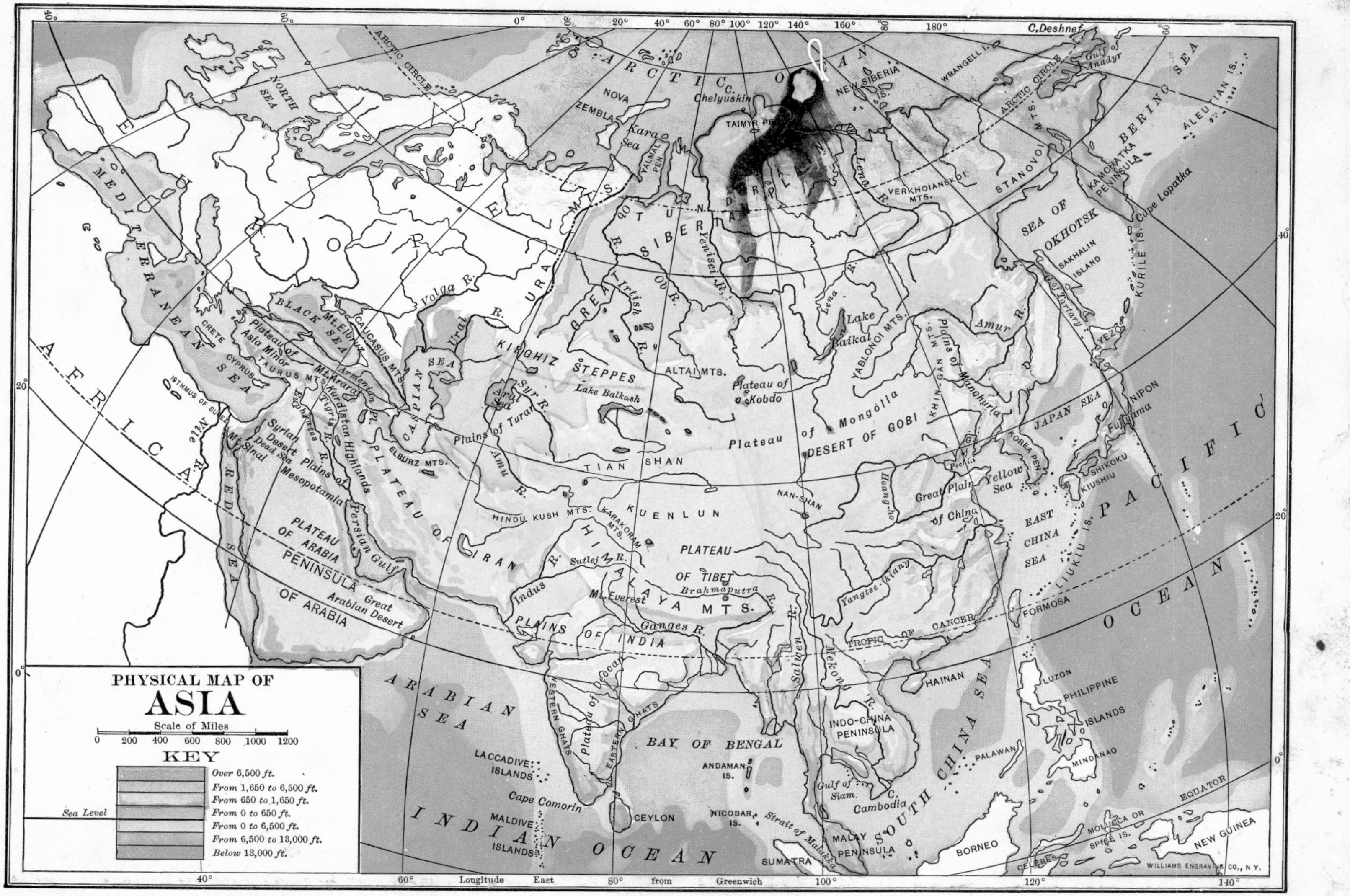
PHYSICAL MAP OF
ASIA
Scale of Miles
0 200 400 600 800 1000 1200
KEY
Over 6,500 ft.
From 1,650 to 6,500 ft.
From 650 to 1,650 ft.
Sea Level
From 0 to 650 ft.
From 0 to 6,500 ft.
From 6,500 to 13,000 ft.
Below 13,000 ft.
Longitude East from Greenwich
ARCTIC OCEAN
PACIFIC OCEAN
INDIAN OCEAN
ARABIAN SEA
BAY OF BENGAL
SOUTH CHINA SEA
EAST CHINA SEA
JAPAN SEA
YELLOW SEA
SEA OF OKHOTSK
BERING SEA
Kara Sea
NORTH SEA
MEDITERRANEAN SEA
BLACK SEA
CASPIAN SEA
RED SEA
Persian Gulf
Aral Sea
Lake Baikal
Lake Balkash
EUROPE
AFRICA
URAL MTS.
CAUCASUS MTS.
ELBURZ MTS.
TAURUS MTS.
HINDU KUSH MTS.
KARAKORAM MTS.
HIMALAYA MTS.
KUENLUN
TIAN SHAN
NAN-SHAN
ALTAI MTS.
YABLONOI MTS.
KHIN-GAN MTS.
STANOVOI MTS.
VERKHOIANSKOI MTS.
WESTERN GHATS
EASTERN GHATS
Mt. Elbruz
Mt. Ararat
Mt. Everest
Mt. Sinai
PLATEAU OF IRAN
PLATEAU OF TIBET
PLATEAU OF ARABIA
Plateau of Asia Minor
Plateau of Kobdo
Plateau of Mongolia
Plateau of Deccan
DESERT OF GOBI
Syrian Desert
Great Arabian Desert
Armenian Pl.
Kurdistan Highlands
Plains of Mesopotamia
Plains of Turan
KIRGHIZ STEPPES
GREAT SIBERIAN TUNDRA PLAINS
Plains of Manchuria
Great Plain of China
PLAINS OF INDIA
PENINSULA OF ARABIA
INDO-CHINA PENINSULA
MALAY PENINSULA
KAMCHATKA PENINSULA
KOREA PEN.
TAIMYR PEN.
YALMAL PEN.
Volga R.
Ural R.
Syr R.
Amu R.
Ob R.
Irtish R.
Yenisei R.
Lena R.
Amur R.
Hoang-ho
Yangtse-kiang
Mekong R.
Salwen R.
Brahmaputra R.
Ganges R.
Indus R.
Sutlej R.
Tigris R.
Euphrates R.
Nile R.
Dead Sea
ISTHMUS OF SUEZ
CRETE
CYPRUS
NOVA ZEMBLA
NEW SIBERIA IS.
WRANGELL I.
C. Chelyuskin
C. Deshnef
Gulf of Anadyr
Cape Lopatka
ALEUTIAN IS.
KURILE IS.
SAKHALIN ISLAND
G. of Tartary
YEZO
NIPON
Fujiyama
SHIKOKU
KIUSHIU
LIUKIU IS.
FORMOSA
G. of Pechili
HAINAN
LUZON
PHILIPPINE ISLANDS
PALAWAN
MINDANAO
BORNEO
CELEBES
MOLUCCA OR SPICE IS.
NEW GUINEA
EQUATOR
SUMATRA
Strait of Malakka
Gulf of Siam
C. Cambodia
ANDAMAN IS.
NICOBAR IS.
CEYLON
Cape Comorin
LACCADIVE ISLANDS
MALDIVE ISLANDS
ARCTIC CIRCLE
TROPIC OF CANCER
WILLIAMS ENGRAVING CO., N.Y.

FIG. 273.

than one fourth of the whole continent

2. Because of the extreme cold in the north —should have been little visited, for most of it is a very cold country. Note how much of it lies in the frigid zone.

plateaus, rather than low plains. One of them, the plateau of Tibet, is from two to three miles above the level of the sea, which is higher than most of the peaks of lofty mountains. You know

Fig. 275. — The Snowy Range in the Himalaya Mountains, the loftiest mountains in the world.

The main slope of this vast plain is toward the north. Trace its three great rivers. What are their names? Like the Mackenzie River in North America, they have been of little help in exploring the country. Why?

For several reasons, the vast central portion of Asia has also been difficult to explore. On Figure 273 ob-

3. Because of the plateaus, mountains, and deserts in the central part serve how many mountain chains are found there. Among them are the Himalayas, just north of India, the loftiest mountain range in the world (Fig. 275). Mt. Everest, the highest peak, rises over twenty-nine thousand feet, or five and one half miles above the level of the sea. Find this mountain on Figure 272. How does it compare in height with Mont Blanc in the Alps? (See table, p. 258.)

There are vast stretches of level land among these mountains, but they are

(p. 25) that the summits of mountains are cold; so, also, are high plateaus. Thus most of the highland of Central Asia has a cool or cold climate.

Much rain and snow falls on the edges of this vast highland. Note the rivers that find their sources there. The three on the north side, crossing Siberia, have already been mentioned. What are their names? What three are found on the east side, emptying into the Pacific? Name several on the south side. From this you see that most of the great rivers of Asia rise in this highland region, just as most of those of western Europe rise in the Alps.

Since the winds lose their vapor on the margin of this great highland, its interior is largely desert or arid land. Find the Desert of Gobi.

A region so mountainous, and so cold and dry as Central Asia, is difficult to explore; and it is not strange that we know little about it even to-day.

From what has been said about the western, northern, and central parts of

4. Because of the character of the people

the continent, it is evident that there can be but few inhabitants in those sections. The vast hordes of people living in Asia must, therefore, dwell in the eastern and southern parts. Most of them live in China, Japan, and India.

How well do we know those parts of the continent? This time it is the character of the people, rather than of the

FIG. 276. — Pilgrims entering Bethlehem on Christmas day. It was here that Christ was born.

country, that has been in the way. The Chinese, for instance, of whom there are such great numbers, are very different from Europeans and Americans, and, until quite recently, they have not wanted anything to do with foreigners. They have not been willing to admit white people into their country even as visitors. How, then, could we find out much about them and their country?

Until about fifty years ago, the Japanese felt and acted the same way toward us. India is better known, because it

has long been under the control of the British.

In recent years the situation has greatly changed, and we are now rapidly becoming acquainted with all the Asiatic people and their continent.

2. Southwestern Asia

Turkey in Europe you have already studied about (p. 213); but much the larger part of Turkey is in

The countries here included

Asia. Trace its boundaries. The other principal countries here included under Southwestern Asia are *Arabia, Persia, Afghanistan,* and *Baluchistan.* Trace the boundaries of each.

The western portion of this part of Asia has long been the part

Why the most familiar part of Asia

of the continent best known to Europeans. One reason for this is that, for centuries before the discovery of America, the trade routes between Europe and the East Indies either crossed this region, or else skirted it on the southwest.

The other reason is the fact that it contains the land once called Palestine. Rome has been of great importance in the world's history, and so has Athens, as we have seen; but the part that has had the greatest influence of all is this tiny Palestine, which has an area of less than a hundred miles square. Here was the early home of the Jews. Here still stands Jerusalem, where Christ was crucified; and near by is Bethlehem (Fig. 276), where Christ was born over nineteen hundred years ago. The many Christian churches have been built in His memory, and Christmas itself is a reminder of His birth.

Palestine is not shown on our map as a separate country, for it is now only a part of the Turkish Empire. One might suppose that so sacred a place would be carefully preserved by the many millions of Christians in the world. They have, indeed, tried to preserve it; thousands and thousands of Europeans have died in the attempt to save Jerusalem from the Turks. Yet the Turks have held it for hundreds of years, and Palestine is now only a part of a little country, called Syria, which belongs to Turkey.

How it happens that Palestine is a part of Turkey

The Turks are *Mohammedans* (Fig. 277), or followers of Mohammed, who was born at MECCA about fourteen hundred years ago. Although they believe in God, their religion is very different from ours, and their holy book is the Koran, not the Bible. Mecca is their holy city. Find it on the map.

The Mohammedans are religious fanatics, and have no patience with any other belief. They detest all Christians, even believing that it is right to kill them. That is one reason why they have wished to capture the holy city, Jerusalem, and destroy whatever reminded them of Christ.

In order to spread their religion, the Turks have often gone to war with neighboring peoples, and have added to their Empire much of the territory that they have conquered. Their country now has a very irregular shape, as you see. What two large rivers do you find? What city is on the lower Tigris?

Extent of the Turkish Empire

If you have ever read "The Arabian Nights," you have read about it.

The reason why not all of *Arabia* is included in the Turkish Empire, is that the Turks have never conquered the inhabitants of the interior of the peninsula. It is an arid and desert plateau,

FIG. 277. — A Mohammedan priest in eastern Asia.

with oases here and there. As in the Desert of Sahara, many of the Arabs are nomads, who wander from place to place tending their flocks of sheep and goats and their herds of horses, cattle, and camels. They live much of the time in the saddle, and are fierce warriors.

One of the products of this region is coffee. You have, perhaps, heard of Mocha coffee; if you look on the map, you will find the city from which it gets its name. Wheat, grapes, olives, figs, dates, oranges, tobacco, and cotton are raised in the Turkish Empire and in *Persia*, usually by the help of irrigation.

Agricultural products of Southwestern Asia

The people of this part of Asia are not advanced enough to carry on much manufacturing;

Manufacturing yet beautiful carpets, rugs, and shawls are made in great numbers, especially in Persia and Turkey. The work is done by hand, and it takes many weeks to make a carpet of the same size as one which could be made in a factory in a few hours. These hand-made rugs and carpets are so beautiful, and wear so well, that they are everywhere highly prized.

Throughout this entire region, which is about two thirds as large as the United States,

Commerce there are very few railways, and even wagon roads are usually lacking. Goods are carried mainly upon the backs of camels, which travel in groups, called *caravans;* and men usually travel on the backs of horses and camels.

The people have advanced very little, and many of their customs are the same as those of the days of Christ. Even to-day, in many parts of this section, it is not safe to travel without a strong guard of soldiers. It is especially dangerous for Christians, since the Mohammedans have so deep a hatred for them.

There are few large cities in this entire region, SMYRNA, in Turkey,

Cities and TEHERAN, the capital of Persia, being the largest. Find the capital of the Turkish Empire.

3. Russia in Asia, or Siberia

This vast country, extending from the Ural Mountains to the Pacific Ocean, is a

Its best-settled part part of the Russian Empire. The best-settled section is in the south, near Persia and Afghanistan. Even this part is thinly inhabited, for the region is arid and desert, like the countries farther south.

The occupations, also, are similar to those of southwestern Asia. In the river valleys, and on the oases, agriculture is carried on with the aid of irrigation; and on the arid lands grazing is important. Meat, hides, wool, and cotton are the principal products. There is scarcely any manufacturing except the making of rugs, shawls, and cloth, by hand. Many hand-made rugs from *Bokhara* and *Khiva* are used in the United States. Find these places on the map.

The northern portion, a land of frozen tundras, is the coldest region on any of the continents. The few people who live there resemble the Eskimos. **Its least-settled part** They keep herds of reindeer, which supply them with milk, meat, and hides, besides serving as draft animals.

The middle part of Siberia is a vast plain which is little settled as yet, but it is the most promising **Its most promising part** section for the future. It has much good soil, and is suited to the production of grains. There is much forest here, and in the mountains valuable minerals are found, including gold and graphite, or "black lead," from which pencils are made.

One reason why this region has not been better settled is the fact that it has been difficult to reach. The rivers, which flow northward, have been of little use, and until lately there have been no railroads. The Russian government has built a railroad all the way across Siberia, so that it is now possible to travel by rail from St. Petersburg to PORT ARTHUR on the Chinese coast. About how far is that? Find IRKUTSK, which is on this railway.

Russia has long used Siberia as a prison, and thousands of prisoners have gone there. Many have been sent not because they have committed any crime, but **Use of Siberia as a prison** because they have said or done something that the Russian rulers did not like. Some, even, have been merely *suspected* of saying or doing something. Many have been seized by officers and thrown into prison without a moment's warning; then, without trial, they.

Fig. 278. — A farming scene in the mountainous region in Siberia.

have been transported to Siberia to work in the mines. Men and women of the highest character have been thus torn from their families and hurried away so secretly that not even their friends knew what had become of them.

Such treatment shows the meaning of a despotic form of government. It also shows us very clearly how fortunate we are in living under such a government as our own.

4. Republic of China

Some of the most important arts that man has ever learned have come from the Chinese. For instance, **Former progress of the Chinese** they made porcelain dishes long before the Europeans knew how, and on that account such dishes are still called *chinaware*, even though manufactured in the United States.

They invented gunpowder, and our firecrackers for the Fourth of July used to come from China. You have doubtless seen the Chinese letters on the outside of packages. They also discovered how to make silk and paper, and they invented the art of printing.

While this strange-looking, yellow race was once among the **Their backwardness now, with reasons** foremost nations of the earth, it is now very much behind the Great Powers of Europe and the New World.

This is partly explained by the fact that they believe that whatever their ancestors did, they must do. This is called ancestor worship. Since their fathers had no railways, telegraphs, or telephones, they have wanted none themselves. Also, owing to their dislike of new things, they have neither traveled much abroad, nor allowed foreigners to visit them. Indeed, they have looked down upon foreigners, or, as they call them, "foreign devils," who have so many strange customs.

A second cause for the backwardness of the Chinese has been their poor government, which until 1912 was an absolute monarchy. Now, however, the government has been changed to a republic.

In spite of these facts, it is quite possible that China with its new government will yet rank as one of the Great Powers.

Possible strength of China in the future
1. Area and population
Her vast population, which is larger than that of all Europe, and five times that of the United States, including Alaska, gives China one great advantage. Her area, which is greater than that of the United States, gives her a second advantage.

There are many kinds of soil, too. There are extensive plains, some of them broad river flood plains and deltas. On the other hand some sections are plateaus, and there are also lofty mountain ranges. In so large a country, with so many differences in climate, soil, and surface features, there are certain to be many resources. Let us see what the principal ones are.

3. The surface features

Fig. 279. — A part of the wonderful Chinese Wall, built centuries ago to prevent invaders from entering the country.

A third advantage is her great variety of climate. Observe through what zones the Empire extends. How much farther south does it reach than our most southern state, Florida? How much farther north, than our most northern states? From this it is plain that the variety of climate is even greater than our own, and that means, of course, that the agricultural products may be even more varied. As in our country, some parts are desert, some arid, and some have abundant rainfall.

2. Variety of climate

In northern and western China, the climate is arid, and there are some extensive deserts. Here the principal products are meat, wool, and hides. South and east of this there is rainfall enough for agriculture. Here the products of the temperate zone, such as wheat, can be raised. What other grains and agricultural products have you found in the northern half of the United States? All these can be raised in this part of China.

4. Resources
(1) Agricultural products

Central China, just south of this section, has a warm temperate climate. Here cotton, rice, millet, oranges, tea, and silk are produced. Rice is one of the chief articles of food for the Chinese, and China produces more raw silk than any other country in the world.

The southern part of the Empire extends into the tropical zone. Here we find tropical fruits, such as grow in Central America and the West Indies. Name several of them.

Thus China produces all the crops that the United States does, and more. Name some of their products that we do not raise.

There are some forest areas, and along the coast there is **(2)** *Lumber and fish* valuable fishing. The Chinese make much use of fish as an article of food, catching them from the rivers as well as from the sea. They even train birds to catch fish for them.

The Chinese have never been noted as miners, and therefore little is known **(3)** *Minerals* about the mineral wealth of the country. Still it is certain that there are vast deposits of coal of the very best quality, some of it hard coal, like that of eastern Pennsylvania. There are also extensive deposits of iron and other valuable minerals.

The natural means of transportation are also excellent. There is an abundance of good harbors, espe- **(4)** *Means of transportation by water* cially at the mouths of the rivers; and these rivers are open to navigation far into the interior. Indeed, even now, the easiest way of getting into the interior of China is by boat, especially on the Yangtse-kiang and Hoang-ho rivers. Trace these rivers.

The Chinese have built a number of canals, and these have been used for centuries. Find the Grand Canal on the map, and tell what cities it connects. Railways and electric cars, being new inventions, have been much disliked by the people. For that reason there are, even now, few of these in this vast Empire.

Fig. 280. — Chinese farming scene. All these level places have been built by the Chinese so that they may cultivate even the steep hill slopes.

Their methods of transportation have been, and still are, very crude. It has been the custom for men to take the place of horses, to a large extent, carrying goods on their backs, and drawing both people and freight in vehicles of various kinds.

One of the principal vehicles is the wheelbarrow (Fig. 281), which has but one wheel, and can therefore be used even where the roads are very narrow. It is said that passengers sometimes make the entire journey from Shanghai to Peking, a distance of six hundred miles, in a wheelbarrow. Labor is so cheap that it costs about twenty cents a day, or at the rate of about half a cent a mile, for each passenger, two traveling in a single wheelbarrow. This is about one fourth as expensive as the passenger rate on some of our railways. The passengers in the wheelbarrow, however, do not go so far in a whole day as we go on our trains in two hours! It is easy to see, too, that they do not travel so comfortably.

Of late, the Chinese are rapidly changing their customs. They are now

Fig. 281. — A Chinese passenger wheelbarrow, on which people are carried long distances.

sending hundreds of their ablest young men to Europe and America to learn about our arts and industries. They are inviting foreigners to their country, are building railroads, and are improving their laws. These signs of progress, together with the change in the form of government already spoken of, show that the Chinese are awakening at last; and it seems likely that they will make wonderful progress in the future.

5. Recent advances

A large portion of the population is massed along the coast and the lower course of the rivers. There are so many people living here that scores of thousands can find no room on the land, and live in house-

Chief cities

boats on the water. Many others dig caves in the hillsides, and live in these burrows.

In this country there are many large cities. Among these are PEKING, the capital; TIENTSIN, its seaport; CANTON, one of the largest cities in China; HONGKONG, a seaport near by; and SHANGHAI, also a seaport. Locate each of these on the map. From the tables on pages 256–258 see how each of these cities compares in size with our largest cities.

5. Japan and Korea

Japan is only a little more than one thirtieth as large as

Fig. 282. — A Chinese lady being carried by two men — a very common way of traveling in China.

China, and has only one-eighth as many inhabitants. It is not much larger than the British Isles in area and population.

Area and population

On the map (Fig. 273) find the two largest islands, Nipon and Yezo, just east of China. Also find Formosa, the most southern island of the Empire.

The Japanese, like their neighbors the Chinese, belong to the yellow race. **Advances since 1853** Like them, also, they for a long time wanted nothing to do with foreigners. In 1853, however, an American naval officer, Commodore Perry, entered the harbor of Yokohama with several war ships, and persuaded the Japanese to allow us to trade with them.

Since that time the Japanese have made wonderful advances. They have built railways and have established lines of steamships to many parts of the world. They have introduced the telephone and the telegraph, have established many newspapers, and numerous schools of all grades. At the same time they have made such progress in manufacturing that they are now one of the leading manufacturing nations of the world.

Only a few years ago Japan engaged in a war with Russia to prevent that Great Power from seizing Korea. The Japanese won the victory and made Korea a part of their own Empire. A few years before that they had a war with China, in which they easily won.

Japan is now far in advance of all other countries in Asia. She ranks as one of the Great Powers of the world, the only one in Asia, and is sometimes called the England of the Orient.

Probably no nation has ever advanced **Reasons for this wonderful advance** more rapidly than Japan has during the last fifty years. Some of the reasons for this astonishing growth are as follows:—

Perhaps the most important of all has been the eagerness of the Japanese to learn. Soon after Commodore Perry's visit, they invited foreigners to come as teachers, and even sent thousands of their young men abroad, to study in the United States and Europe. **1. Eagerness to learn**

The valuable resources of the country are a second reason for the advance of Japan.

The climate is everywhere moist enough for **2. The natural resources of the country**

FIG. 283.— A scene in Japan. The mountain peak is the very perfect cone of the volcano Fujiyama.

agriculture, and, although much of the surface is mountainous, there is a great deal of excellent soil. The people have learned to cultivate it very carefully, too, allowing no land to lie idle that can possibly be used for crops.

The long distance over which the islands extend from north to south, makes it possible to raise many different kinds of crops. Measure to see how far it is from Yezo, on the north, to Formosa, on the south. What is the latitude of the northern and southern boundaries? The crops in the north are the products of the

Q

cool temperate zone ; those in the south, and especially in Formosa, are such as

FIG. 284.—This building was torn in pieces by the shaking of the earth during one of the destructive Japanese earthquakes.

are common to the tropical zone. Japan, like China, produces a great deal of silk, rice, and tea.

This small country has important mineral resources, including gold, copper, iron, coal, and petroleum. The two latter are useful as fuels, and there is also excellent water power for use in manufacturing.

Japan suffers some serious drawbacks, to be sure. For example, many of the islands are very small, and all of them are very mountainous. They are really the crests of a great mountain range rising from the bottom of the sea, and some of the peaks are volcanoes. The mountains are still rising, too, and as they rise, the rocks now and then break apart and change their positions, causing earthquakes. Sometimes these shocks are so powerful that houses are thrown down, and there is great destruction of life and property. Japan has been visited by many such terrible earthquakes (Fig. 284).

A third reason for the wonderful progress of Japan is that labor is very cheap there, as in China; **3. Cheap and skillful labor** and that the Japanese are very skillful workmen. In the United States one often sees especially beautiful fans, parasols, napkins, dolls, and screens that were made in Japan. Whatever the Japanese make, they try to make beautiful.

In silk manufacturing, especially, they have taken high rank. They are also very skillful in pottery making, and they manufacture much cotton and woolen cloth, as well as iron goods, such as machinery and ships.

A final reason for the rapid advance of Japan is the opportunity that it has en-

FIG. 285.—Japanese ladies drinking tea in their home.

joyed for ocean commerce. In this respect Japan reminds us of the British

4. Advantages for commerce Isles. The coast is very long, and there are plenty of good harbors, so that the products may be easily shipped in various directions.

FIG. 286. — Yoshihito, Emperor, or Mikado, of Japan.

The principal city of Japan is the capital, TOKYO, where the Emperor, or **Principal cities** *Mikado* (Fig. 286), lives. It is situated on the largest island, and is about the size of Chicago. YOKOHAMA, the seaport of Tokyo, is a city of about one third of a million inhabitants.

Korea was an independent kingdom until a few years ago, when Japan seized it during her war with Russia. Like China, it is a very backward nation, and, until recently, foreigners were not allowed to enter the country. The chief industry is agriculture, but there are extensive forests and valuable mineral deposits.

6. India and the Countries East of it

India, the central one of the three peninsulas on the southern side of Asia, is about half as large as the **Area and population** United States, but it contains more than three times as many people.

The peninsula east of India includes several countries, with many millions of inhabitants. The largest of these is *French Indo-China*, which is larger than France and England together, while *Siam* is almost as large. *Burma*, also on this peninsula, is a part of the Indian Empire.

FIG. 287. — A Burmese working woman carrying her child.

The greater part of these two large peninulas is under the control of European nations. The lion's **The control** share belongs to the British, **of this vast** who rule India and much of **region** the peninsula east of it. On Figure 310 trace the British possessions; the French possessions. Siam is an independent country.

This is the part of the world that Columbus was seeking when he discovered

Fig. 288. — Natives of India picking tea leaves on a tea plantation.

America. He undertook his voyage in order to find a short and easy route for **Why these possessions are valuable** bringing to Europe the silks, dyewoods, spices, perfumes, ivory, and precious stones that had long been reaching Europe from the Indies.

These same valuable products are still brought from this region, but other products as well now come from here. One reason why India is of special value to England is that it produces much cotton, which is shipped to the British Isles to be made into cloth. Wheat is another important crop in India. Why should Great Britain welcome this (p. 190)? Other crops are rice, tea (Fig. 288), coffee, sugar, and poppies, from which opium is made.

The peninsula east of India, and the East Indian Islands, supply many precious stones, and produce many spices, such as pepper, nutmeg, and cinnamon, besides tropical woods and fruits. Many of these products are shipped to Europe from the principal seaport, Singapore. This is an English city on an island at the very southern tip of the Malay Peninsula.

The native inhabitants of this region, like the Chinese, have long been highly civilized. They have many **Benefits to the native inhabitants** beautiful buildings that are centuries old. Even before the time of the Roman Empire, and of the Republic of Athens, the people of India were far advanced in civilization. But, like the Chinese, for a long time they did not cultivate the arts and sciences as Europeans have done. In many ways, therefore, it has been to their advantage to come under the control of European countries.

The British, for instance, have caused many excellent roads and railways to be built in India. They have also established a number of manufacturing industries. Another important work has been to improve the system of irrigation; for much of western and central India is arid, and some of it is even a desert.

Eastern and southern India, where the winds blow from the ocean, have abundant rain. Because of the dampness and the tropical heat, there are extensive forests here, forming a dense tangle, or *jungle*. In this jungle the tiger lives; also the elephant, and other large and fierce animals. There are great numbers of poisonous serpents, too, and thousands of people die every year from their bites. The English government has done much to make life safer and more agreeable in this section.

In spite of these benefits, one wonders how so large a country, **Reasons why the British can control India** with so vast a population, can be kept under control by the English. India is about fifteen times as large as Great Britain, and has about seven times as many inhabitants.

Many of the people of India are, in truth, dissatisfied with the English rule, and wish for independence; but they have not been able to obtain it, for India is very weak. One main cause for its weakness is the *caste* system; for people there belong to different classes, or castes. Men belonging to one caste will have almost nothing to do with those of a lower caste; they will not even eat at the same table with them. There are also different races and customs among the Indian people. These differences among them have made it impossible for the natives to expel the English, as they certainly could if they were to unite.

Several very large rivers rise in the Himalayas and flow across northern India

and Burma. What are their names? Describe the course of each. The Indus is the river from whose name **Principal rivers and cities** both the word *India* and the word *Hindu* comes. The natives are sometimes called Hindus.

Fig. 289. — A temple in India, in which the natives worship.

The river that flows toward the southeast is the Ganges, on which the largest city, Calcutta, is situated. The other leading cities of India are Bombay, Madras, and Delhi, the capital. Bombay has an excellent harbor. The two principal cities on or near the eastern peninsula are Bangkok and Singapore. Locate each of these cities.

What islands lie east of French Indo-China? Name their capital. You have already learned something about these in your study of the United States; for you remember that the Philippine Islands form one of our colonies (p. 161).

General facts about Asia
Questions

1. Give some idea of the area and population of Asia. 2. Why might we expect that Asia would be well known? 3. What kind of land is found in the south-west? How has this kept us from knowing more about the continent? 4. What conditions in the north have made it hard to find out much about Asia? 5. Why has the central part become little known to us? 6. How has the character of the people prevented us from knowing more about them?

Southwestern Asia
1. Questions

1. What countries are here included? Locate each. 2. Why is this the most familiar part of Asia? 3. How does it happen that Palestine is now a part of Turkey? 4. What is the extent of the Turkish Empire? 5. Name the agricultural products of Southwestern Asia. 6. Tell about the manufacturing there. 7. The commerce.

2. Suggestions

1. What stories in the Bible have you read, that tell about places mentioned in this geography? 2. What is meant by the date 1909? 3. Find out whether your grocer sells "Mocha" coffee. 4. Examine a Turkish or Persian rug.

Siberia
1. Questions

1. State some facts about the best-settled part of Siberia. 2. About its least-settled part. 3. About its most promising part. 4. Tell about the use of Siberia as a prison.

2. Suggestions

1. Of what advantage will the Siberian railway be to Russia? 2. How does that railway compare in length with those crossing the United States? 3. What object do you see in having the eastern terminus, Port Arthur, so far south?

Republic of China
1. Questions

1. Tell about the former progress of the Chinese. 2. What is their present form of government? 3. What about the area and population of China? 4. What kinds of climate are there? 5. What are the surface features? 6. What resources has China? 7. Describe its recent advances. 8. Name and locate the principal cities.

2. Suggestions

1. How can you distinguish a Chinaman from other men? 2. How might railways in China help greatly to prevent the awful famines that they sometimes have there? 3. Find out about the Great Wall of China. 4. What reasons can you see for or against the free admission of Chinese to the United States?

Japan and Korea
1. Questions

1. Compare Japan with China and the British Isles in area and population. 2. What advances have been made by Japan since 1853? 3. Give four reasons for such advances. 4. Locate the capital and Yokohama. 5. Tell about Korea.

2. Suggestions

1. Make a collection of Japanese articles, such as paper napkins, fans, etc. 2. Examine them to see in what respects they are artistic or beautiful. 3. Collect pictures of Japanese houses and people.

India and countries east of it
1. Questions

1. State some facts about the area and population of this region. 2. What nations control it? 3. Mention some ways in which this region is valuable to the nations that control it. 4. Mention some benefits that the native inhabitants have received from British rule. 5. Give a special reason why the British are able to control India. 6. Name and locate the principal rivers and cities.

2. Suggestions

1. Find out about foreign missions to India, or to other parts of Asia. 2. How far was Columbus from India when he discovered America? 3. What route should he have taken if he had continued his voyage to India? 4. On a globe find which is the shortest water route from Bombay to London. 5. Read Kipling's "Jungle Book."

General review

1. Name the principal countries of Asia, and locate each. 2. What routes might you take in going to Peking? 3. What great cities of Europe and North America are in nearly the same latitude as Peking? 4. Name the principal rivers in Asia, and describe their courses. 5. Name and locate the chief cities of Asia. 6. Draw an outline map of Asia, putting in the boundaries of the principal countries. 7. Put in, also, the principal mountains, rivers, and cities. 8. Make a sand map of the continent, showing its shape and its main slopes.

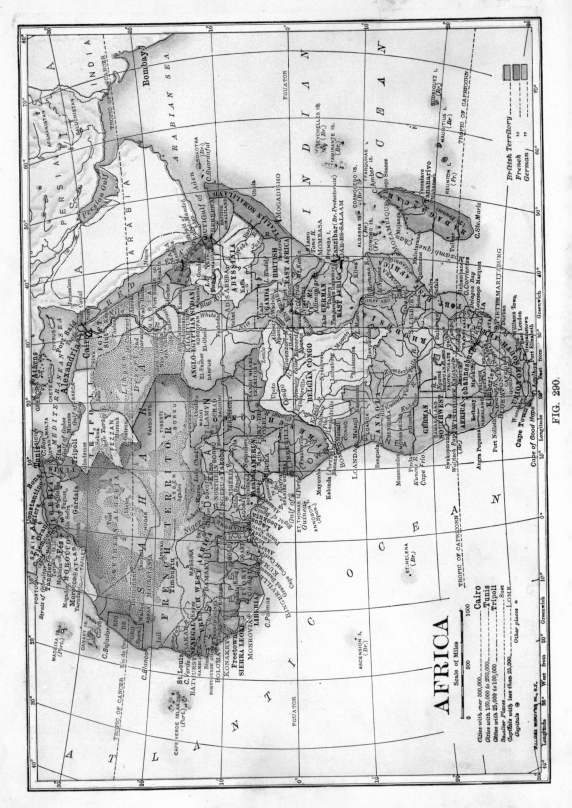

AFRICA

Scale of Miles

0   500   1000

Cairo
Tunis
Tripoli

Cities with over 300,000...........
Cities with 100,000 to 300,000....
Cities with 25,000 to 100,000.....
Smaller Places
Capitals with less than 25,000....
Capitals

FIG. 290.

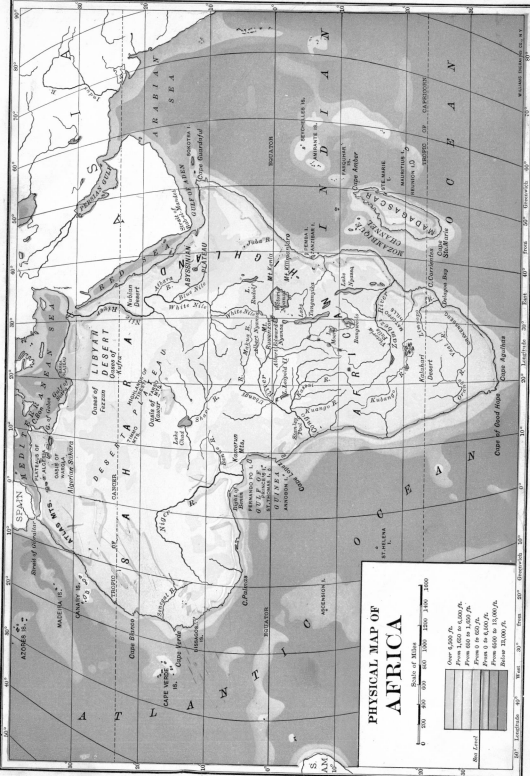

FIG. 291.

PHYSICAL MAP OF
AFRICA

Scale of Miles

0 200 400 600 800 1000 1200 1400 1600

Over 6,500 ft.
From 1,650 to 6,500 ft.
From 650 to 1,650 ft.
From 0 to 650 ft.

Sea Level

From 6500 to 13,000 ft.
Below 13,000 ft.

XIV. AFRICA

1. What continent does Africa most resemble in shape? 2. In what parts are the chief **Map study** mountain ranges (Fig. 291)? 3. Name and trace the three largest rivers. 4. About how much of Africa lies in the torrid zone? Is this an advantage or a disadvantage? Why? 5. How does its coast line compare with that of Europe in regularity? 6. What influence must that have

continents that history tells us about, and it lies so near Europe that the two almost join at the Strait of Gibraltar; yet it is the least known of all the continents.

There are several reasons why so little is known about Africa. In **Why Africa is** the first place, there is a **so little known** vast desert south of the Mediterranean

FIG. 292. — A caravan of camels crossing the Sahara Desert, bearing a load of the products of the tropical region of Central Africa.

upon the harbors? 7. What large island lies east of southern Africa? 8. What three groups of small islands lie west of northern Africa?

1. General Facts about Africa

Probably one reason why Africa is called the *dark continent* is the fact that **Why called the** it is the home of the black **dark continent** man. Another reason is that until recently we have known so little about it. It is one of the oldest

Sea (Fig. 292). It extends east and west across the continent from the Atlantic Ocean to the Red Sea; and from north to south it is a thousand miles wide.

This vast region, most of which is called the Sahara Desert, is very difficult to cross. It has no roads or railways, and the only way to travel over it is **1. The great** on camels. There are so few **desert in the** oases that the watering places **northern part** are usually many miles apart, so that both camels and men may perish from thirst. Frightful sand storms sometimes arise, continuing for hours and even days; and in these the sand is drifted about by the winds, filling the air and sometimes even burying the caravans. If these perils are escaped, there is still the danger of attack from the fierce nomads who live in the desert, and who rob the caravans, often showing no mercy to travelers.

It is not strange, therefore, that Europeans have failed to become well acquainted with Africa by entering it from the north.

One of the largest cataracts is Victoria Falls (Fig. 293), in the lower Zambezi River. It is larger even than Niagara, and is one of the grandest waterfalls in the world. The Nile also has several rapids; and there is a great cataract in the Congo. Thus the rivers have been of little use in exploring the continent.

A third reason why we know so little about Africa is its unhealthful climate. Notice where the Tropics of Cancer and Capricorn cross the continent. From this you see that most of Africa is in the tropical zone. Indeed, the equator crosses it not far from the center, and only the northern and southern parts are in the temperate zones.

3. The unhealthful climate

In this tropical region, the low coast lands have too hot and damp a climate for white men; and there is much malaria, as

Fig. 293.—The Victoria Falls in the Zambezi River of South Africa.

One might expect the large rivers to offer a good means of reaching the interior. Trace the Nile, Niger, Congo, and Zambezi, and notice how far they extend into the continent. If these could be navigated far up toward their sources, as our Hudson and Mississippi rivers can be, they would make excellent highways to the interior; but this cannot be done, for all of them have rapids and and falls in their lower courses.

2. The rapids and falls in the rivers

The reason for these falls is that the interior of Africa, like that of both Mexico (p. 176) and Spain (p. 209), is mainly a plateau, whose elevation is from a quarter to a half mile above the level of the sea. In descending from this plateau, the rivers tumble in cataracts and falls.

well as other diseases that thrive in a hot, damp climate. Generally, therefore, Europeans can live with comfort only upon the high land of the interior. This fact has helped to keep foreigners out of Africa; for settlements in new countries are usually first made along the coast. It is dangerous even to cross the narrow strip of low coast land.

A part of Central Africa, where the rainfall is very heavy, is covered by a dense forest like that in the Amazon Valley (p. 182). This forest extends north and south for a full thousand miles, and is very difficult to traverse.

4. The forest jungle, the wild animals, and the savages

Besides this, there are many wild animals in the forest and on the open plains to the north and south of it. Among these are the lion, elephant, rhinoceros, hippopotamus, and giraffe as well as many serpents. Some of these animals, like the lion, are very fierce and dangerous.

Another difficulty comes from the great numbers of savage black men, or Negroes, many of whom are dangerous men to meet. For centuries the Negroes have been seized and carried away as slaves to various parts of the world. Even to-day, the Arabs seize many of them for that purpose. Such treatment has not helped to make them friendly to white men.

Why the southern part is best known Strange as it may seem, the best-known part of Africa is the very southern tip, the part farthest from Europe. You will notice that this region lies in the temperate zone, which is one reason why Europeans have gone there. Another reason is that, in former days, ships going from Europe to India had to sail around the Cape of Good Hope. In this way men learned about that section; and long before other parts of the continent were occupied by Europeans, the Dutch had colonies in South Africa. This is now the best developed part of the continent.

Parts of Africa recently seized by Europeans Only during the last half century has there been much exploration and settlement in other parts of Africa. In that time, however, some of the countries of Europe have been very active, and have laid claim to a large part of the continent, just as they laid claim to North America several centuries ago.

You can see from the map that Africa is divided into many more countries than our continent ever was. What parts are owned by Great Britain (Fig. 310)? By Germany? By France? What other countries have colonies there (Fig. 290)? Make a sketch of Africa, showing the sections owned by the three Great Powers of Europe just mentioned.

Fig. 294. — A negro hut in Africa.

Improvements made by Europeans Now that so much of Africa is under the control of Europeans, people are going there to explore and settle, just as people have come to our own country. Thus the continent is rapidly becoming known.

In the past, in most parts of Africa, there have been very few wagon roads. Goods had to be carried either on the rivers or along paths or trails. The natives themselves usually carried these goods on their backs. Now, however, roads, railways, and telegraph lines are being built.

You will see three large lakes on the eastern side, south of the equator. What are their names? Each of these is important for navigation, for upon them steamboats can go long distances. The rivers are also more used for navigation. Above and below the waterfalls of the Congo, Nile, and other rivers, boats can run long distances. By build-

portant cities along the coast of northern Africa.

Later, Arabs from Asia spread westward over that section, and their descendants still occupy the region. Like the Turks (p. 219), they are Mohammedans, and they still make pilgrimages to the holy city, Mecca, in Arabia. Their manners and customs are very different

Fig. 295. — A group of nomads and their tent on the northern border of the Sahara Desert in Algeria.

ing railways around the falls and rapids, these rivers are now becoming of great value for transportation.

The boldest plan of all is to build a railway from the Cape of Good Hope to Cairo in Egypt. How far is that? It is called the Cape-to-Cairo route. Doubtless one will in time be able to travel by rail all the way from Cape Town to the Mediterranean Sea.

2. Northern Africa

The northern part of Africa has long been settled by the white race. Indeed,
Character of the people in early days, when the Greeks and Romans were flourishing, there were large and im-

from those of Europeans. Indeed, they still live much as the people of western Asia did in the time of Christ. They know little about the rest of the world, and carry on scarcely any trade with other people. Their manufacturing is done by hand, and the chief products of the country are those needed for the simplest food, clothing, and shelter.

The best-known country in this section is *Egypt*, which is crossed by the Nile River. Trace its Egypt, the oldest ccuntry boundaries. CAIRO is its capital and largest city, and ALEXANDRIA is the chief port.

This is the country over which the Pharaohs, the kings of Egypt, used to

FIG. 296. — One of the pyramids of Egypt, built of huge blocks of stone to a height of several hundred feet. They were used as tombs for kings who lived thousands of years ago.

provides the water necessary for crops. Thus each year the river both waters and fertilizes a vast tract of level, fertile land. In this way, for thousands of years, millions of people have been supported in the midst of the desert.

Egypt lies just north of the Tropic of Cancer, and therefore it has a warm temperate climate. It is so warm there that crops like those of our Southern States can be produced. Among the principal products are grain, cotton, and sugar cane. Cotton and wheat are sent to European countries, especially to England; for the British have some control over Egypt, although they do not fully govern it.

3. The agricultural products

rule. Ruins of their buildings, and their immense pyramids (Fig. 296), built thousands of years ago, may still be seen. Here, the Bible tells us, Moses once lived; and Joseph, also. What stories do you remember about them?

1. Its ancient history

Egypt is a desert country, like Arabia to the east and the Sahara to the west. Yet Joseph's brothers, you may remember, went down into that country from Palestine, to get food. It is still a great agricultural region.

2. How the Nile River supports the inhabitants

The fact that Egypt is so productive is due to the Nile River. Every year floods cause the river to rise until it overflows its banks. The water, carrying a large quantity of sediment, has built a fertile flood plain on either side of the river, and a broad delta at its mouth. The annual floods spread over these broad plains. Each overflow leaves a thin layer of rich mud, and at the same time

The eastern part of Egypt includes the Isthmus of Suez, which connects Africa with Asia. Because of this narrow neck of land, ships sailing from Europe to Asia were long compelled to go all the way around Africa. In 1869 a canal eighty-seven miles long, and wide and

4. The Suez Canal

FIG. 297. — A ship in the Suez Canal.

deep enough for large ocean ships, was opened across the Isthmus. On a globe, estimate how many miles are saved by the Suez Canal (Fig. 297) in making a journey from London to Calcutta.

Name the countries west of Egypt along the Mediterranean coast. What **Other countries** are their capitals? Most of **of northern** these countries, like Egypt, **Africa** are controlled by European nations. Algeria, which is a French colony, is the most important.

Farming and grazing are the principal industries of this whole region, and the products are similar to those of Egypt and southern Europe. There are also some mineral deposits, but the people are so unprogressive that little is done with them.

3. Central Africa

In the northern part of Central Africa is the *Sudan*, a broad strip of country extending across the continent from east to west. Its northern edge is arid, for it grades into the Sahara Desert on that side; but farther south it receives plenty of rain during one season of the year, while the other season is dry. This prevents the growth of forest, except along the rivers, for trees cannot live through the dry season. Agriculture, however, is possible here, and even the Negroes raise crops.

Abyssinia, one of the few parts of Africa not controlled by European nations, lies in this belt. Point out this country. The land is high here, making the temperature cooler than it would otherwise be.

The climate of the Sudan changes toward the south, and near the equator an abundance of rain falls at all seasons. It is here that the dense tropical forest exists (p. 232), and in it many valuable tropical plants grow, including the rubber tree. Among the wild animals, the ele-

phant is especially important, for its ivory tusks are very valuable (Fig. 298). One of the chief reasons why caravans cross the Sahara Desert is to obtain this ivory.

A number of the countries in Central Africa belong to European nations. Name these countries. Find Belgian Congo. What great rivers do you find? What lakes?

Fig. 298. — Negroes of Africa carrying the huge ivory tusks of the elephant.

4. South Africa

Much of South Africa was first claimed by the Dutch of Holland. The English, however, long ago **Why largely** got possession of Cape of **owned by the** Good Hope; and by war **English** they obtained the other Dutch countries of South Africa. They are now united under the name, The Union of South Africa.

What other European countries have possessions in South Africa? What important rivers do you find here?

What does the latitude tell you about the climate of this region? Which is **Its climate** the coolest part? Why? Along the eastern coast there is abundant rainfall, for the winds here blow from the Indian Ocean; but the winds lose their vapor on the eastern slopes, and the interior and the western side of South Africa are therefore arid. In fact, parts of this section are as desert as the Sahara.

Grain is the most important crop, but ranching is the leading **Its agricultural products** industry on the arid plateau and on the low mountains that rise above it here and there.

A peculiar industry in South Africa is ostrich raising (Fig. 299). The ostrich, which is the largest of birds, is unable to fly, but on its wings and tail it has large, delicate, and beautiful feathers, which are very valuable. For what purpose are they used? The home of the ostrich is the desert of northern Africa, where it runs wild; and ostrich feathers are one of the products of the Sahara. The feathers are so costly that it pays to raise these birds to obtain them.

fully washed, in order to separate the precious stones from it. These mines produce more diamonds than any other part of the globe.

The diamonds are so small that one valued at several hundred dollars might easily be hidden and carried away by a workman. In fact, men have been known to swallow them in order

FIG. 299. — Ostriches on an ostrich farm in South Africa.

One reason why South Africa has been so attractive to the English is its **Its chief attraction for the English** great mineral wealth. This is the richest gold-mining region in the world, producing even more gold than all the mines of the United States. JOHANNESBURG is in the center of the gold district.

Farther south, at KIMBERLEY, diamonds are found in the decayed rock. This rock is dug out (Fig. 300) and care-

to carry them away without being detected. To prevent such theft, the men are not often allowed to leave the works. They are furnished with homes and food by the company, and, when they wish to leave, they are carefully examined to see that none of the precious stones are being taken away.

1. Why is Africa called the Dark Continent? 2. How has the Sahara Desert prevented the exploration and settlement of Africa? 3. How have the rapids **Review Questions** and falls in the rivers interfered with its exploration? 4. State how the climate has had a similar effect. 5. How have the

forests, animals, and peoples likewise kept Europeans away? 6. How does it happen that South Africa is the best-known part? 7. What parts of Africa have been recently seized by Europeans? By what nations? 8. What improvements have been made by Europeans? 9. Tell something of the character of the people in northern Africa. 10. Name and locate the chief cities of Egypt. 11. What do you know about the ancient history of Egypt? 12. Explain how the Nile River helps to support the inhabitants. 13. Name the agricultural products of Egypt. 14. Tell about the Suez Canal. 15. Name and locate the other countries of northern Africa. 16. What is the character of Central Africa? 17. Name the products. 18. How does it happen that South Africa is largely owned by the English? 19. Describe its climate. 20. What are its agricul-

largest cities in Africa be located on the Nile River near its mouth? 4. Find some object made of ivory, and show it to the class. 5. Examine an ostrich feather and a diamond. 6. Why are there no tributaries to the northern half of the Nile? 7. Find out about the war between the Boers and the British. 8. Read the story of Joseph in the Bible, beginning in Genesis, Chapter 37. 9. Draw an outline map of Africa and put in the principal countries and colonies, rivers, and cities.

XV. AUSTRALIA, THE EAST INDIES, AND OTHER ISLANDS OF THE PACIFIC

1. Find Australia on a globe, and show how you would reach it by ship from New York. Through what waters would you pass (Fig. **Map study** 106)? 2. How would you reach it from San Francisco? 3. In what part are most of the mountains? 4. The rivers? 5. The cities? 6. In what zones is Australia? What does this tell you about its temperature? 7. What parts of South America and Africa are in the same latitude as southern Australia? 8. What are the principal islands of the East Indies? 9. In what direction are the Philippine Islands from Australia? Estimate the distance. 10. Find the Hawaiian Islands; New Zealand.

FIG. 300. — A diamond mine at Kimberley in South Africa. Many thousands of dollars' worth of diamonds have been taken out of this pit.

tural products? 21. Its mineral products? 22. Name and locate the cities. 23. Tell about diamond mining.

Suggestions 1. What reasons can you give why Timbuktu, on the Niger River, should be an important trade center? 2. Beginning with the western Sahara, trace the desert country that extends eastward across Africa and Asia. 3. Why should the two

1. Australia

The names of the three eastern divisions of Australia — Victoria, New South **Ownership of** Wales, and Queensland — **this continent** suggest the country to which Australia belongs. What one is it? The British control only a part of the other continents, but Australia, the smallest of all the continents, they have entirely to themselves.

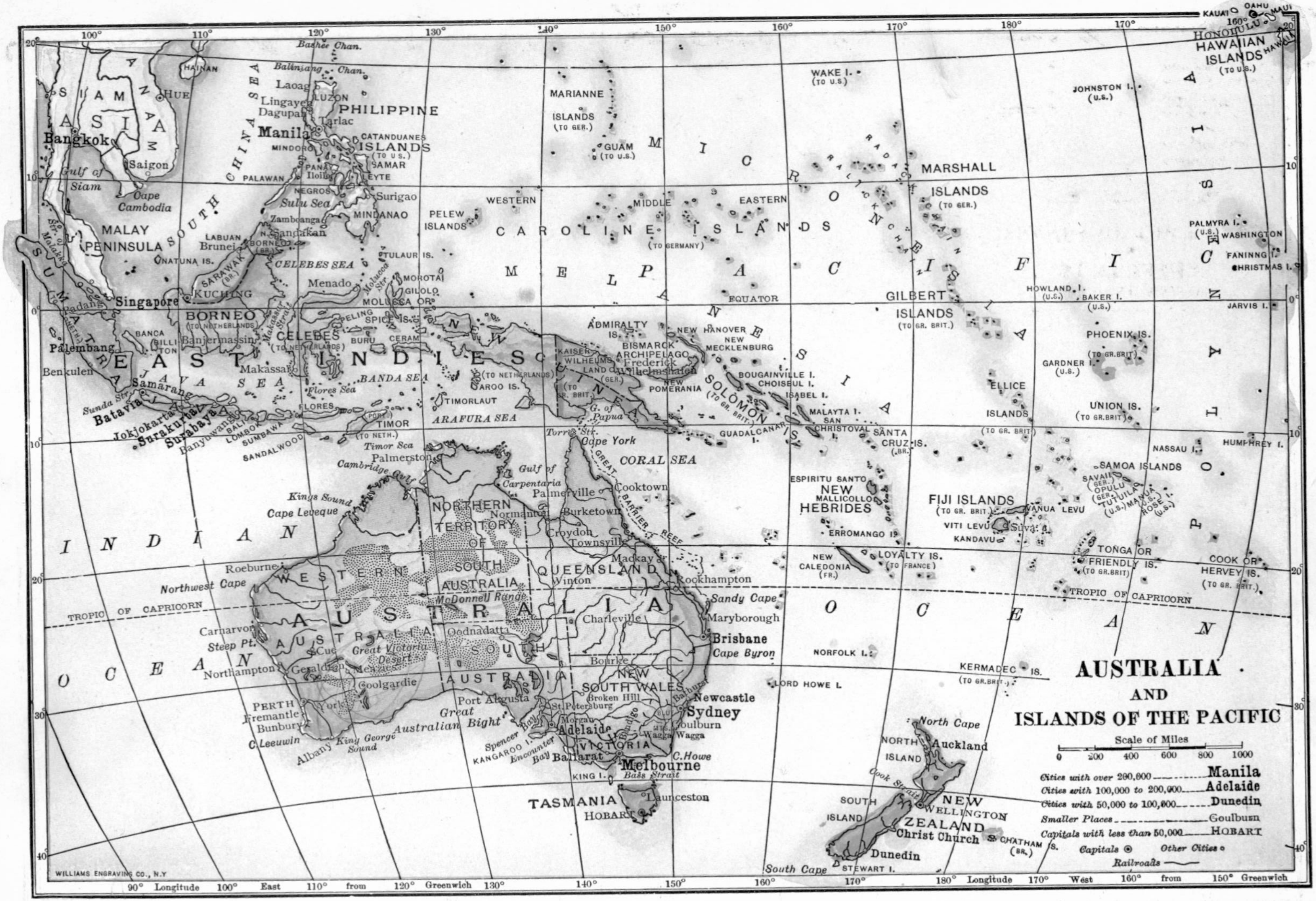

AUSTRALIA
AND
ISLANDS OF THE PACIFIC

Scale of Miles
200 400 600 800 1000

Cities with over 200,000 .... **Manila**
Cities with 100,000 to 200,000 ...... **Adelaide**
Cities with 50,000 to 100,000 .... Dunedin
Smaller Places .... Goulburn
Capitals with less than 50,000 ...... HOBART
Capitals ⊙   Other Cities ○
Railroads _____

FIG. 301.

WILLIAMS ENGRAVING CO., N.Y.

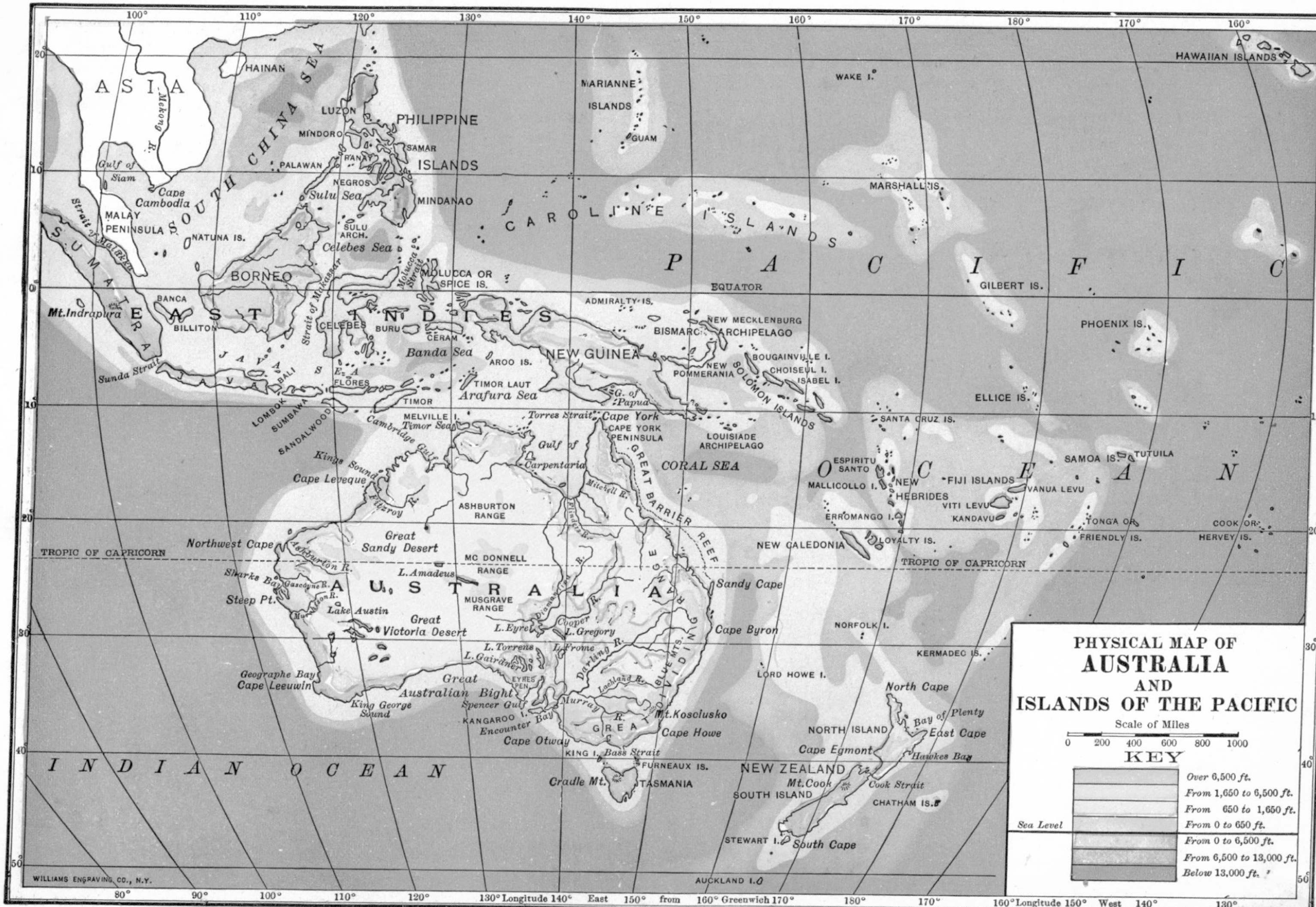
PHYSICAL MAP OF
AUSTRALIA
AND
ISLANDS OF THE PACIFIC
Scale of Miles
0 200 400 600 800 1000
KEY
Over 6,500 ft.
From 1,650 to 6,500 ft.
From 650 to 1,650 ft.
From 0 to 650 ft.
Sea Level
From 0 to 6,500 ft.
From 6,500 to 13,000 ft.
Below 13,000 ft.
ASIA
SOUTH CHINA SEA
PHILIPPINE ISLANDS
EAST INDIES
CAROLINE ISLANDS
PACIFIC OCEAN
INDIAN OCEAN
AUSTRALIA
NEW GUINEA
NEW ZEALAND
CORAL SEA
GREAT BARRIER REEF
TROPIC OF CAPRICORN
EQUATOR
HAWAIIAN ISLANDS
MARIANNE ISLANDS
GUAM
WAKE I.
MARSHALL IS.
GILBERT IS.
PHOENIX IS.
ELLICE IS.
SAMOA IS.
TUTUILA
FIJI ISLANDS
VANUA LEVU
VITI LEVU
KANDAVU
TONGA OR FRIENDLY IS.
COOK OR HERVEY IS.
SANTA CRUZ IS.
NEW HEBRIDES
ESPIRITU SANTO
MALLICOLLO I.
ERROMANGO I.
LOYALTY IS.
NEW CALEDONIA
NORFOLK I.
KERMADEC IS.
LORD HOWE I.
North Cape
Bay of Plenty
East Cape
Hawkes Bay
NORTH ISLAND
Cape Egmont
Cook Strait
CHATHAM IS.
Mt. Cook
SOUTH ISLAND
STEWART I.
South Cape
AUCKLAND I.
ADMIRALTY IS.
NEW MECKLENBURG
BISMARCK ARCHIPELAGO
NEW POMMERANIA
BOUGAINVILLE I.
CHOISEUL I.
ISABEL I.
SOLOMON ISLANDS
LOUISIADE ARCHIPELAGO
G. of Papua
Torres Strait
Cape York
CAPE YORK PENINSULA
Gulf of Carpentaria
Mitchell R.
Flinders R.
HAINAN
Mekong R.
Gulf of Siam
Cape Cambodia
MALAY PENINSULA
Strait of Malakka
SUMATRA
Mt. Indrapura
NATUNA IS.
BANCA
BILLITON
BORNEO
Sunda Strait
JAVA
BALI
LOMBOK
SUMBAWA
SANDALWOOD
FLORES
TIMOR
LUZON
MINDORO
PALAWAN
PANAY
SAMAR
NEGROS
MINDANAO
Sulu Sea
SULU ARCH.
Celebes Sea
CELEBES
Strait of Makassar
Molucca Strait
MOLUCCA OR SPICE IS.
BURU
CERAM
Banda Sea
AROO IS.
TIMOR LAUT
Arafura Sea
MELVILLE I.
Timor Sea
Cambridge Gulf
Kings Sound
Cape Leveque
Fitzroy R.
ASHBURTON RANGE
Great Sandy Desert
Northwest Cape
Ashburton R.
Sharks Bay
Gascoyne R.
Steep Pt.
Murchison R.
MC DONNELL RANGE
L. Amadeus
MUSGRAVE RANGE
Lake Austin
Great Victoria Desert
L. Eyre
Cooper R.
Diamantina R.
L. Gregory
L. Torrens
L. Frome
L. Gairdner
Darling R.
Lachlan R.
BLUE MTS.
GREAT DIVIDING RANGE
Geographe Bay
Cape Leeuwin
Great Australian Bight
EYRES PEN.
Spencer Gulf
King George Sound
KANGAROO I.
Encounter Bay
Murray R.
Mt. Kosciusko
Cape Howe
Cape Otway
KING I.
Bass Strait
FURNEAUX IS.
TASMANIA
Cradle Mt.
Sandy Cape
Cape Byron
WILLIAMS ENGRAVING CO., N.Y.
Longitude East from Greenwich
Longitude West

FIG. 302.

FIG. 305. — A flock of sheep in the sheep raising country of New South Wales in Australia.

forests. Between this and southern Australia, sugar, cotton, and rice are raised.

Australia is a noted mineral region, producing gold especially. For many **Minerals** years this continent has ranked as one of the leading gold-producing regions of the world. Silver, copper, iron, coal, and other mineral products are also mined here.

Manufacturing is not yet greatly developed in Australia, so that most **Manufactures** of the wool, hides, and metals, are exported; and since this is a British colony, they go mainly to England. Some of the imports, many of which are received from England, you can probably name. Gradually, however, the Australians are developing manufacturing, and are thus coming to depend upon themselves.

Since the people and industries are found mainly in the humid southeastern part of Australia, we see why **Principal cities** several large cities have grown up in that section. The largest is SYDNEY, the capital of New South Wales. Next in size is MELBOURNE, the capital of Victoria and the principal seaport. ADELAIDE, the capital of South Australia, is the third city in size. Each of these cities has an excellent harbor. What is the capital and chief city of Tasmania? Of Queensland?

2. New Zealand

Southeast of Australia are two large islands forming the British colony of New Zealand. How far is New Zealand from Australia? It does not form a part

R

of the Australian Commonwealth, just as Newfoundland does not form a part of the Dominion of Canada (p. 175).

The surface of these islands is very rugged, and there is much wonderful

Fig. 306.—One of the grand fiords on the coast of New Zealand, where there is some of the finest scenery in the world.

scenery (Fig. 306). The mountains are very grand, and some of the highest peaks are volcanic cones. Heavy snow falls upon the high mountains, and from these snow fields large glaciers descend through the mountain valleys. There are also hot springs and geysers here, as in our Yellowstone National Park (p. 156).

The climate of New Zealand resembles that of Australia, although it has more abundant rainfall. The products, also, are much the same. It is a very progressive country, with many valuable resources and much manufacturing.

3. The East Indies

Area and names of these islands

Between Australia and Asia there are hundreds of islands, most of them too small to be shown upon the map. Some of them, however, are very large. Java, for instance, is about the size of the

state of New York, and Borneo is about six times as large. All these islands together form a group, or archipelago, known as the East Indies. What other large islands do you find among them? In what zone do they lie? What, therefore, is their climate? In what direction from them are the Philippine Islands?

Their products

On the East Indian Islands, with their hot, damp climate, there are extensive forests containing many kinds of valuable tropical woods. Also, besides Java coffee, which is well known, tea, spices, indigo, rice, sugar cane, tobacco, cotton, and grain are important products. From the very earliest times, too, this region has been noted for its precious stones (p. 228).

Their ownership

It was these islands, as well as India and the Malay Peninsula, that Columbus was trying to reach. Their products are so valuable that the European nations have eagerly taken possession of them. England, as usual, has a part. Point it out. This time, however, she has not obtained the lion's share. That belongs to the little country of Holland. Name the large islands that are controlled wholly, or in part, by the Dutch.

4. Islands of the Pacific

Those belonging to the United States

There are many hundreds of islands in the Pacific Ocean. You have already learned the names of some of these which are possessions of the United States (p. 163). Give their names and locate them on the map (Fig. 106).

One of the largest islands in this region is New Guinea, just north of Australia, **New Guinea** which is not usually classed as one of the East Indian Islands. In what zone does it lie? Among what three nations is it divided? All of its products are tropical, and it is covered with a dense forest, inhabited by fierce savages. Very few Europeans live there.

Among the smaller groups are the Fiji Islands. Find these. To what country do they **Other islands** belong? What two groups lie west of the Fiji Islands? Northeast of the Fiji Islands are the Samoa Islands, one of which, as you know, belongs to the United States.

Review Questions
1. Describe the government of Australia. 2. What is there peculiar about the native plants, animals, and people? 3. What use was first made of Australia? 4. What is the population? 5. In what part of Australia do most of the inhabitants live, and why there? 6. What are the agricultural products? 7. The minerals? 8. Tell about the manufactures. 9. Locate the principal cities. 10. Tell about New Zealand. 11. Where are the East Indies? 12. What are the names of the principal islands? What about their size? 13. What are their products? 14. What countries control them? 15. Name several groups of islands in the Pacific that belong to the United States. 16. Tell about New Guinea. 17. Name other island groups in the Pacific.

Suggestions
1. What other countries, besides Australia, are especially noted for cattle and sheep? 2. For gold mining? 3. Read about the trouble caused by rabbits that were imported into Australia. 4. Name and locate the principal desert regions on the earth. 5. Make a sketch map of Australia, putting in the principal mountains, rivers, and cities. 6. Find what spices are used in cooking at your home.

XVI. REVIEW OF THE UNITED STATES AND OTHER GREAT POWERS

We have seen that there are six nations of Europe that are called Great Powers, or World Powers. Name each of them **The Great Powers of the** (p. 188). The United States **world, and** makes a seventh World **their forms of** Power, and Japan an eighth. **government** Give the principal boundaries of each. Which two have a republican form of government? Which one is an absolute monarchy (p. 203)? What form

Fig. 307. — A village in New Guinea, where the houses are built on posts rising above the water.

of government have the other five? Each of the other nations on the earth is called a "Minor" or Lesser Power, being much weaker than any one of the eight World Powers.

On what continent is each of the eight World Powers located? **Continents and** What continents, therefore, **zone to which** contain no Great Powers? **the World** In what zone does the **Powers belong** United States lie? In what zone is the main portion of the other World Powers? Can you give any reasons why the chief nations of the earth are found in the temperate zone?

The greatest of these eight Powers,

sions of the United States, as shown in Figure 310. Of Russia ; Germany; France.

It should be remembered that the eight World Powers mentioned are not

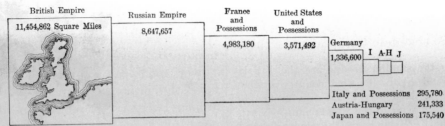

FIG. 308. — The areas controlled by the eight World Powers (1910).

United States compared in area and population with other Great Powers

in area, is the British Empire, as seen in Figure 308. What is the rank in area of each of the others?

In Figure 309 the British Empire is seen also to have the greatest population of the eight. What is the rank of each of the

the eight *largest* nations of the earth. They are simply the eight *strongest* nations. China, for instance, has a much larger area and population than most of these eight. Yet it is a backward nation, for reasons that we have already studied. What are they

Other large and promising countries of the world

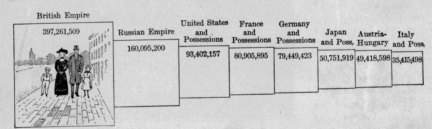

FIG. 309. — Population of the eight World Powers (1910).

others in population? What is the rank of our country in area and population compared with the other World Powers?

The Power that has the greatest foreign possessions is the British Empire.

Dependencies of the Great Powers

In Figure 310 point out the principal foreign possessions of the British. Can you account in any way for the fact that the British have control over so much of the earth? Point out the foreign posses-

(p. 221)? China, however, is a very promising nation for the future. Why (p. 222)? What do you know about its occupations (pp. 222-223) ?

Argentina is the most promising country in South America. What can you tell about it (p. 182)? What other two nations of that continent might be compared with Argentina in importance (pp. 182, 184)? Tell the principal facts about each. How does Brazil compare

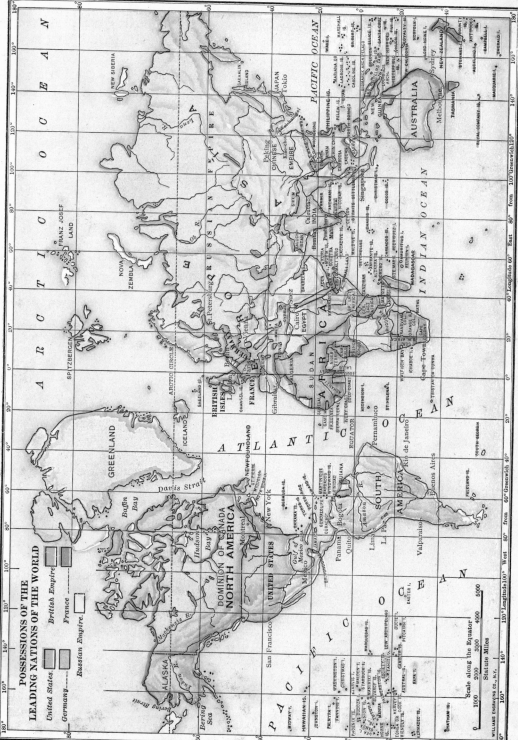

POSSESSIONS OF THE
LEADING NATIONS OF THE WORLD

United States.
British Empire.
Germany............
France
Russian Empire.

FIG. 310.

with the Great Powers in area? (See table on p. 255.)

About one person in eight now living in

cultural products? Where is each raised? What parts of our country receive too little rain for farming? What is the

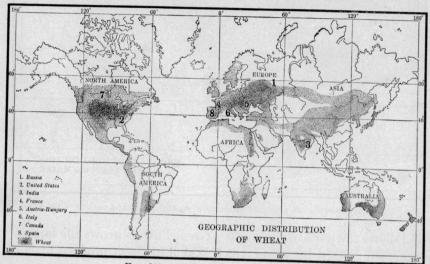

FIG. 311. — Wheat regions of the world

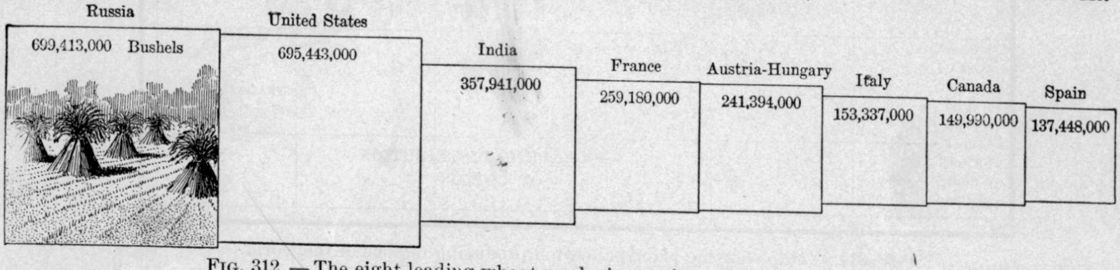

the United States came here from some other land. Figure 235 shows which country has been sending us the greatest number. **Immigrants to the United States** Which ranks second in this respect? Can you name other countries not named in this diagram that have sent us immigrants? Which of the Great Powers has been sending us most immigrants? Which have sent very few?

Agriculture is the greatest industry **Agriculture in the leading countries** in the United States, giving occupation to more than one third of all the workers in the country. What are our chief agri-

leading industry there? In what parts is irrigation important?

✗What are the principal agricultural products of the British Isles (p. 189)? Of Germany (p. 193)? Of France (p. 195)? Of Russia (p. 203)? Of Italy (p. 198)? Of Austria-Hungary (p. 201)? Of Japan (p. 225)? Which of these nations depends most upon foreign countries, or upon its dependencies, for food?

In what countries is *wheat* extensively raised (Fig. 311)? Note the rank of the leading wheat-producing countries of the world (Fig. 312).

Russia	United States	India	France	Austria-Hungary	Italy	Canada	Spain
699,413,000 Bushels	695,443,000	357,941,000	259,180,000	241,394,000	153,337,000	149,990,000	137,448,000

FIG. 312. — The eight leading wheat producing regions of the world (1910).

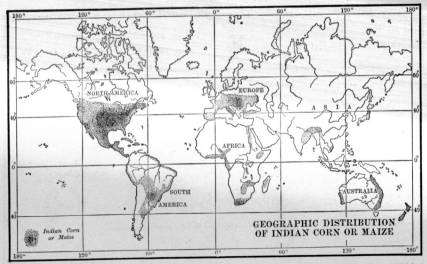

Fig. 313. — Map showing the principal Indian corn (maize) producing regions of the world.

Figure 313 shows the parts of the world that produce *corn*. Which one of the Great Powers grows the largest amount? Which of them produce little of it?

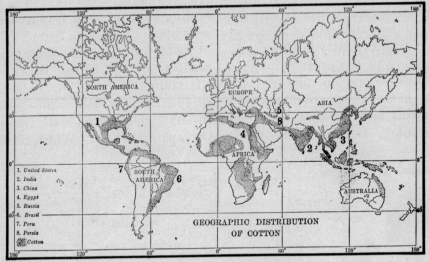

Fig. 314. — Map showing principal cotton producing regions of the world.

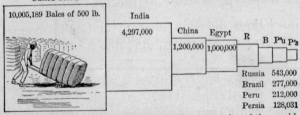

Fig. 315. — The eight chief cotton producing countries of the world (1910).

Is cotton more, or less widely cultivated than corn (Fig. 314)? What parts of the world mainly produce it? Which of the Great Powers raise a large amount of it? What do you learn from Figure 315?

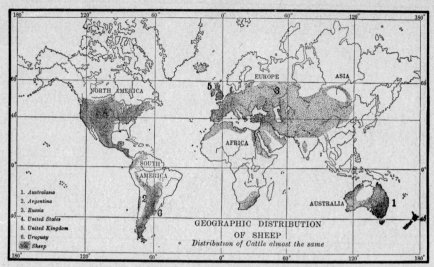

Fig. 316. — Map to show the principal sheep raising sections of the world.

In Figure 316 note the distribution of cattle and sheep. What countries are important for grazing? What useful products are obtained from these animals besides meat? From your study about the countries of the world, name some which produce quantities of sugar

What about mining in the United States? In the British Isles (p. 190)? In Germany (p. 194)? In France (p. 196)? In Russia (p. 203). In Italy (p. 198)? In Austria-Hungary (p. 202)? In Japan (p. 226)?

Mining in the leading countries

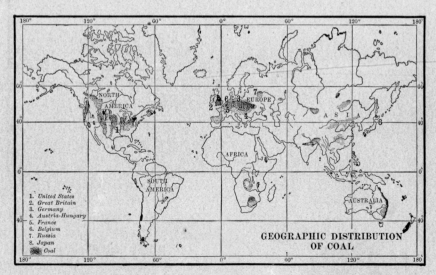

Fig. 317.— Map to show the principal coal bearing regions of the world.

cane; grapes; oranges; tobacco; coffee; tea; rice; raw silk; lumber; rubber.

Figure 317 shows the parts of the world that have much coal. Which of the Great Powers are important in that industry? Which one is not? No- | are World Powers? Which of the World Powers have little iron ore?

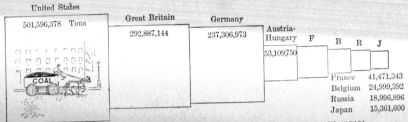

FIG. 318. — The eight leading coal producing countries of the world (1910).

tice the rank of the Great Powers in coal production as shown in Figure 318. | What about manufacturing in the United States? In the British Isles

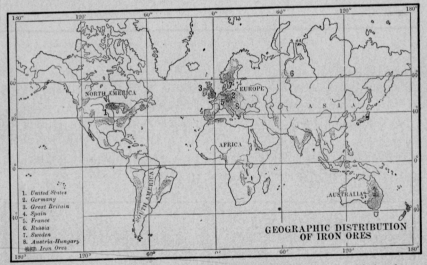

FIG. 319. — Map showing the principal regions of the world where iron ore is found.

In Figure 319 iron ore is shown to be widely distributed. What countries produce much of it? Figure 320 shows the rank of the six leading iron-mining countries. Which of these countries | (p. 190)? In Germany (p. 194)? In France (p. 196)? In Italy (p. 198)? In Austria-Hungary (p. 202)? In Russia (p. 203)? In Japan (p. 226)? Manufacturing in the leading countries

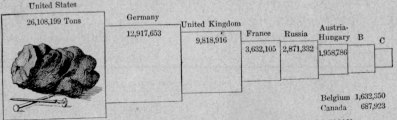

FIG. 320. — The six leading iron producing countries of the world (1910).

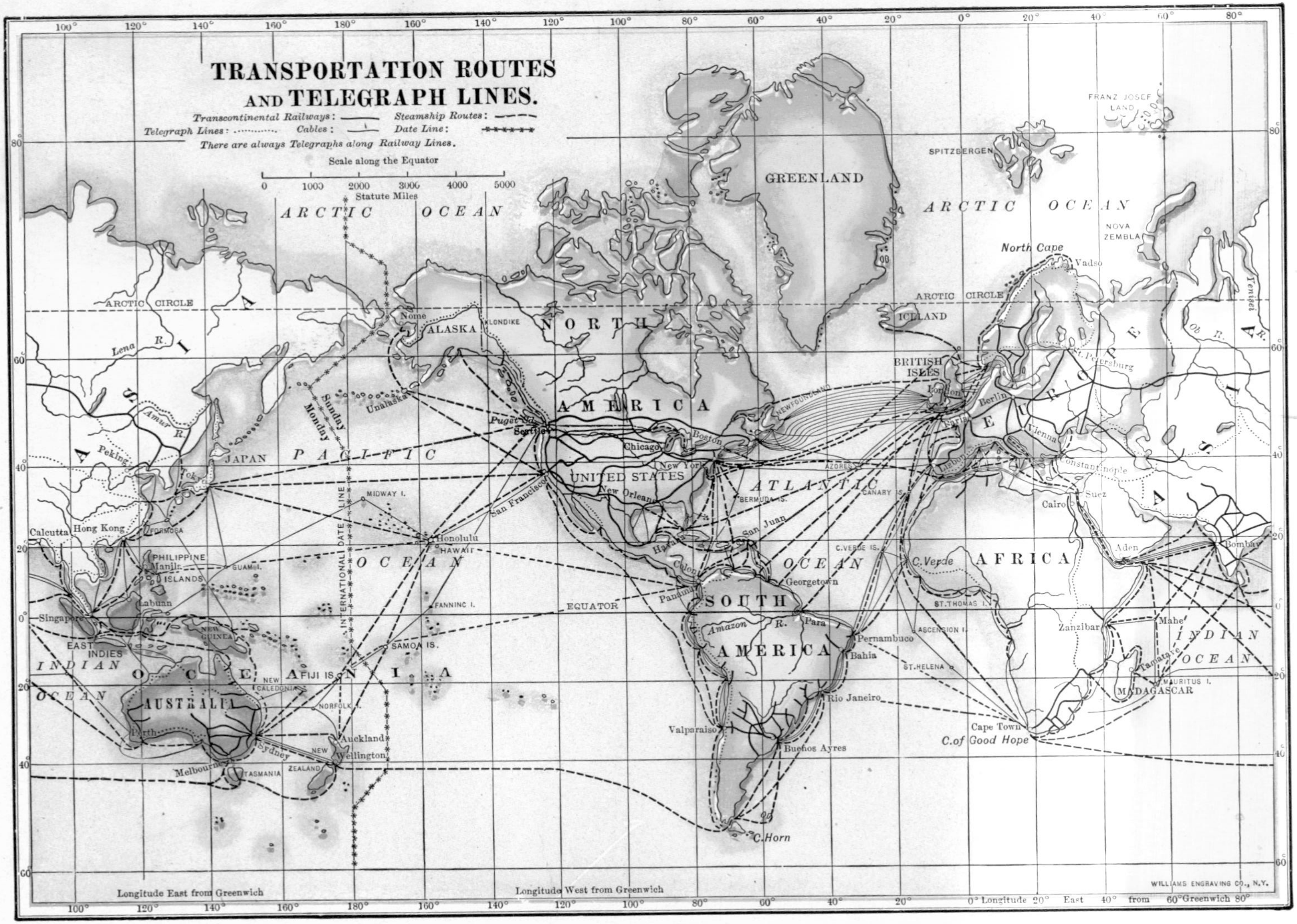
TRANSPORTATION ROUTES AND TELEGRAPH LINES.
Transcontinental Railways:
Steamship Routes:
Telegraph Lines:
Cables:
Date Line:
There are always Telegraphs along Railway Lines.
Scale along the Equator
0 1000 2000 3000 4000 5000
Statute Miles
ARCTIC OCEAN
GREENLAND
NORTH AMERICA
UNITED STATES
SOUTH AMERICA
AFRICA
EUROPE
ASIA
AUSTRALIA
OCEANIA
PACIFIC OCEAN
ATLANTIC OCEAN
INDIAN OCEAN
ARCTIC CIRCLE
EQUATOR
INTERNATIONAL DATE LINE
Sunday
Monday
Longitude East from Greenwich
Longitude West from Greenwich
WILLIAMS ENGRAVING CO., N.Y.

FIG. 323.

According to Figure 321, what parts of the world are very important in manufacturing? Which of the Great Powers have little of it? What Lesser

what you can about each of the twenty-five.

Figure 323 shows the principal transportation routes of the world. Which

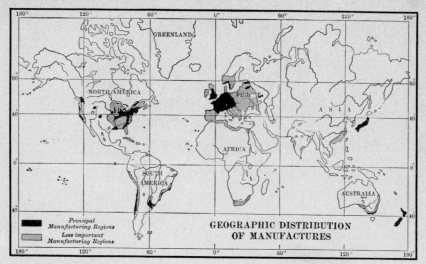

FIG. 321.— Map to show the principal manufacturing sections of the world.

Powers of Europe do much manufacturing (pp. 208, 212)? Note the rank of the leading manufacturing countries of the world in Figure 322.

Tell about trade and transportation, or commerce, in the United States;

Commerce and largest cities of the leading countries
in the British Isles (p. 191); in Germany (p. 194); in France (p. 196); in Italy (p. 199); in Austria-Hungary (p. 202); in Russia (p. 204); in Japan (p. 227).

In the Appendix, page 257, you will find a list of the twenty-five largest cities of the world. Locate each of them. How many of these cities has each of the World Powers? Which of them belong to the Lesser Powers of the world? Tell

ocean has the greatest commerce? Why? What cities are connected by the lines showing routes across the Atlantic Ocean? What are the chief routes of commerce on the Pacific? How is the importance of the Suez Canal shown

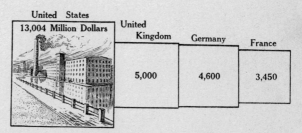

FIG. 322.— In this diagram is given the number of million dollars' worth of manufactured goods produced by the four leading manufacturing nations in the world.

in this figure? What countries will be greatly benefited by use of the Panama Canal.

APPENDIX I

REFERENCES TO DESCRIPTIONS, IN PROSE AND POETRY, OF TOPICS TREATED IN THIS GEOGRAPHY. FOR TEACHER AND PUPIL

McM. means The Macmillan Co., New York; *Ginn*, Ginn & Co., Boston, Mass.; *A.B.C.*, American Book Co., New York; *S.B.C.*, Silver, Burdett & Co., New York; *Heath*, D. C. Heath & Co., Boston; *E.P.C.*, Educational Publishing Co., Boston; *Scribner*, C. Scribner's Sons, New York; *L.S.*, Lothrop, Lee, Shepard, Boston; *Ap.*, D. Appleton & Co., New York; *R.Mc.*, Rand, McNally & Co., Chicago; *E.P.D.*, E. P. Dutton & Co., Boston.

METHODS AND AIDS. — Geikie, "The Teaching of Geography" (McM., $0.60); King, "Methods and Aids in Geography" (L.S., $1.20); Parker, "How to Study Geography" (Ap., $1.50); Trotter, "Lessons in the New Geography" (Heath, $1.00); McMurry, "Special Method in Geography" (McM., $0.70); Frye, "The Child and Nature" (Ginn, $0.80); Frye, "Teacher's Manual of Methods in Geography" (Ginn, $0.50); Redway, "Manual of Geography" (Heath, $0.65).

JOURNALS. — *Journal of School Geography* (R. E. Dodge, Teachers College, Columbia University, New York City, $1.00 per year); *National Geographic Magazine* (Washington, D.C., $2.50; includes membership to Society).

STANDARD REFERENCE WORKS. — "The Statesman's Year Book," published each year, gives latest statistics, etc. (McM., $3.00); Mill, "Hints to Teachers and Students on the Choice of Geographical Books" (Longmans, Green & Co., New York, $1.25); Mill, "International Geography" (Ap., $3.50).

GEOGRAPHY READERS, ETC. — Strong, "All the Year Round" (Ginn, three volumes, $0.30 each); Carpenter, "Geographical Readers" (A.B.C., $0.60 per volume); Payne, "Geographical Nature Studies" (A.B.C., $0.25); Fairbanks, "Home Geography for Primary Grades" (E.P.C., New York, $0.60); Youth's Companion Series (Ginn, $0.25 to $0.40); Starr's "Strange Peoples" (Heath, $0.40); Lyde, "Man and His Markets" (McM., $0.50); Herbertson, "Man and His Work" (McM., $0.60); Pratt, "American History Stories" (E.P.C., four volumes, $0.36 each); Pratt, "Stories of Colonial Children" (E.P.C., $0.40).

COMMERCIAL AND PHYSICAL GEOGRAPHY. — Chisholm, "Commercial Geography" (Longmans, Green & Co., New York, $0.90); Adams, "Commercial Geography" (Ap., $1.30); Shaler, "First Book in Geology" (Heath, $0.60); Tarr, "Elementary Geology" (McM., $1.40); Tarr, "New Physical Geography" (McM., $1.00).

FOOD, CLOTHING, AND SHELTER. — Fairbanks, "Home Geography," the following topics: "Our Homes, "Homes of the Animals," etc. (E.P.C., $0.60); Chamberlain's "Home and World Series," four vols. (McM. $0.40 each); Payne's "Geographical Nature Studies," "Shelter," "Our Shelter," etc. (A.B.C., $0.25); Starr, "Strange Peoples," "Eskimo," "Negroes," etc. (Heath, $0.40); Youth's Companion Series, "Strange Lands Near Home," "The Play of Eskimo Boys," "The Home of the Icebergs" (Ginn, $0.25); Youth's Companion Series, "Under Sunny Skies," "Across the Desert," "From Tangier to Tetuan," etc. (Ginn, $0.25).

THE SOIL. — King, "The Soil" (McM., $1.25); Tarr, "Elementary Geology," Chapters VI, XI, and pp. 475–487 (McM., $1.40); Shaler, "First Book in Geology," pp. 24–29 (Heath, $0.60). *Nature Study Quarterly*, No. 2, October, 1899 (Cornell University, College of Agriculture, Ithaca, N.Y. Free on application); Kingsley, "Madam How and Lady Why," Chapter IV, "The Transformation of a Grain of Soil" (McM., $0.50); Frye, "Brooks and Brook Basins," section on "How Soil is Made and Carried" (Ginn, $0.50).

HILLS AND VALLEYS. — Whittier, "Among the Hills" (poem); Whittier, "The Hilltop" (poem); Hutchinson, "The Story of the Hills" (McM., $1.50); see also under "Rivers and River Valleys."

MOUNTAINS. — Avebury, "The Beauties of Nature," Chapters V and VI (the former on forests) (McM., $1.50); Jordan, "Science Sketches," section on "The Ascent of the Matterhorn" (A. C. McClurg & Co., Chicago, $1.00); Tarr, "Elementary Geology," Chapter XVII (McM., $1.40); Tarr, "New Physical Geography," Chapter VI (McM., $1.00); Shaler, "First Book in Geology," Chapter V (Heath, $0.60); Kingsley, "Madam How and Lady Why," Chapter V, "The Ice Plough" (McM., $0.50); Fairbanks, "Home Geography for Primary Grades," sections on "The Story of a Mountain," and "What We Learned by Climbing a Mountain" (E.P.C., $0.60); Youth's Companion Series, "Strange Lands Near Home," section on "A Growing Mountain" (Ginn, $0.25); "Under Sunny Skies," section on "Mount Vesuvius" (Ginn, $0.25).

RIVERS AND RIVER VALLEYS. — Tarr, "Elementary Geology," Chapters VI–X (McM., $1.40); Tarr, "New Physical Geography," Chapter IV (McM., $1.00); Shaler, "First Book in Geology," Chapter VI (Heath, $0.60); Payne, "Geographical Nature Studies," sections on "Valleys," "Plants of the Valleys," and "Animals of the Valleys," etc. (A.B.C., $0.25); Kingsley, "Madam How and Lady Why," Chapter I, "The Glen" (McM., $0.50); Frye, "Brooks and Brook Basins" (Ginn, $0.50); Avebury, "The Beauties of Nature," Chapters VII and VIII (McM., $1.50); Parker and Helm, "Uncle Robert's Geography," Vol. III, Chapters XII and XIV ($0.50); Poems: "The Brook," Tennyson; "The Mad River," Longfellow; "The Falls of Lodore," Southey; "The Brook and the Wave," Longfellow; "A Water Song," E. G. W. Rowe; "The Endless Story," A. K. Eggleston; "The Impatient River," E. G. W. Rowe; the last three in Payne's "Geographical Nature Studies" (A.B.C., $0.25).

PONDS AND LAKES. — Shaler, "First Book in Geology," pp. 125–129 (Heath, $0.60); Tarr, "Elementary Geology," pp. 188–193 (McM., $1.40); Tarr, "New Physical Geography," Chapter IX, (McM., $1.00); Avebury, "The Beauties of Nature," Chapter VIII (McM., $1.50); Payne, "Geographical Nature Studies," section on "Pools, Ponds, and Lakes" (A.B.C., $0.25); "The Lakeside," poem, by Whittier.

THE OCEAN. — Shaler, "Sea and Land" (Scribner, New York, $2.50); Tarr, "New Physical Geography," Chapters X, XI (McM., $1.00); Avebury, "The Beauties of Nature," Chapter IX (McM., $1.50); Andrews, "Stories Mother Nature Told Her Children," section on "Sea Life" (Ginn, $0.50); Holland, "The Sea Voyage," in "Arthur Bonnicastle"; Dickens, "David Copperfield," Chapter V; "Robinson Crusoe," Chapter III; Taylor, "The Waves," "Wind and Sea," in Marble's "Nature Pictures by American Poets" (McM., $1.25); Coleridge, "The Ancient Mariner."

THE AIR. — Tarr, "New Physical Geography," Chapters XII–XIV (McM., $1.00); "A Summer Shower," "Cornell Nature Study Bulletin," No. 1, June, 1899 (free on application to College of Agriculture, Cornell University, Ithaca, N.Y.); Murché, "Science Reader," Book III, sections on "Air," "Vapor in the Air," "Vapor; What Becomes of It?" "What the Atmosphere Is," "Ice, Hail, and Snow" (McM., $0.40); Frye, "Brooks and Brook Basins," sections on "Forms of Water" and "The Atmosphere in Motion" (Ginn, $0.50); Strong, "All the Year Round," Part II, sections 33–39 (Ginn, $0.30); Andrews, "Stories Mother Nature told Her Children," section on "The Frost Giants" (Ginn, $0.50); Payne, "Geographical Nature Studies," many excellent stories and poems (A.B.C., $0.25); Marble, "Nature Pictures by American Poets"; "Summer Shower," Dickinson; "Rain," De Land; "Song of the Snowflakes," Cheney; "Cloudland" (McM., $1.25); Wilson, "Nature Study in Elementary Schools," Second Reader, the following poems: "The Rain Shower," "The Wind Song," "The Bag of Winds," "The Sunbeams," "Snowflakes," "Signs of Rain," "The Rainbow" (McM., $0.35); Lovejoy, "Nature in Verse," the following poems: "Merry Rain," "The Clouds," "The Dew," "The Fog," "The Rain," "The Snow," "The Frost," "Jack Frost," "Little Snowflakes" (S.B.C., $0.60); Shelley, "The Cloud"; Whittier, "The Frost Spirit"; Bryant, "The Hur-

ricane"; Whittier, "Snow-bound"; Irving, "The Thunderstorm" (prose).

INDUSTRY, COMMERCE, AND GOVERNMENT. — Payne, "Geographical Nature Studies," sections on "Occupations," "Trade or Commerce," "Transportation by Land," "Transportation by Water," School and Country. (A.B.C., $0.25); Andrews, "The Stories Mother Nature Told Her Children," section on "The Carrying Trade" (Ginn, $0.50); Whittier, "Songs of Labor"; Brooks, "Century Book for Young Americans" (Century Co., New York, $1.50); Brooks, "The Story of the United States" (The Lothrop Publishing Co., Boston, $1.50); Wilson, "Nature Study in Elementary Schools," Second Reader, section on "Boyhood of Lincoln" (McM., $0.35); Payne, "Geographical Nature Studies," section on "Government" (A.B.C., $0.25).

MAPS. — Excellent outline maps of states and continents, costing 1½ to 2 cents each, can be purchased from D. C. Heath & Co., Boston; Rand, McNally & Co., Chicago; and other publishers. Maltby, "Map Modeling," (A. S. Barnes & Co., New York, $1.25); Kellogg, "Geography by Map Drawing" (same publishers, $0.30); Redway, "The Reproduction of Geographical Forms" ($0.30) and "Teacher's Manual of Geography" ($0.65) (both by Heath); Frye, "The Child and Nature" (Ginn, $0.80); Frye, "Sand and Clay Modeling (A.B.C., New York, $0.10); Frye, "Teacher's Manual of Methods in Geography" (Ginn, $0.50); Kellogg, "How to Teach Clay Modeling" (A. S. Barnes & Co., New York, $0.25); King, "The Picturesque Geographical Readers," First Book, Lesson XIII (L.S., $0.50).

FORM AND SIZE OF THE EARTH. — Andrews, "Seven Little Sisters," section on "The Ball Itself" (Ginn, $0.50); Irving, "Life and Voyages of Christopher Columbus" (G. P. Putnam's Sons, New York, $1.75); for Columbus, Magellan, etc., see various school histories. Also, poem on "Columbus" by Tennyson, D'Anvers, "Science Ladders," Vol. I (E.P.C., $0.40); Gee, "Short Studies in Nature Knowledge," section on "The Great Globe Itself" (McM., $1.10).

DAILY MOTION OF THE EARTH AND ITS RESULTS. — Redway, "Manual of Geography," Chapter VI (Heath, $0.65); "Daybreak" (poem), Longfellow.

THE ZONES. — Eggleston, "Stories of American Life and Adventure," section on "Adventures in Alaska" (A.B.C., $0.50); Andrews, "Seven Little Sisters," sections on "The Little Brown Baby," "Agoonack, the Esquimau Sister," and "How Agoonack Lives" (Ginn, $0.50); Schwatka, "The Children of the Cold" (E.P.C., $1.25); Ballou, "Footprints of Travel," Chapters XXIX and XXX (Ginn, $0.60); King, "The Picturesque Geographical Readers," First Book, Part 2 (L.S., $0.50).

THE CONTINENTS AND OCEANS. — Andrews, "Seven Little Sisters" (Ginn, $0.50); Ballou, "Footprints of Travel" (Ginn, $0.60); Kelly, "Leaves from Nature's Story Book," Vol. III, "A Visit to the Bottom of the Ocean" (E.P.C., $0.40); Shaler, "The Story of Our Continent," section on "Coral Reefs" (Ginn, $0.75); Tarr, "Elementary Geology," p. 251 (McM., $1.40); D'Anvers, "Science Ladders," Vol. III, Lesson VIII (E.P.C., $0.40); Youth's Companion Series, "Strange Lands Near Home" and "The Wide World" (Ginn, each $0.25); Andrews, "Each and All" (L.S., $1.00); Miller, "Little People of Asia" (E.P.D., $2.50); Schwatka, "Children of the Cold" (E.P.C., $1.25); Shaw, "Big People and Little People of Other Lands" (A.B.C., $0.30); Poems: Shelley, "A Vision of the Sea"; Longfellow, "The Secret of the Sea"; Longfellow, "The Wreck of the Hesperus"; Holmes, "The Chambered Nautilus"; Byron, "The Ocean."

NORTH AMERICA.— Shaler, "The Story of Our Continent" (Ginn, $0.75); Lyde, "North America" (McM., $0.50); McMurry, "Excursions and Lessons in Home Geography," (McM. $0.50); Adams, "An Elementary Commercial Geography" (Ap., $1.10); Gannett, Garrison, and Houston, "Commercial Geography" (A.B.C., $1.25); Rocheleau, "Geography of Commerce and Industry" (E.P.C., $1.00); Carpenter, "Geographical Reader," North America (A.B.C., $0.60); Chase and Clow, "Stories of Industry," Vols. I and II (E.P.C., $0.40).

THE UNITED STATES.— Brooks, "Century Book for Young Americans" (The Century Co., New York, $1.50); Brooks, "The Story of the United States" (L.S., $1.50); Channing, "Students' History of the United States" (McM., $1.40); Ballou, "Footprints of Travel," Chapters I and XXV (Ginn, $0.60); Gannett, "The United States," Stanford, "Compendium of Geography" (Scribner, $5.50); Eggleston, "Stories of American Life and Adventure," "Stories of Whaling," and "A Whaling Song," "A Story of Niagara," "How Frémont Crossed the Mountains," "The Finding of Gold in California," "Descending the Grand Cañon," and several Indian stories, (A.B.C., $0.50); Chase and Clow, "Stories of Industry," Vol. I, "Lumbering," "Ship Building," "Marble and Granite," "Slate and Brick," etc., Vol. II, "Manufacturing," "Fisheries," "Whaling," etc. (E.P.C., each volume $0.40); King, "The Picturesque Geographical Readers," Third and Fourth Books (L.S., $0.50); Carpenter, "Geographical Readers," "North America" (A.B.C., $0.60); Wilson, "Nature Study in Elementary Schools," Second Reader, "The Tree," by Björnson (McM., 0.35); McMurry, "Pioneer Stories of the Mississippi Valley" (Public School Publishing Co., Bloomington, Ill., $0.50); Ballou, "Footprints of Travel," Chapter XXV (Ginn, $0.60); Chase and Clow, "Stories of Industry," Vol. I, several sections on "Mines and Mining" (E.P.C., $0.40); Shaw, "Big People and Little People of Other Lands," section on "The Indians" (A.B.C., $0.30); Youth's Companion Series, "The Wide World," section on "Barbarian Babies" (Ginn, $0.25); Poems: Whittier, "Mogg Megone," "Pentucket," "The Bridal of Pennacook," "The Merrimack," "The Norsemen"; Longfellow, "The Woods in Winter," "The Building of the Ship," "The River Charles"; Emerson, "Boston"; Riley, "When the Frost is on the Punkin," "Knee Deep in June"; Bryant, "The Prairies," "The Hunter of the Prairies"; Whittier, "The Pass of the Sierra"; Joaquin Miller, "In the Yosemite Valley"; Holmes, "Our Country."

ALASKA.— Ballou, "Footprints of Travel," Chapter XXVI (Ginn, $0.60); Eggleston, "Stories of American Life and Adventure," "Adventures in Alaska" (A.B.C., $0.50); Carpenter, "Geographical Reader," North America (A.B.C., $0.60); Youth's Companion Series, "The Wide World," section on "The Alaska Eskimo" (Ginn, $0.25).

OTHER COUNTRIES OF NORTH AMERICA.— Coe, "Our American Neighbors," Chapters I–XVII (S.B.C., $0.60); Andrews, "Seven Little Sisters," the two sections on "Agoonack" (Ginn, $0.50); Schwatka, "The Children of the Cold" (E.P.C., $1.25); Gee, "Short Studies in Nature Knowledge" (McM., $1.10); Peary, "The Snow Baby" (Stokes, New York, $1.20); Shaw, "Big People and Little People of Other Lands," section on "Greenland" (A.B.C., $0.30); "An Arctic Vision," Bret Harte; "Evangeline," Longfellow; Lyde, "A Geography of North America" (McM., $0.50); Ballou, "Footprints of Travel," Chapters XXIII, XXIV, XXV, XXVII, and XXVIII (Ginn, $0.60); Youth's Companion Series, "Strange Lands Near Home," and "The Wide World," section on "The Boys of Mexico" (Ginn, $0.25).

SOUTH AMERICA.— Ballou, "Footprints of Travel," Chapters XXIX–XXXI (Ginn, $0.60); Coe, "Our American Neighbors" (S.B.C., $0.60); Youth's Companion Series, "Strange Lands Near Home" (Ginn, $0.25); Carpenter, "Geographical Reader" "South America" (A.B.C., $0.60); Starr, "Strange Peoples," section on "South American Peoples" (Heath, $0.40).

EUROPE.— Lyde, "A Geography of Europe" (McM., $0.50); Ballou, "Footprints of Travel," Chapters X–XXII (Ginn, $0.60); Coe, "Modern Europe" (S.B.C., $0.60); Pratt, "Northern Europe" (E.P.C., $0.40); Lyde, "A Geography of the British Isles" (McM., $0.60); King, "The Picturesque Geographical Readers," Sixth Book (L.S., $0.60); Pratt, "Stories of England" (E.P.C., $0.40); Andrews, "Seven Little Sisters," "The Little Mountain Maiden," and "Louise" (Ginn, $0.50); Reynolds's "Regional Geography," "Europe" (A. & C., Black, London, 2s.); Rocheleau, "Geography of Commerce and Industry" (E.P.C., $1.00); Shaw, "Big People and Little People of Other Lands" (A.B.C., $0.30); Youth's Companion Series, "Northern Europe" and "Under Sunny Skies" (Ginn, $0.25 each); Chase and Clow, "Stories of Industry" (E.P.C., $0.40); Carpenter, "Geographical Reader" on "Europe" (A.B.C., $0.60); Poems: Alice Cary, "The Leak in the Dike"; Longfellow, "Venice," "The Belfry of Bruges," "Nuremberg," "To the River Rhone," "To the Avon"; Joaquin Miller, "Sunrise in Venice," "In a Gondola," "To Florence"; Shelley, "Ode to Naples."

ASIA.— Ballou, "Footprints of Travel," Chapters III, VIII, and IX (Ginn, $0.60); Andrews, "Seven Little Sisters," "The Story of Pen-se," also "Gemila" (Ginn, $0.50); Smith, "Life in Asia" (S.B.C., $0.60); Pratt, "Stories of India" (E.P.C., $0.40); Pratt, "Stories of China" (E.P.C., $0.40); Rocheleau, "Geography of Commerce and Industry" (E.P.C., $1.00); Youth's Companion Series, "Toward the Rising Sun," and "The Wide World" (Ginn, $0.25 each); Carpenter, "Geographical Readers," "Asia" (A.B.C., $0.60); Miller, "Little People of Asia" (E.P.D., $2.50); Poems by Whittier;

"The Holy Land," "Palestine," "The Pipes of Lucknow."

AFRICA.—Lyde, "A Geography of Africa" (McM., $0.50); Ballou, "Footprints of Travel" Chapters IX and X (Ginn, $0.60); Badlam, "Views in Africa" (S.B.C., $0.65); Andrews, "Seven Little Sisters," section on "The Little Dark Girl" and "Gemila" (Ginn, $0.50); Rocheleau, "Geography of Commerce and Industry" (E.P.C., $1.00); Youth's Companion Series, "The Wide World," sections on "Some Little Egyptians," "A School in Cairo" (Ginn, $0.25); Carpenter, "Geographical Readers" on "Africa" (A.B.C., $0.69); Chase and Clow, "Stories of Industry," Vols. I and II (E.P.C., $0.40).

AUSTRALIA, etc.—Ballou, "Footprints of Travel," Chapters II, IV, V, VI, VII (Ginn, $0.60); Kellogg, "Australia and the Islands of the Sea" (S.B.C., $0.68); Pratt, "Stories of Australasia" (E.P.C., $0.40); Rocheleau, "Geography of Commerce and Industry" (E.P.C., $1.00); Redway, "Commercial Geography" (Scribner, $1.25); Starr, "Strange Peoples" (Heath, $0.40); Chase and Clow, "Stories of Industry," Vols. I and II (E.P.C., $0.40); Poem, "Western Australia," O'Reilly.

APPENDIX II

TABLES OF STATISTICS

NOTE. — The figures 1900, 1910, etc., refer to the year in which the Census was taken or the estimate was made. Most of the figures are obtained from the U. S. Census Reports, the "Statesman's Year Book," or from Gannett's "Statistical Abstract of the World."

SIZE OF THE EARTH

LENGTH OF THE EARTH'S DIAMETER at equator (miles)	7,926
LENGTH OF THE EQUATOR (miles)	...24,902
THE EARTH'S SURFACE (square miles)	**196,940,000**
Pacific Ocean (square miles)	...55,660,000
Atlantic Ocean (square miles)	...33,720,000
Antarctic Ocean and the great southern sea surrounding the south pole (square miles)	...30,605,000
Indian Ocean (square miles)	...16,720,000
Arctic Ocean (square miles)	...4,781,000
The Sea (square miles)	**141,486,000**

CONTINENTS AND PRINCIPAL COUNTRIES

	Area in Square Miles		Population
NORTH AMERICA	**8,500,000**		**125,000,000**
United States	3,026,789	1910	91,972,266
United States (with Alaska, etc.)	3,624,122	1910	93,402,151
Mexico	767,005	1910	15,063,207
Canada	3,603,910	1911	7,192,338
Newfoundland	42,734	1910	237,531
Central America	200,865		5,077,169
Cuba	44,000	1910	2,150,112
Panama	31,500	1909	419,029
SOUTH AMERICA	**7,400,000**		**49,000,000**
Brazil	3,218,991	1908	21,461,100
Argentina	1,135,840	1911	7,171,910
Peru	695,733	1908	4,500,000
Chile	292,580	1910	3,329,030
Colombia	435,100	1910	4,320,000
Bolivia	605,400	1910	2,267,935
Venezuela	393,976	1911	2,713,703
Ecuador	116,000	1910	1,500,000
Paraguay	171,204	1910	752,000
Uruguay	72,210	1910	1,112,000
EUROPE	**3,600,000**		**439,000,000**
Russia	1,862,524	1910	135,859,400
German Empire	208,780	1910	64,903,423
Austria-Hungary	261,100	1910	51,323,921
France	207,054	1911	39,601,509
British Isles	121,390	1910	45,469,564
Italy	110,659	1910	34,269,746
Spain	194,783	1910	19,503,068
Turkey in Europe	65,350	1909	6,130,200
Norway	124,130	1910	2,392,698
Sweden	172,876	1910	5,521,943
Denmark	15,582	1911	2,775,076
The Netherlands	12,648	1910	5,945,155
Belgium	11,373	1910	7,516,730
Portugal	35,490	1900	5,423,132
Switzerland	15,976	1910	3,741,971
Greece	25,014	1907	2,631,952
Bulgaria	38,080	1910	4,284,844
Roumania	50,720	1910	6,966,000
Servia	18,650	1910	2,911,701
Montenegro	3,630	1909	250,000
ASIA (with East Indies)	**21,000,000**		**901,000,000**
Republic of China	4,277,170	1909	439,214,000
India	1,766,642	1911	315,132,537
Burma	236,738	1911	12,115,217
French Indo-China	309,980	1909	16,317,000
Siam	195,000	1909	6,686,486
Japan	147,655	1910	50,751,919
Korea	86,000	1911	13,125,027
Turkey in Asia	693,610	1909	17,688,500
Siberia	4,786,730	1911	8,220,100
Persia	628,000	1909	9,500,000

	Area in Square Miles		Population
Arabia	170,330		1,050,000
Afghanistan	250,000		5,900,000
Baluchistan	131,855	1901	829,712
AFRICA	**11,000,000**		**125,000,000**
Abyssinia	432,432	1910	5,000,000
Belgian Congo	909,650	1910	15,500,000
Egypt	400,000	1907	11,139,978
Algeria	343,500	1911	5,563,828
Morocco	219,000	1910	5,000,000
Tripoli	398,900	1906	1,000,000
Tunis	45,779	1910	1,923,217
Cape of Good Hope	276,995	1911	2,122,982
Transvaal	110,426	1911	1,676,611
AUSTRALIA, COMMONWEALTH OF	**3,000,000**		**4,400,000**
New South Wales	310,372	1910	1,621,677
Victoria	87,884	1911	1,315,551
Queensland	670,500	1910	572,654
South Australia	380,070	1910	412,808
Tasmania	26,215	1910	186,860
Western Australia	975,920	1911	282,114
New Zealand	104,751	1910	1,048,347

AREA AND POPULATION OF THE UNITED STATES

	Area in Square Miles	Population in 1900	Population in 1910
Alabama	51,998	1,828,697	2,138,093
Alaska	590,884	63,592	64,356
Arizona	113,956	122,931	204,354
Arkansas	53,335	1,311,564	1,574,449
California	158,297	1,485,053	2,377,549
Colorado	103,948	539,700	799,024
Connecticut	4,965	908,420	1,114,756
Delaware	2,370	184,735	202,322
District of Columbia	70	278,718	331,069
Florida	58,666	528,542	752,691
Georgia	59,265	2,216,331	2,609,121
Guam	210	8,561	11,973
Hawaiian Islands	6,449	154,001	191,909
Idaho	84,313	161,772	325,594
Illinois	56,665	4,821,550	5,638,591
Indiana	36,354	2,516,462	2,700,876
Iowa	56,147	2,231,853	2,224,771
Kansas	82,158	1,470,495	1,690,949
Kentucky	40,598	2,147,174	2,289,905
Louisiana	48,506	1,381,625	1,656,388
Maine	33,040	694,466	742,371
Maryland	12,327	1,188,044	1,295,346
Massachusetts	8,266	2,805,346	3,366,416
Michigan	57,980	2,420,982	2,810,173
Minnesota	84,682	1,751,394	2,075,708
Mississippi	46,865	1,551,270	1,797,114
Missouri	69,420	3,106,665	3,293,335
Montana	146,572	243,329	376,053
Nebraska	77,520	1,066,300	1,192,214
Nevada	110,690	42,335	81,875
New Hampshire	9,341	411,588	430,572
New Jersey	8,224	1,883,669	2,537,167
New Mexico	122,634	195,810	327,301
New York	49,204	7,268,894	9,113,614
North Carolina	52,426	1,893,810	2,206,287
North Dakota	70,837	319,146	557,056
Ohio	41,040	4,157,545	4,767,121
Oklahoma	70,057	790,391	1,657,155
Oregon	96,399	413,536	672,765
Panama Canal Zone	474	Population varies	

	Area in Square Miles	Population in 1900	Population in 1910
Pennsylvania	45,126	6,302,115	7,665,111
Philippine Islands	127,853	7,360,551	8,276,802
Porto Rico	3,435	962,019	1,118,012
Rhode Island	1,248	428,556	542,610
Samoan Isds. (U. S. Territory)	77	3,800	6,780
South Carolina	30,989	1,340,316	1,515,400
South Dakota	77,615	401,570	583,888
Tennessee	42,022	2,020,616	2,184,789
Texas	265,896	3,048,710	3,896,542
Tutuila	54	3,800	('09) 6,780
Utah	84,990	276,749	373,351
Vermont	9,564	343,641	355,946
Virginia	42,627	1,854,184	2,061,612
Washington	69,127	518,103	1,141,990
West Virginia	24,170	958,800	1,221,119
Wisconsin	56,066	2,069,042	2,333,860
Wyoming	97,914	92,531	145,965

TWENTY-SIX LARGEST CITIES OF THE UNITED STATES

	Population Census of 1900	Population Census of 1910
1. New York, N.Y.	3,437,202	4,766,883
2. Chicago, Ill.	1,698,575	2,185,283
3. Philadelphia, Pa.	1,298,697	1,549,008
4. St. Louis, Mo.	575,238	687,029
5. Boston, Mass.	560,892	670,585
6. Cleveland, O.	381,768	560,663
7. Baltimore, Md.	508,957	558,485
8. Pittsburgh, Pa.	321,616	533,905
9. Detroit, Mich.	285,704	465,766
10. Buffalo, N.Y.	352,387	423,715
11. San Francisco, Cal.	342,782	416,912
12. Milwaukee, Wis.	285,315	373,857
13. Cincinnati, O.	325,902	364,463
14. Newark, N.J.	246,070	347,469
15. New Orleans, La.	287,104	339,075
16. Washington, D.C.	278,718	331,069
17. Los Angeles, Cal.	102,479	319,198
18. Minneapolis, Minn.	202,718	301,408
19. Jersey City, N.J.	206,433	267,779
20. Kansas City, Mo.	163,752	248,381
21. Seattle, Wash.	80,671	237,194
22. Indianapolis, Ind.	169,164	233,650
23. Providence, R.I.	175,597	224,326
24. Louisville, Ky.	204,731	223,928
25. Rochester, N.Y.	162,608	218,149
26. St. Paul, Minn.	163,065	214,744

CITIES OF THE UNITED STATES AND ITS DEPENDENCIES MENTIONED IN THIS BOOK

	Population Census of 1900	Population Census of 1910
Akron, O.	42,728	69,067
Albany, N.Y.	94,151	100,253
Annapolis, Md.	8,525	8,609
Astoria, Ore.	8,381	9,599
Atlanta, Ga.	89,872	154,839
Augusta, Me.	11,683	13,211
Austin, Tex.	22,258	29,860
Baltimore, Md.	508,957	558,485
Bangor, Me.	21,850	24,803
Baton Rouge, La.	11,269	14,897
Berkeley, Cal.	13,214	40,434
Birmingham, Ala.	38,415	132,685
Bismarck, N.D.	3,319	5,443
Boisé, Idaho	5,957	17,358
Boston, Mass.	560,892	670,585
Bridgeport, Conn.	70,996	102,054
Brockton, Mass.	40,063	56,878
Brooklyn, N.Y.	1,166,582	1,634,351
Buffalo, N.Y.	352,387	423,715
Butte, Mont.	30,470	39,165
Cambridge, Mass.	91,886	104,839
Camden, N.J.	75,935	94,538
Carson City, Nev.	2,100	2,466
Charleston, S.C.	55,807	58,833
Charleston, W.Va.	11,099	34,014

	Population Census of 1900	Population Census of 1910
Chattanooga, Tenn.	30,154	44,604
Cheyenne, Wy.	14,087	38,537
Chicago, Ill.	1,698,575	2,185,283
Cincinnati, O.	325,902	364,463
Cleveland, O.	381,768	560,663
Colorado Springs, Col.	21,085	29,078
Columbia, S.C.	21,108	26,319
Columbus, O.	125,560	181,548
Concord, N.H.	19,632	21,497
Cripple Creek, Col.	10,147	6,206
Dallas, Tex.	42,638	92,104
Dayton, O.	85,333	116,577
Denver, Col.	133,859	213,381
Des Moines, Iowa	62,139	86,368
Detroit, Mich.	285,704	465,766
Dover, Del.	3,329	3,720
Duluth, Minn.	52,969	78,466
Evansville, Ind.	59,007	69,647
Fall River, Mass.	104,863	119,295
Fort Wayne, Ind.	45,115	63,933
Fort Worth, Tex.	26,688	73,312
Frankfort, Ky.	9,487	10,465
Galveston, Tex.	37,789	36,981
Gloucester, Mass.	26,121	24,398
Grand Rapids, Mich.	87,565	112,571
Guthrie, Ok.	10,006	11,654
Harrisburg, Pa.	50,167	64,186
Hartford, Conn.	79,850	98,915
Helena, Mont.	10,770	12,515
Honolulu, Hawaiian Isds.	39,305	52,183
Houston, Tex.	44,633	78,800
Indianapolis, Ind.	169,164	233,650
Jackson, Miss.	7,816	21,262
Jacksonville, Fla.	28,429	57,699
Jefferson City, Mo.	9,664	11,850
Jersey City, N.J.	206,433	267,779
Juneau, Alaska	1,864	1,644
Kansas City, Mo.	163,752	248,381
Key West, Fla.	17,114	19,945
Knoxville, Tenn.	32,637	36,346
Lansing, Mich.	16,485	31,229
Lawrence, Mass.	62,559	85,892
Leadville, Col.	12,455	7,508
Lincoln, Neb.	40,169	43,973
Little Rock, Ark.	38,307	45,941
Los Angeles, Cal.	102,479	319,198
Louisville, Ky.	204,731	223,928
Lowell, Mass.	94,969	106,294
Lynn, Mass.	68,513	89,336
Madison, Wis.	19,164	25,531
Manchester, N.H.	56,987	70,063
Manila, Philippines		234,409
Memphis, Tenn.	102,320	131,105
Miami, Fla.	1,681	5,471
Milwaukee, Wis.	285,315	373,857
Minneapolis, Minn.	202,718	301,408
Mobile, Ala.	38,469	51,521
Montgomery, Ala.	30,346	38,136
Montpelier, Vt.	6,266	7,856
Nashville, Tenn.	80,865	110,364
Newark, N.J.	246,070	347,469
New Bedford, Mass.	62,442	96,652
New Haven, Conn.	108,027	133,605
New Orleans, La.	287,104	339,075
New York, N.Y.	3,437,202	4,766,883
Nome, Alaska	12,486	2,600
Norfolk, Va.	46,624	67,452
Oakland, Cal.	66,960	150,174
Ogden, Utah	16,313	25,580
Oklahoma City, Ok.	10,037	64,205
Olympia, Wash.	4,082	6,996
Omaha, Neb.	102,555	124,096
Pasadena, Cal.	9,117	30,291
Paterson, N.J.	105,171	125,600
Pensacola, Fla.	17,747	22,982

	Population Census of 1900	Population Census of 1910
Peoria, Ill.	56,100	66,950
Philadelphia, Pa.	1,293,697	1,549,008
Phœnix, Ariz.	5,544	11,134
Pierre, S.D.	2,306	3,656
Pittsburgh, Pa.	321,616	533,905
Ponce, Porto Rico	27,952	35,027
Portland, Me.	50,145	58,571
Portland, Ore.	90,426	207,214
Providence, R.I.	175,597	224,326
Pueblo, Col.	28,157	44,395
Raleigh, N.C.	13,643	19,218
Reading, Pa.	78,961	96,071
Richmond, Va.	85,050	127,628
Rochester, N.Y.	102,608	218,149
Rutland, Vt.	11,499	13,546
Sacramento, Cal.	29,282	44,696
Saginaw, Mich.	42,345	50,510
St. Augustine, Fla.	4,272	5,494
St. Joseph, Mo.	102,979	77,403
St. Louis, Mo.	575,238	687,029
St. Paul, Minn.	163,065	214,744
Salem, Mass.	35,956	43,697
Salem, Ore.	4,258	14,094
Salt Lake City, Utah	53,531	92,777
San Antonio, Tex.	53,321	96,614
San Diego, Cal.	17,700	39,578
San Francisco, Cal.	342,782	416,912
San José, Cal.	21,500	28,946
San Juan, Porto Rico	32,048 ('99)	48,716
Santa Fé, N. Mex.	5,603	5,072
Savannah, Ga.	54,244	65,064
Scranton, Pa.	102,026	129,867
Seattle, Wash.	80,671	237,194
Sitka, Alaska	1,396	1,036
Somerville, Mass.	61,643	77,236
Spokane, Wash.	36,848	104,402
Springfield, Ill.	34,159	51,678
Springfield, Mass.	62,059	88,926
Stockton, Cal.	17,506	23,253
Superior, Wis.	31,091	40,384
Syracuse, N.Y.	108,374	137,249
Tacoma, Wash.	37,714	88,743
Tallahassee, Fla.	2,981	5,018
Tampa, Fla.	15,839	37,782
Terre Haute, Ind.	36,673	58,157
Toledo, O.	131,822	168,497
Topeka, Kan.	33,608	43,684
Trenton, N.J.	73,707	96,815
Troy, N.Y.	75,057	76,813
Vicksburg, Miss.	14,834	20,814
Washington, D.C.	278,718	331,069
Wheeling, W.Va.	38,878	41,641
Wilkes-Barre, Pa.	51,721	67,105
Wilmington, Del.	76,508	87,411
Wilmington, N.C.	20,976	25,748
Worcester, Mass.	118,421	145,986
Youngstown, O.	44,885	79,066

TWENTY-FIVE LARGEST CITIES IN THE WORLD

				Population
1.	London, England	1910		4,872,702
	Greater London	1910		7,537,196
2.	New York, U.S	1910		4,766,883
3.	Paris, France	1911		2,846,986
4.	Tokyo, Japan	1908		2,186,079
5.	Chicago, U.S.	1910		2,185,283
6.	Berlin, Germany	1910		2,070,695
7.	Vienna, Austria-Hungary	1911		2,004,291
8.	St. Petersburg, Russia	1910		1,907,708
9.	Canton, China *			1,600,000
10.	Philadelphia, U.S.	1910		1,549,008
11.	Moscow, Russia	1909		1,481,200
12.	Buenos Aires, Argentina	1911		1,326,994
13.	Calcutta, India	1910		1,216,514
14.	Constantinople, Turkey			1,125,000
15.	Osaka, Japan	1908		1,117,151
16.	Shanghai, China *			1,000,000
17.	Tientsin, China *	1910		1,000,000
18.	Rio de Janeiro, Brazil	1909		1,000,000
19.	Bombay, India	1910		972,892
20.	Hamburg, Germany	1910		936,000
21.	Budapest, Austria-Hungary	1910		880,371
22.	Glasgow, Scotland	1911		784,455
23.	Warsaw, Russia	1909		781,179
24.	Liverpool, England	1910		767,606
25.	Barcelona, Spain	1911		700,000

IMPORTANT FOREIGN CITIES

			Population
Adelaide, Australia	1910		192,000
Alexandria, Egypt	1907		332,246
Algiers, Algeria	1906		138,240
Amsterdam, Netherlands	1910		573,983
Antwerp, Belgium	1910		320,640
Arequipa, Peru	1908		{ 35,000 { 40,000
Asuncion, Paraguay	1910		84,000
Athens, Greece	1907		167,479
Bahia, Brazil	1909		230,000
Bangkok, Siam	1909		628,675
Barcelona, Spain	1911		700,000
Basel, Switzerland	1910		131,914
Batavia, Java	1905		138,551
Belfast, Ireland	1910		391,167
Belgrade, Servia	1910		84,285
Berlin, Germany	1910		2,070,695
Berne, Switzerland	1910		85,264
Birmingham, England	1910		570,113
Bogota, Colombia	1909		150,300
Bombay, India	1910		972,892
Bordeaux, France	1911		261,678
Bremen, Germany	1910		246,872
Brisbane, Australia	1909		148,077
Brussels, Belgium	1910		665,806
Bucharest, Roumania	1908		300,000
Budapest, Austria-Hungary	1910		880,371
Buenos Aires, Argentina	1911		1,326,994
Cairo, Egypt	1907		654,476
Calcutta, India	1911		1,216,514
Callao, Peru	1908		31,000
Canton, China			1,600,000
Cape Town, Cape Colony	1911		67,000
Caracas, Venezuela			72,429
Cayenne, French Guiana	1910		12,426
Cettinje, Montenegro	1906		4,500
Christiania, Norway	1910		242,801
Cologne, Germany	1910		516,167
Constantinople, Turkey			1,125,000
Copenhagen, Denmark	1911		462,161
Dresden, Germany	1910		546,882
Dublin, Ireland	1910		402,928
Edinburgh, Scotland	1911		320,315
Fez, Morocco	1910		140,000
Florence, Italy	1911		232,860
Frankfort, Germany	1910		414,598
Georgetown, British Guiana	1911		53,000
Geneva, Switzerland	1910		125,520
Genoa, Italy	1911		272,077
Glasgow, Scotland	1911		784,455
Hague, The, Netherlands	1910		280,515
Halifax, Nova Scotia	1911		46,000
Hamburg, Germany	1910		936,000
Havana, Cuba	1910		302,526
Havre, France	1911		136,159
Hobart, Tasmania	1911		27,719

* The populations of Chinese cities are very uncertain. The latest estimates give them a far smaller population than was formerly given.

		Population
Hongkong, China	1911	366,145
Irkutsk, Siberia	1908	108,060
Jerusalem, Turkey in Asia	1910	70,000
Johannesburg, Transvaal	1910	158,580
Kabul, Afghanistan	1906	60,000
Kimberley, Cape Colony	1911	13,656
La Paz, Bolivia	1909	78,856
Leipzig, Germany	1910	587,635
Lima, Peru	1908	140,884
Lisbon, Portugal	1900	356,009
Liverpool, England	1910	767,606
London, England	1910	4,872,702
London, Greater	1910	7,587,196
Lyon, France	1911	523,796
Madras, India	1910	518,660
Madrid, Spain	1910	571,539
Malaga, Spain	1910	133,045
Manchester, England	1910	716,354
Mandalay, Burma	1910	138,299
Marseille, France	1911	550,619
Mecca, Turkey in Asia		80,000
Melbourne, Victoria	1910	591,830
Mexico City, Mexico	1910	470,659
Milan, Italy	1911	599,200
Mocha, Turkey in Asia	1900	5,000
Montevideo, Uruguay	1909	291,465
Montreal, Canada	1910	466,000
Moscow, Russia	1909	1,481,200
Munich, Germany	1910	595,053
Naples, Italy	1911	723,208
Odessa, Russia	1909	478,900
Ottawa, Canada	1911	86,000
Para, Brazil		65,000
Paramaribo, Dutch Guiana	1910	35,082
Paris, France	1911	2,846,986
Peking, China		1,600,000
Pernambuco, Brazil	1906	150,000
Perth, Western Australia	1908	54,354
Prague, Austria-Hungary	1910	223,741
Quebec, Canada	1910	78,000
Quito, Ecuador	1909	70,000
Riga, Russia	1908	318,400
Rio de Janeiro, Brazil	1909	1,000,000
Rome, Italy	1911	538,634
Rotterdam, The Netherlands	1910	426,888
St. John, Canada	1911	42,000
St. John's, Newfoundland	1901	31,501
St. Petersburg, Russia	1910	1,907,708
Santiago, Chile	1907	332,724
São Paulo, Brazil	1909	400,500
Seoul, Korea	1911	278,958
Shanghai, China		1,000,000
Singapore, Straits Settlements	1911	311,985
Smyrna, Turkey in Asia		350,000
Sofia, Bulgaria	1910	102,769
Stockholm, Sweden	1910	341,986
Sucre, Bolivia	1909	23,416
Sydney, Australia	1910	621,100
Teheran, Persia	1905	280,000
Tientsin, China	1910	1,000,000
Timbuktu, Sudan		20,000
Tokyo, Japan	1908	2,186,079
Toronto, Canada	1911	376,000
Trieste, Austria-Hungary	1910	229,475
Tripoli, Tripoli	1909	30,000
Tunis, Tunis	1906	227,519
Turin, Italy	1911	427,733
Valparaiso, Chile	1907	162,447
Vancouver, Canada	1911	100,000
Venice, Italy	1911	160,727

		Population
Vera Cruz, Mexico	1910	29,164
Victoria, Canada	1911	32,000
Vienna, Austria-Hungary	1911	2,004,291
Warsaw, Russia	1909	781,179
Wellington, New Zealand	1911	70,729
Winnipeg, Canada	1911	135,000
Yokohama, Japan	1908	394,303
Zurich, Switzerland	1910	189,088

HEIGHT OF A FEW MOUNTAIN PEAKS

	Feet
Mount Everest, Himalaya Mountains, Asia	29,002
Kanchanjanga	28,156
Aconcagua, Andes Mountains	22,860
Mt. McKinley, Alaskan Mountains, Alaska	20,464
Mt. Logan, Coast Ranges, Canada	19,539
Orizaba, Sierra Madre, Mexico	18,314
Mt. Elbruz, Caucasus Mountains, Russia	18,200
Mt. St. Elias, Coast Ranges, Alaska	18,025
Mont Blanc, Alps Mountains, France	15,781
Mt. Whitney, Sierra Nevada Mountains, California	14,502
Mt. Rainier, Cascade Mountains, Washington	14,363
Mt. Shasta, Cascade Mountains, California	14,380
Pikes Peak, Rocky Mountains, Colorado	14,111
Mauna Loa, Hawaiian Islands	13,675
Frémont Peak, Rocky Mountains, Wyoming	13,790
Fujiyama, Japan	12,365
Mt. Mitchell, Appalachian Mountains, North Carolina	6,711
Mt. Washington, White Mountains, New Hampshire	6,279
Mt. Marcy, Adirondack Mountains, New York	5,344

SOME OF THE LARGEST RIVERS OF THE WORLD

Name	Country	Length in Miles	Basin Area Square Miles	Ocean
Missouri-Mississippi	United States	4,300	1,257,000	Atlantic
Nile	Africa	3,400	1,273,000	Atlantic
Amazon	South America	3,300	2,500,000	Atlantic
Ob	Siberia	3,200	1,000,000	Arctic
Yangtse-Kiang	China	3,200	548,000	Pacific
Congo	Africa	2,900	1,200,000	Atlantic
Lena	Siberia	2,800	950,000	Arctic
Hoang-Ho	China	2,700	570,000	Pacific
Niger	Africa	2,600	563,300	Atlantic
Plata	South America	2,580	1,200,000	Atlantic
Mackenzie	Canada	2,000	590,000	Arctic
Volga	Russia	2,400	563,300	Caspian
St. Lawrence	North America	2,200	530,000	Atlantic
Yukon	Alaska	2,000	440,000	Pacific
Indus	India	1,800	372,700	Indian
Danube	Europe	1,770	300,000	Atlantic

TEN OF THE GREAT LAKES OF THE WORLD

Name	Length in Miles	Breadth in Miles	Area in Square Miles	Country
Caspian	680	270	169,000	Russia
Superior	390	160	30,829	U. S. and Canada
Victoria Nyanza	230	220	30,000	Africa
Aral	225	185	26,900	Asiatic Russia
Huron	250	100	22,322	U. S. and Canada
Michigan	335	85	21,729	United States
Tanganyika	420	50	12,650	Africa
Baikal	397	45	12,500	Siberia
Erie	250	58	9,990	U. S. and Canada
Chad (a shallow lake which grows very large in the rainy season and shrinks in the dry season)			about 10,000	Africa

APPROXIMATE AVERAGE HEIGHT OF SOME PLATEAUS

	Feet
Tibet	10–15,000
Bolivia	10–13,000
Spain	2–3,000
Mexico	5–6,000
Western United States Plateau	5–6,000
Brazil	2–2,500

INDEX AND PRONOUNCING VOCABULARY

KEY TO PRONUNCIATION

(Webster's International Dictionary)

ā, as in āle ; ȧ, as in senʼāte ; â, as in câre ; ă, as in ăm ; ä, as in ärm ; ȧ, as in ȧsk ; ɑ, as in fiʼnɑl ; ạ, as in ạll ;
ē, as in ēve ; ĕ, as in ĕ-ventʼ ; ē, as in ĕnd ; ẽ, as in fẽrn ; e, as in reʼcent ; ī, as in īce ; ĭ, as in ĭ-deʼa ; ĭ, as in ĭll ;
ō, as in ōld ; ŏ, as in ŏ-beyʼ ; ô, as in ôrb ; ŏ, as in ŏdd ; ū, as in ūse ; ů, as in ů-niteʼ ; ụ, as in rụde ; u, as in full ;
ŭ, as in ŭp ; û, as in ûrn ; y̆, as in pitʼy̆ ; ōō, as in fōōd ; o͝o, as in fo͝ot ; ou, as in out ; oi, as in oil ; N, representing
simply the nasal tone of the preceding vowel, as in ensemble (äNʼsäN'bʼl), ' (for voice glide) as in pardon (pärʼdʼn) ;
g (hard), as in go ; s (sharp), as in so ; z (like s sonant), as in zone ; ch (= tsh) as in chair ; sh, for ch, as in
machine ; zh (= sh made sonant), for z, as in azure ; j (= dzh), for g, as in gem ; k, for ch, as in chorus ; kw,
for qu, as in queen ; ks (surd), for x, as in vex ; gz (sonant), for x, as in exist ; f, for ph, as in philosophy ; hw,
for wh, as in what ; t, for ed, as in baked ; ng, as in long ; ṇ (like ng) for n before the sound of k or hard g, as
in bank ; n (ordinary sound), as in no ; th (sonant), for th, as in then ; th (surd), as in thin.

The primary accent is indicated by a short, heavy mark (ʼ), the secondary by a lighter mark (').
The numbers refer to pages. Where several references are given, the pages on which the principal description
is to be found are indicated by heavier type.

A

Abyssinia (ăbʼĭs-sĭnʼĭ-ȧ), 236.
Aconcagua, Mt. (-ä'kŏn-käʼgwȧ), 184.
Adelaide (ădʼē-lād), 241.
Adirondack Mountains (ădʼĭ-rŏnʼdăk-), 110.
Adriatic Sea (ădʼrē-ăt'ĭk- or āʼdrĭ-), 200, 202.
Afghanistan (ȧf-gănʼĭs-tänʼ), 218.
Africa (ăfʼrĭ-kȧ), 93, 94, 95, 96, **231–238**; central part, see Central Africa ; climate, 3, 232 ; deserts, 7–9, 235, 236 ; mountains, 25 ; nomads, 8, 9 ; northern part, 234–236 (see Egypt) ; plant life, 3–4, 7 ; portions explored and settled by Europeans, 233 ; rainfall, 3, 236 ; rivers and waterfalls, 232 ; Sahara Desert, 231–232 ; southern part, 233 (see South Africa) ; surface features, 7–9, 232, 235–236.
Agriculture, 1–2, 65 ; comparisons regarding, in leading countries, 245–246. See also subdivision under names of countries, etc.
Air, the, 54–59 ; importance of, to life, 54–55 ; movement of, or winds, 55–56 ; taking up of water by, 56.
Akron (Ohio) (ăkʼrŭn), 142.
Alabama (ălʼȧ-bäʼmȧ), 123, 125.
Alameda (Cal.) (ä'lä-mäʼdȧ), 153.
Alaska (ȧ-lăsʼkȧ), 101, **158–160** ; acquisition of, by United States, 102, 158 ; agriculture, 158 ; fishing, 159 ; mining, 159 ; towns, 160 ; trade, 152 ; transportation, 159–160.
Albany (N.Y.) (ạlʼbȧ-nĭ), 114, 117.
Aleutian Islands (ȧ-lūʼshȧn-), Fig. 106.
Alexandria (ălʼĕgz-ănʼdrĭ-ȧ), 234.
Alfalfa (ăl-fălʼfȧ), Western States, 147.
Algeria (ăl-jēʼrĭ-ȧ), 197, 236.
Allegheny (Pa.) (ălʼē-gäʼnĭ), 112.

Alps Mountains (ălps-), 26–28, 186, 198, 201, 211.
Amazon River (ămʼȧ-zŏn-), 182, 183.
Amsterdam (ămʼstēr-dămʼ), 208.
Andes Mountains (ănʼdēz-), 180, 181, 183, **184.**
Andorra (ȧn-dŏrʼrȧ), 361, 375.
Animals, in Arctic regions, 5 ; Australia, 239 ; Central Africa, 4, 233 ; Central States, 134–135 ; forests of the Sudan, 236 ; Indian jungle, 229 ; Northeastern States, 109 ; Russia in Asia, 220 ; Sahara Desert, 8 ; Southern States, 124 ; Yellowstone National Park, 157.
Antarctic Circle (ănt-ärkʼtĭk-), 92.
Antarctic Ocean, 98.
Antilles (ăn-tĭlʼlēz or äNʼtēlʼ), 178.
Antwerp (ăntʼwẽrp), 209.
Apennines Mountains (ăpʼen-nīnz-), 198.
Appalachian Mountains (ăpʼpȧ-lāʼchĭ-ȧn- or lăchʼĭ-ȧn-), 104, 110, 117, 121, 143.
Apples, in Central States, 134 ; New York State, 110 ; Northeastern States, 110 ; Western States, 146.
Apricots, California and Pacific Coast, 146.
Arabia (ȧ-rāʼbĭ-ȧ), 218, 219.
Aral Sea (ärʼal-), 216.
Archipelago (ärʼkĭ-pĕlʼȧ-gō), East Indian, 242.
Arctic Circle (ärkʼtĭk-), 91.
Arctic Ocean, 5, 97–98, 175, 204.
Arequipa (ä'rȧ-kēʼpȧ), 184.
Argentina (är'gĕn-tēʼnȧ), 180, **182**, 184.
Arizona (ărʼĭ-zōʼnȧ), 147, 150, 155, 156.
Arkansas (ärʼkan-sạ), 121.
Asbury Park (N.J.) (ăzʼbēr-ĭ-), 47.
Asia (äʼshĭ-ȧ), 95, 186, **216–230** ; absence of knowledge concerning, and reasons, 216–218 ; area, 216 ;

arid and desert land, 216 ; character of people, 218 ; immigrants to United States from, 107 ; population, 216 ; surface features, 217 ; trade of Pacific coast states with, 152. See also under countries of Asia.
Asphaltum (ăs-fălʼtŭm), production of, 185.
Astoria (Ore.) (ăs-tōʼrĭ-ȧ), 149.
Athens (ăthʼĕnz), 212.
Atlanta (Ga.) (ăt-lănʼtȧ), 127, **130.**
Atlantic City (N. J.) (ăt-lănʼtĭk-), 47.
Atlantic Ocean, 47, 96–97.
Atmosphere. See Air.
Austin (Texas) (ạsʼtĭn), 130.
Australia (ạs-trāʼlĭ-ȧ), 93, 96, **238–241** ; agriculture, 240–241 ; animals, 239 ; cities, 241 ; climate, 239–240 ; deserts and rivers, 240 ; manufacturing, 241 ; mining, 241 ; population and its distribution, 239 ; rainfall, 239–240 ; stock-raising, 240 ; surface, 240 ; vegetation, 239.
Austria-Hungary (ạsʼtrĭ-ȧ hŭṇʼgȧ-rĭ), 188, **200–202** ; agriculture, 201 ; area, 200, 244 ; cities, 202 ; climate, 201 ; commerce, 202 ; government, 200–201, lumbering, 201 ; manufacturing, 202 ; mining, 201–202, 248 ; mountains, 201 ; parts of country, 200 ; population, 244 ; surface, 200 ; transportation, 202.
Avalanches, 27, 30, 42.
Axis, rotation of earth on its, 89–90.

B

Bahamas (bȧ-häʼmȧs), 178.
Bahia (bȧ-ēʼȧ), 183.
Balkan Countries (bȧl-känʼ- or bạlʼkan-), 213.
Baltic Sea (bạlʼtĭk-), 204, 205.

259

THE following pages contain advertisements of a few of the Macmillan books on kindred subjects

BAKER AND CARPENTER
LANGUAGE READER SERIES

Primer

123 pages. 12mo. 25 cents net

By FRANKLIN T. BAKER, Professor of the English Language and Literature in Teachers College, the late GEORGE R. CARPENTER, and MISS JULIE T. DULON, Teacher in Public School No. 151, New York City.

First Year Language Reader

xiv + 138 pages. 12mo. 25 cents net

By FRANKLIN T. BAKER, GEORGE R. CARPENTER, and MISS KATHARINE B. OWEN, Instructor in the Charlton School, New York City.

Second Year Language Reader

xiii + 152 pages. 12mo. 30 cents net

By FRANKLIN T. BAKER, GEORGE R. CARPENTER, and MISS KATHARINE B. OWEN.

Third Year Language Reader

xvi + 284 pages. 12mo. 40 cents net

By FRANKLIN T. BAKER, GEORGE R. CARPENTER, and MISS MARY E. BROOKS, Supervisor of Primary Work in Brooklyn.

Fourth Year Language Reader

xiv + 345 pages. 12mo. 40 cents net

By FRANKLIN T. BAKER, GEORGE R. CARPENTER, and MISS IDA E. ROBBINS, Instructor in Horace Mann School, New York City.

Fifth Year Language Reader

xv + 477 pages. 12mo. 45 cents net

By FRANKLIN T. BAKER, GEORGE R. CARPENTER, and MISS MARY F. KIRCHWEY, Instructor in Horace Mann School, New York City.

Sixth Year Language Reader

xxiii + 482 pages. 12mo. 50 cents net

By FRANKLIN T. BAKER, GEORGE R. CARPENTER, and MISS JENNIE F. OWENS, Instructor in Jersey City Training School.

LEADING FEATURES

1. Teachers agree as to the value of good literature as the basis of the English work. But the classics are often either not related at all to the work in expression, or the relationship is indicated in a vague and desultory fashion.

The Language Readers make the relationship close and vital, without rendering the work in expression pedantic, or killing the enjoyment of the reading.

2. Each Reader has some dominating interest in its subject-matter.

In the first two books, where the main problem is to teach the beginnings of reading, much must be sacrificed to interest and simplicity, and these books deal with simple story and poetry, mostly of folk-lore and child-life.

In the third book, the dominant element is the fairy-story and the folk-tale.

In the fourth book, the animal-story and the tale of adventure are given the leading place.

In the fifth book, the great myths of the world, the hero-stories of the nations, are retold.

In the sixth book, a selection of stories, poems, and essays serves as an introduction to general literature.

3. The standards of good literature and the interests of the normal child have been kept in mind.

Great care has been taken that the books shall be *good readers,* independent of the language work introduced.

The language work has been so handled as not to make it obtrusive in appearance or impertinent in comment.

4. In grading the reading and language work, the editors have had the assistance of able and experienced teachers from both public and private schools.

5. Illustrations have been freely used.

Color Work—by the newer processes—adds special charm to the four lower books.

THE MACMILLAN COMPANY
64-66 FIFTH AVENUE, NEW YORK

BOSTON   CHICAGO   SAN FRANCISCO   ATLANTA

CHANCELLOR'S
GRADED CITY SPELLERS

Year by Year Edition	7 Books		Each, 12mo	Cloth	
Second Year Grade	.	.	.	54 pages.	15 cents *net*
Third Year Grade	.	.	.	52 pages.	15 cents *net*
Fourth Year Grade	.	.	.	68 pages.	15 cents *net*
Fifth Year Grade	.	.	.	64 pages.	15 cents *net*
Sixth Year Grade	.	.	.	68 pages.	18 cents *net*
Seventh Year Grade	.	.	.	80 pages.	18 cents *net*
Eighth Year Grade	.	.	.	89 pages.	18 cents *net*

Two Book Edition	Each, 12mo	Cloth	
Book One — Second, Third, and Fourth Year Grades . . .	166 pages.	25 cents *net*
Book Two — Fifth, Sixth, Seventh, and Eighth Year Grades . . .	299 pages.	30 cents *net*

Paper Cover Edition	10 Books	Each, 12mo		
Second Year Grade, Part I	.	.	30 pages.	6 cents *net*
Second Year Grade, Part II	.	.	28 pages.	6 cents *net*
Third Year Grade, Part I	.	.	28 pages.	6 cents *net*
Third Year Grade, Part II	.	.	28 pages.	6 cents *net*
Fourth Year Grade, Part I	.	.	36 pages.	8 cents *net*
Fourth Year Grade, Part II	.	.	36 pages.	8 cents *net*
Fifth Year Grade, Complete	.	.	64 pages.	12 cents *net*
Sixth Year Grade, Complete	.	.	68 pages.	12 cents *net*
Seventh Year Grade, Complete	.	.	80 pages.	12 cents *net*
Eighth Year Grade, Complete	.	.	89 pages.	12 cents *net*

CHANCELLOR'S GRADED CITY SPELLERS constitute the first attempt to provide **spelling lessons by grades**, from the time that the spelling book is first placed in the hands of the pupil until the completion of the grammar school course.

CHANCELLOR'S GRADED CITY SPELLERS are **published in two different forms**, bound in full cloth, one series being in seven books, a book for each year from the second to the eighth year of the elementary school course ; while the other series consists of two books, the first volume grouping together the work of the second, third, and fourth years, and the second volume embracing the work of the fifth, sixth, seventh, and eighth years.

The general plan of the series includes a review of drill words from the lessons of the preceding year, daily advance lessons, the use of all important words in suitable sentences, frequent reappearance in the sentences of the difficult words, syllabication of all spelling words, and systematic reviews at regular intervals.

The words to be learned are presented in three different ways :

(*a*) **Alone,** not syllabicated, for recognition as they ordinarily appear.

(*b*) **Combined** with other words in sentences, thus revealing the significance of the new words.

(*c*) **Syllabicated,** for the analysis of the literal elements.

The series is **rich in all the ordinary forms of word study.** *Prefixes and suffixes* are treated with clearness and completeness. *Synonyms, homonyms,* and *antonyms* are matters of exercise at frequent intervals, and the various forms of *word-building* based upon the relation of *stems and roots* are presented with a fullness not surpassed in any other spelling series.

THE MACMILLAN COMPANY
64-66 FIFTH AVENUE, NEW YORK

BOSTON   CHICAGO   SAN FRANCISCO   ATLANTA

THE MODERN ENGLISH COURSE

By Henry P. Emerson, Superintendent of Education, Buffalo, New York, and Ida C. Bender, Supervisor of Primary Grades, Buffalo, New York.

BOOK I

ELEMENTARY LESSONS IN ENGLISH

12mo   Cloth   ix + 246 pages   40 cents net

BOOK II

A PRACTICAL ENGLISH GRAMMAR

12mo   Cloth   xiv + 400 pages   60 cents net

This series has been named "The Modern English Course," because the books aim to present the subject of language in accordance with modern principles of teaching, and because they are based on a study of the usage of the best writers and speakers of modern English.

These books aim to give the young (1) ability to express their own thoughts and to understand the thoughts of others; (2) a clear insight into the structure of the English sentence; (3) effectiveness in the use of language; (4) an appreciation of its higher uses in literature.

The books are written in good English. The authors are masters of an excellent style of writing, and they have given their work a quality and finish which is educating and refining in the highest degree. The illustrative sentences in both books have been selected with great care from standard literature, and they are valuable in themselves either for the information or the suggestive thought they contain.

The definitions are short, clear, concise, and within the comprehension of the pupils. As far as definitions are given in Book I, they are identical with Book II. In general the two books are consistent; there are no contradictions; they are harmonious in aim, in method, in explanation, and in definition.

Book I is designed for the fourth to sixth years, and Book II for the seventh and eighth years of the Elementary course.

In the *first* book emphasis is placed on matters of human interest, — the family, the school, social relations, and nature. The aim has been to produce subject-matter of genuine interest to children, and yet of intrinsic value. The fact is recognized that a knowledge of technical grammar without abundant exercises, both oral and written, exerts very little influence either on the daily speech or on the written composition of children. Constant effort is made to increase their vocabulary, to teach them variety of expression, and to make expression easy and natural. To bring about these results, there is a rational use of imitation to give mastery of proper forms. The exercises are adapted to the age of the pupil, and the forming of habits of correct oral speech is given the same attention as written composition. The explanations are lucid and clear; the exercises, copious and suggestive.

In the *second book* the illustrative sentences have been specially prepared by the authors. The sentences that make up the exercises are especially apt as illustrations of the principles in hand; they have literary merit, being drawn largely from standard literature. In deference to a growing conviction that composition should be a subject of study distinct from grammar, a separate part of the book is devoted to this feature of language study. All exercises are "workable"; every sentence in every exercise illustrates the principle under discussion. Review questions are grouped at convenient intervals throughout the book.

THE MACMILLAN COMPANY

64–66 FIFTH AVENUE, NEW YORK

BOSTON   CHICAGO   SAN FRANCISCO   ATLANTA

FOR SUPPLEMENTARY READING

HISTORY AND BIOGRAPHY

Dickson's From the Old World to the New . . . . 50 cents *net*
    A Hundred Years of Warfare . . . . 50 cents *net*
Hart's Source Readers in American History
    No. 1, Colonial Children . . . . 40 cents *net*
    No. 2, Camps and Firesides of the Revolution . . . . . . 50 cents *net*
    No. 3, How Our Grandfathers Lived . . . . 60 cents *net*
    No. 4, The Romance of the Civil War . . . . 60 cents *net*
Hawthorne's Grandfather's Chair . . . . 25 cents *net*
McMurry's Pioneer History Stories
    Pioneers on Land and Sea . . . . 40 cents *net*
    Pioneers of the Mississippi Valley . . . . 40 cents *net*
    Pioneers of the Rocky Mountains and the West . . . . . . 40 cents *net*
Tucker's The Universal School Reader . . . . 45 cents *net*
Wilson's History Reader for Elementary Schools . . . . . . 60 cents *net*

GEOGRAPHY

Chamberlain's Home and World Series
    How We are Fed . . . . 40 cents *net*
    How We are Clothed . . . . 40 cents *net*
    How We are Sheltered . . . . 40 cents *net*
    How We Travel . . . . 40 cents *net*
McMurry's Excursions and Lessons in Home Geography . . . . 50 cents *net*
    Type Studies from the Geography of the United States . . . . 50 cents *net*
    Larger Types of American Geography . . . . 75 cents *net*

MYTHS AND FABLES

Cole's Heroes of Olden Time . . . . 40 cents *net*
    Story of the Golden Apple . . . . 40 cents *net*
Hawthorne's Wonder Book . . . . 25 cents *net*
    Tanglewood Tales . . . . 25 cents *net*
Keary's Heroes of Asgard . . . . 25 cents *net*
Kingsley's Heroes; Greek Fairy Tales . . . . 25 cents *net*

NATURE STUDY AND SCIENCE

Holden's Real Things in Nature   65 cents *net*
Kingsley's Madam How and Lady
    Why . . . . . 50 cents *net*
Millard's The Wonderful House
    that Jack Has . . . 50 cents *net*
Murché's Science Readers
    Book I . . . . 25 cents *net*
    Book II . . . . 25 cents *net*
    Book III . . . 40 cents *net*
    Book IV . . . 40 cents *net*
    Book V . . . 50 cents *net*
    Book VI . . . 50 cents *net*

Murché's Science Readers
    Book VII . . . 50 cents *net*
Shallow and Cullen's Nature Study
    Made Easy . . . 40 cents *net*
Wilson's Nature Study in Elementary Schools
    First Reader . . . 35 cents *net*
    Second Reader . . 35 cents *net*
Wright's Heart of Nature Series
    I. Stories of Plants and Animals 30 cents *net*
    II. Stories of Earth and Sky . 30 cents *net*
    III. Stories of Birds and Beasts . 30 cents *net*

THE MACMILLAN COMPANY

64-66 FIFTH AVENUE, NEW YORK

BOSTON   CHICAGO   SAN FRANCISCO   ATLANTA